Praise for *The Art of Tim*

'Griffiths' luminous new work underlines the inarguable point that if we are truly to understand our history, we must get to know those who wrote it. A must-read for anyone interested in Australia's past.'
— TIM FLANNERY

'Erudite but honest. Generous yet discerning. Warm, perceptive and nothing if not elegant. A soulful meditation on the people who have shaped our past into the stories we call history, by an historian who himself is at the top of his game. Tom Griffiths reveals that the beating heart of history rests in the humanity of those who write it.' — CLARE WRIGHT

'Tom Griffiths' study of fourteen historians greatly enriches our understanding of Australia past and present. The book teems with fresh insights into our history. The author, himself an eminent environmental historian, keeps his subjects close to earth. Like much of his work, the book adds new meaning to the word "country".'
— KEN INGLIS

'A series of subtle and penetrating intellectual portraits of Griffiths' teachers, forebears and peers. As we read, we are brought into communion not only with the minds of these thinkers, but with the mind of Griffiths himself, an historian at the height of his powers, with insights that range far beyond history to the meaning and significance of modernity itself. This book is not only a meditation on the past, but a rallying cry for the future, in which Australia's history might be a source of both unflinching self-examination and poetic wonder.' — BRIGID HAINS

'For too many decades Australian history has been a cacophony of "too many notes". Tom Griffiths has the rare, reconciling capacity – and a collegial historian's generosity – to envisage it as a symphony, created by many voices, the discordant as well as the harmonious, that tells an evolving, bracing story of who we are.' – MORAG FRASER

'Tom Griffiths reveals the crucial importance of history to our humanity. A rare feat of imagination and generosity, *The Art of Time Travel* will remain relevant for decades to come.' – MARK MCKENNA

'By exploring the intellectual and emotional backstories of fourteen people who have crafted Australian history, Tom Griffiths shows how and why it is done. In the process, he has created a beautiful work of history.' – JULIANNE SCHULTZ

'Sharp insights, thoughtful judgment, a generous spirit – *The Art of Time Travel* has the hallmarks of all Tom Griffiths' scholarship. His panorama of Australian historians shows why any similar survey conducted in the future will include his own artful work among the honoured.' – STEPHEN J. PYNE, Arizona State University

'An enthralling account of the intellectual rediscovery of Australia, vividly brought to life by a gifted interpreter. Griffiths' lyrical prose is mesmerizing.' – DAVID LOWENTHAL, University College London

'Liberates the study of historians and historiography from the dry, soulless confines of the academy to demonstrate the creative and imaginative craft at its best. If there were one single volume to encapsulate this dramatic, complex, entangled and exciting field, *The Art of Time Travel* is that book. Certain to become an instant classic.' – JANE CARRUTHERS, University of South Africa

THE ART

HISTORIANS AND THEIR CRAFT

OF TIME

TOM GRIFFITHS

TRAVEL

Black Inc.

Published by Black Inc.,
an imprint of Schwartz Publishing Pty Ltd
Level 1, 221 Drummond Street
Carlton VIC 3053, Australia
enquiries@blackincbooks.com
www.blackincbooks.com

National Library of Australia Cataloguing-in-Publication entry:
Griffiths, Tom, 1957–, author.
The art of time travel / Tom Griffiths.
9781863958561 (paperback)
9781925203127 (ebook)
History—Australia.
994

Cover design by Peter Long
Text design and typesetting by Tristan Main
Cover image © Daniel Schoenen: Image BROKER: age fotostock

For Michael, Julie, Mardie and Dominic

Contents

Prologue

A couple of years ago, when I was walking a pilgrimage route in rural France, I was invited to share the evening meal with three fellow walkers, all of them French. Conversation eventually got around to how we earned our livings. One was an air-conditioning salesman, one was a nurse and the third a psychological counsellor. When they discovered that I was a historian, there was a chorus of approval, even, dare I say it, a frisson of serious regard – something unexpected for scholars in Australia. And, as proud French citizens, they were ready with their natural next question: 'Who are your favourite French historians?'

The question beautifully fulfilled one of the stereotypes we have of French culture – that the general public knows and reveres its nation's intellectuals. It was predicated on the confidence that they would know the names I managed to present to them. Even the adjective 'favourite' acknowledged that there were many possibilities of which they were aware, and that my answer would reveal something about myself. The question also sweetly assumed that I, as a historian living in Australia, was part of a global scholarly community, and would surely be familiar with the historians of France. They awaited my answer – I am not exaggerating – with strong interest.

I gave them two names. The first was Fernand Braudel. This was greeted with satisfaction and approval. Yes, they replied, *The Mediterranean* was a landmark work, a history with prodigious scale and depth, a book they all knew.[1] My second offering was Emmanuel Le Roy Ladurie. 'Oh yes! The author of *Montaillou!*' they rejoiced.[2] I had hit the jackpot here, and there was much to discuss about the intimate eye on medieval society that Ladurie had given us all. My stocks went up even further when I was able to say that I had heard Ladurie speak just a week earlier, at a conference in Munich. Now I was boasting. Before the meal was over, they had pressed me for the titles of *my* histories and regretted that they were not 'yet' translated into French. I knew they never would be, but how exhilarating that they considered it likely.

Over the next week or two, as I strode across the Aveyron, I happily pondered this heady conversation, which had unexpectedly united my scholarly and recreational lives. Would I ever be asked this question in Australia, I wondered. And how would I reply? What is the role of historians in our national conversation and what exactly is it that they do?

This book is a quirky, serious and personal exploration of the art and craft of history in Australia since the Second World War. I have chosen to illuminate my discipline in the way my French table companions found most congenial: by nominating some of my favourite historians and trying to describe how they work. I am keen to show that writing history is a highly creative act and that its artistic aspirations are perfectly consistent with the quest to represent the past truthfully. Good history is a high-wire, gravity-defying act of balance and grace that fills me with awe. Rather than investigating this process abstractly, I am going to observe how particular historians construct a body of work out of a lifelong dialogue between past evidence and present experience. Historians tend to be dedicated, passionate citizens who seek to make a difference by telling true stories. They scour their own societies for vestiges of past worlds, for cracks and fissures in the pavement of the present, and for the shimmers and hauntings of history in everyday action. They begin their enquiries in a deeply felt present. But as time travellers they have to forsake their own world for a period – and then, somehow, find their way back.

∽

If, at the dinner table, I had named a third favourite French historian, it would have been Marc Bloch. A French Jew who fought in both world wars, Bloch was a senior member of the French Resistance in Lyon who was captured by the Gestapo, imprisoned, tortured and murdered in 1944. Together with Lucien Febvre, he founded in 1929 the Annales School of historians, which pioneered 'the new social history' with its integration of social science techniques and interest in long-term changes in social structures and collective mentalities. Bloch was a gifted student of rural society, and his *French Rural History* (1931) and *Feudal Society* (1939) remain greatly admired. But perhaps his most famous works were those written during the German occupation of France, when he was mostly stranded from his sources except for the grim stimuli of oppression and imprisonment. In 1940 he wrote *Strange Defeat*, an urgent but reflective analysis of his country's 'terrible collapse' under the German invasion. He also began writing *The Historian's Craft* – but it was unfinished on the evening he was taken in a truck to be executed with twenty-seven other Resistance prisoners. The manuscript survived, and it began with the question, 'What is the use of history?' The book was his response: a heartfelt but calm self-examination at a time when many felt betrayed by history. Bloch's tenacious integration of civic engagement and critical scholarship amidst such trauma was an inspiration to many of the historians studied in this book.[3]

Historians are often challenged about the usefulness of their discipline – and they frequently challenge themselves. The Australian historian Graeme Davison, himself inspired by Marc Bloch's practical sense of history as a craft, took up the challenge of 'the utilitarian age' of the late 1990s to write his insightful book *The Use and Abuse of Australian History*.[4] Another Australian historian, Hugh Stretton, besieged by rising economic rationalism in the 1980s, treasured history as a discipline because it has 'three qualities which have been scarce in modern social science': it is 'holist, uncertain and eclectic'. 'Who study societies of every kind,' he asked, 'study them whole, know most about how they conserve or change their ideas and institutions, write in plain language, and generally know how uncertain and selective their knowledge is at best? Historians do.'[5]

History is a form of knowledge that tends to be subtle, humble, complex and contextual and therefore less amenable to generalisation, prediction or application. A decade ago, when I was writing a history of Antarctica and researching human experience in remote places, I read the medical and psychological studies of life in isolated communities and kept coming up against the limits of faceless, nameless, clinical accounts of deeply personal and cultural matters. In the name of objectivity, rationality and generalisation, real people were gutted and meaning ebbed away. History, by contrast, spills over with illuminating, verifiable examples that you can argue with. *This person did that here, then, because.* History's commitment to contingency and particularity has often been seen to weaken its usefulness. But to understand the rigours of the long polar night – and to survive it – people need vivid tales of winters past.

Historians welcome questions about usefulness because history is a democratic practice that cherishes its connection with the people and the polity. History can be constructed at the dinner table, over the back fence, in parliament and in the streets, and not just in a tutorial room or at the scholar's desk. Historians generally don't try to hide behind jargon or intimidate others with professional bullying. They aim to give voice to common experience and seek to communicate with the widest audience. Ironically, it is this very inclusiveness that can expose their authority to challenge. History is so important, so ubiquitous, so integrated with our public and personal lives – with the very substance and art of living – that it is possible to take it for granted and overlook its power. It so seamlessly underpins everything we do that it can be hard, sometimes, to detect its daily revolutionary influence.

This is why historians cultivate wonder as a technical skill. Wonder is a mechanism by which we might make the familiar strange. I agree with the American historian Caroline Walker Bynum when she says that 'we write the best history when the specificity, the novelty, the awe-fulness, of what our sources render up bowls us over with complexity and significance.' Or, as the American environmental historian Richard White put it: 'Any good history begins in strangeness. The past should not be comfortable ... The past should be so strange that you wonder how you and people you know and love could come from such a time.'[6]

So here is our double historical quest: to be astonished as well as to understand. This tension goes to the heart of the historical enterprise – a tension between the past as familiar (and continuous with our own experience) and the past as strange (and therefore able to widen our understanding of what it means to be human). The essence of good history is this balance between empathy and perspective, intimacy and distance. Historians immerse themselves in context; they give themselves wholly and sensually to the mysterious, alchemical power of archives. As well as gathering and weighing evidence, piece by piece with forensic intensity, they sensitise themselves to nuance and meaning, to the whole tenor of an era, the full character of a person. Historians move constantly between reading and thinking their way into the lives and minds of the people of the past – giving them back their present with all its future possibilities – and seeing them with perspective, from afar, with a bracing sense of their strangeness.

It seemed right that I was prompted to think of those three French historians while I was on foot in an agricultural region that has famously resisted modernisation and where one is keenly aware of the inertia embedded in peasant society. All three historians were fascinated by rural and material life, by preindustrial society and the deep, organic sources of French identity. The dinner-table conversation took place not far from the centre of Bloch's war-time resistance and the field of grass where he was murdered. I was also walking Braudel's great divide in French culture and history between the north and the south, a long linguistic frontier where the French language once splintered into a myriad patois, producing a variety of pronunciation that accommodated even my Australian accent.[7] And I later discovered that I was traversing Ladurie's favourite region in the whole world. This was the place into which he would, if he could, take the planet time travelling. Writing of the Aveyron, he confessed, 'My wish for our planet, where the majority of people are poor peasants, is the opposite of most futuristic Utopias: namely a rural and probably impossible one. I should like, in the twenty-first century, to see the whole world looking more like the Aveyron in about 1925. It would not be at all bad as a brave new world.'[8] On the pilgrim paths of the Aveyron, 1925 does not feel all that far away. It is separated from the twenty-first century by just one or two ratchets of the great engine of social change, the workings of which most fascinated the historians of the Annales School.

Braudel's history, like Bloch's, was shaped by war. He was taken prisoner by the Germans in 1940 and he drafted his great work *The Mediterranean* in captivity. The book's startling innovation was the distinction, within historical time, of 'a geographical time, a social time, and an individual time'. Reeling from the horrors of war, Braudel reacted against the dominance of political history and the conventional short timespan of historians, instead championing the study of the *longue durée*, the slow-moving structures and rhythms of centuries. 'Can there be any humanism at the present time,' he wrote in 1946, 'without an ambitious history, conscious of its duties and its great powers?'[9] His own experience of war-time captivity propelled him to seek escape from the grim immediacy of the history of events, and to reject the short timespan, itself a sort of imprisonment. So he participated in that urgent postwar search for a history to live by, one that found human commonality beyond the categories of 'nation' or 'race', and one that pushed history back into 'prehistory'. Australian historians, as we shall find, have been on a parallel but distinct journey.

Historians often take time for granted even though it is their medium. Time flows steadily; it dictates chronology; it lazily supplies causation. It relentlessly propels us into the future, snatching the present from us, making the past strange. In spite of this apparent agency, we often assume that time is inert and flat, without form, colour or contours. In this book, Australian historians travel in time but also analyse time itself, finding that it has a topography and history of its own. Bloch rebelled against seeing time as nothing more than a measurement. 'In contrast,' he argued, 'historical time is a concrete and living reality with an irreversible onward rush. It is the very plasma in which events are immersed, and the field within which they become intelligible.' 'In truth,' agreed Braudel, 'the historian can never get away from the question of time in history: time sticks to his thinking like soil to a gardener's spade.'[10]

Bloch (1886–1944) was the teacher of Braudel (1902–1985), and Braudel was the teacher of Ladurie (1929–), so I found myself reflecting on three generations of French history, and thus on the collaborative and filial character of my craft. History is an international discipline but it has nations, generations and families, teachers and students, mentors and rebels. Ideas and styles are shaped by imitation, admiration and loyalty as well as by argument and reaction. This book finds echoes of French history in Australian practice as well as other intellectual influences from abroad, but most of all it portrays a vigorous and confident Australian intellectual culture, one that draws its dynamism from our own ecological and historical opportunities.

As the American Jeremy Popkin has observed, Australian historians may be unusually reflective and autobiographical in practice. The Australian Americanist David Goodman adds that 'history has been possessed in Australia in particular of unusual cultural authority.' He notes that history in Australia has been moderately 'popular' in its productions, in a way that many of the other humanities are not; and that historians have been 'the last of the generalists, the last of the bearers of a general interest in the whole of society and culture, or in any of its parts'. He believes that 'without quite knowing why, Australians have turned to historians to answer some of the very largest questions about their national and social life.'[11]

This book's selection of historians in Australia – not all of whom are Australian historians – is a personal one and certainly not representative. I anticipate and hope that it will prompt the question, 'Why didn't you include so-and-so?'[12] Manning Clark, for example, the subject of two recent brilliant biographies, mischievously appears here only as a minor character in the study of a novelist. There are many other striking omissions. The people I've chosen have, along with others not portrayed here, inspired and influenced me, and my life has intersected with theirs, as I explain along the way. Together they make a bid for Australians as key thinkers in history, and I hope they make a case for the distinctive character and quality of our historical imagination.

The American writer William Faulkner famously said that 'The past is never dead. It's not even past.' This simple, powerful quote declares what we know to be true, that the past is never gone or left behind; we are never free of its burden or its inspiration. Since we can't disentangle ourselves from its power, we might as well wrestle with it intelligently.

The past is a quarry of ideas, an archive of possible future scenarios. Physicists say the same of time. In the fundamental laws of physics, time forward and time past are treated as equal. 'It's not that the past has gone,' says physicist Brian Greene in explaining the fabric of the universe. 'All of time exists in much the same way that all of space exists ... every moment is as real as any other, every moment exists on the same footing as every other.'[13] The theory of relativity leads us to the conclusion that the experience of time flowing relentlessly in a particular direction is an illusion of human perception. Physics puzzles over this illusion: 'Why do we remember the past and not the future?' asks Stephen Hawking in his bestseller, *A Brief History of Time* (1988).[14] Physicists can wonder over the causes of time's arrow, but it is up to historians to make sense of our experience of it.

After the development of Einstein's general theory of relativity in 1915, it became meaningless to talk about space and time as absolute, as transcending the limits of the universe; instead, they became dynamic qualities of the universe itself. In effect, the universe became finite and historical; it was no longer unchanging but had a beginning and an end – a life. Without absolute time, each individual has their own personal measure of time that depends on where they are and how they are moving. Physicists and historians agree on this. In the year of the fall of the Berlin Wall, the Australian historian of Russia David Christian began to teach a course on 'Big History' at Macquarie University, which offered a history of the universe over 13.6 billion years from the Big Bang to the present. Christian's course was built on the insight I have been describing, and was inspired also by the belief that historians needed to reclaim their traditional role as global storytellers.[15]

John Lewis Gaddis, in *The Landscape of History: How Historians Map the Past* (2002), observes that 'the methods of historians are closer to those of certain natural scientists than to those of most social scientists.'[16] Marc Bloch, E H Carr and Keith Hancock each made the same observation. The hope of the humanities to become scientific, and to be objective and predictive about human cultural and social change, faltered from the beginning of the twentieth century, although the quest goes on in some social sciences today. Subjectivity, reflexivity, context and contingency were rediscovered as scholarly virtues. What is fascinating is that the natural and physical sciences also moved in this direction at the same time. Narrative complexity made a comeback and historical thinking became pervasive. We might say that this was 'the historical revolution' to balance 'the scientific revolution' of the seventeenth and eighteenth centuries.

Gaddis uses the gravitational phenomenon known as a 'singularity' to understand the flow of time. Singularities exist within black holes and transform everything that passes through them; a singularity was the initial state of the universe before the Big Bang. Gaddis suggests that the present is a singularity through which the future must pass in order to become the past. On the future side of the singularity, continuities and contingencies are fluid and indeterminate; however, as they pass through it they fuse and cannot be separated.[17] The present locks these swirling possibilities and shifting relationships into place and they can't be unzipped. This compelling image captures the gravitational power of the past and the exhilaration and terror of living. It reminds us that the present, to which we pay so much lip service, snaps into solidity in a moment. The past is our only anchorage and our chief source of meaning.

So there is all of time to explore. Fictional time travellers have been propelled into the past by drugs, dreams, knocks on the head, pacts with the devil, lightning bolts and thunder claps, or with the help of a space craft, time machine or tardis.[18] The craft that historians use is their own beloved discipline, cobbled together at a desk with pen, paper, screen, dust and data, augmented by talking, walking, looking and listening, and infused with a critical imagination. You don't need Doctor

Who's tardis or Dr Emmett Brown's flux capacitor if you've got Professor Dening's exercises (see Chapter 6) or Dr Smith's trowel (Chapter 14). Gaddis argues that 'historical research has capabilities well beyond that of a time machine', for historians have greater selectivity, can be in several places at once and can zoom in and out.[19]

One of the primary launch pads for the historian's time travel is the archive. The act of pilgrimage to a repository, the rituals and protocols of access, the reverent quiet of the room, the whispered request to the librarian and the donning of white gloves are all purifying preparations for silent communion with fragile paper, where the magic begins. Then there are emanations from the documents themselves, which the historian sometimes exposes to the light for the first time since they were preserved. The great French historian of the nineteenth century Jules Michelet celebrated his transformative engagement with the catacombs of manuscripts in the Archives Nationales of Paris with these words: 'As I breathed their dust, I saw them rise up. They rose from the sepulchre ...' It is unclear whether it was the documents or the dead that arose, but it was definitely Michelet who breathed life into them.[20] It is the historian's rare experience of power. I'm lucky that one of my first jobs as a historian was in a magnificent archive – the Manuscripts and Pictures collections of the State Library of Victoria – where I was part of a process whereby private family documents entered a public collection and became national history. I was steeped in the excitement of dealing with the material legacy of the past and was exposed (and contributed) to the fashions and contingencies of preservation. Even in the age of the internet, the archive remains a defining site where historians know who they are and what they do. Our students must be weaned from the screen and propelled into these enchanted places.

'Being there' – in place as well as time – entails adventure and exploration. It means visiting not just the archives, but the people with documents or memories and the places where it all happened. Manning

Clark was famous for his journeys in search of place and atmosphere: examining the faces of portraits and statues, visiting the capes and bays named by Cook in his journal, taking long walks around London to understand William Charles Wentworth, and following the path of Burke and Wills from Royal Park in Melbourne to Mootwingee and Tilpa and eventually to the Dig Tree on the Cooper. As his biographer Mark McKenna put it, 'For more than three decades, he walked almost every line of *A History of Australia*.'[21] The writers in this book have done the same; they are keen, in some cases legendary, walkers, and when they step outside they are equipped with boots, cameras, maps and pocket notebooks.

Historians are sometimes expected to be aloof from the present because of their pursuit of the past. But the opposite is more often true; they are frequently active citizens and wide-eyed travellers. If they are not, good teachers make them so. 'I would give trainee historians the chance to travel the world,' declared Theodore Zeldin. 'I am an historian. Therefore I love life,' announced Bloch's friend Henri Pirenne.[22] 'Imagination has its deepest roots in the lust for life,' affirmed Keith Hancock. He added:

> When we encounter a pupil [with an antipathy to theory] ... we should not inflict theory upon him but should encourage him to spend equivalent time in climbing mountains and wading rivers, joining archaeological 'digs', making music and listening to it, producing plays and acting in them, learning languages, reading novels and poetry – not all of these things, of course, but some of them.

Why? Because, as Hancock told his students, 'No imagination, no history.'[23] And he probably added: 'No passion, no scholarship.' Professional time travellers have to know intimately the culture and coordinates of their own time – so that they can get back to it! And so that they can speak to the present with sensitivity and discernment.

At the beginning of this inquiry I wondered if people I might casually meet in Australia would so readily ask me to name my favourite historians as did the French ramblers. Recently when I walked three weeks of the Heysen trail in South Australia with my adult children, we arrived after six days in McLaren Vale, looking forward to a glass of red wine. There a friend gave us accommodation for the night and we spent the evening talking with locals around an open fire under the stars, mostly about music, wine and politics. A builder and budding vigneron whose wine I was enjoying, on learning that I was a historian, told me that his favourite book was Eric Rolls' *A Million Wild Acres* (see Chapter 8) and asked me what I thought of it. Although we had just met, we immediately found common ground in the grapes of the Vale and the soil of the Pilliga.

History – that unending dialogue between the present and the past – is essential to human consciousness. It is conducted as part of the daily business of living, of knowing oneself, of grappling with memory and of finding meaning. It is also a systematic and reflective intellectual discipline with academic traditions and scholarly conventions. Thus there is a vast spectrum of historical consciousness that includes forms of knowledge both instinctive and learned. The more richly we can integrate these various influences, the better and more thoughtful our scholarship will be. It is not inconsistent to advocate history as the highest of arts and the most demanding of scholarly pursuits at the same time as recognising it as an everyday search for meaning for which there is an insatiable personal and public hunger.

I have long been fascinated by historical consciousness, and twenty years ago wrote a book, *Hunters and Collectors* (1996), which explored popular patterns of memory and history-making in Australia, particularly beyond the academy. Here, by contrast, I am looking at people who together build disciplinary knowledge about the past – my subjects are not necessarily trained or professional historians (although most studied here are) but they are all people who research the past with a reflective, scholarly purpose. I begin with a novelist and end with an archaeologist and there's a poet and a farmer in the mix, but most identify as historians and have made their careers in practising history. However, rather than 'career', they would speak of 'vocation' or 'calling' – terms that capture the lifelong dedication and almost spiritual quest that drive many writers of non-fiction. So there is a self-conscious academic discipline at the heart of this book that we might also call a craft, another word favoured by many of the people portrayed.

'Craft' evokes the combination of intellectual, artistic and technical skills that attract many to history, and captures the tactile, sensual dimension of working with archives as well as the experience of writing as a form of sculpture. In writing history I find that one must first amass the clay, the raw material of reality, building up the rough form, gathering much more than one can eventually keep. Then begins the careful paring away, the sculpting and moulding, the tweaking out of detail. The final reality emerges, and one could believe that it was always there, trapped in the clay, awaiting discovery and release. This book aims to investigate the art of non-fiction, the distinctive creative challenges of telling stories that try to be as true as they can be. How does the writing of history differ from fiction, what is the interplay of evidence and imagination, and what styles of art might we discern in scholarship – impressionism, still life, pointillism, cubism, magic realism?

I write this book with the conviction that indeed something magical happens in the writing of great history. Just what that magic is, or might be, these chapters attempt to explore. I think the best way to examine this process is through its varied practice, by watching gifted historians at work and looking over their shoulders as they travel into the past. History is sometimes depicted as a static, hidebound package of dates and facts, already given, that must be learned. Anyone who researches and writes history, however, discovers that the past is alive and shifting. It is both elusive and malleable. Its chameleon quality is disturbing and raises questions about ethics and responsibility. One learns to draw on the past delicately and with a sense of responsibility. It is a lifetime commitment. And it is completely collaborative and collegial, for every insight depends upon others. We talk often of writing, which is the enduring measure of academic productivity, but the most generous thing a scholar can do is read. Read thoughtfully, widely and in context so that a whole body of work might be seen in the making. That is the journey these chapters take.

ONE

The Timeless Land: Eleanor Dark

ennilong and his father, Wunbula, gazed out to sea from the clifftop, searching the horizon for the boat with wings. Wunbula remembered the moment he had first seen the magic boat borne along the ocean like a bird. He had been participating in a ceremony south of his country when it appeared. His heart had leaped and his pulses hammered; he had felt both fear and rapture. The boat had flown into the harbour, folded its great white wings and come to rest. Mysterious beings with faces pale as bones, and with coverings on their heads, feet and bodies, had come ashore. After staying for many days, the *Bereewolgal* (strangers) suddenly left. Wunbula, who had by then returned to his own country, watched from a headland as the boat passed by on its journey north. He had etched an image of it into the sandstone and into his memory, and he had made a corroboree to tell of it. In the seasons following, Wunbula and Bennilong came secretly and often to the high cliffs to look for its return.

It is with this powerful image of a young Bennilong watching and waiting on the edge of a silent continent that the novelist Eleanor Dark begins her book *The Timeless Land* (1941).[1] The bird with wings that appeared mysteriously from over the unending water teases Bennilong with intimations of another land that he might one day hope to visit.

He grows up with a feeling that is half longing and half dread and that holds a vague sense of destiny: that the winged boat will return, that his life will somehow entwine with the lives of these strangers, and that he might discover that the water is not unending after all.

Wunbula dies in battle and Bennilong becomes a young man, and the memory of the magic boat dims. Yet still he comes often to the clifftop to gaze. And one day, it returns. Bennilong feels cheated that he did not see it first, hearing instead the excited stories from further south. But soon he does see it from the same rock he had visited with his father. 'The shadow world of dreams and spells and spirits had become real, ratified by a white sail against the blue water; and the real world grew misty, dimmed by a miracle, shaken by magic made visible.' His eyes never move from the approaching sail and he feels a dreadful apprehension. 'Steadily it came nearer. Sometimes, dipping in the swell, its wings swung and turned golden in the afternoon sunlight, like the wings of the gulls which swooped about them.'

Dark's fiction takes us to this eastern Australian clifftop in the late eighteenth century, this precipice of human history, the moment when peoples with immensely long and intimate histories of habitation encountered the furthest-flung representatives of the world's most industrialised nation, when the circle of dispersal of modern humans out of Africa more than 70,000 years earlier was finally closing.

Eleanor Dark dramatised this epic encounter as the coming of time to a timeless land.[2] Here on Bennilong's clifftop, she explained, 'life was marooned, and Time, like a slowly turning wheel, was only night and day, night and day, summer and winter, birth and death, the ebb and swell of tides.' The 'passing centuries ... had evolved in their brains no machinery for the understanding of Change.'[3] Time here was only the unvarying cycle of nature; its inertia threatened the momentum of the invaders.

She portrayed their leader, Governor Arthur Phillip, as restless and disturbed. He stood on the deck of the HMS *Supply* at anchor in

Sydney Cove in late January 1788 and regarded the dark land in the sinking twilight.

> There was no sense of Time here. To-night – was it Now, or a thousand years ago? What was it in the life of a man which gave him that reassuring sense of the passage of time? On his little journey from the cradle to the grave, how comforting to feel that Time moves forward with him – how chilling, how strange, how awesome, to feel, as one felt here, that Time was static, a vast eternal, unmoving emptiness through which the tiny pathway of one's life ran from darkness into darkness, and was lost! … 'To-morrow,' he said briskly to himself, but the word was empty. The ageless land had drained it of its meaning and its promise.[4]

Time is capitalised in these musings, as is Change, and also Man and Nature, which are in opposition. And in Australia, the colonists find that Nature is in troubling ascendancy. 'Undisturbed and unchallenged for countless centuries,' it had attained a might, a stature that diminished Man. The British immediately sensed the profound difference of the land and the threat it held to their equanimity. Dark imagines one of the First Fleet officers, Captain Watkin Tench, expressing it thus: 'Its difference was indifference. This place did not welcome you, like Rio; it did not look particularly fertile, and it was certainly not languorous. Nor did it repel you, like Table Bay; it offered no enmity, no resistance. It simply waited.'[5]

The antidote to such passivity and disempowerment was human order, action, noise and industry. The Aboriginal people watched the feverish activity of the white invaders with puzzlement. 'They were like bees or ants, these white people … They toiled and they swarmed, always moving, always going hurriedly from one place to another, always dragging things about, building, struggling, making a labour of their life.'[6] And Nature was to be their first conquest; the removal of trees was the colonists' priority and the sound of the axe declared their arrival in the silent, timeless land.

Eleanor Dark, a novelist, was probably Australia's most influential historical writer of the twentieth century. *The Timeless Land*, the first book in her trilogy of historical novels, was widely read, studied in schools and prescribed for matriculation reading in Victoria. It was translated into Swedish, German, Italian and Spanish and selected for the Book of the Month Club in the USA, making it a bestseller. It went through eight editions and has remained in print.[7] *The Timeless Land* introduced many foreigners to Australia and many Australians to their own history. When the novel was published in late 1941, readers and 'newshounds' wanted to know about the book *and* they wanted to know about Australia's past.

I am interested in the relationship between history and fiction and want to explore how such an influential novelist set about her historical task (see Chapters 5 and 12 for further discussion of this issue). I agree with the novelist James Bradley that we mustn't value fiction for its non-fiction: we 'mustn't make research the thing that matters about fiction'.[8] But it is significant that, for Dark in *The Timeless Land*, facts were her foundation and she wanted to imagine into and within the known past.

Eleanor Dark never claimed to be a historian but she took the craft of history very seriously. Her preface to *The Timeless Land* began: 'My aim has been to give a picture of the first settlement of Sydney, which is always true in broad outline, and often in detail, but I make no claim to strict historical accuracy either in my dealings with the white men or the black.' The original first sentence in her earlier draft (which appears in some later published editions) was: 'This book has borrowed so much from history that it seems advisable to remind readers that it is fiction.'[9]

We are fortunate that Eleanor Dark has attracted several skilled biographers – in particular Drusilla Modjeska, Barbara Brooks (with Judith Clark) and Marivic Wyndham.[10] In spite of this attention, Dark has often been seen to be 'neglected' – as a female writer, as a social critic, as an Australian novelist. I would add that she has also been neglected

as a historian. Dark's turn to historical fiction in the 1930s is acknowledged as a turning point in her reputation and influence, but her
biographers have kept their focus on her fiction and depicted her history
as an instrument of the novelist.[11] While literary studies have empha-
sised the fictiveness of *The Timeless Land*, historians have quite reasonably
bypassed her, as a writer of fiction, in their accounts of the emerging
discipline of history in Australia. But *The Timeless Land* wielded power
and influence also as a work of history – and it could do so because of
the author's dedicated research and serious historical purpose. Her friend
the historian Dorothy Fitzpatrick wrote Eleanor frank, detailed and critical letters in which she wrestled with the novel as a work both of fiction
and of history. In December 1941 Fitzpatrick observed that *The Timeless
Land* 'will be read by a far wider public than had ever read accurate
Australian history before'.[12] So in this chapter I am writing about a significant work of art and scholarship without worrying about how to
categorise it. I am not arguing that Eleanor Dark was a historian, nor
am I assessing *The Timeless Land* as a work of history; rather, I am por-
traying how and why a writer of fiction came to invest so deeply in an
empirical quest for historical understanding.

Eleanor and Eric Dark moved to Katoomba in the Blue Mountains in
1923 and bought a house a short walk from the giddy canyon depths
and swirling clouds of the escarpment. The home was already named
'Varuna' after a powerful god of Hindu mythology who is associated
with the Moon, but also with the airs and waters of Earth.[13] Eventually
the weatherboard house was replaced by a large, white, two-storey home
designed by Eleanor. 'She is in the clouds,' wrote her friend Jean Devanny,
intending the double meaning.[14] The separate world of the mountains
and the elemental majesty of the cliffs, gorges and skies were to shape
this writer's retreat, and her writing.

From her high, white sanctuary on the sandstone plateau, Dark imagined looking out towards the breaking wave of British colonisation on the eastern shore and, in three long books written over a decade and a half, described the incoming tide of invasion until it was lapping at the base of her own mountains. In her historical trilogy, the early colonists are always looking west towards the lavender-coloured range of hills. Somewhere in the heart of those mountains, they thought, a noble river must rise. And what lay beyond? It was 'a flat purple range running north and south, a barrier which might hide anything – or nothing'.[15] The line of hills beckoned and drew them, but it was like a mirage that receded before their strenuous efforts. The characters in the novels constantly look up towards their creator, to the escarpment where Dark was toiling away, conjuring them alive. Up there, somewhere, dreams one settler, is a house on a hilltop, 'Alone. White in the blueness.'

We can see the historical trilogy as an account of the gradual penetration of this mountain fastness by the newcomers, by the society whose values the novels throw into critical relief. 'Here was someone looking out, not looking in,' as Manning Clark was to say of Eleanor Dark.[16] The novels are full of the detail gathered from Eleanor's familiar backyard – the sheer difficulty of progress through the bush, the wayward creeks and marshes, the giant trunks of falling trees, the rocks that shredded boots – lovingly evoked, sometimes with comic purpose. The stumbling of the invaders is watched from the other side of the frontier; there is giggling in the bush as they lose their way, and the official expeditions inland always lag well behind the unofficial infiltrations. By the time Mr Gregory Blaxland and his party finally 'cross' the mountains in 1813 at the end of the trilogy, the reader has already been taken into the gorges and mountains many times, and knows that the trails of campfire smoke that the 'explorers' observe in the distance include the hearths of settlers as well as Aborigines. The reader of Dark's trilogy knows that the British ambition to be the 'first' to cross the mountains is an arrogant vanity, for as one bush dweller explains, 'There's been natives crossin' back and forth maybe for hundreds of years.'

When the publishers of *The Timeless Land* wanted some author photos, the only ones Eleanor could supply were of her camping and bushwalking. The Darks loved exploring their mountains, and it was a wonderful respite from desk work: 'Went with E. for walk round Golf Links & Cyclorama Point – feeling dopey from being too long indoors over the b. book.'[17] A respected rock climber, Eric formed a climbing club called the Blue Mountaineers (known locally as the Katoomba Suicide Club), and Eleanor would join them for tough walks of 30 to 40 kilometres a day.

When Eleanor was writing *The Timeless Land*, she and Eric packed rucksacks and camping gear and set out to retrace the steps of the first colonists to venture into their realm. In 1789 Governor Phillip ordered Lieutenant William Dawes to lead a party inland from the plains of the Nepean River to Round Hill, now known as Mount Hay. It was the first attempt by the British to ascend the Blue Mountains. In late May 1940 Eleanor, Eric, Frank Walford, Michael Dark (aged eleven) and his friend Geoff Sinclair (thirteen) left Emu Plains on the Nepean and roughly followed the route of Dawes' party. With this long bushwalk Eleanor aimed not just to travel in time so as to better imagine and describe the terrain of the 1789 expedition. She was also connecting her mountain home in space to the world of the novel. She was walking the beeline of her narrative from the settling of the coastal plain to the bridging of the escarpment. Hanging on the walls at Varuna were paintings that made the same connection – they were landscapes by Elioth Gruner, whose *plein air* pastoral scenes of the banks of the Nepean River at Emu Plains made him famous in the early twentieth century.[18]

In 1789 Dawes' party retreated after five days, bemused by the labyrinthine ridges and gorges and unable to find a way through or over them. In *The Timeless Land*, Dark described how the exploring party found the

gullies getting deeper and more precipitous every day, and how Round
Hill, occasionally glimpsed 'rising stolidly from its wild chaos of lesser
hills', hardly grew closer. The views remained the same: 'Trees, trees,
trees ... Nothing else.' The Darks did not follow Lieutenant Dawes into
all the gorges and dead-ends; they kept to the main ridge and managed
to avoid confronting cliff faces. 'Started off from foot of mts at about ¼
to 9,' recorded Eleanor in her diary. 'Walked all day. Camped at night in
Faulconbridge Creek in v. good cave.' They found pleasant camping and
good rock overhangs each night. Four days later they reached the Mount
Hay track, where they were met by a car and returned to Katoomba.

The successful expedition was reported in *The Sydney Bushwalker*
by Marie Byles, who concluded: 'I am sure that Governor Phillip would
be gratified to know his commands had been at length carried out albeit
a century and a half after they were given.'[19] The Dark party, although
they experienced 'many vicissitudes' on the approach to Mount Hay,
efficiently completed the trek that defied official British expeditions for
a quarter of a century.

The walk offered a welcome respite from the war. On 29 May 1940
Eleanor recorded the arrival home in her diary: 'Back to "civilization"
again with news of bombings, sinkings, killings, & surrender of Belgian
army! Oh for the bush!'[20] Her mountain home was Eleanor's retreat from
distractions to her writing but also from a world going mad in the 1930s
and '40s. Dark's fiction gave voice to her critique of the ascendancy of
material values over human values. The visible misery of the Depression,
the international rise of fascism, the sense of social and political crisis and
the spectre of another war disturbed Dark, as it did many Australian
writers of this period. They wondered about the opportunities and dangers of nationalist literature at such a time. Sitting one day on the grass
of Hyde Park in central Sydney correcting the proofs of *The Timeless Land*,
Eleanor was 'driven away by a particularly strident recruiting truck'.[21]
Was her turn to history another kind of retreat? I don't think so.

Eleanor's biographers agree that *The Timeless Land* was a change of direction that reflected the Darks' increasing interest in history, politics and socially engaged writing at a time of fascism and looming conflict.[22] Many of the Darks' friends were turning to historical writing in the 1930s: Marjorie Barnard and Flora Eldershaw in *A House is Built* and *Phillip of Australia*, Brian Penton in *Landtakers*, H V (Bert) Evatt in *The Rum Rebellion*, Vance and Nettie Palmer, Katharine Susannah Prichard and historians Dorothy and Brian Fitzpatrick. Eric gave Eleanor a copy of H G Wells' *Outline of History* for her birthday in 1936.[23] History was a way to understand the changes that were so rapidly overtaking their own society. Yet, as the war throttled Australian life at home and as Eleanor wrote her eighteenth-century story into the unused pages of Eric's medical appointments diary (paper was rationed), Eleanor wondered whether writing was futile, especially writing about the distant past.[24] She told her American publisher, James Putnam, that 'during the long and often tiresome process of writing it I was continually bothered by the feeling that all writers *should* be writing about momentous contemporary events; and yet I did realise that so-called "modern" problems are not new, but only old problems now reaching culmination point, and that they were already well rooted in the times of which I was writing.'[25] Drusilla Modjeska identified Dark's 'attempt to write about a society at the point of crisis, but by exploring its origins' and felt that *The Timeless Land* recognises 'a heritage of humanism and anti-fascism in Australian history and holds out the possibility that it could be continued, despite the weight against it'.[26] The book which brought the ships with wings to Bennilong's shore was published just a month before Australia declared war on Japan and came under threat from another foreign invasion. *The Timeless Land* examined an earlier annexation and investigated Britain's moral right to its antipodean acquisition.

❧

By the time Dark was beginning to write *The Timeless Land*, she had added two further retreats to the sanctuary that was Varuna. Each expressed an impulse that shaped her writing. One was a magnificent, yawning cave in a great sandstone cliff above Govett's Creek. She and Eric had observed it from the other side of the gorge, as a gash in a distant rockface, on one of their regular bushwalks and climbing excursions in their mountain backyard. They were looking for a cave to make their own, and about a year later they set out to find the dark, promising shadow in the cliff they remembered. In early January 1937 Eleanor recorded: 'Eric & I for walk to explore Gusty Gorge, & search for cave.'

They found it and were delighted with it. It was two caves really, one a sunlit high-roofed cavern with a dress-circle view of two headlands opening onto a deeper gorge, and the other a darker cave in a gully with its own waterfall. They quickly moved in, keeping its location secret by taking different paths to its mouth, and using the cavern as a kitchen and sunroom and the gully cave for sleeping. They cleared the floor of the cave with crowbar and mattock and by dynamiting the largest rocks and then levelled it with earth they brought in from termite mounds. 'E and boys brought down packs of ant-bed after breakfast & then E and I and Mike laid it, (finishing floor of main cave) while boys went off to swim,' Eleanor recorded in her diary in early January 1938.[27] The waterfall cave had a stream, and the creek below could be dammed to create a swimming hole.

It was a weekender, a place of refuge, a 'summer resort' where Eleanor and Eric could take friends and enjoy exploring the bush, and where the children could play and swim. But they created domesticity there too — Eleanor enjoyed 'pottering about the cave', did household 'chores' there just as she did at Varuna, cut grass for bedding, made a vegetable plot, watered her parsnips, potatoes and pumpkins, built a fireplace with cemented shelves, and installed furniture, cooking equipment and some mattresses.

When I visited it a year or two ago, it felt immense, remote and in a world of its own, and even on a day of swirling mists, it was infused with a great sense of space and light. It is an exhilarating setting, enfolded within the range and also a lookout. The descent to the cave is steep and still little known, but it has become a site of quiet pilgrimage. A collection of old boots and billies from Eleanor's time is respectfully tucked away on a natural shelf above the sleeping platform in the waterfall cave, and an old meat safe is still suspended between boulders.

The eye of the cave looks out onto the great gorge and sandstone cliff faces of Govett's Creek and the sounds of the bush resonate in the overhang: 'Heard large rock-fall somewhere during night,' Eleanor wrote.[28] They listened to lyrebird concerts, sheltered from storms that made their own little waterfall thunder 'like Niagara', and moved from the main cave to the waterfall cave in high winds. Once during the night 'some beastie, probably goanna, stole three out of four of our hard-boiled eggs,' and on another trip Eric and the boys killed a snake and ate it.

They called the place Jerrikellimi, a name that sounded Aboriginal but which was a combination of their own names: John, Eric, Eleanor and Mike. This invented name, with its evocation of Aboriginality, had resonances of the Jindyworobak poets, a group that formed in Adelaide in the same year Eleanor found her cave and, like her, drew inspiration from Aboriginal words, images and understandings of landscape. Dark, for example, referred to Australian writers and artists as 'the corroboree-makers'. False local legends about the cave grew: that it was used by Eric as a guerrilla training base during the Second World War, that they had a year's supply of food hidden there, that they sought refuge in the cave for several months during the Bay of Pigs crisis, and that the name was indeed Aboriginal and meant 'the retreat of the Dark People'.[29]

Another legend of the cave is that Eleanor wrote *The Timeless Land* there. She certainly found it the year she began the book, and dwelling under the arching roof of stone must surely have strengthened her imaginative empathy for Aboriginal life. It expressed a strong impulse in her writing: to offer an insider view, to evoke her country in sensual detail and to draw on the 'inexhaustible legend' of Australia's antiquity. She may have recorded notes and ideas in the cave, perhaps even on the slab of rock they used for a table. But her daily discipline of words was exercised at home, at her desk, and from 1938 in another retreat for which she had longed.

She called it 'my room', a room of her own. It was her new writing studio in the garden at Varuna. In early August 1938, with the writing of *The Timeless Land* gathering momentum, she moved in: 'In afternoon moved desk & chair & books over to room ... [and two days later] Home in afternoon, lit fire in my room & sat here.'[30] A woman who had as a child lived just down the road from Varuna remembers how kind the Darks were to her family and that they also allowed them to play on the tennis court: 'My only memory of Eleanor is that when we arrived, and we arrived very quietly, she would disappear with almost a tragic look on her face into her little cottage.'

This was surely the haunted look of the writer. Not tragic so much as bitten. Once 'bitten' by the bug of an idea, Eleanor reflected, the writer lived with a perpetual sense of guilt, feeling guilty when she is writing and feeling guilty when she is not, engaged in the lifelong burglary of 'stealing time'. 'Most novelists – in Australia at all events – find that writing is compelled to take second, third, fifth or sixteenth place,' she reflected. Eleanor would slip away to the one place where writing was a sanctioned priority, to her workroom, separate from the house and where she was not to be interrupted. Although she cherished the seclusion, it was often an ordeal: 'no schoolboy ever crept to school as unwillingly as I creep to my desk!'[31] She generally felt that the only truly joyful moment of the writing life was the ten minutes after completion of a book, the short-lived relief before the next bug bit. Writing was physically hard work – transcribing notes, copying out drafts, typing the manuscript – and it all depended on mental labour too. The historical trilogy, with its extra burden of research, was especially exhausting. The physical finality of posting the completed manuscript of *The Timeless Land* was exhilarating and liberating: 'Went up with E. to send M.S. away ... Can hardly believe it's finished & GONE!!'[32]

The cottage was furnished with an impressive desk and chair, a comfortable armchair, cupboards and drawers for her manuscripts and notebooks, and bookshelves for her key sources. This room of her own was an assertion of Eleanor's need for independence as an artist and as a woman, and therefore expressive of her feminist politics. Its apartness from the domestic household and even from her cherished role as mother was crucial. 'I covet a brass door-knocker,' she confessed in 1946, 'but as the one great salient point of the whole thing is that nobody is ever to knock upon pain of death, I think I shall have to do without it.'[33] One day, when her son Michael knocked in desperation on the door of the cottage, he pleaded with his mum: 'This is a life or death situation. I'm hungry.'[34]

Varuna is now superbly managed as a writers' house. Some years ago I had the good fortune to work there, and was assigned Eleanor's cottage as my writing room. It is her other 'cave': simple, elegant, with a hearth and a bay window looking over the garden. The few steps from the kitchen through the back door and across the lawn to the inviolable place of work were indeed focusing and liberating. As well as absorbing the atmosphere of the studio, with its collection of volumes of the *Historical Records of Australia*, I relished the opportunity to browse in the Darks' home library. One day I noticed a brown-paper-covered volume hidden at the far edge of a locked bookcase in the main house. When I was able to retrieve it, I discovered it was Eleanor's annotated copy of *The Timeless Land*. In the margins of the pages, she had footnoted her fiction. This fact, she wrote, was from David Collins' account, this one from Watkin Tench's narrative, this event was described in the governor's dispatch, this interpretation of Aboriginal society was drawn from Threlkeld, and that from Professor Elkin. She wanted to honour the known past as well as to inform it with her imagination. Her quest was as much historical as literary.

In her fiction, Dark was increasingly fascinated by time; the uneven flow and fabric of it was a mysterious and palpable part of her narratives. Following early-twentieth-century physics, modernist writers often depicted life in terms of fluidity and uncertainty rather than linearity and order. In her daily diaries, Eleanor gave her own experience of time a cyclical dimension by writing her diary in a round: there were five, six or seven years to a diary and she would return each year to the start of the volume and record her entries under those of the years before. A glance up the page reminded her of the rhythmical routines and seasons of life. In her novel *Waterway* (1938), Dark played with the subjectivity of time, its capacity to stretch or intensify in individual experience. In *The Timeless Land*, she explored time as a shared cultural and historical property.

Waterway focused on Sydney Harbour and featured quotes from colonial documents at the head of its sections, implicitly drawing parallels between Sydney Cove present and past. When Dark was finishing the novel she was sometimes distracted by history, recording in her diary in December 1936: 'I began to work but got reading History of NSW instead.'[35] In the middle of 1937, as *Waterway* moved into production, Eleanor threw herself into researching the life of Caroline Chisholm for a chapter in *The Peaceful Army*, a book edited by Flora Eldershaw for the 150th anniversary of British settlement that aimed to recognise the role of women in Australian history. Dark was attracted to a woman who believed in family and also in bravely advocating social change. Studying Chisholm took her into the heart of colonial history and Dark

identified 'three black shadows' across the bright picture of early
Australia: 'the treatment of convicts, the treatment of emigrants, and
the treatment of the aborigines'.[36] It was her first piece of sustained historical research and she was 'bitten', hooked on history. 'Mitchell Library
all day,' she recorded in her diary in May 1937, 'working on Caroline.'
'Whole day at Library', 'grappled with Caroline till after 1 am again',
'final struggle with Caroline'.[37] There was a new competitive presence
in the household. Young Mike asked: 'Will you read to me or have you
got to do some Caroline?'[38]

As soon as Eric had posted 'Caroline' to Miss Eldershaw, the Darks
sailed for the United States and Canada, Eleanor's first and only trip
overseas. Eric was visiting hospitals to learn about heat treatments and
Eleanor would meet her American publishers. The Darks were away for
three months, and Eleanor was counting the days to her return. On
Saturday, 23 October 1937, she was 'up at crack of dawn to see first of
coastline! Stayed on deck till inside Heads.' So Eleanor had the experience of arriving by sea to her own country and beholding it through
strangers' eyes, and perhaps feeling both insider and outsider. It was she
who was on the boat with wings — well, an ocean liner — nosing its way
through the Heads into Port Jackson, *and* she was coming home.

The first weekend after their return to Katoomba, they got up early
and set off for Jerrikellimi. A few days later, Eleanor was reading and taking notes about Aborigines. The writing of *The Timeless Land* had begun.

Eleanor Dark's working days in the writing of the book were like those
of a historian, with trips to Sydney and long hours with the archive shaping her routine: 'To town in morning & worked at Mitchell. Lunch in
gardens, Mitchell in afternoon.'[39] The Mitchell Library was a centre of
networks for writers and independent scholars, especially women:
Marjorie Barnard wrote to Miles Franklin in 1937 declaring, 'I'm living

there at present (with Governor Phillip).'[40] Eleanor had a loose-leaf book for her research notes, organised chronologically, a page for each date, with the action or event noted and the source recorded. Another notebook recorded customs and traditions of Australian Aborigines, organised alphabetically into sections on 'Ceremonies', 'Kinship' and 'Language'. Eleanor was captivated, but she also felt the burden of this scholarly mission, 'a type of mental effort which doesn't come naturally to me' and which ultimately left her 'with a sort of loathing of my desk'.[41] Percival Serle, when completing his *Dictionary of Australian Biography* in 1949, wrote to Eleanor about *Storm of Time* (1948) saying, 'Your history seemed excellent to me,' and offering some minor corrections to historical facts. But Dark was able to show that he was wrong and also drew his attention to 'a curious mistake' in the *Historical Records of New South Wales*. Serle replied that Dark 'could have done an infinitely better book' on Macquarie than Malcolm Ellis had.[42] Her fiction was disciplined with referenced facts – too disciplined, some of her readers and critics thought of the later books in the trilogy. As the historical novels took over her life, she became a slave to her respect for past reality.

Dark found herself sickened by the complacency of Sydney's celebration of the sesquicentenary of British settlement in 1938. Aborigines, convicts and women were forgotten or suppressed in a triumphal national story that celebrated free white male pioneers planting the flag on a virgin continent. Professional historians, the few who existed, were doing little to unsettle this complacency, applying their expertise mostly to imperial history and situating Australian history as a footnote to it. Women were mostly outside or on the edge of universities, had their own research networks, and worked in libraries on local primary sources; thus they tended to be more critical of orthodox views of empire. Eleanor Dark wanted to write a more radical historical account, one from the inside, looking out from her cave in the sandstone escarpment towards the swelling tide of invasion. Beginning her novel with Wunbula and Bennilong standing on an eastern headland scanning the horizon, watching for the return of the great ship with wings, was a stunning imaginative leap from the ships to shore, to the view from the edge of the trees.[43]

American readers received *The Timeless Land* as speaking to something universal. It was 'a racial drama'. 'For the first time, I believe,' wrote Hassoldt Davis in *The Nation* in New York, 'we see in graphic full scale the initial conflicts and adjustments of a dark race with a white one ... Bennilong, the proud, the furious, is a unique character in fiction.'[44] Dorothy Canfield, writing in *The Bookman*, explained that:

> Americans are not only ignorant of, but honestly not very much interested in early days in Australia ... But the American public is going to be interested in this unique and moving novel. What it does is to throw open the window of our imagination and let in a flood of understanding on the heaped up piles of facts all too familiar to us in our own past ... Have we ever had, before, from a truly able writer of fiction, a creative divination of what the first contacts really were, in human terms, between simple savages and the complex exacting society of the white man?[45]

Dark was decades ahead of Australia's historians in realising that the big story about British colonisation at Port Jackson was that of the encounter between settlers and Aborigines. When Manning Clark set out on what he sometimes called his 'journey without maps' and began writing his multi-volume *A History of Australia*, one of the few scholarly influences he acknowledged was *The Timeless Land*.[46] In the week he gave his first lecture in Australian history at the University of Melbourne in 1946, he read the work of 'the creator ... of the image of the "winged bird"' and recognised someone who was 'no spiritual exile' but who felt at home in Australia, someone who 'belonged'.[47] In 1946 he and his wife, Dymphna, visited the Darks at Varuna and left inspired, and in 1948, Manning invited Dark to lecture to his history students at Melbourne University, a visit remembered by one of his students that year, John Mulvaney (see Chapter 3).[48] In 1963 Clark sent Dark a copy of the new edition of volume 1 of his *A History of Australia* with this explanation: 'The reason for this is that if there is any value in the work at all this comes in part from the inspiration in reading *The Timeless Land*, and I would like you to accept the book in gratitude for all that I owe to your own work.'[49] In 1976 he again visited Eleanor in Katoomba and recorded in his diary: 'So moved to speak to her again that I kissed her goodbye. That bond between people who are aware of things in life that do not bother other people.'[50] In 1980 Clark sent Dark a telegram: 'Still deeply moved by the majesty of your creation.'[51]

Yet Clark's own histories remained relatively impervious to the cross-cultural human drama that Dark had researched and explored. Such was the power of disciplinary thinking, even on a maverick such as Clark. History became professional and academic in the late nineteenth century by developing a science of the document and servicing the increasingly powerful nation state, itself a generator and organiser of documents. It was aligned with literacy and nationalism, and enforced a rupture between history and prehistory, civilisation and 'the primitive', humans and animals, culture and nature.[52] The Dark side of Clark remained, at that time, outside of history. As did the dark side of colonial Australia.

Eleanor was now spending many weekends sleeping beneath a rock overhang, listening to the echoing sounds of the bush. She began *The Timeless Land* with 'the idea of Australia' ('an alarmingly large idea but alluring') and an Aboriginal character, Bennilong, whom she had encountered when reading David Collins' account of the British settlement.[53] She recalled that 'the personality of the man emerged and gripped me. He became a living person to me. So much so that I collected all the items and began to weave a story around him. And I couldn't write about Bennilong without writing about his environment, and so the book took shape.'[54]

Dark told her publisher that her purpose was 'to tell a story of the white settlement partly from the black man's point of view'. Her first title for the book was 'Black Man's Burden'. And the third book in her trilogy, *No Barrier*, was originally called 'Land of Plunder'. Exploitation of the land was a powerful theme of the novels, and Bennilong would carry the burden of that story too. Eleanor had originally drafted a prologue to *The Timeless Land* that depicted the ancient continent as it existed in the European imagination before 1770. But her publisher, William Collins, wanted to cut the prologue because the manuscript was too long, and encouraged her instead to begin with her description of Bennilong and his father.[55] So the reflections on time and destiny at the start of the book were folded into the exploration of Bennilong's consciousness as he kept watch with Wunbula on the headland.

In the sesquicentenary of 1938, Aboriginal people in Sydney declared a Day of Mourning in protest at the celebrations. Eleanor's novel, taking shape at the same time, used the word 'invasion' for British colonisation. A few years later she would debate this version of Australian history with the publisher Sydney Ure Smith, who challenged Dark's use of the phrase 'we stole the land' to describe British settlement. In 1944 Ure Smith had commissioned Dark to write an essay on 'Australia and the Australians' for a book for an American audience, but her contribution was rejected by the publishing director of John Sands because it was 'too self-critical'. Ure Smith then offered to publish it in a different collection, with one proviso:

> The only thing I'm sorry about is that you feel so strongly about the use of the word 'stole'. My objection to its use at this particular time is that we are still at war – and I dislike the idea of pointing out our own weaknesses at such a time. In peace time it is different – but

anything which aids and abets our enemies – or enemy sympathis-
ers – somehow sticks in my gizzard. If we had not taken the
land – some other nation would have done so – and I doubt if the
natives would have had more consideration. I also do not like to
subscribe to anti-British sentiment ...[56]

Ure Smith's argument was threefold: that overseas war trumped any
'war' or 'theft' on colonial soil, that the land was going to be taken anyway, and that the British were better masters than most. These arguments
would regularly reappear in conservative critiques of Aboriginal history
throughout the century. But Ure Smith's final tactic was to pretend to
disdain history altogether: 'Frankly,' he concluded, 'I am not so interested
in our past as in our future.' Yet that single past participle – 'stole' – mat-
tered very much to him. He asked Eleanor to 're-consider my objection
to one word'. But she did not. And the word was published.

Bennilong's perspective enabled Dark to examine, and see as
strange, the imperial and material foundations of her own Western liberal society. She wanted to analyse the impulses of conquest that were
playing out so dramatically on the world stage as she wrote her novel.
The Timeless Land was as much about nature as about Aborigines, and
Dark depicted the two as in harmony, in a state of equilibrium that she
felt her own society had lost. At a time when overstocking, drought and
erosion were producing dramatic dust storms, Dark observed that
Aboriginal people did not 'battle with the soil'. In a talk entitled 'The
"Conquest of Nature"', Dark regretted the term and reflected: 'It is use-
less at this stage to hunt back through history for the moment when
man made that first false step in this matter, but most likely it occurred
during that period when he first began to diverge mentally from the
rest of the animal world.' Her inquiry seeks the primitive, animal source
of Aboriginality even as she exalts the humanity of Indigenous
Australians. Hunting for that moment – that schism – might be 'use-
less' but it was nevertheless a quest that underpinned Dark's fascination

with early colonial Australian history. Aboriginal Australia, she suggested, offered 'a human community which may serve as a kind of "control"' in understanding that first false step towards dominating nature.[57] Her Aboriginal people were 'primitive' in a material sense, and their conditions of life seemed like those of animals, but there was something noble in their spirit. 'I do not want to be taken for a "back-to-nature" advocate,' she wrote in the preface to *The Timeless Land*, 'nor for one who, in these disillusioned times, regards our own civilisation as inevitably doomed; but I do believe that we, nine tenths of whose progress has been a mere elaboration of the technique, as opposed to the art of living, might have learned much from a people who, whatever they may have lacked in technique, had developed that art to a very high degree.'

Dark's opening portrait of Bennilong and Wunbula depicts a state of innocence and contentment that is disturbed by something beyond the horizon, something outside known space and time. So *The Timeless Land* tells the story not only of an invasion, but also of a Fall. Bennilong is introduced to the reader as a six-year-old boy with a destiny that is somehow bound up with the boat with wings. Bennilong senses it, and so does Wunbula as he looks down on his son drawing in the sand. Between Bennilong and the magic boat 'there stretched a thread of contact – frail, invisible, intangible'. As a grown man when the boat returns, Bennilong is drawn to the white people, but he is also curiously reticent because he knows in his heart that there is no rush – for the fateful meeting, and all that will follow from it, surely awaits him. Thus the stage is set for the tragedy of Bennilong.

Bennilong's tragedy is his people's tragedy. The novel describes the devastating impact of smallpox on the Indigenous people of Port Jackson from the autumn of 1789. Probably more than half the Aboriginal population died from this disease. Smallpox quickly and tragically wrought a reduced and much-altered Aboriginal society: 'far fewer old people, fewer mature women, proportionally more young men and youths'.[58] Colonists were dealing, almost from the beginning of the encounter, with an Indigenous society that was coping with dramatic and catastrophic change. In the years and decades that followed, violence, murder and dispossession enforced the invasion.

But Bennilong's tragedy, as explored by Dark in her novel, focuses on a more personal turmoil. Even as a boy Bennilong feels the stirrings of an addiction that will bring him down. He is vulnerable and corruptible. As a man on the frontier, drawn to the theatre of encounter, he relishes the adrenalin of performance. The alcohol of the white people gives him lucidity and visions. Near the end of *The Timeless Land*, Bennilong fulfils his destiny and sails on a boat with wings out of the harbour, bound for a distant land, past the headland where he and his father had gazed at the ocean horizon years before.

The book ends with an epilogue depicting Bennilong's return from London to Australia three years later. 'Once, he thought, life was whole, like the body of a man. Once the past, the present, and the future were intricately woven together, and with them was entwined the life of man, body and spirit, one life ... But now something had assailed it. Change had gashed it like a knife, and the spirit flowed out of it like blood.' A drunk and angry Bennilong, caught between cultures, returns to the eastern headland where he had watched his father etch a stone carving of the boat with wings, and he defaces it. The sun sets on his defeat and 'an exhausting and unendurable sense of loss sweeps over him.' He falls and cuts his arm on the broken bottle of drink, and the blood from his wound runs into the disfigured grooves of Wunbula's drawing.

In the final volume of the trilogy, *No Barrier* (1954), Laetitia Mannion, whose housemaid is Bennilong's daughter, is reading the *Sydney Gazette* in January 1813 when her eye is caught by a strange but familiar name.[59]

It is a report of Bennilong's death at Kissing Point, penned by an anonymous journalist, which Eleanor found at the Mitchell Library and which has been used extensively by writers and historians since. The death notice declared: 'Of this veteran champion of the native tribe little favourable can be said. His voyage to and benevolent treatment in Great Britain produced no change whatever in his manners or inclinations, which were naturally barbarous and ferocious ... In fact he was a thorough savage, not to be warped from the form and character that nature gave him, by all the efforts that mankind could use.'[60] For Laetitia, Bennilong's life was proof of the intractability of the black race, in spite of British kindness and indulgence. Aboriginal scholar Marcia Langton recently declared this 1813 obituary 'a vicious tract that failed to mention his services to the colony'.[61]

Dark acknowledged her reliance on accounts of Aboriginal culture by A P Elkin, Phyllis Kaberry, Mary Gilmore, Herbert Basedow and Daisy Bates. And in her preface to *The Timeless Land*, she declared: 'The race is nearly gone ...' But the very years she was writing saw the beginnings of a profound change in the way white society viewed the past and future of Australian Indigenous peoples. It was a watershed in public opinion about Aborigines; opposing ideas were brought in closest proximity and sometimes met at the divide. In some ways, racism was increasingly entrenched, but it was also articulately challenged by Aboriginal activists, white humanitarians and anthropologists. Aboriginal people, it was realised almost with a shock, had 'survived', or at least could 'be preserved' if proper action was taken by white Australians. Racism and sympathy met in this injunction to 'preserve', for it sustained the image of Aboriginal culture as delicate and vulnerable, passive and static, an object rather than a subject of history.

But in another sense, the acceptance of survival was an acknowledgement that Aborigines were historical beings, and thus it left more room for intimations of the longevity of the Indigenous occupation of

Australia.[62] Perhaps people had been here for thousands of years, rather than hundreds? Extinction and lack of antiquity both collapsed chronology; they were the twin traits of a timeless people. White Australians abandoned these beliefs at about the same time, in the very years that Dark was beginning her book. *The Timeless Land*, even as it depicted a changeless pre-European world and saw Bennilong as doomed, also fostered the new understandings by dramatising the individuality and humanity of real Aboriginal historical figures. As Dorothy Fitzpatrick wrote to Eleanor in 1941, 'It is very important for most people to have it brought home to them that they could have lived a life just like these primitive people are recorded to have lived, and still have remained the same sort of human being.'[63] And so we might even see Dark's description of a 'timeless' culture as a sympathetic literary evocation of the Dreaming: a world view that was cyclical, self-renewing, and bound to intimately known landscape and nature. The timelessness that Dark evoked was not outside of culture; it was a powerful humanistic vision, the key to another way of seeing, another way of relating to land, and another spirituality.

It was Eleanor Dark who conjured Bennilong alive again for twentieth-century Australians, and who framed his life as a tragedy, with help from the original *Sydney Gazette*. Inspired by the real Bennilong for whom she had looked in the historical documents – and Dark was to write the *Australian Dictionary of Biography* entry on him in 1966 – she imagined him as a cheeky, curious, strategic man grappling with circumstance and a sense of destiny, but caught and lost between cultures. In her *ADB* entry she wrote that, following his return from London in 1795, the sources are scanty but 'it is clear that he could no longer find contentment or full acceptance either among his countrymen or the white men.'[64] In her novel, Bennilong became an emblematic figure, and one generally paired – on equal terms – with that other icon, Governor Arthur Phillip. Each came to be seen as representative of their culture, and their foundation dialogue and individual fates were seen to determine the future of cross-cultural relations in Australia.

Inga Clendinnen's *Dancing with Strangers* (2003), an ethnographic history of the first years at Port Jackson that features 'Baneelon', brings this template of interpretation into the twenty-first century. Despite many new insights, Clendinnen remained wedded to the trope of tragedy and was unwittingly loyal to Dark's narrative framework, even though Clendinnen herself dismisses the novel. She concluded of Baneelon: he 'fumed his way to an outcast's grave. He should have died earlier, in the days of hope.'[65] Such is the enduring power of *The Timeless Land*, even over those who feel beyond its influence. In 2008 Marcia Langton, writing of the arrival in 1788 of 'giant canoes with wings', made a powerful case for Bennilong's agency in the colony's affairs, but also portrayed his eventual decline to 'a weak, defeated man'.[66] In the decades following the novel's publication, the mercurial Bennilong, although celebrated in life as a chameleon, remained trapped in just one kind of death. The sun always sets on his defeat.

But there is ebullient life in the Wangal warrior Woollarawarre Bennelong yet (his name now spelt with an 'e'). In the last few years, historians have reinterpreted his achievement. In 2001 Keith Vincent Smith published a biography of Bennelong, and in 2009 the journal *Aboriginal History* offered new insights into his life and death from Kate Fullagar, Emma Dortins and Smith.[67] In the same year, Grace Karskens introduced us to a more complex Bennelong as part of a portrait of the Eora people in her wonderful history of early Sydney, *The Colony*. Karskens observes that 'in settler history we seem to be constantly searching for beginnings ... But in Aboriginal history of the colonial period so often the search is for endings.' In Karskens' portrait of early Sydney, 'the space "between cultures" was not a void. It was full of possibilities.'[68] Bennelong, it now seems, did not fall into alcoholism and despair but returned to his people at Kissing Point, renewed his Eora clan networks, remarried, had another child, regained leadership and died an honoured and mourned elder. His elusiveness in the white sources after his return from Britain can be seen as a kind of escape. As Smith put it, 'He was one of the first to face the dilemma of knowing two cultures. In the end he chose his own.'[69]

It was Eleanor Dark who reintroduced Australians to the figure on the headland and made us feel for him and with him, and her tragic biographical mode has endured even against the grain of evidence.[70] In the years since Dark's imaginative leap, we have come to know this remarkable Aboriginal man differently and more fully – and, as our understanding of his people and their history and future has changed, so has Bennelong. His destiny keeps unfolding with our own, and that 'thread of contact' that Dark imagined he felt on the headland continues to weaves its way through Australian history.

In her perceptive biography of Eleanor Dark, Marivic Wyndham warns that 'reading *The Timeless Land* as a piece of history' violates 'the spirit as well as the thrust of the story'.[71] I cannot agree. Dark never called it a piece of history, never claimed to be a historian and was diffident about her skills as a scholar. But she was driven to understand the real past. She was a dedicated and pioneering researcher of the archive. She was respectful of chronology and context as well as reflective about the character of time itself. When questioned about the historical content of her trilogy, she never took refuge in her status as a novelist but responded with what she knew from the sources. She worked hard to align her fiction with the known facts and she imagined intelligently into the spaces. Historians who were her contemporaries evaluated her work as history as well as fiction. *The Timeless Land* deserves recognition not only as a great novel but also as a path-breaking work of the historical imagination.

TWO

The Journey to Monaro: Keith Hancock

'If there were a Nobel Prize for History,' observed Stuart Macintyre in 2010, 'Hancock would surely have won it.'[1] In the mid-1960s in Canberra, when he was approaching the age of seventy, Professor Sir William Keith Hancock returned to the study of his own country's history and began to write a book that would be hailed as a pioneering work of environmental history in Australia. It was called *Discovering Monaro* (1972) and focused on the high rolling plains and mountain ranges of the Australian Alps. Environmental history was a new field that gained identity and strength in the 1960s and '70s, focusing on the changing relations between people and nature and the entwined human and natural history of places. Hancock enjoyed the thought that, after a lifetime of working in imperial and Commonwealth history, he was embarking on the intellectual equivalent of the classic retirement occupation, that of cultivating his own backyard.[2] A doyen of his discipline, a highly respected professor and academic leader at ease in recording and interpreting world affairs, he had turned to that most antiquarian of pursuits, to that marginal and often-disdained academic endeavour: local history. *Discovering Monaro* is consciously, proudly 'parochial' – Hancock used the term positively. He wished to enrich Monaro's life and pastures with 'a good historical tilth'.³ The book is suffused by a certain bravado; 'discovering' was part of the Hancock lexicon of moral, scholarly engagement along with other favourite words such as 'attachment', 'craft', 'justice', 'span' and 'witness'. He considered himself a discoverer. Discovery, he wrote, 'is not a once-for-all achievement, but rather is a continuing effort, whose end – if ever there is an end – still lies far beyond sight'.⁴ It is a process that connects the historian not only to the past, but also to the future.

Hancock famously felt a tension between birthplace and career, origins and opportunity, Australia and England, home and 'Home'. Enshrined in the title of the first volume of his autobiography, *Country and Calling* (1954), the conflict was peculiarly colonial and specifically Australian. It can also be seen to represent the poles of rural and urban existence, one (literally 'the country') evoking his upbringing and preferred habitat, and the other denoting the regulated, built environment of the professional. But his eloquent opposition of country and calling is also, I believe, expressive of a universal scholarly tension between emotion and intellect, practice and theory, poetry and science that underpins all his work. 'Country', in the Aboriginal sense of the word, was not just Australia or even his birthplace of Gippsland; it was also childhood, innocence, earth and experience – the organic past. And 'calling' was not just career and overseas opportunity, but also the impersonal discipline of profession, argument and abstraction – the idealist present. Hancock continually searched for a rapprochement between these two worlds of practice as he did between the two soils he loved, Australia and Europe. He expressed it in his notion of history as a craft, his profession as a guild, his sources as 'witnesses', his brief as 'taking sides', 'thinking and doing', 'inquiry and narration', and his enthusiastic approval of conducting history 'with boots on'.

So Hancock gave equal weight to both words in the title of *Discovering Monaro*. The book is as much about how and why he delves into that region as it is about what he finds there. My only conversation with Hancock, two years before his death, was about this book, and I was able to tell him that I had walked the Jagungal plain and the Kosciuszko high country carrying it in my rucksack. I am interested in the emotional origins of Hancock's environmental history. In what ways might we see the book as a projection of his career and sensibility? In his discovery of Monaro, Hancock returned to source, emotional and geographical, and here I will do the same by unpacking three scenes that recede in time – Australia in the 1960s, England in the 1940s, and Italy in the 1920s – seeking in each the seeds of *Monaro*.

AUSTRALIA: 1966

It is a balmy day in the summer of 1966. Two men are setting off from Canberra for a day's fishing in Monaro. They are both historians, one Sir Keith Hancock, recently retired professor of history in the Research School of Social Sciences at the Australian National University, and the other Dr Robin Gollan, a senior fellow in the same institution and a distinguished scholar of radical and labour movements in Australia. They choose a bank of the Gudgenby River and cast their lines. At first they have little luck. But towards midday, after Hancock makes 'a perfunctory cast on to the rippled surface of a wide ford', a big trout rises and takes him by surprise. Hancock misses him. 'Never mind,' he says, 'let's have lunch.' As they eat and smoke their pipes, the two talk about Hancock's next research project. He is less than a year away from finishing the second volume of his biography of the South African leader Jan Smuts, a task that has occupied him for fifteen years. What is to be his next task, his next question? (Hancock always asked students and colleagues 'And what is your question?'[5]) The acclaimed author of *Australia* (1930) wants to write again about his own country, but this time with more 'news than views', and his question is: 'How, for good or for ill, have Australians used the land on which they live?' But such a sweeping inquiry needs a precise and exhaustive focus, a specific region of study. Over lunch Bob Gollan, gesturing to the river and the blue Brindabellas, says, 'You love this country, why don't you write about it?' They tidy the camp and Hancock makes a careful cast into the ripples. The big trout plays with his ambitions and rises again. This time he nets him – and is netted by him. 'In that moment,' recalled Hancock, 'Monaro became my quest.'[6]

The Monaro (pronounced *Mon-air-oh*) was Hancock's 'particular place'. It backed onto his childhood domain of Gippsland, which lay just over the mountains. In *Country and Calling* he had celebrated that rural upbringing and comforted himself in his mature years with the thought that, from a block of land he bought in 1948 on the north-eastern slopes of the Dandenongs, he could follow mountain ridges all the way to the east Gippsland coast of Croajingolong.[7] The Monaro is also Canberra's hinterland. It is one of the legacies of the placement of the national capital that scientists and scholars, since the war, have swarmed into the high country. In the alps, as in Burley Griffin's Canberra, systematic, intellectual ways of knowing preceded, paralleled and often prompted emotional attachment. Hancock was ambivalent about Canberra. In 1930 he wrote, 'There is something very attractive about garden cities; but it is difficult to pretend that they are nobler than Pericles' Athens.'[8] In 1948, on a brief return to the city, he confessed, 'Canberra, now that I saw it again, both irritated and charmed me, as it had always done.'[9] He once famously derided it as 'a good sheep station spoilt' but he later came to admire the emergent form of the city that Walter Burley Griffin designed, and perceived 'within the basin of the Molonglo River an intricate yet orderly man-made landscape framed by the inviolate hills of "the timeless land"'.[10] Discovering Monaro was his way of intellectually deepening an uneasy attachment to Canberra.

Hancock always wrote self-consciously as a historian, continually reflecting on the skills and orientation of his own craft.[11] He believed the cardinal virtues of the historian were attachment, justice and span,

where 'span is a consciousness of the relations of things'.[12] Although
he championed cross-disciplinary inquiry, it was to historians and students of history that he ultimately spoke. His book was certainly not
the first to offer a fine-grained regional analysis of land use, and it
neglected to incorporate many of the insights afforded by the neighbouring discipline of geography. But it probably *was* the first study of
land use to be so artfully grafted by a senior academic historian onto
the traditions of professional historical inquiry.

The rise of environmental politics in the late 1960s brought ecology and history closer together, directly stimulating historical scholarship
and giving the new environmental history an occasionally apocalyptic
and moralistic tone. Hancock placed *Discovering Monaro* in this new
political and scientific context through his engagement with the insights
of ecologists and also his twin invocation of the local and the global, a
dialectic that bypassed nationalism, the central concern of Hancock's
earlier work. Whereas Hancock, in this book, declined to place his
scholarship in an Australian geographical or historical tradition, he
readily linked the Monaro with the emerging international politics of
environmentalism. Manning Clark, writing in the *Bulletin*, considered
it 'the first significant look at our past through what might be called
the "pollution and ecology window"'.[13] The geographer Oskar Spate
observed, 'This is a story with a moral, or any number of morals; one
is tempted to think that the whole book is designed just to lead up to
a restrained but eloquent conservationist polemic.'[14] *Discovering Monaro*
is an extended historical and philosophical parable about 'man and
nature', informed not only by global environmental politics but also
by the Bible, for it was in retirement that Hancock renewed his study
of biblical and early church history. It is no surprise, then, that Hancock's
model for the writing of *Monaro* was not a fellow academic but a judge,
Leonard Stretton, Royal Commissioner into the Black Friday bushfires
(1939) and forest grazing (1946), a man who called witnesses, who

projected a powerful moral vision, and who wielded biblical language in the service of public policy.[15]

One of the heroes of *Monaro* is Baldur Byles, a forester who worked above the treeline and showed Hancock the mountains.[16] Byles walked the high country for six months, got down on his hands and knees to examine the evidence of soil erosion and strenuously advocated the protection of the water catchments from grazing cattle. Byles had originally supported grazing in the mountains but was converted by the evidence of his eyes, becoming a dedicated champion for conservation and the abolition of the 'snow leases'. Influenced perhaps by his older sister, Marie, a Buddhist and bushwalker, Baldur Byles developed a practical management philosophy that drew on both the arts and the sciences. He wanted parts of the mountains to be 'sacred places'. Hancock admired the forester's physical engagement with the place and was attracted to the fact that he was a poet as well as a scientist. Near the end of *Discovering Monaro*, Hancock quoted from Byles' unpublished eulogy to the snow gum, the tree that, like Byles himself, was at home in the high country:

> We cannot appreciate anything fully until we understand it, until we pick up its wave length so to speak, until we learn to think the way it thinks ... So, if we wish to understand this particular Australian tree we must try to understand its point of view, realising that it is a living organism, like you and me ... We must try to understand its manner of living, its philosophy of life, its place in the world of natural things and the spirit that keeps it going in spite of great adversity.[17]

Byles was 'thinking like a snow gum', reminiscent of the American forester and conservationist Aldo Leopold, who in the 1940s advocated 'thinking like a mountain' in order to understand the holism of ecology. Hancock likened Byles to the botanist Maisie Fawcett and to Judge Stretton: all three shared a practical wisdom, a bureaucratic fearlessness and a commitment to applied ecology that he admired and hoped to emulate in his work on the Monaro.[18]

Discovering Monaro has become widely regarded as one of the foundation texts of Australian environmental history. But if one were to choose the most path-breaking environmental history of the 1970s and early '80s, you might turn as well to J M Powell's *Environmental Management in Australia* (1976), or Eric Rolls' *They All Ran Wild* (1969), or – especially in terms of regional history – Rolls' masterpiece, *A Million Wild Acres* (1981), an environmental and human history of the Pilliga Scrub in northern New South Wales (see Chapter 8). Organic rather than schematic, *A Million Wild Acres* revealed the storytelling power of an ecological sensibility, reached the heights of great literature with its laconic and vernacular style, and – in Les Murray's words – burnt off derivative or imported forms of ecological consciousness.[19] Although, by contrast, *Discovering Monaro* focused conventionally on land use, it also anticipated the cooperative alliance of historians and ecologists that flowered most notably in the 'forest history' of the 1980s and '90s.[20]

Another pioneer of the new environmental history was George Seddon, a connoisseur of landscape, whose book *A Sense of Place* (published in the same year as *Discovering Monaro*) was concerned not just with the physical patterns of the Swan River coastal plain but also with the imaginative apprehension of the land, bringing together science, history and aesthetics. In *Searching for the Snowy* (1994), Seddon worried eloquently about how to write 'an environmental history' of a river and its catchment. An early exponent of regional history was Margaret Kiddle in her 1961 study of pastoralism on Victoria's western plains. Kiddle and the Western District, Seddon and the Snowy, Hancock and the Monaro, Rolls and the Pilliga: here we can discern a strengthening lineage of regional history with a moral and environmental edge.

Hancock's book of the 1970s, written by a repatriated professor with European longings, is still caught – in some ways – in the ebbing tide of the cultural cringe. Eric Rolls' book of the 1980s, written by a farmer about his own land, is by comparison homegrown, almost unconsciously indigenous. And, to take an example from the 1990s, Tim Flannery's *The Future Eaters* (1994), an influential ecological history written by a zoologist and offering a provocative Australian history of the world, could be characterised as 'the cultural strut'. Historian, farmer, zoologist; Europe, Australia, the world: here is an interesting essay in the changing relationships of country and calling, of nature and nation.

Let me turn now to analyse Hancock's European longings, for they suggest other ways that we might place his achievement and explain his enduring impact. I'll return, as Hancock continually did in his imagination and emotions, to Tuscany. But we go there, again as Hancock did, via England.

ENGLAND: 1949

It is a sunny day in the spring of 1949. The vice-chancellor of the newly established Australian National University, Douglas Copland, has just arrived in London from Canberra and is sitting with another man on a bench in St James's Park. The man is Keith Hancock, Gippsland boy, author of *Australia* (1930) and professor of economic history at Oxford University. Hancock is also a member of the Academic Advisory Committee of the new Australian National University and has been invited to take up the position of foundation director of the Research School of Social Sciences in Canberra. He has lived in Britain for fifteen years and longs to return to Australia; in fact, he has already given preliminary notice of his intention to resign his Oxford chair. The vice-chancellor opens the talk on the park bench, and Hancock responds. In his autobiography, Hancock recalls, 'Within ten minutes everything is finished between the Australian National University and me.'[21] He is plunged into misery. Postwar England shadows and engulfs him and his separation from Australia appears absolute and irrevocable. 'I felt myself all at once cut off from home.'[22]

It is an enigmatic moment in Australian university politics, especially for a man who made his anguished love for his country the central relationship of his life. The scene on the park bench attracted the attention of his reviewers, who became fascinated by his 'mysterious' silence on this exchange. '"Friction" Costs Us Historian', 'Canberra Lost a Brilliant Brain' and 'No Job Here for This Historian' were amongst the headlines greeting the publication of his autobiography.[23] What transpired during those minutes on the park bench in St James's Park and what do they say about Hancock's love for Australian soil and his later scholarly study of it?

In the mid-1990s I was a 'professional Australian' working as a lecturer at the Menzies Centre for Australian Studies, which was then part of the Institute of Commonwealth Studies at the University of London. I taught British youth about Australia and helped to present Australian perspectives to the British public and media. My office looked out onto Russell Square, which, under the first pale rays of English summer sunshine, was transformed annually into a sunbaking studio for London office workers, stripped to their underwear. In the Institute's tea room, where everyone but the Australians wore ties, stood a bust of Sir Keith, who became the first director of the Institute of Commonwealth Studies in 1949 after the collapse of his conversation on the park bench. In the library I was delighted to find Hancock's draft manuscript of *Country and Calling*, which he wrote while at the Institute. The easy fluency of Hancock's writing is impressive.[24] The sequence and flow of the published book are already there; the notebooks are ordered and numbered, and so are most of the pages. The corrections that Hancock makes are largely to expression and tone, rarely to the order of argument or narrative. He uses pencil but seldom rubs it out. The only significant deletions occur in his elucidation of the park bench scene. Here there are an unusual number of false starts; large slabs of the handwritten version have been eliminated from the published text, and some pages have been removed. His discomfort is clear, and he confesses as such in the book: 'In an earlier draft of this chapter I did try to make those explanations but found myself unable to make them adequately because I knew only one side of the story.'[25]

The issue of friction that Hancock would not mention in his book was 'academic recruitment'. Two and a half years earlier, Hancock, Sir Howard Florey, Professor Marcus Oliphant and Professor Raymond Firth had been invited by the Interim Council of the new university to constitute themselves as an Academic Advisory Committee; each one, in Hancock's words, 'was the potential director of a School'. In March 1948, after an eight-day journey from Britain on a Sunderland flying boat to attend meetings about the future of the university, Hancock perhaps had a greater sense of the isolation of Canberra than did Council members, and, together with his own ambiguous feelings about the city and even about the 'novel' experiment that was the ANU, a stronger insight into the difficulties of attracting people to the invented capital.[26] But he also had an expatriate's prejudice against homegrown academic talent. 'Write some time and tell me whether the dice are loaded against the research school of social studies at Canberra,' he wrote to his Melbourne friend and former Adelaide student Colin Badger in 1947. 'Can you pursue social studies creatively in such a limited society?'[27] Hancock was aware of the university's obligation to supply 'a new creative impulse' and fulfil a truly national mission in order to meet the expectations and soothe the sensitivities of 'the state universities' (a term still current in Canberra).[28] When his friend Raymond Firth declined the new university's invitation to head the School of Pacific Studies, Hancock immediately proposed himself as head of Pacific Studies as well as Social Sciences. He felt exhilarated: Australia was within his grasp, as was a leading role across all the humanities. It was at this point that he gave verbal notice of his intention to resign his Oxford chair.

The talk on the London park bench, whether it lasted 'ten minutes' or 'four hours' (which was Copland's estimate), settled the matter. Jim Davidson, in his biography of Hancock, has superbly analysed the tensions underlying this meeting.[29] Hancock had long awaited it, the vice-chancellor had flown far, and the outdoor discussion was decisive. According to Hancock's unpublished account, Copland told him that the Interim Council could not 'under any circumstances' accept his offer to act as head of Pacific Studies and Social Sciences together: the invitation was to direct the School of Social Sciences alone. 'So that was that,' concluded Hancock.

His compass was spinning. He felt now that he 'had no roots anywhere at all'. Neither country nor calling seemed to have triumphed in this messy negotiation. Why did he not seek more information? Why did he not pursue a compromise? 'I had no false dignity to hold me back but somehow I lacked the spirit,' he wrote. This was his puzzlement and regret. Why had his homesickness been insufficient to draw him through this difficulty; why had politics and pride overwhelmed his emotional geography? Was he 'only half-Australian', as Nettie Palmer had judged?[30]

I am interested in this moment because it was part of Hancock's journey to Monaro. At the heart of his park bench crisis was his uncertainty about his 'country'. He had left Australia fifteen years before and, although he yearned for it in many ways, going home was a leap into the unknown. Then there was Canberra, a place Hancock would learn to love, a place he would contrive to possess – through his contribution to the ANU, his discovery of the Monaro and his fight to save Black Mountain from a telecommunications tower – but about which he had always held profound doubts. 'And the place?' he had questioned Badger in 1947. 'Is it possible to get service? Is there any conversation?'[31] Restless in Adelaide and Birmingham, Hancock liked camping in the bush or dining with heads of government, but could not see any merit in provincial society.[32] He worried about his wife, Theaden: 'What sort of life would it be for her?' And how would she fare in a frontier, academic society?[33]

Then there were 'the social sciences', a term and concept with which Hancock was uncomfortable (he preferred 'social studies'). The university proposed four postgraduate institutes or schools of scientific research. 'It would have no Greek,' commented Hancock. And a 'university that was all post-graduate Science (and the adjective 'social' would be only a partial mitigation) seemed to be hardly a *universitas*'.[34] Hancock was uneasy with the 'fashionable junk' that was the social sciences: 'Although I have had much traffic with social scientists of one tribe or another,' he wrote, 'I am, as I have already explained at some length, an historian belonging to none of the tribes.'[35] He was scathing about 'the pretentious mumbo jumbo that was called sociology' and dismissive of the uses of psychology for historians.[36] Hancock sometimes considered himself a frustrated 'artist' or 'poet', 'compelled [by career] against his bent in the direction of science'.[37] That is not to say that he did not value scientific techniques in the humanities; there was a strong element of positivism in his thinking. He was an economic historian after all and, as Michael Roe has reflected, 'WKH liked *spine* almost as much as span.'[38] But his preferred science was natural rather than social. If he was going to work with the sciences, then it would be with the more prestigious natural and physical ones rather than with the territorially competitive social ones. Working with natural scientists enabled the historian to 'belong to none of the tribes', to place his discipline at the centre of the arts and humanities, reaching cooperatively across C P Snow's 'two cultures'.[39]

Many of the interdisciplinary endeavours he later initiated at the Research School did just this – the Wool Seminar, the Murray Waters Study, the Botany Bay Project, and one must add Monaro – and they (like Monaro) drew on Canberra's strength as a community unusually rich in the scientific elite.[40] These were strategic scientific alliances with which Hancock was intellectually comfortable, and with which he could maintain History's dominance in the face of the burgeoning social sciences. And so one also suspects that, sitting on the park bench, he was happier to start the two schools together because the Research School of Pacific Studies would have provided him with a ballast of empirical, regional responsibilities to balance the more abstract and potentially threatening social sciences.

Country and Calling has been called 'the longest job application in history', and consulting the draft confirms that impression.[41] Hancock was very conscious of his distant Australian audience, beginning his manuscript with an injunction to 'Remember the Audience' and heading the list with Vance and Nettie Palmer, champions of Australian literature. He wrote at a time when Canberra, although lost to him, still beckoned. It is hard not to see the book as driven by regret at that missed opportunity, that failure to realise an imagined destiny. But it is deeper than that, for *Country and Calling* is about a greater loss: it is a lament for a lost Australia, for childhood, innocence, uncomplicated virtue; a feeling that he has paid the price, finally, for absence. 'Mediterranean latitudes, not English ones, are the ones for me ...', Hancock wrote. 'How can a man feel at home in latitudes so murky that he is unable to admire his own halo?'[42] He may have considered calling the book 'Once an Australian' — it is scratched in one of the notebooks beside 'Country and Calling' on a play-page of jottings — and it is a title, intriguingly, that historian Ian Britain gave his portrait of four Australian expatriates, Barry Humphries, Clive James, Germaine Greer and Robert Hughes.[43] The implied ending, 'Always an Australian', confirms this sense of Hancock's fatalistic view of nationality as destiny.

In *Country and Calling*, Hancock wanted to excuse the apparent carelessness with which he let Canberra slip, yet not burn any bridges. In the end, he uncharacteristically wasted his words. The deleted passages are, at times, too self-justificatory, and Hancock, a master of tone, knew he was protesting too much. They were more severe than the published version on the Interim Council of the University and the vice-chancellor. That, too, he knew might be unwise. But they also reveal that he was not a victim of politics or circumstance or distance, but of his own pride and, more fundamentally, of vacillation about 'country' and specifically about Canberra. When he did finally come, eight years later, he was determined to make amends for his private betrayal of country, and looking to make an intellectual investment not just in Australia but in the high country.

ITALY: 1923

It is a blazing hot day in the summer of 1923. Two young men in shirts, shorts, sandals and broad peasant hats are on a walking tour – a three-week pilgrimage – in Tuscany, winding their way two or three hundred miles south-east from Florence to Assisi and beyond. They sleep in haystacks, olive groves and humble beds. They are both Commonwealth men, Keith Hancock from Australia and Reid McCallum from Canada, both carrying books in their packs. Their rural idyll is darkened by their encounters with a bullying xenophobia amongst Italy's citizens under the newly ascendant Mussolini. Hancock is compelled to question the origins of fascism, and the historical relations between liberalism and nationalism – in this, his favourite landscape.[44]

Hancock's Tuscan interlude resonates throughout his life, not just in an abiding love of Italy and Europe, and in his sustained professional scrutiny of nationalism, but also in a reverence for the worked landscape, one etched and shaped by the rhythms of labour and self-sufficiency. And his Tuscan experience also informed that famous 'lust for life', the scholarly expression of which was his commitment to the archive of the feet, to the practical inspiration and tutorship of crisp air, good talk and dirty boots. As we know, Hancock enthusiastically promulgated the injunction – which he attributed to R H Tawney – that good historians need strong boots, and he tells the story that Monaro people identified him so closely with that phrase that later, when he was a guest of honour at a dinner at Cooma, the flowers on the dining tables were cunningly inserted into boots of all sizes and types.[45] Teaching today in Hancock's School of History in Canberra, I commemorate this prank by bringing a boot-bouquet to my annual class on environmental history for new doctoral students.

So Hancock is also discovering, or rediscovering, the youthful exuberance that he first celebrated in Tuscany. After forty and more years of being driven by large, unwieldy public projects, including prolonged war-time wrestling with 'a brute documentary mass', Hancock in his retirement again finds the freedom to choose his subject, and the exhilaration of seeking his scholarly inspiration out-of-doors.[46] As well as fieldwork, interviews and serious use of the historian's boots, he employs that other important tool of the mountain scholar, the fly-fishing tackle. His is a conscious and contrastive courtship with country: 'I imagine,' he confessed at the beginning of his Monaro study, 'it will take a good deal of patience over a good many years to feel at home with grasses and bushes.'[47]

Hancock was not only discovering Monaro and rediscovering his youthful, outdoor self, or at least its sources of energy; he was also discovering Italy in Australia, and thereby seeking again to reconcile his lifelong tension. 'In Monaro,' he declared, 'I have rediscovered the Tuscan rhythm.'[48] Here is Hancock's account of a dinner on a property near Cooma:

> At the dinner table that evening there were about a dozen people, all of them deeply rooted in the land yet well acquainted with the wider world of men and books. They encouraged me to talk history; two or three of them invited me to go fishing with them; one of them, an Olympic ski-runner, insisted that I was not yet too old to

put on skis again and join him on a *langlauf*. The talk was spacious, like the landscape; crisp like the air. I told my friends when I returned home that I had been in Tuscany.[49]

Historian Ros Pesman has drawn suggestive parallels with David Malouf, Kathleen Fitzpatrick, David Martin and Peter Porter, and sees Hancock's sentiments as part of the longing of an immigrant people for a harmony in their land with which they can identify, one that they can claim.[50] In 1970s Australia, a scholar like Hancock, while awakening to the ancient Aboriginal presence and influence, looked for that harmony in European echoes in the south-eastern corner of settled, pastoral Australia. From the 1990s a scholar was more likely to seek that harmony in the continuing Indigenous land-use traditions of the continent's centre and north.

During his writing of *Monaro* Hancock was living through the dramatic beginnings of a revolution in understanding Aboriginal Australia. In the late 1960s, as the next chapter explores, the great antiquity of Aboriginal civilisation in Australia was confirmed. Hancock, who had characterised colonisation as 'invasion' as early as 1930, drew excitedly on this revelation – comparing the 600 generations of black Australians who had lived in Monaro with the six generations of white – and he also quickly incorporated into his work the insights into Aboriginal burning regimes that archaeologist Rhys Jones had described in 1969 as 'fire-stick farming'. In Canberra in the 1960s and early '70s Hancock was at the heart of an archaeological and anthropological research frontier. But he remained trapped in his culture's blindness about frontier violence. Although he acknowledged the general pattern of violent European conquest, he claimed that in the Monaro 'as almost nowhere else, resistance and retaliation did not ensue'. It was the classic local historian's apologia: *it didn't happen here.* But Mark McKenna's history of Eden-Monaro, *Looking for Blackfella's Point* (2002), draws on diaries, letters and newspaper records to reveal a state of sporadic warfare and

'reckless barbarity' on Hancock's particular frontier and argues that
Aboriginal people of the region 'fought tenaciously against the invasion
of their land'.[51]

Hancock also overlooked the unyielding endurance of Aboriginal
identity in his region: he recorded the death of Biggenhook in June 1914
and declared that 'with him died the Ngarigo'.[52] Christine Hansen, in
her study of Aboriginal social history in Eden-Monaro, analysed 'the
tenacious grip of the Monaro's extinction narrative', a vice that Hancock
did not escape. He overlooked the active role of Aboriginal people in
the pastoral industry as well as evidence collected by linguist Luise
Hercus about the Ngarigo language spoken by people living in Orbost
in the 1960s. Hansen reflects that a good conversation might have transpired if Hancock had met Alex Brindle, a high plains Ngarigo black-
tracker who worked in his country for the New South Wales Police,
raised a large family in Cooma and died in the late 1960s while *Discovering
Monaro* was being written. She also explores the intriguing possibility
that the Man from Snowy River was actually a Koori.[53] These alternative stories and lineages were only just emerging as Hancock walked the
paddocks of Monaro. In any case, he was more concerned to reconcile
his love of two soils, one of which was on the other side of the world.

In searching for Tuscany in Australia, Hancock was seeking an
Australian peasantry. Hence his admiration for those he met in Monaro
who were, as he put it, 'deeply rooted in the land'. He was renewing
his long-term economic interest in peasant agriculture; amongst the
historians he most admired were Marc Bloch and R H Tawney. His
first book, *Ricasoli and the Risorgimento in Tuscany* (1926), was dedicated to Antonio Cecconi, 'a peasant in a remote corner of Tuscany'.
Hancock's imagery of Tuscany was often lyrical and romantic: 'the Old
Testament pot ... hangs over every peasant's fireplace,' he wrote. 'One
may find young girls of sixteen singing with the sheep like the shepherd-
esses of the *Eclogues*.' (The French historian Bloch was also a student

of the countryside and an admirer of the peasantry – and he too quoted from Virgil's *Eclogues*.[54]) 'Lovers of Virgil,' Hancock continued, 'are surprised and excited when they discover Tuscan peasants using that same wooden plough which is described in one of the more difficult passages of the *Georgics*.'[55] And so on. And in Monaro – another landscape where soil was a precious resource – he gleefully found properties where the horse had survived the motor car, not just out of sentiment, but out of ecological circumstance and regional utility; he celebrated long family continuities of ownership and care that fostered an accommodation of local environmental realities; he described 'a kind of Metayer system' for dairy farmers; he honoured and reproduced Bukalong's century and more of rainfall records; he drew attention where he could to the success of small-scale farming; and he cherished any evidence of landscape connoisseurship and commemoration.[56] Baldur Byles, the forester and hero of *Monaro*, was – as Jim Davidson has observed – the Australian equivalent to Cecconi, the Tuscan peasant to whom Hancock dedicated *Ricasoli*.[57]

Yet Monaro had few farmers. It offered a cameo of pastoral Australia and a warning of the difficulties of agriculture and even diversity of production. Wool and meat were the staples, and 'Monaro people could no more compete with their neighbours to the east in producing butter than they could compete with their neighbours to the west in growing wheat.' It was vulnerable to drought, land degradation and falling wool and livestock prices. Hancock recommended that 'Bad times in Monaro' would make a rewarding project of historical research.[58] But overall he was characteristically, and perhaps misleadingly, optimistic. Stephen Dovers has argued that the basalt downs – Hancock's focus in his analyses of land tenure and management – are the areas of Monaro that most escaped erosion. Elsewhere in Monaro, overgrazing and rabbits, in association with drought and small property sizes (with the push for closer settlement), have meant that Monaro is one of the worst-afflicted regions of soil erosion in New South Wales.[59]

But Hancock's interest in folk culture and worked landscapes in Australia, however romantic, was a fruitful result of his European yearnings, and possibly a further dimension of the book that made it original and unusual in its time. Monaro became a courtroom in which Hancock could judge the opposing forces that had ruled his own life, that of 'the stagnation which ensues when there is too little movement' and 'the disintegration which too much movement causes'.[60] His own estranged relationship to country made him search for evidence of belonging. He anticipated debates about sense of place, cultural landscapes, bioregionalism and reconciliation when he wrote: 'People in Monaro do not merely own their land, they belong to it.'[61]

As environmental history took off in the 1970s, particularly in America, its focus was conservation history, the wilderness aesthetic and national parks. A dichotomy grew, still evident in the environmental movement today, between the unused landscape and the misused one, the pristine landscape and the exploited and degraded one, the deserted landscape and the desertified one.[62] In 1974 Hancock indulged his anti-Americanism by making fun of what he saw to be that nation's mutually exclusive histories – he styled them as either The Epic of America or The Rape of America.[63] And the moral landscape of the conservation movement has similarly tended to be a language of extremes. Hancock, with his Tuscan dreaming, his interest in the rhythms of spoiling, restoring and improving, and his intuitive attachment to a landscape wrought by culture, charted a different course, one that has become more compelling with the years.

THREE

Entering the Stone Circle: John Mulvaney

Late one glorious summer evening near the end of the Second World War, nineteen-year-old John Mulvaney was cycling in the limestone hills of the Cotswolds in England. Suddenly the 'brooding, mysterious' Rollright Stones appeared before him – a weathered, prehistoric stone circle on the edge of a ridge, once described by the eighteenth-century antiquarian William Stukeley as 'corroded like worm-eaten wood, by the harsh jaws of time'.[1] It is a beautiful Neolithic site several thousands of years old, a place of reputed solar sightlines and subtle energies that has generated some strange experiences of light and weather for local farmers. Folklore says it is impossible to count the Stones and arrive at the same number each time. Megalithic enthusiasts believe the location of the circle was chosen because the lie of the land is 'associated perhaps with some special union of earth and sky'.[2] It was here that John felt the thrill of his 'first encounter with the deep past'.

A year or so before, in the week he turned eighteen, Mulvaney had enlisted in the Royal Australian Air Force, not out of patriotism, as he explained later, but out of 'escapism'. The war freed him from 'two unhappy years' as a trainee rural primary schoolteacher, and also enabled him to circumnavigate the world 'at the King's expense'. He later ranked his enlistment as one of the crucial decisions of his life. In John's words, 'Time and fortune prevented me from dropping any bombs in anger, because Hitler's war ended just as I was posted to a Lancaster bombing base.'[3]

So his war-time memories are of 'gentler things', of visiting English historic places, of exploring the green, romantic landscape continually evoked in his Australian rural education. Perhaps the war sharpened John's appreciation of this early human past. Returning to Australia at the end of the war, he gratefully accepted the government's offer of a place at Melbourne University for 1946, under terms of a rehabilitation training program for ex-servicemen. It was another liberating opportunity provided by the war, a rare chance to make up for lost schooling, and John plunged into the study of ancient history. In 1948 he sat in Manning Clark's class, where, as well as attending closely to primary documents, he was advised 'to read novels which conveyed the ethos of a period'. *The Recollections of Geoffrey Hamlyn* by Henry Kingsley (1859) and *For the Term of His Natural Life* by Marcus Clarke (1874) 'were advocated because they illustrated both truth and error'. *The Timeless Land* was praised and Eleanor Dark addressed the class.[4]

War and 'the deep past': these two experiences were entwined, and their emotional and intellectual chemistry shaped Mulvaney's career, and his discipline. John returned to contemplate the Rollright Stones on nearly all of his subsequent visits to England. In Australia in the 1950s he was to encounter a rather different 'stone circle', and would begin to discover an even deeper human past.

ᖰ

Australia has a settler history of resistance to the intimations of Aboriginal antiquity and adaptability. From the beginnings of colonisation, there was reluctance amongst colonists to acknowledge the depth of belonging of a people whose continent they had usurped. Aborigines, it was commonly thought, had no history. They were caught in the fatal thrall of nature's continental museum. Instead of history, Aborigines had myths, the mark of the 'primitive'. For Europeans, time was the essence of history; for Aborigines it was place that was historical. Yet even that attachment was denied them. They were dispossessed both physically and intellectually, for they were branded nomadic as well as timeless. Aboriginal people hadn't been there *long* and they never came from *here*: this was the thinking. The real nomads, however, came in boats with wings and brought their expansive, imperial history with them.

The invaders' historical habits of mind persist in disturbing ways. In the Grampians mountains of Victoria, the state's most significant Aboriginal rock art site, Bunjil's Cave, is protected from vandalism by a cage of iron bars, terrible in its symbolism.[5] The sacred site was for a long time disparaged by local whispers that when white people first came to live in the district, no sign of a painting existed in the cave.[6] Martin Thomas and Grace Karskens have written with insight about another significant rock art site, the Bull Cave south-west of Sydney, also caged since 1982, where white art competes with black, and where Aboriginal history and title are challenged by violent graffiti. As Karskens perceives, this 'is not "mindless" vandalism: it's too pointed, too deliberate, too articulate.'[7] Even benign signage can perpetuate absence and silence. Outside Alice Springs, the Northern Territory Parks and Wildlife Service, which employs many Aboriginal people and advocates cross-cultural awareness, erected a sign in 2014 celebrating the Owen Springs cattle station as having been established 'in country where few people had been before'. In north-east Tasmania, where Aboriginal history now laces tourist experiences, a local Aboriginal woman entered a takeaway store in 2015, admired a historical display inside that celebrated European pioneers, and struck up this conversation:

> 'What an interesting display,' I remark to the shopkeeper.
> 'Yes,' she replies. 'We have a very interesting history and many of the original families still live in the area.'

'What about the Aboriginal people who lived here?' I ask.
'Do you have any information on those people?'
'No,' she replies. 'I don't think there were any around here.'[8]

Colonial scientists and collectors found human antiquity in Australia elusive because the typical cultural clues were absent. There were no shards of pottery, no tools of different metals, no buildings or 'monuments' that Europeans recognised, and there seemed to be no domesticated plants or animals other than the dingo. The questions continually asked by natural historians in the nineteenth century were: Did humans have a geological history in Australia? Could artefacts be found by digging? If Aborigines were 'primitive', were they also ancient? Had large animals become extinct as in Europe, and, if so, had they once been contemporary with Aborigines? Did people watch the volcanoes blow? What were the local clues to antiquity?

Until the mid-twentieth century many Australians believed that Aboriginal people had occupied the continent for only a few thousand years, and some argued for an even briefer presence.[9] And there was an assumption that Aboriginal culture had been unchanging, its environmental impact minimal. 'The Stone Age' was the term most used to characterise Aboriginal culture in the first half of the twentieth century. It was the first of three ages of European prehistory defined in 1819 by the Danish archaeologist and curator Christian Thomsen, a chronological sequence that progressed from Stone to Bronze to Iron. The Stone Age became a powerful metaphor of primitiveness, for it conveyed the image of a static culture, one that was unmalleable, impermeable, discrete, inorganic. But the phrase more appropriately describes the early twentieth-century obsession of settlers with stone-tool collecting. Donations of Aboriginal stone artefacts literally filled the National Museum of Victoria. During the Second World War truckloads of them were removed to an outside store to clear museum space. John Mulvaney remembers how, in 1957, when he tried to study where the stone hatchet heads in these collections came from, he found them piled in a vast mound on a storeroom floor.[10] They were still there, roughly gathered in boxes, inscrutable and uncatalogued, when I went looking for them in 1992. Their partial labelling linked them not to the places where they were found but to the donors who picked them up. These amateur collectors competitively scoured the country for stone tools and removed them. They did not dig because they believed there was nothing to find: they expected no depth to the human record. And a 'good' collector left very little for others to discover. One enthusiast boasted in 1961 of his two-week 'hunting trip' to outback New South Wales: 'In all we sent home 13 Banana crates full weighing 2 Hundred weight to the case … A most successful trip.'[11] Mulvaney recalled learning of one collector who tipped his unwanted finds down a disused mineshaft so that competitors would not find them. Thus the cairns of stones amassed in museums were more eloquent memorials to this circle of collectors – we might call them a 'stone circle' – than to the people who made and used the artefacts.

At the same time that scientific resistance to Aboriginal antiquity was solidifying, stratigraphic archaeology was making its first break-throughs in Australia. In 1929 an archaeological dig at Devon Downs rock-shelter on the banks of the Murray River in South Australia demon-strated the existence of a stratified site of some antiquity. Norman Tindale and Herbert Hale, both of the South Australian Museum, exca-vated to a depth of six metres, and identified evidence of cultural and environmental change.[12] From 1935 at the Lapstone Creek Rockshelter (Emu Cave) near Sydney, George Bunyan, C C Towle and Frederick McCarthy, the last from the Australian Museum, demonstrated past cul-tural change by the excavation of a stratified series of different stone tool types.[13] Nothing demonstrates the conservatism of the stone tool collectors so well as the efforts they put into marginalising or discred-iting these new and exciting approaches. Change over time – *history* – was an explanatory tool rejected by most of the amateur collectors.

They also disdained Aboriginal informants. Their collection work assumed extinction, often of the people, and certainly of their useful knowledge. '[W]e are not much better off,' wrote Kenyon in 1911, 'than the British Archaeologist delving amongst the barrows and mounds of his native isle.'[14] The collectors were self-made detectives who turned their backs on living testimony. Some such as George Murray Black, who gathered artefacts with a large truck and dug up Aboriginal skeletons from burial mounds along the Murray River from 1929 to 1951, plotted his 'poaching' expeditions to avoid the 'Mission half castes and abos' and any other 'busy bodies' who might have been relatives of the dead bodies. The stone-tool collections were built upon an invention of cultural discontinuity, upon the severance even of Aboriginal tradition and memory. The collectors did not want to recognise living Aborigines because it would mean the end of their detached 'science' and lead them into the disturbing terrain of the humanities.

As we saw in Chapter 1, the 1930s were a watershed in Australian public opinion about Aborigines. The acceptance that Aboriginal people had survived colonisation – a slow, late insight of settler Australians – opened the way for acknowledgement of the antiquity of Aboriginal occupation. The author of *The Timeless Land*, in spite of her title, helped settlers to see Aborigines as historical beings. The scientific discovery of Aboriginal antiquity, always known by Aborigines themselves, was not just a product of radiocarbon – it awaited the recognition that the original colonisers of Australia also had a future.

❧

Anthropologists and archaeologists occasionally used to proclaim the discovery of 'a new man', by which they meant a distinct stream of ancient humanity, generally represented by some newly uncovered fossil evidence. In the 'stone gossip' of the 1950s and '60s collectors began to refer to 'the new man'.[15] His name was John Mulvaney, now in his thirties and recently returned from his archaeological studies at Cambridge University. Although profoundly Australian in manner and outlook, to stone-tool collectors paranoid about overseas theoretical influence he initially seemed to be 'the European', bringing the Cambridge model of field archaeology to the bush.[16] In the early 1950s, while studying in Britain, John saw himself as representing a fresh approach in archaeology as a whole, which he believed had for too long fixated on things at the expense of the people who made them. As a consequence, the essential humanity of the deep past had been lost. He was also critical of the 'incalculable' harm done to antiquities by 'the early discoverers of buried civilisations' who carelessly removed objects from their original cultural context. He was already aware that Australian archaeology defied European categories of the Palaeolithic and Neolithic: 'If only the theorists had examined the axes of the Australian aborigines they would have been shocked,' he wrote from Cambridge in 1952. He preferred the term 'pre-historian' over 'archae-ologist' because he saw himself as, above all, a *historian* of pre-literate societies.[17] In Britain, Europe and Libya Mulvaney had experienced 'thrilling' fieldwork but he was determined to apply his training in Australia. 'I hankered after the Iron Age,' he later wrote, 'but knew I must return to Stone.'[18]

It is Mulvaney's name, above all, that we identify with the archae-ological revelation that Australia has a Pleistocene past. 'No segment of the history of Homo sapiens,' wrote John, 'had been so escalated since Darwin took time off the Mosaic standard.' The 1960s were, in Mulvaney's words, the decade of 'the deluge', 'the golden years', 'the Dreamtime' of Australian archaeology. At Kenniff Cave in southern Queensland in 1962, Mulvaney dramatically confirmed a minimal radio-carbon date of 13,000 years. Samples from a test dig at the cave in 1960 had been sent overseas for analysis, and the results were finally heard over an expedition breakfast during a second dig in July 1962 when a telegram was picked up on the party's transceiver set. Mulvaney at first suspected a transmission error of an additional nought.[19] The minimal age of human occupation in Australia became 20,000 in 1965, over 30,000 by 1970, and reached a probable 40,000 by 1980. From the 1990s, 60,000 or more years became the likely horizon.[20]

Mulvaney's archaeological career directly coincided with the radio-carbon revolution. Carbon-14 dating was a tool tailor-made for some professional magic. It was a scientific method of dating that bypassed the field typologies of the amateur and connoisseur and brought laboratory science into the heart of humanistic archaeology. The techniques of the nuclear age would decipher a 'stone age'; radiocarbon would illuminate what John called 'the dark continent of prehistory'. He enthusiastically hailed carbon-14 as 'A New Time Machine'. It not only introduced a novel chronology, but also revolutionised understandings of social evolution. Ancient humanity was revealed to be dynamic rather than passive, wrestling constantly with a rapidly changing environment. 'Australians,' wrote Mulvaney in 1952, 'can expect to find the history of the aborigines unfolded.'[21]

When Mulvaney returned home from Cambridge and began to introduce professional archaeological practice and perspectives to the study of ancient Aboriginal history, his instinct was to work respectfully with the white collectors and curators who had preceded him. In the 1950s and '60s, these were the people with whom he had to negotiate over access to Aboriginal sites and information in south-eastern Australia, rather than Aboriginal people themselves. These white antiquarians claimed a sort of possession of Aboriginal sites, through priority of collection and also through a growing sentimental attachment to the places of their own hunting and gathering. Thus Mulvaney's double intellectual enterprise was launched: to apply objective scientific techniques to the chronology of ancient Australia, and at the same time to understand those who had previously studied or mediated the Aboriginal past and whose work and ethics he often needed to criticise or transform. It is a key to Mulvaney's character, and a testimony to his commitment to both history and archaeology, that he spent much of his life trying to understand the culture of collection that he helped to overturn. In evaluating this legacy he also hoped to free himself from it. In systematically digging the earth, in establishing human antiquity, in demonstrating cultural and environmental change over Australian time and space, and in championing the protection of Aboriginal sites and heritage, he upended the world of his predecessors.

Yet there were continuities that served him well. Like the collectors, Mulvaney was empirical in orientation, fieldwork-driven and fascinated by artefacts. Like them, he was accused of being too interested in stone technology. Mulvaney's common interests with the collectors, his commitment to cross-disciplinary partnerships in research, and his slightly delayed professional training, made him a sensitive intermediary between amateur and professional at a critical time in Australian archaeology. In practice, he minimised his professional status, or used it to give recognition to the most rigorous of his predecessors – in particular, Norman Tindale, Frederick McCarthy and Edmund Gill.

Through his research, Mulvaney crusaded against the straitjacket of Social Darwinism that gripped Aboriginal studies for nearly a century, and this led him to become an informed critic of evolutionary thinking. He considered racism a 'fatal flaw in the Australian psyche', and was keen to articulate a humanitarian tradition in Australia and a positive, moral vision of race relations. This powerful interest in the history of ideas about Aboriginal Australia enabled him to become a sympathetic biographer of intelligent men of the frontier – Alfred Howitt, Collet Barker, Baldwin Spencer, Frank Gillen, Ernest Cowle, Patrick Byrne and Paddy Cahill. Mounted Constable Cowle and the telegraph official Pado Byrne were outback bushmen with legendary thirsts – and Mulvaney, ever the archaeologist, found evidence of the drinking feats of his heroes in a trail of broken glass that you can still find out there today. Professor Baldwin Spencer (1860–1929) 'moved in' to Professor Mulvaney's home for decades and made his presence felt at the family dinner table. In 2000 John thanked his first wife, Jean, 'for her patience across thirty years, during Baldwin Spencer's presence as a virtual house guest'.[22]

The social and political context of archaeology changed dramatically in John Mulvaney's lifetime. Living in Victoria in the 1950s, he believed he 'had never met an Aboriginal person'. 'I mean,' he said, 'they just didn't "exist".'[23] However his wife, Jean Campbell, had known Aboriginal people in Warrnambool, Victoria, and had worked with them in northern and western Australia (and gone on nightly crocodile hunts with them on paperbark rafts) while completing a cycling trip around the continent in 1949–50. In 1965 John made a two-month 'epic' trip around northern Australia researching Macassan sites and establishing further contact with Aboriginal people. By the late 1960s he was realising that he had 'underestimated the possibilities for research amongst living communities', and by the early 1970s he was urging fellow archaeologists that priority be given to 'Aboriginal-oriented research', by which he meant working with the people themselves.[24] Soon he was feeling his way towards a new scholarly ethic. He welcomed the reassertion of Aboriginal cultural identity as 'one of the most significant developments in Australian intellectual history'.

In a world recoiling from the horrors of Hitler's war, human antiquity became a measure of human unity, a way of escaping from racial discourse and of locating a common, global past. Aboriginal antiquity became universal human heritage. But to Indigenous peoples, the quest for antiquity often seemed a distancing device, 'a kind of political physics' denying them ownership of a past that they feel is ever-present.[25]

The scientific search for antiquity can be problematic for Aboriginal people for the very reason that it tethers ancient Australia to the world. It generalises a local story into a global one; it draws boundaries between the ancient past and the custodial present; it sketches historical, migratory connections between Aboriginal people and other humans, and ultimately finds Australia's human beginnings elsewhere. For Aboriginal people, the scientific discovery of antiquity – when it finally came – was politically useful and sometimes full of significance, but it was also occasionally threatening. Time still seemed to be the 'gift' of the invaders.

Mulvaney's commitment to seeing ancient Australian history as part of a global human saga led him to resist some Aboriginal assertions of local heritage rights. In 1990 he strongly protested the Museum of Victoria's unconditional return of the ancient Kow Swamp collections of human remains to the Echuca Aboriginal community for reburial. Mulvaney argued for a 'Keeping Place' – a place managed by Indigenous people for repatriated cultural material – and believed that this option would have future benefits to Aboriginal, as well as non-Aboriginal people. He looked back on this dispute as 'my career's most distressing episode'.[26] The racial discourse that he had devoted his career to dissipating, and which 'prehistory' with its awesome timescale seemed uniquely destined to make irrelevant, seemed to crystallise again right under his trowel as some Aboriginal people claimed exclusive ownership of their past.

Mulvaney set out to use archaeological techniques and perspectives to humanise the past. He therefore always gave special value to documenting the history, spirituality and humanity of Indigenous societies, as well as their antiquity. In the newly professional field of archaeology in mid-twentieth-century Australia, Mulvaney was often identified as 'the scientist', bringing objective techniques to a world dominated by conjecture and prejudice. Yet he was also the humanist educating the collectors, and later some of his professional colleagues, to the human

drama of ancient Australia. In this way he brought together his two
great intellectual influences – Max Crawford's School of History at the
University of Melbourne (especially the teaching of Kathleen Fitzpatrick
and John O'Brien) and the Cambridge School of Archaeology, which
brought him in contact with Glyn Daniel, Grahame Clark and Charles
McBurney. For Mulvaney, enthusiasm is the paramount virtue of the
teacher, imagination the essential gift of the scholar, and 'literate fluency' the fundamental responsibility of the intellectual. He not only
pioneered the discovery of Australian human antiquity, but as Bain
Attwood has recognised, John also challenged the entire scale and shape
of conventional Australian history.[27] In 1969 Mulvaney began his account
of *The Prehistory of Australia* with the words: 'The discoverers, explorers
and colonists of . . . Australia, were its Aborigines.'[28]

Inspired by John, I've also made regular returns to the Rollright Stones
when in England – while driving across the Midlands, when walking
the Cotswold Way, and once on a long walk from Stratford-upon-Avon
to Oxford. I'm always moved, as John was when he happened upon the
Stones in 1944, by the romantic ambience of the site. But thanks to
John's work and the generation that followed him, I see the Stones as
a relatively recent monument in the long history of humanity. As an
Australian gazing at that circle, my mind travels to the far deeper human
past that feels ever-present in my own country but which Europeans
took so long to see and accept. The Rollright Stones are still old and
corroded by time, but John helped make them younger in our eyes.

And one can still feel their mystery. My first visit to the Stones was
in the spring of 1996, when I planned to photograph them for a book
that Tim Bonyhady and I were preparing about John's work.[29]
Photographing a sacred site can feel a little sacrilegious, but I expected
it would be simple to capture an image of the light-coloured stones

against the green sward. The day was calm and sunny and the sky blue and cloudless as I approached the grassy hillside upon which the 30-metre-wide circle of limestones stood. But as I passed through the hedge and entered the field, a sharp wind gust heralded a sudden change of atmosphere. A small, dark cloud appeared from nowhere above the Stones and, as I walked towards them, it unleashed a furious hailstorm that turned the circle white. Within minutes the assault was over, the cloud disappeared and sunshine glistened innocently on a grainy, silver mantle enclosed by the Stones, now in disguise.

FOUR

The Magpie:
Geoffrey Blainey

Geoffrey Blainey is the great phrase-maker of Australian history. The title of his 1966 book, *The Tyranny of Distance*, became part of the language, and in 1993 his description of critical views of Australia's past as 'black armband history' entered the political lexicon. He is a master of narrative history who can evoke the material reality of past daily life with telling detail, whether it be of a mining landscape in the 1850s or a household kitchen in the early 1900s. His writing distils powerful metaphors and often evokes mechanical or rhythmic polarities: a 'great seesaw' of ideas in the Western world, a swinging pendulum of fashion, the ebb and flow of tides of opinion, the two sides of a coin, a ledger of national account, a balance sheet of history. He constantly weighs positive and negative cultural legacies and offers a calculus of achievement. Blainey disarmingly admits that 'one of my difficulties is that I'm half a determinist', explaining that 'somewhere in my background, in my training or in my makeup, I have a preference for hundred to nought answers.'[1] His quizzical determinism and literary grace have together made him one of Australia's most influential and best-known historians – a prophet even – and definitely the subject of dinner-table conversations.[2]

He has also made his career as a contrarian. When the tide of opinion is flowing and the pendulum of fashion is swinging, his inclination is to go in the other direction. He uses history to demonstrate large economic and social patterns over time and thus to make present enthusiasms suspect. He often claims to speak for a silent majority, one that he believes is being drowned out by a noisy ephemeral faction. This style of public activism whipped up a storm in March 1984 when Blainey addressed Rotary International in Warrnambool and criticised the federal government's immigration policies, stating that there was unfair discrimination in favour of applicants from Asia and that the influx of Asian immigrants living 'at the taxpayers' expense' threatened social coherence at a time of unemployment. Blainey explained that he was drawing on his expertise in Australian history; he was also confident he knew the hearts of his fellow citizens, especially 'the old Australians', and he received many letters supporting his stand. Under attack, his views became more extreme: he used the metaphor of 'a secret room' to allege government manipulation of the immigration intake.[3]

In a manifesto about his scholarly style first delivered in 1968 and later called 'Antidotes for History', Blainey explained that he was wary of 'stock responses', those habitual, readily available, convenient answers that we turn to because original thinking 'is an arduous occupation'.[4] Blainey looked instead for what was missed by others. Introducing a history of Gembrook written by local farmer-naturalist Bill Parker, he recalled: 'I had the privilege at the age of fifteen of walking behind his horse-drawn plough and picking up loose potatoes that had been missed by the potato diggers a few months previously.'[5] It is tempting to see this activity as a metaphor for Blainey's scholarly life, for he has delighted in finding the golden potatoes that other foragers have failed to unearth, especially the ones at their very feet, unobserved but tripping them up. In his histories, he gets great pleasure from revealing the obvious but unseen, the alluvial gold. When reviewers accuse him of identifying what is self-evident, I hear him chuckling.

A metaphor he himself uses for his research is another natural one, that of the magpie. Apart from the inappropriate football connotations (he barracks for Geelong), this metaphor works well. Blainey prods the earth inquisitively, feeds quirkily, collects sustenance in a proudly idio-syncratic way. He scavenges bright details and oddments that catch his eye. His voice is rich, his song mellifluous! He flies above the terrain and perceives broad patterns below. And as the bird books warn us, he doesn't concede ground and can launch surprising attacks, especially in defence of his nest. Furthermore, this is a bird that, to quote ornithol-ogist Graham Pizzey, has 'benefited greatly from land-clearing and establishing of crops, pastures, waterholes'.[6] Farmed land, mined land, developed land is his preference.

Geoffrey Blainey often evokes rural landscapes and his personal and childhood experiences of them in country Victoria. Whether they are the hills of South Gippsland or the mullock heaps of the goldfields or the forests and farms of the Dandenongs, they have shaped his writ-ing and his politics. He offers his own memories of them as a tribute to country people, as an acknowledgement of the lyrical power of nature, and to remind us that he grew up with soil under his fingernails. And he often expresses admiration for rural folk, especially for reminiscing old-timers, that rump of pioneering Australia that Blainey's histories celebrate. These people are both his sources and his constituency. He values, and perhaps seeks to emulate, the confluence of reflection and experience in their lives, the apparently natural elision of art and life, of poetry and practicality. He is therefore an eloquent champion of Henry Lawson's writing, which he admires for its 'rich mosaic of detail' and evocation 'of an Australian way of life that has vanished' – and he offered his own elegy for that lost world in a book about everyday life between the first gold rush and the First World War called *Black Kettle* and *Full Moon: Daily Life in a Vanished Australia* (2003). It 'begins with billy tea and candles, and ends with ice cream and the telephone'. Like Lawson, Blainey is 'the eavesdropper on a thousand conversations'.[7] Of his Gembrook friend Bill Parker, he wrote: 'He experienced so much that he has written about or he learned it firsthand from old-timers who are now dead.' This is an organic, inherited lineage of pioneering set-tler experience of which Blainey feels himself to be a part, and for which he is a voice.

At the age of twenty he was commissioned to write the history of the Mount Lyell Mining and Railway Company in Queenstown, a job arranged by Professor Max Crawford from the University of Melbourne, where Blainey completed his honours in history. Blainey's three years on the west coast of Tasmania made him 'intensely sympathetic to mining fields, their traditions and way of life' and included playing football on the white gravel ground for Smelters FC and participating in Australia's longest wheelbarrow race (from Zeehan to Queenstown). He strapped on a miner's lamp and was shown through old underground workings, and he made arduous walking expeditions to mining sites with just a tin of peaches and two eggs carried in a spare woollen sock (he would eat the peaches then boil the eggs in the tin).[8] He said he learned at Queenstown what he did not learn at university: that ordinary people could be pre-cious sources. At a time of rapidly increasing professionalism and specialisation in the discipline of history, Blainey never despised the pub-lic: as an academic he has always been a loner; as an urban intellectual he championed people on the land; as a writer he took on the mantle of speaking for ordinary Australians; and as a literate man he celebrated their occasional illiteracy (for he found the unlettered to have sharper memories). He was a 'public historian' before his time.

One of Blainey's early writings was a short biographical study of Sir Samuel Wadham, a professor of agriculture at the University of Melbourne who retired in 1956 and whom Blainey called 'one of the

most influential men in Australia's rural history'. In his affectionate
portrait of Wadham we can discern a prophecy of the kind of intellectual Blainey himself was to become, a manifesto for his own public life.
When Wadham arrived in Melbourne from Cambridge in 1926 to take
up the chair in agricultural science, Wadham was not a practical farmer
and himself doubted whether he could work a plough, yet he was soon
in the country, touring the wheat belt of north-western Victoria, advocating the close study of 'seasons, soils and sales', deeply interested in
the economics and sociology of the countryside. He was 'a man so often
seen yarning with farmers, his foot propped on a fencing wire, his shirt
tail waving in the breeze'. Blainey's portrait continues:

> [Wadham's] articles and speeches and broadcasts (and they number
> hundreds) justified his place even if he had taught no students.
> Perhaps no other professor in the history of the university had so
> enlarged the influence of his chair and formed such close contacts
> with the particular community he represented ... He could have
> shut himself up in the university, rarely visited the country, and he
> could have issued few public utterances and avoided the turbulence
> of public controversy ... he has no wish to be provocative or to appear
> intellectually superior; he merely states what he believes to be true.

And Blainey concludes that perhaps the greatest testimonial to Wadham
'are the countless letters which he has received from country people'.[9]

In the mid-twentieth century, French historian Fernand Braudel championed the multiplicity of time, and the need for historians to look
beyond 'social time' or *l'histoire événementielle*, the history of events, in
order to embrace *la longue durée*, the slower-moving structures and
cycles of centuries. He saw the history of events as 'a surface disturbance, the waves stirred up by the powerful movement of tides. A
history of short, sharp, nervous vibrations ... A world of vivid passions,

certainly, but a blind world, as any living world must be, as ours is, oblivious of the deep currents of history, of those living waters on which our frail barks are tossed ...' Geoffrey Blainey was one of the pioneers of *la longue durée* in the Australian setting. He embraced this interest in long-term, little-noticed economic and social cycles, and delineated geographical patterns and changes in material life that reached beyond a generation.

It is one of the stances that makes his histories quirky and surprising. *The Tyranny of Distance* (1966) was a great and innovative essay on the social and economic history of space and time, about how distance shaped Australian history. *The Causes of War* (1973) analysed worldwide patterns of peace, trying to get beneath 'the short, sharp, nervous vibrations' of conflict. *The Great Seesaw* (1988) offered an intellectual history of the Western world, an intriguing long-term, cyclical dance between economy and ideas, in which Australia was quite naturally a partner. *A Land Half Won* (1980), written before the full discovery of El Niño, wrote climate into Australian history. *Triumph of the Nomads* (1975) made history of prehistory, offering a humanist narrative of what had been the scientific, Aboriginal preface to the Australian story (Blainey had been a field assistant on John Mulvaney's dig at Fromm's Landing in 1956). 'It is now my view,' wrote Blainey in 2015, 'that the great rising of the seas [from 13,000 years ago] which began long after Aborigines arrived, is the most important event in the human history of Australia.'[10] It was Blainey, provoked by Mulvaney, who vividly evoked the clockface of human time in Australia and the last few minutes that represented Europeans, and who finished his history of ancient Australia with an Indigenous glimpse of approaching British ships on the eastern horizon. The boats with wings were, in Blainey's account, 'Sails of Doom'.

In *A Short History of the World* (2000), he fulfilled his desire to encompass all human time; he acknowledged that it was in some ways

The Tyranny of Distance writ large.[11] It is revealing that Blainey did not push these histories, even his world history, back beyond humans. Yet, from the end of the twentieth century, histories of Australia began to include dimensions of 'deep time', not just the ancient past of Aboriginal peoples but the awesome millennia of pre-human Australia and its geological antecedents. For example, Stephen Pyne's *Burning Bush: A Fire History of Australia* (1991) began with an evolutionary history of Gondwana and the eucalypt, and ended with the new ideas brought to Australia by the flood of diverse immigrants following the Second World War, thus transcending 'the standard dichotomy' of the Aboriginal and British peoples.[12] The opening chapter of Stuart Macintyre's *A Concise History of Australia* (1999) was a vivid essay on 'Beginnings' that took the reader from imperial history to the Dreaming, from the idea of a sleeping land brought to life by Europeans in the eighteenth century to an account of the supercontinent of Pangea and the later landmass of Sahul (greater Australia in the last ice age) as the site of a civilisation of unique longevity.[13] At the turning of the millennium, the first volume of Eric Rolls' 'biography' of *Australia* (2000) began with the creation of the universe and was devoted entirely to this part of the planet as it was before people came here.[14]

Blainey's histories remain determinedly human. The limits to his time travelling remind us that there is little place in his histories for biology or ecology, even though he was one of the first Australian historians to write attentively and fondly of the environment. He is interested in economy but not in ecology. He attends more to the inorganic moon than the dynamic sun, to the expansive mystery of the sea rather than the known diversity of the land, to the economics of space instead of the ecology of place. And so his Indigenous world is one of economic nomadism rather than spiritual and ecological territoriality. His natural world is one of landscapes, elements and resources; it is there for humans to use for their profit or neglect to their peril; it helps shape human character and provides constraint and opportunity for human society, but it is rarely populated with other living creatures or with its own evolutionary history, specificity and dynamism. His ABC Boyer Lectures about Australia were entitled *This Land Is All Horizons*.[15] His concern is with the physics and geography of the globe more than with the biology and ecology of the Earth.

Innovative in so many anecdotal ways, Blainey's *A Short History of the World* nevertheless resisted the radical opportunities provided by the preceding three decades of scientific and historical research. David Christian, the pioneer of Big History, a genre of world history that embraces ecological and geological time and takes the story back to the origins of the universe, reviewed Blainey's *A Short History of the World* and was disappointed with its unselfconscious use of the metaphors of social evolution and its unreflective approach to progress and directionality in history.[16]

Blainey therefore stands apart from emerging environmental narratives that undermine dominant imperialist accounts of Australian origins and which attend to our distinct geological and biological inheritance. The discovery of ecological deep time entails a journey into the continent itself; it means adopting an 'inside' view of Australia. We have broken down the old imperial image of the tyranny of distance and found correctives to our assumed history of isolation and containment. The Australian writer David Malouf has remarked that one of the imaginative gifts of Europeans to the land of Australia was their vision of the continent as an island: it 'was not just a way of seeing it, and seeing it whole, but of seeing how it fitted into the rest of the world'.[17] This was an imported, imperial vision, a view from the outside and one looking longingly to very distant shores, one which conceived of Australia (to quote Blainey) as 'like a huge barren rock in an ocean' with useful strategic promontories and harbours bordering a meaningful maritime map and backing onto emptiness.[18] The continent also turned its back – its huge humpback of desert – on Asia, and looked east across the Pacific Ocean and south to the Great Circle sailing route of high latitudes that linked it to Europe. 'If Aborigines are a land-dreaming people,' David Malouf concludes, then 'what we latecomers share is a sea-dreaming'.[19] This particular invention of Australia – and Blainey was its most prominent exponent – saw it as the island continent, upside-down at the other end of the world, surrounded and defined by the sea, emotionally linked to the world by the sky, ruled by the tyranny of distance, and inhabited by Aboriginal peoples who had been trapped and impoverished by its isolation. For an admirer of technology such as Blainey, the cross-cultural encounter on Australia's beaches in the eighteenth century was between 'people who could not boil water' and 'the nation which had recently contrived the steam engine'.[20]

In the half-century since Blainey's *Tyranny of Distance* was published, settler Australians continued to sever formal ties with Britain and grew more receptive to Aboriginal perspectives, more diverse in cultural identity and more alert (and vulnerable) to the economic power of Asia. And we discovered our own long, green Gondwanan past, a dynamic biological and geological genesis in our own hemisphere. Thus the story of Australian colonisation, recognised as 'invasion', tilted on its axis to meet new realities. We are now more inclined to claim that our isolation has been exaggerated, that it is Europe rather than Australia that is the 'New World', ecologically speaking, and that technological differences in the ancient Aboriginal past were not a consequence of isolation, but were an environmentally informed choice. In this re-invention of Australia, it is the savanna and not the sea that represented the barrier. It was not the simple geographical boundary of open ocean that primarily shaped Australian civilisation, but the complex ecological reality of soil and climate. Australia was not so much physically isolated by the sea as ecologically distinguished by the land. Full of contemporary social and environmental implications, this insight emerged from an Australian history of deep time and required an overturning of the tyranny of distance. Blainey, however, continued to stand apart from it, as his history of the world showed: if the seas had not risen, he insisted, Australia would probably have become agricultural and more like New Guinea.[21]

Geoffrey Blainey, with his powerful geographical imagination and his Braudelian interest in capitalism, material life and *la longue durée*, pioneered the injection of environmental sensibilities into Australian history. But from the late 1960s, green politics overtook him in a way that clearly irritated him, just as multicultural politics did a little later. Hence much of his later work seems to be written defensively and combatively, trying to maintain his vision of society and environment in the face of ideas whose power – and darkness – he resented.

There were two great watersheds in Geoffrey Blainey's professional career. One is well recognised: that fateful year, 1984, when he drew trenchant criticism for his comments about Asian immigration. The other was the late 1960s, the era of 'the counter-culture', the term he uses to describe the decade's distinguishing characteristic. This seems to me to be the moment when a man of innovative thinking suddenly found himself out of sympathy with the dynamic ideas of his generation. In the late 1970s he began writing *The Great Seesaw: A New View of the Western World, 1750–2000*, which can be seen as an attempt to make sense of what had happened to him. He was trying, I think, to historicise and therefore to distance and control a social and intellectual movement whose power surprised him, whose politics worried him, and whose lack of a sense of history annoyed him.[22]

In *The Great Seesaw*, Blainey drew attention, as is his wont, to a powerful but 'rarely noticed' social and political pattern, this time a seesaw of ideas and attitudes that became influential from the eighteenth century. The tension, the balance at the heart of the seesaw is that between wilderness and the machine, between the romantics and 'the believers in reason and progress', between a faith in nature and a faith in technology. A swing towards nature, explained Blainey, is usually accompanied by changes in attitudes to nakedness, a warm climate and clothing styles, as well as an increasing respect for 'primitive peoples', a term he chose to retain. The swing between technology and nature is also a swing between optimism and pessimism, with those believing in technology being defined as the optimists.[23]

Blainey is most convincing where he shows – as for example with Henry Thoreau, Aldo Leopold or the greenhouse effect – the way ideas had to await the favourable tilt of the seesaw to become influential, or an unfavourable tilt to become dangerous. His book is a sustained argument about the way in which ideas and the economy interact, and about how a serious cultural analysis could be used to foresee economic trouble, and might eventually moderate the swings of the seesaw. A cautious mental climate, he shows, can be as economically vital as raw statistics of production, and may lead the swing. It is a pattern not unlike El Niño: although irregular, it has predictive potential.[24] You can never be sure of the length of the cycles, but once the indicators start lighting up, once the Southern Oscillation Index or the Pessimism Quotient rises, then a recognisable process is underway. Although not a theorist, Blainey does like producing generalisations about human behaviour. He is keen for history to prove itself capable of yielding general truths like economics or sociology: 'History as a discipline should be more confident,' he declared in 1984. 'It shouldn't be so cautious and timid.'[25] *The Great Seesaw*, like *The Causes of War*, aims to use history to alleviate future social and political crisis. It is a stance that is both idealistic and conservative.

The counter-culture of the 1960s made Blainey think about intellectual fashion and what it was to be outside it. The immigration debate of 1984 must have intensified his interest in historical patterns that dictate the social limits of discussion. The debate took off in the middle of his writing of *The Great Seesaw*, so it is not unexpected to find him exploring in it a history of what he calls 'prevailing intellectual taboos'.[26] And, on a smaller timescale, why should comments he made at Warrnambool in that year, so like comments he'd made elsewhere and earlier, be suddenly noticed there and then? His own academic interest in the swings of intellectual fashion and in the predictive potential of history made him, I think, less careful in the way he defended and extended his position on immigration, less alert to the immediate local, social consequences of his arguments, more determined to push the limits of prophecy, to unearth the extremes, more wilfully curious to test the taboos of his attackers.

In the seesaw, Blainey felt that he had identified a locomotive of fashion. He had found a way of making sense of a disconcerting period of history he was living through – a sudden, otherwise inexplicable reversal of the values that had reigned during the quarter-century from 1945 to 1970, the period of his coming of age, a period he calls 'the great success story of recorded economic history'. As he says on the opening page of the book: 'The seesaw has been tilting up and down since at least the eighteenth century, and at times it reaches an extreme angle. We recently experienced a tilt of the seesaw, so sudden that cultural and economic life temporarily seemed to lose its sense of direction.'[27]

His lack of sympathy with the counter-culture was unmistakable. The prosperity of that earlier era, he wrote, 'was such that it could even finance the new opponents of material success'. 'If economic times had been harsh, and if technology had been simpler and less productive, most of the young people who went to Woodstock and to the rallies against the Vietnam War and the crusades in favour of nature would instead have been working hard for a living.'[28] A long-term view of the swings of the seesaw allowed him to depict his own era as extreme, a time when two new strands of Australian nationalism – 'the black and the green', Aboriginal land rights and green politics – had gained ascendancy. Both were encouraged by international law and conventions that had diminished the power of Australian parliaments. But the seesaw would inevitably (and reassuringly) swing back. 'There is a brittle quality in these extreme moods,' he concluded.[29]

In this analysis, a set of ideas critical of economic development becomes a fashion; a powerful set of ideas with which Blainey disagrees becomes an 'influential minority'; a *dangerously* powerful set of ideas becomes a religion, a cult, a crusade – and it has an altar, worshippers, a halo, the sacred, a Garden of Eden, and guilt.[30] It is with these metaphors that he depicts the green movement.

In Australia, the five years between 1968 and 1973 indeed witnessed a dramatic swing of the seesaw, from a minerals boom to a petroleum crisis, from the Little Desert to Lake Pedder, from conservation to environmentalism. This is how, in 1994, Geoffrey Blainey summarised green politics in modern Australia:

> By 1970 nature had won tens of thousands of converts ... The 'light greens', believing in economic development as well as in preserving rare species and places of rare beauty, were still in the ascendancy. Later they would become the unconscious captives of the small numbers of dedicated and professional 'dark greens' who opposed all kinds of economic development. The dark greens, seeing nature as the Garden of Eden, breathed a religious fire.[31]

There are some familiar strategies in this condensed narrative. Here, the dark greens are presented as sinister, even conspiratorial. They are not only a cult, they are professional, too; they are a vocal minority, they reject all economic development, and they make reasonable people 'unconscious captives'.

But there were few 'unconscious captives' in the green movement. Instead, there was a robust, confrontational and at times bitter debate. In her book *Defending the Little Desert* (1998), Libby Robin analysed the way many of the older-style conservationists – people Blainey would label light green – fought and felt betrayed by the radical environmentalists who gained power in the early 1970s. The dark greens not only thought differently, they worked differently. They rejected the old patriarchal establishment networks of the earlier utilitarian conservationists (another form of 'professionalism'), and introduced an organisational style that was participatory and egalitarian. As Robin puts it: 'A left-wing model that gave voice to the "little people" was foisted on a conservation movement that had run for two decades on a "who-knows-who" basis.'[32] Foresters were the clearest example of conservationists alienated by the new environmentalists. They considered themselves 'the first conservationists' and were shocked to find themselves stranded on the 'other side' of environmental debates.[33]

Blainey's environmentalism has also been shaped by this feeling of shock, this loss of power, this sense of hurt to establishment networks. He is, like the foresters, defending history, deriding the dark greens for not knowing any, for failing to acknowledge and respect a conservation legacy. Blainey commented that his friend Bill Parker was 'an observer of nature from his early years – it was enthusiastically studied in many primary schools long before the rise of the green movement – he still watches lyrebirds that live in the bush near his farm'. So Blainey again reminds us of how old is the new, and of how tiresome is the new that does not acknowledge the old. And he also invokes that great divide between ephemeral urban fashions and enduring rural experience.

The contrast between dark and light greens also suggests the emotional polarities of optimism and pessimism, sun and shadow, that Blainey has both studied and lived through. The anti-humanism of deep ecology and of aspects of the green movement has disturbed scholars from both the left and the right. Socialist scholar Murray Bookchin condemned what he saw as deep ecology's suicidal lack of faith in humanity.[34] Historian Simon Schama depicted American environmental historians as the generators of a 'dismal tale' about world history, as

the writers of 'penitential histories'. He found that environmental history 'inevitably tells the same dismal tale: of land taken, exploited,
exhausted'; of harmonious traditional cultures displaced by the capitalist
aggressor.[35] British historian John MacKenzie considers that Clive
Ponting's *A Green History of the World* (1991) presents a strikingly doom-
laden picture: 'In his reading, it is not only a case of "Apocalypse Now",
but also of "Apocalypse Then".'[36] This brand of scholarship was exemplified in Australia by William Lines in his book *Taming the Great South
Land* (1991), and especially in his *False Economy* (1998). These 'dark green'
histories were dramatic counter-progressivist narratives that depicted
'world history as one long free fall, with imperialism as its global accel-
erator'.[37] Their chief value is that they do not flinch from telling the
genuinely disturbing story of modern humanity's relationship with
nature, which, in Australia, offers dramatic examples of species extinction and land and water degradation. But, at their worst, their polemic
can also flatten the past into an undifferentiated and hateful caricature,
beyond redemption, where ordinary men and women have no control
over their lives. The result is bad history, for there is no meaning, no
agency and no hope. It patronises the past and strands the future. Blainey,
by contrast, has not only been a historian of optimism; he has also been
an optimistic historian, a Panglossian prophet, 'the sunniest of our leading historians', a champion of the positive ledger of national life.[38]

But it can be just as simplifying and disempowering to impose a
progressivist template on history. The great difference between the light
greens and the dark greens, in the Blainey view, is that while both have
a genuine concern for the environment, the dark greens 'believe that
the traditional goal of economic development must be subordinated'.[39]
The dark greens are seen to threaten not only Australia's economic future,
but also the legitimacy of its past. As Tim Rowse has observed, Blainey's
'thinking about the history of the colonists' land use is sometimes driven
by the nagging question of how dispossession can be justified'.[40] In 1993

Blainey attacked the High Court's judgement on native title in *Mabo*, claiming that it rested on 'prejudice and misguided research'.[41] In 2003, he favourably reviewed *The Fabrication of Aboriginal History* (Vol. 1, 2002) by Keith Windschuttle, a controversial book that argued that widespread frontier violence against Aboriginal people was an invention of modern academic historians. Windschuttle's book was shown to be flawed and was strongly criticised by most experts in the field (see Chapter 7). In welcoming such a book, Blainey – one of the earliest of recent historians to write of 'the war on the grasslands' (in *A Land Half Won*) – now signalled his view that the pendulum had swung too far.

Blainey's insistence on the balance sheet of history, a metaphor at once economic and biblical, is his response to this anxiety about dispossession.[42] He also made a fundamental distinction between land as 'nature' and land as 'resources'; in Blainey's evolutionism, it is an admired characteristic of advanced society to convert one into the other.[43] Europeans made the land productive for more people than did Aborigines; they converted neglected resources into exports. These achievements are posted as positives on the national ledger, balancing the negative weight of dispossession and violence and environmental degradation. 'Australia was more a success story than a failure,' he judges.[44] It is a peculiar competition and an impossible arithmetic. How do we 'match ecological and economic realities', as H C Coombs put it in an essay written in the midst of that seesaw swing of the early 1970s?[45] How do we measure human suffering or ecological loss, particularly as the full dimensions of both are still becoming apparent?

Early in *The Great Seesaw*, Blainey offers this reflection on intellectual fashion – and, one senses, on his experience of the 1960s:

> In nations where freedom is accorded to ideas there will always be minority attitudes as well as majority viewpoints. Belatedly I learned an essential truth when I realised that in certain decades the dynamic ideas – those that gave the flavour and even the ultimate label to the

decade — were held by only a vocal minority. Nonetheless those ideas forced the majority viewpoint to defend itself, and thereby dictated the intellectual and cultural agenda for that decade. Sometimes, in christening and labelling an age, we emphasise what is new rather than what is common.[16]

Blainey has always been more interested in what is common than in what is new. From his ingenious fossicking and gleaning, from his magpie-like collection of evidence, he selects 'what seems to have been typical rather than what was exotic'.[47] He generally identifies himself as the articulator of less vocal, unobserved, rarely noticed, more stable majorities; perhaps many of them are Robert Menzies' 'forgotten people': this is his populism.

∾

Blainey is a genuine contrarian who has always relished a bit of social and academic mischief. So this pioneer climate historian — in 1971 he wrote an article called 'Climate and Australia's History' — found himself in the twenty-first century inclined to be a sceptic about climate change. In 2005, in his 500-page history of the twentieth century, he gave the discovery of anthropogenic global warming just one short paragraph, explaining that 'we still stand in the dark' about its causes. (For a very different history of the twentieth century, see John McNeill, *Something New Under the Sun*, published in 2000).[48] In 2009 Blainey cautiously endorsed a book by climate science critic Ian Plimer, *Heaven + Earth: Global Warming — The Missing Science* (2009) with the words: 'Those who say that the latest "climate change" is unique are really making a profound appeal to history. Professor Ian Plimer is a leading historian of climate change, and takes his evidence from the layers of rocks. He strongly challenges the prevailing theory of human-induced global warming.' It is not a ringing endorsement, but Blainey is happy to set the cat amongst the pigeons.[49]

Australians have always had a healthy scepticism about their intellectuals, but in the early twenty-first century, intellectual expertise of any kind was commonly disdained for political purpose. The 'History Wars' and the 'Climate Wars' were both manifestations of this shift. Systematic, disciplined knowledge was disparaged, and accused even of wilful conspiracy and fraud. Historians and scientists were both depicted as willing to sacrifice scholarly integrity for politics and profit.

The parallels in these public debates about historical knowledge and climate science are striking. People have a daily, socialised experience of myth and memory just as they have a daily embodied experience of weather, and this is the source of their genuine expertise and the basis upon which they assert judgements independent of scholarly historians and scientists. But history is to memory what climate is to weather: detailed research over time reveals other truths. The leading Australian critics in these two debates – Keith Windschuttle and the geologist Ian Plimer – also had much in common. Each savagely changed allegiances in public politics during their lifetimes; each gained his notoriety from claiming to be a whistleblower on an entire profession; each attacked what was deemed 'the orthodox school'; each reduced the contest of ideas to a phoney, distracting debate about numbers; and each was self-published and rejected peer review. Both were promoted by the Murdoch press; both attracted the support of John Howard; and both were given a nudge along by Geoffrey Blainey.

For Blainey, climate science is an intellectual fashion that has gone too far – eventually the pendulum will swing back. He perceives another brittle and extreme mood, another fashion about to recede. He resents the exclusive authority of the climate scientists, and positions himself – as he did in the immigration debate in 1984 – as the champion of the everyday perceptions of ordinary people, of experience over theory, of weather over climate. His four great-grandfathers dug for gold and his long career as a historian of mining, mining companies and mining towns

(Queenstown, Broken Hill and Mount Isa) schooled him in the economic importance of mining and inclined him to defend it from attack. He is critical of the interference of international bodies in his country's sovereignty. And he still probably carries a deep emotional wound from the attacks on him by his professional colleagues about his views on Asian immigration. Marginality was suddenly no longer his choice and he developed sympathies for the underdog and whistleblower in intellectual battles. The climate debate was sure to attract his contrarianism, for it involved a prominent 'consensus' of 'experts' represented in an 'international body' (the IPCC) that is championed by 'greens'. But he is unable or unwilling to separate environmentalism and climate science. Thus this ardent champion of Western science and technology has found himself rejecting modern science's gravest insight. Contrarianism has been an immensely creative scholarly style for Blainey, and a successful professional strategy. But there is a studied naivety and innocence about him, and a carelessness for the consequences of the game he is playing.

❧

At the turn of the millennium, I spent some weeks in the Channel Country of south-west Queensland, a country of legends, where white landowners celebrate achievements Blainey would endorse: they are making marginal land productive in a global economy and take pride in 'feeding the world'. Yet, by the late 1990s, these pastoralists on Cooper's Creek were beginning their sentences with the words 'I'm not a radical greenie, *but* ...' It was because they had recently successfully fought a battle to keep the Cooper unregulated and to defend their region from cotton farmers. In this campaign their allies were Aboriginal people and urban greenies. They were defending the largest inland draining system in the world. Many of the Cooper pastoralists now talk of pasture management as much as stock management, of firing the grasses, of huge paddocks kept only for emergency feed, of planning for drought and accepting flood as a bonus, of going with the flow. Cotton production, with its chemicals and thirst for water, is far more disruptive of ecological processes than pastoralism has ever been. The mayor of the Barcoo Shire described his rivers with words like 'braided', 'ephemeral' and 'anastomosing' (vein-like) because this is the language with which he can defend a fragile economy of water that he knows intimately but needs to argue for scientifically. One Cooper pastoralist, full of genuine wonder, called the channels 'anasto*mazing*'.[50]

If we were to draw up Blainey's balance sheet of history on the banks of the Cooper today, we would have to bow to the might of the cotton farmers, for they have the money, the imperial power and the transforming technology. The people sacrificed would be those very battlers on the land whom Blainey has spent so many fine words celebrating, and who were themselves dispossessors. He would have to acknowledge that the Channel Country is now less intensively inhabited than in Aboriginal times. His balance sheet could not properly calculate the cost of the cotton farmers' invasion: the dams, the salinity, the chemical pollution, the community disintegration. Such a template would prematurely rule a judgemental line across the ledger and limit the opportunities for creative and cooperative solutions to environmental and social problems.

When struggling to explain great social and intellectual transformations, especially the one in his own lifetime, Blainey turned repeatedly to the great seesaw. It is an exhilarating metaphor and illuminating in the connections it makes across the vast terrain of history, but it is also a mechanism that poses simple binaries and reduces novelty to passing fashion. Like his assessment of climate science, it allows little room for ecological reality or cultural surprises. While Blainey is brilliant at finding forgotten insights in the old, his metaphor of social change does not readily accommodate the truly new.

FIVE

The Cry for the Dead: Judith Wright

I n the 1970s, Judith Wright decided she needed history. Wright was arguably Australia's best known and most admired poet of the twentieth century. From the 1940s her poems quickly entered the national literary consciousness. Her early poetry was popular and critically acclaimed because of its distillation of white pioneer mythology, yet she was to become a critic of that inheritance. When her activism quickened in the 1960s, Wright's poetry was judged to have suffered. One of the ways that her career has been characterised is that she sacrificed her writing for her politics; her politics not only stole time from her writing, but it was also perceived to diminish the quality of what writing she could do. But I think there has been insufficient attention paid to the new kinds of writing she *was* doing. The two fires, the two passions that burned within her, were art and activism, and one way that Wright came to reconcile them was to choose a different kind of art, that of history. Poetry and politics came together to produce disciplined non-fiction.

This is the story of how and why that transformation came about, a tale of two very different books by the same author about the same subject written decades apart. The first was a semi-fictional novel about her grandparents called *The Generations of Men*, written in the 1940s and '50s, and the second was a history of the frontier on which they lived, *The Cry for the Dead*, published in 1981. When Wright decided in the 1970s to travel back again to the time of her pastoral ancestors, she did so with an urgent political purpose and with the help of a new kind of writing.[1]

In the drought and war and deep cold of the winter of 1942, Judith Wright returned to New England, the country of her childhood, to work the land with her father. One day they searched together for an old track leading from the coast to the tableland, and they happened upon a sheer cliff called Darkie Point near Point Lookout, where they had often camped as a family. Her father told her that this had been the place where, in revenge for the killing of cattle, a whole group of Aboriginal men, women and children had been driven over the cliff.[2] That story, as Wright recalled, 'had sunk more deeply into my own life than he would perhaps have liked, and was to influence me forever'.[3] In her poem 'Nigger's Leap, New England' she asked: 'Did we not know their blood channelled our rivers, / and the black dust our crops ate was their dust?'

The year and a half she spent in this region in 1942–43 was critical in shaping Judith's literary preoccupations and sensibilities. She had left New England eight years earlier and was now rediscovering the land as her own, indeed as part of herself, as her 'blood and bone'. The threat of Japanese invasion sharpened her sense of belonging: she felt the land 'under her own ribs'.[4] And she reinhabited it at a time when it was visibly hurting – the dramatic dust storms and drought of the early '40s engulfed the land. Also, she was exposed through her father to the stories of Aboriginal dispossession. So she was doubly haunted: by the fate of the Indigenous people whose land was now her family's, and by the fate of that land – her extended body – falling apart. She began at this time to write a novel based on her family history, but abandoned it until her discovery of twenty-three surviving volumes of her grandfather's diaries suddenly gave it substance and direction. Albert Wright had written devotedly of his life on the land, and it was this daily record that delivered into Judith's hands an opportunity to evoke the historical detail of her grandparents' lives. Therefore, a remarkable historical manuscript lies at the heart of her novel. Because of those crucial diaries, Albert Wright became the man at the centre of *The Generations of Men*.

Judith Wright was the daughter of a pastoral dynasty. She was, as she put it herself on many occasions, 'a fifth-generation descendant of pastoralists on both sides' of her grand-parentage.[5] Her grandparents' forebears both came to Australia from England, in 1828 and 1840 respectively, to become farmers in the Hunter Valley. All her ancestors, claimed Judith, 'had much the same kind of background of fairish wealthy English family with too many sons'. *Too many sons*: thus her family history was already being shaped by 'the generations of men'. The younger sons had little prospect of land in England and had to leave home to get it. In Australia they could dispossess another people, establish their own lineage, and assume the management of a rather different kind of land. It is the ethical and environmental responsibilities of that new tenure that Judith Wright made it her life mission to analyse.

In *The Generations of Men*, Judith writes of her grandmother's grand-father, George Wyndham, as a radical escapee from 1820s England turned conservative by the experience of raw egalitarianism on the Australian frontier. George felt that something had gone awry with his plans, but could not put his finger on exactly what. It was not just his fellow Australian colonists who had made him retreat into his Englishness; it was also the land itself and its original peoples: 'the country, he could not trust it. It had something up its sleeve, he felt obscurely. "We should have left the place to the blacks!" his old friends would sometimes burst out, half-seriously, at news of droughts, bushrangers, speared cattle, rust in the wheat.'[6]

One suspects that the title of the book is a kind of *trompe-l'oeil*. As a woman in a pastoral dynasty, the actual land would never come to Judith. Perhaps this freed her to examine its ethical and spiritual legacy? Mary Durack, Margaret Kiddle, Elyne Mitchell, Mary Bennett, Alice Duncan-Kemp and Barbara York Main are further Australian examples of pastoral daughters who became famous family or pastoral chroniclers.[7] Judith Wright was, however, the beneficiary of one extraordinary financial legacy because of her gender. Judith's grandmother, May Wright, left money especially for her granddaughters. After her husband Albert's death, May Wright had managed the family property in New England for so long that she had money in her own right, and it was her bequest that enabled Judith to study at the University of Sydney and then to travel to Europe for a year.[8] *The Generations of Men* was written, surely, in tribute to this remarkable woman to whom Judith was so indebted. And indeed, May Wright begins and ends the book and is its hero – and her written reminiscences provided crucial source material. In spite of the title of the book – or more likely, in deliberate tension with it – *The Generations of Men* is actually about a woman. A woman on the masculinist, pastoralist frontier – the world and predicament into which Judith was herself born. So although this book seems at first to be the work of a dutiful daughter, it is suffused with a subtle feminism.

The book's drama is twofold. There is the love story between May and Albert, and there is the battle with the land. May grew up in the Hunter Valley in relative poverty because her father had gambled on pastoral country on the Tropic of Capricorn in Queensland in the 1860s. He had been lured by reports of good land to purchase a run, which he called May Downs after his daughter, but he was caught by the great Queensland slump of that decade and was bankrupted. As a child, May Mackenzie had shared her father's excitement about this new frontier, but they were soon forced back to the Hunter Valley to eke out a living on the land of her grandfather. In 1871, aged sixteen, May Mackenzie met Albert Wright, almost fifteen years her senior, at the wedding of her friend and his sister.

Albert had been managing two stations inland from Rockhampton that had been repossessed in the Queensland slump. One of them, situated on the Dawson River, was called Nulalbin; its previous owner had died of fever and worry and it was Albert's job to assess the land and its assets for sale by an agent. He was there to close the books and abandon the land – to return it, as his father might have said, 'to the blacks'. The original owners were still there, and Albert worked closely with several Aboriginal stockmen and relied on their judgement and assistance. The previous owner had tried sheep and failed, but it looked like a good season when Albert arrived in 1868, and because the cattle began to improve, their sale was delayed. Albert began to nourish an idea. He had come to respect this country – he knew the run, he worked well with old Captain, the Aboriginal head stockman, and he had decided that it was good cattle country. He wondered if he could borrow the money needed to take over the mortgage. Albert nailed a sapling over the door of the quarters, went south to talk business and, in November 1869, returned as the new owner of Nulalbin.

Thus when Albert met May in 1871 and they courted one another for an intensive few days following his sister's wedding, Albert stood before her not just as any land-owning suitor but as a man whose life was already entwined with the very Queensland frontier that had both ruined May's father and excited her as a child. *The Generations of Men* tells these twin stories, then, these entwining strands of May and Albert's relationship and of their battle with the land.

Albert and May together struggled to secure and maintain Nulalbin throughout the 1870s and early 1880s, in the face of economic uncertainty, drought and a land that delighted and defied them. Aboriginal people both helped them and haunted them. They were the stockmen and the housemaids, but they were also profoundly alien. In the novel, they appear through May's eyes as unreliable and mysterious, more like animals than humans. May doubts that they have souls, she compares their noisy presence to a flying fox camp, she despises them for eating with the dogs, and she sees their seasonal migrations as being like those of birds.[9] Judith Wright the novelist uses her forebears to portray a fatal psychological relationship between Aborigines and invaders. May feels a 'deep emotional repulsion that was half attraction' for the Aboriginal way of life. Her fear was 'the kind of fear that had prompted the white men to kill and kill, not because of the little damage the blacks could do them materially, but because of a threatened deeper damage, the undermining of a precarious way of life that existed by denying what the aboriginals took for granted'. And Albert, who learned some of their dialects and respected their knowledge, is also shown resenting their psychological power over him: 'They had scarcely made even the show of resistance,' he reflected. 'Looking back, he could see how it had been necessary to the whites to magnify that resistance, to keep alive in their minds the memory of the few killings, the few hostilities, to imagine dangers that had never existed. Only in that way could they justify themselves for killing, keep their own self-respect ... To forgive oneself – that was the hardest task.'[10]

Albert, like his father-in-law, had his own ill-fated northern venture in the late 1870s, taking a leap of financial faith in new country being opened up further north on the Atherton Tableland and in the Gulf Country. It was a bad gamble and sent him back into deep debt after the few hard-won gains at Nulalbin. By the mid-1880s, and following the death of their young son and an agonising drought, Albert and May retreated to cooler, greener country on the New England plateau in northern New South Wales, maintaining Nulalbin from a distance. In 1890, in his fiftieth year, Albert died of pneumonia. The central tragedy of the book is thus Albert's defeat in his battle with the land. May – against advice – continues to manage their properties, out of both loyalty to Albert and belief in herself. She takes over Albert's work, and even his diary. The last quarter of *The Generations of Men* portrays how May secures financial and farming success on her New England property, Wongwibinda, even purchasing the neighbouring country, Wallamumbi, and imagining establishing a landed dynasty stretching from New South Wales into Queensland. The hardships of the frontier recede, a glow of triumph and nostalgia is allowed, and the book ends in 1929, the year of May's death, as she looks back with a quiet satisfaction on a solid century of her family's presence in Australia.

In the twenty years following the publication of *The Generations of Men*, Judith Wright increasingly devoted her time and energy to public causes. She was a co-founder of the Wildlife Preservation Society of Queensland and fought campaigns against exploitation of the Great Barrier Reef and against sand mining at Cooloola in the Noosa district and later Fraser Island. She was a foundation member of the Australian Conservation Foundation from 1966 and a member of the Whitlam government's Hope Inquiry into the National Estate, which reported influentially in 1974. She protested against Australia's involvement in the Vietnam War and became a patron of the Campaign Against Nuclear Power. She fought against damming and woodchipping in Tasmania in the 1970s and became national president of the Campaign to Save Native Forests. She supported Aboriginal writers and became a close friend of the poet Kath Walker, later known as Oodgeroo Noonuccal. Wright was a campaigner for land rights as well as a member of the Aboriginal Treaty Committee formed in 1978. She was a friend, lover and confidante of 'Nugget' Coombs, who was chair of that committee.

Judith had always been political, and many of her views were shaped by her intellectual collaboration with writer and philosopher Jack McKinney, whom she met in Brisbane in 1944 and lived with from 1946 until his death in 1966.[11] She was disturbed by the arms race of the Cold War, but also by the materialism of the postwar years and by 'the effects of the technological and industrial invasion of the land [she] loved'.[12] In her own words, she became 'part of a kind of resistance movement, called conservation'. In opposing rampant development she was also advocating a philosophical stance that she shared with McKinney, a view that the scientific and rational thinking of modern Western culture held the seeds of its own destruction and needed to be replaced by a 'feel-ing-intuitive or emotional view of the world'.[13] Thus her poetry was part of her politics, and a 'crisis of language' was integral to her wider sense of global crisis.[14] So too was her family history a part of her politics, for much of her activism had its roots in her lifelong quest to understand the ambiguities of her pastoral inheritance. Her twin concerns of Aborig-inal rights and the environment found positive as well as negative sources in her family background. Her grandfather, Albert, had been unusual in paying his Aboriginal workers. Her father, Phillip, was a pioneer con-servationist, a national park advocate, an early prophet of the threat of soil erosion and land degradation, and a man committed to public life.

But, in spite of the emotional and intellectual confluence between her art and her activism, they were indeed separate and mostly irrec-oncilable tasks. She *was* torn; she constantly regretted that her political commitments prevented her from writing more. The precious hours of the creative day leaked away. Tim Bonyhady, speaking in 2005 at the inaugural Two Fires Festival in Braidwood, which honours Wright, reflected on the way Judith's activism went well beyond her political writing, the way she 'bore the grind of daily campaigning'.[15] She was, for a period around 1970, 'a full-time conservationist', speaking, organ-ising, crusading, carrying the heavy administration of activism. To read through her voluminous papers in the National Library is to dis-cover that she was prey to constant demands and solicitations, both political and poetic; she was often thoughtful and gracious in response, sometimes firm and dismissive, and when the issue appealed to her, passionate and active. She knew that, as a renowned and popular poet she had 'curiosity value' to the environmental movement, and this status was one she both exploited and resented. As someone who had habitually sought the margins, she was uncomfortable with publicity, yet there was always a relish in challenging taboos. She wrote in 1982 to the historian A L Rowse that 'being female I am not supposed to express my dislike and indeed trained not to do so from birth.'[16] Well, now she could. Her 'curiosity value' gave her a delicious freedom to say what she thought, and to be heard.

The adversarial context of her campaigning created a need for a different kind of writing, something that would go beyond metaphorical or poetic truth; she needed words that would be legally and historically defensible. I think this is a fascinating moment in the career of a great writer. Judith had to turn the powerful poem about 'Nigger's Leap, New England' into a coolly researched and verifiable history of the frontier.[17] In the years that she was finishing *The Cry for the Dead*, the Aboriginal Treaty Committee was formed with Judith a foundation member. This committee, led by 'Nugget' Coombs, 'called for a Treaty, within Australia, between Australians'. In words that sound like Judith's, the Treaty Committee lamented that there was no 'documentary recognition of the quality and courage of those who were conquered'.[18] The Treaty would be concerned not only with land rights, but also with political rights. Judith, while working for that committee, was writing a book that gave a secure scholarly foundation to its political campaign. Her alternative title for *The Cry for the Dead* was 'A Right to the Soil?'

Let's see how Judith Wright sets about becoming a historian. She had always sought a peripheral status, institutionally as well as geographically, and, as Australian literature professor Philip Mead puts it, Wright 'was to harbour a kind of anti-academicism all her life'.[19] Yet, just as she had found the university useful in the early stages of establishing herself as a writer, so in the late 1970s did she again court disciplinary knowledge. From her research notes in her papers, we can look over her shoulder as she reads her way through squatting history and local Queensland pioneering chronicles. Writing *The Generations of Men* had made her realise that her education had not equipped her to understand the great pastoral migrations in which her forebears had taken part.[20] Now, twenty to thirty years later, she found a mountain of new material generated by the explosion in Australian history since the 1950s. She was especially interested in the new work on the frontier being done in the 1970s by Raymond Evans and Henry Reynolds. She read Reynolds' book, *The Other Side of the Frontier*, in manuscript, and it was published in the same year as hers. Alongside this historical scholarship, she was reading texts in Aboriginal anthropology, both old and new – A W Howitt's *Native Tribes*, Edward Curr's *The Australian Race*, the work of A P Elkin (who had once been her teacher), John Mulvaney and Jack Golson on *Aboriginal Man and Environment in Australia* and Mulvaney and E B Joyce's archaeological work at Kenniff Cave, as well as scientific perspectives that emerged in the 1960s on Aboriginal burning regimes. She also read Claude Levi-Strauss as she tried to find ways to empathise with, describe and understand a different civilisation, looking for intelligent contrasts between hunter-gatherer societies and her own. Above all, she trawled the regional archives and newspapers.

This was a scholarly enterprise she was embarked upon, and the task she set herself was to master the literature that might enable her to strengthen and enrich her particular narrative. Looking back on 1949 and *The Generations of Men*, she concluded, 'My views have not changed. But my knowledge has.'[21] 'My reading and research', she wrote, 'took me into dark places, into which historians are only recently beginning to throw some light.'[22] It was depressing work. She needed unique, grounded and localised truths that she could go out and do battle with. She needed to be able to show that this happened exactly here, precisely then.

In October 1977, Judith and her daughter Meredith hired a car and
set off for the Dawson Valley in Queensland, where her grandfather
Albert ran cattle on 'Nulalbin', 'to check some final details' in the writing of *The Cry for the Dead*.[23] Judith had been there before, with Jack
McKinney in a hot January just after the war, when they had been 'care-
less and moneyless'. By the time of this second trip, however, she was a
public figure and she told Len Webb, rainforest ecologist and dear friend,
that she felt the need to appear 'convincingly harmless' to the locals. She
feared that none of them would talk to her because of her known views
about history and the treatment of Aboriginal people. But the trip passed
amicably: Judith reported to Len that she 'met a lot of the "old hands",
aristocratic and otherwise, but [they] didn't take any baits. I did my
poodle-faking act very well' and Meredith 'kept discreetly silent'.[24]

She found the mood of the people unsympathetic: 'Rural misery
flourishes, as do complaints about unions and demands for the troops.'[25]
And the landscape depressed her: 'They have just about ruined that
country,' she wrote, 'mostly sand underlain with clay, creeks deep in
sand and only spear-pumps get water ... a real mess,' though she did
see 'some excellent regrowth', especially on the black soils. On Goomally
station, what had been 'open forest' in the 1920s had become thickly
overgrown and only about a third of the country was usable for grazing.
She found all the creeks on Nulalbin 'deeply sanded', and only one
lagoon survived. The string of waterholes teeming with life had gone.[26]
Judith's eye was searching for precise detail and understanding; she
wanted to know the lie of the land. She recorded the fall of the Dawson
range north and south, the colour of the clays (red, yellow, white), the
creeks that were 'all dry' (Spring, Blackboy, Pearl, Lily), the ant and bird
life. Meredith remembers how Judith kept on stopping the car, getting
out and taking photos. Meredith, who was seeing the country for the
first time, would notice a wonderful tree, but her mother was out there
photographing soil erosion.[27]

With her new eyes and purpose – and the change in her politics and art – Judith begins to embed the story of her grandparents in a broader cross-cultural and environmental narrative. Her main characters in this new book, no longer larger than life, shrink back to size and become figures in a landscape. This adjustment of focus allows other figures, hitherto very much in the background, even ghostly, to be rescued from our peripheral vision and claim our attention. There is an uncompromising directness about her prose; it is 'thicker, darker, heavier'.[28] As historian Michael Roe puts it, the sublimated sorrow of *The Generations of Men* has been turned into active pain and anger.[29] Wright becomes an elegant slave to fact and context, rarely venturing beyond what she finds in the record, yet always enlarging the telling with interpretive insight and context. Albert and May are transformed from warmly imagined and partly fictionalised ancestors into slightly distanced and partially known historical people in a dynamic landscape. Their personal curiosities, concerns and consciences about Aboriginal society, which were portrayed in the earlier book, are now used to analyse these anxieties more broadly in settler society. The adjustment of focus from interior lives to the broader landscape of colonial experience better illuminates the shifting terrain between private and public in frontier culture. In relinquishing the semi-fictional form, some elements of her storytelling are lost: we miss the novelist's confident access to thoughts and feelings. But other dimensions are gained: the story has greater gravity and a wider canvas, and uncertainty and silence become a part of the narrative.

As Inga Clendinnen has said of the writing of history, 'Were this fiction, I would know that all things said and left unsaid, all disruptions, were intended to signify. But this is not fiction, and I cannot be sure.'[30] So the moment Judith Wright chooses history, she enables herself to speculate about silences. Her grandfather's diary becomes more than a mine for the novelist; it is transformed into a finished but incomplete artefact, a piece of evidence whose gaps must be tested. In the summer of 1868–69, there was violent conflict over the possession of waterholes in south-eastern Queensland. Albert recorded tersely in his diary: 'About sixty Blacks were shot at Grosvenor last week.' In that month of January, Albert – who seldom missed filling in his diary entries, unless sickness prevented him – found himself condemned to silence for three whole weeks.[31] 'What happened during that time,' wrote Judith, 'and the reason for that silence, can only be guesswork.'

As the author's lens draws back, the ghostly Aboriginal figures of her poems and the alien creatures of her novel come into focus as a people. The dark shapes haunting the brigalow and the puzzling individuals helping May in the house and Albert on horseback become *the Wadja*, a people with culture and history, the long-term inhabitants of deeply known country who also defend it fiercely from invasion. As Graeme Davison has observed, 'The union of land and lineage that [Wright] celebrated in her own forebears' history is now relocated to the Aborigines they dispossessed.'[32] Gone is the earlier view that Aborigines offered little resistance. The intruding whites also come into a different focus. Wright offers us a view of them through Aboriginal eyes: as a race with few women and almost no children, a people defiant against the laws of sharing, building elaborate structures of wood and stone in which they shut themselves away, and constantly, ruthlessly, breaking the body of the land.[33] The balance of the narrative shifts a little earlier to the 1860s, the decade of most conflict and tension on the south-east Queensland frontier. May Mackenzie does not appear in the book until two-thirds of the way through. Albert is unquestionably the main character but he shares the stage with other white men trying to wrest a living from the land, and their preoccupying relationship is with the Aboriginal people. And the Wadja do not just fade away: as late as the 1870s, Albert Wright recorded a gathering of about 500 Aborigines on the banks of the Dawson.[34] On another occasion, May Wright wondered 'why they did not kill us all, they were so many and we so few'.[35]

Judith was frustrated that she could not tell more of the Aboriginal story. Her publisher, Frank Eyre, pointed out that she was unable to fulfil her promise to capture the Indigenous experience. She replied:

> If you had any idea of the quantity of notes, books, documents, archival documents, etc. I have consulted or of the size of my card index and the amount of material I have copied, you would be taken aback. Poor Kathleen Fitzpatrick's struggles over Sir John Franklin had nothing on mine. I have had to educate or re-educate myself in not only history, but anthropology, ecology, geography, geology – you name it . . . May Hell admire me, as the bushrangers used to say, but I wished often I hadn't taken it on at all![36]

In the absence of many surviving written documents about the Wadja, Wright turned to the document of the land as another way of evoking their lives. 'My object of course,' she wrote to Frank Eyre, 'has been to tell the story of their country and what happened to it – which is essentially the story of the Aborigines' own destruction.' So the land must bear witness to its people.

The Cry for the Dead is relatively uncelebrated as a pioneering environmental history, yet it was deeply attentive to the story of ecological change. Environmental and Indigenous politics were so entwined in Wright's campaigning that in 1991 she resigned as patron of the Wildlife Preservation Society of Queensland because of its failure to support Aboriginal land rights. She saw the emergent 'wilderness' politics of the 1980s as incompatible with the recognition of Indigenous history. In *The Cry for the Dead*, the story of the land is inextricable from the story of its original people and equally revealing of what the invaders were doing, or not doing. It was a double ignorance and silence Wright was dealing with: 'If the English settlers were contemptuously ignorant of the realities of Aboriginal life, they were equally ignorant of the country itself.'[37] In *The Cry for the Dead*, Albert's personal battle with the land, a land of droughts and flooding rains that frustrates his ambitions and finally defeats him, becomes a more complex social and environmental history of a land destabilised by European pastoral occupation, a land that retaliates with hoof-hardened soils, drying swamps, sanded-up rivers and creeks, revengeful spear grass, resurgent eucalypts sprawling onto the flats, and introduced prickly pear run rampant.[38] Several reviewers at the time recognised this dimension: T B Millar wrote: 'Here is an account of the brooding land's revenge upon its desecrators.'[39] Edmund Campion's joint review in the *Bulletin* of Wright's new book and Eric Rolls' *A Million Wild Acres* was titled 'The Land Which Fought Back for its Tribes', and he observed that 'The land itself has become a major character in recent books of Australian history.'[40] Randolph Stow welcomed the book as perhaps the first history to detail the ecological changes caused by the white invasion.[41]

Wright's book also drew responses from readers offended by her politics. In August 1982 the book was reviewed in the *Guardian* in England. The reviewer, Terry Coleman, a journalist on the staff of the paper and also a historian, was dismissive and disdainful of Wright's work. 'She is of the Bury-My-Heart-at-Wounded-Knee school of history,' he wrote. Coleman rebutted Wright's history with words and concepts that became familiar years later when Australia's History Wars gathered pace. In response to *The Cry for the Dead*, Coleman defended the British settlement of Australia in the following way:

> The early governors of New South Wales considered the blacks as much subjects of His Britannic Majesty as the white convicts of the penal settlements. The first governor took Bennelong, an aborigine, into Government House and dressed him like a gentleman, and Sydney Opera House today stands on Bennelong Point. The third governor, King, sketched aborigines with obvious affection.
>
> But it was a hopeless business, and the impact of the white

settlement was obviously going to be a fatal one. A few blacks killed whites, the whites revenged themselves, and from then on, though whites were hanged for murdering aborigines, the outcome was inevitable.

But it was emphatically not an extermination. It was the inevitable result of a collision between civilised Europe (though Europe might carry a rifle) and the stone age, for the aborigines, even today, are, most of them, the local representatives of the Stone Age. Very few have wanted to enter Australian society.[42]

The words that frame the death of Aborigines are these: 'inevitable', 'obviously' and 'hopeless'. Settlers – represented by benevolent kings and governors – offered kindnesses that were rejected or unappreciated. Aborigines initiated the violence; settlers responded only out of revenge; and British justice and the rule of law – although fairly applied – was in vain. This was not an encounter of civilisations, but a collision between a cultured people and a primitive and unredeemable race.

Eighteen years after Coleman, Keith Windschuttle argued that historians invented frontier violence in the post-1960s period to serve the needs of their strengthening left-wing politics.[43] Wright's history was indeed a product of post-1960s politics, as we have seen. But Windschuttle and Coleman argue that historians made up frontier violence out of nothing; it was an artefact of the counter-culture, even an academic conspiracy. The long, agonising history of the white conscience is inconvenient to this theory, so Windschuttle and his defenders have no interest in, and no sensitivity to, the sinews of settler memory (see Chapter 7). Yet this is exactly what Judith Wright's work is about, and why it has such enduring and haunting relevance. She shows that the whites were as human as the blacks. Wright portrays a frontier caught, from its very beginnings, in a web of intrigue, curiosity, violence and anxiety, a fatal psychological embrace, and she shows how the tensions between history and memory, and between public and private, are ingrained in Australian frontier experience.

In order to illustrate this powerful dimension of Judith's work, it is helpful to look at a rather different response to *The Cry for the Dead*. It is a letter written to Judith Wright by a fellow descendant of the south-eastern Queensland pastoral pioneers, a man named James Henry, whose father was born in 1881 not far from Nulalbin when Albert and May Wright were living there.[44] Henry wrote to Judith in 1982 of the way her book treats the violence of the Australian frontier:

> The odd thing is, you know, that we always knew the theme in our bones, as only children can. Those legendary unspoken horrors, those sins cherished by successive generations, were essential to us; they added value to our conspiracy of silence, our annual dues at the bushman's club. We suffered much from a simpleton's concept of loyalty, lived our lives at very exalted levels of guilt and fear. Ours was, I suppose, an odd inheritance: the preservation, in silence, of truths suppressed by our elders and betters, the old pastoral nomads who, in their way, did have something to hide. We valued that legacy – rightly. Without it we might have seen ourselves for what we were. Dusty industrialists, masquerading as bushmen. Spending our lives gambling tooth and nail against the climate, the markets, the neighbours. There was – it's hard to say this, but it's so – more style to any one of the old hands who also helped to destroy the blacks, than there is to be found among their successors who, with demonstrable imbecility, destroy the land stolen on their behalf. There are, I gather, some honourable exceptions. I have not met them.
>
> I read *The Generations of Men* and *The Cry for the Dead* once more, in that order, after I wrote to you. The two books, though separated by 30 years in execution, make a beautiful diptych, don't they – a special form for conveying a sort of truth to people at a particular time, especially to those who fear it most. Like me and the bush people, still in thrall to our imaginary audience of fine old pioneers and other phantoms.
>
> As you see, you have revived my memories and put upon the past a set of values which I had despaired of ever being able to experience as my own, though I knew of their existence. I am profoundly grateful to you.

P.S. It looks to me, reading this rather incoherent letter, as if the belief systems I acquired as a boy are breaking up, or down as the case may be. There are many like me to whom this will occur when they catch up with the passionate ironies which form, like holograms, in the angle between your two books. I expect there'll be the devil to pay, but there's a rare elation I quite like in the air.[45]

Judith must have treasured this letter. Here, her reader recognises that *The Generations of Men* and *The Cry for the Dead* are complementary books, bound together like the two sides of a frontier, each exploring a different angle of truth. Henry's letter also expresses some of Judith's own ambivalence about an Australian pastoral inheritance, the pride as well as the unease. In 1981, the year that *The Cry for the Dead* was published, she wrote that 'these two strands – the love of the land we have invaded, and the guilt of the invasion – have become part of me. It is a haunted country.'[46] James Henry keenly describes the mortal embrace that Judith Wright was trying to loosen. She must have hoped that he would prove right, that there would indeed be 'the devil to pay' in the wake of the book – but apart from Terry Coleman's disdain, there was minimal disturbance. Judith regretted that the book 'sank like a stone' – although she also felt a 'grim pleasure' that this reception confirmed the endurance of the silence she had studied.[47]

And today we are keenly aware that 'the rare elation' that James Henry felt in the air has remained rare, and that some of the belief systems that propped up pastoral Australia are stubborn and persistent, even as the economic, social and ecological systems that supported it are crumbling.

The Cry for the Dead took its title from the Aboriginal chant in honour of the recently deceased, generally uttered just before daybreak. As another reviewer, Axel Clark, observed, Wright's book was a lament for all the dead – for the Wadja first of all, but also for the living land and its other inhabitants – the birds, marsupials, even the marauding stock – and a lament, too, for the white people who dispossessed the blacks.[48] Where are the white pioneering families now? This is the unexpected twist in the plot – it is a windfall of Judith's decision to write a history that stays with the land. 'We too have lost our dreaming,' she grieved when reflecting on her ancestors' eventual abandonment of pastoral lands in Queensland.[49] The Cry for the Dead tells of the loss of Wright's stolen inheritance by 'traders and stock-exchanges': she mused that 'what's stolen once is stolen again'.[50] In a Queensland parliamentary debate in 1902, in the midst of devastating drought, one politician asked 'Where are the pioneers?' and mourned that the country was fast passing into the hands of the mortgagees.[51] In her poem 'Two Dreamtimes' (1973), which was addressed to the Aboriginal poet Oodgeroo Noonuccal, Wright reflected that, although 'a knife's between us', she and her black sister shared 'grief for lost country ... poisoned now and crumbling'. Wright concluded The Cry for the Dead with the observation that 'None of the descendants of Albert and May Wright now own land on the plain or beyond it; and perhaps none of the Wadja, if any remain, have seen the country that once was theirs.'[52] The Generations of Men moves with Albert and May to new country and a more hopeful family future, while The Cry for the Dead stays with the Dawson Valley as it is doubly dispossessed of its people.

So a eulogy became a lament. Judith and her editor at Oxford University Press discussed how the two books were different. 'That was a personal story,' wrote Frank Eyre of The Generations of Men, 'this is a tragic history of a country.'[53] T B Millar reviewed the later book for the Canberra Times, and declared: '[Wright] has discarded the poet's pen and its romantic temptations for the discipline of the historian ... As such she has written a far more important book than Generations of Men could possibly be, if less literary and comfortably readable.'[54]

But sometimes scholars mistakenly assume the power of books and underestimate the gulf between popular and learned understandings of history. In 2003 I made a journey rather like the one Judith and Meredith made in 1977. I travelled to the Dawson Valley, to the heart of Wadja country, and I took with me *The Generations of Men* and *The Cry for the Dead*. They are still the only substantial published sources on the history of that country. I, too, was anxious about how to play the local politics, but keen to learn about the books' reception amongst their most important readers. Regional networks soon delivered me into the hands of the local historian, a thoughtful, well-read man living in Baralaba, and we spent several hours talking about the history of his country, especially the period of his own lifetime. He knew of Albert Wright and of *The Generations of Men*, but he had never heard of *The Cry for the Dead*. He promised to order it from the library bus. So this local historian knew the novel but not the history, which itself is cause for reflection.

From his house, and with his encouragement, I rang the owners of Nulalbin and organised a visit that afternoon to see the foundations of the Wrights' old home. But a short time later, the woman rang back. She had talked to her husband; there was nothing to see, he said, and they didn't know any history. But I did get to spend a night on another part of the old run, for Nulalbin had been reduced to many smaller holdings. I stayed on a farm owned by a couple, one of them locally born, who took in backpackers and made it their job to introduce visitors to the history of their land, and to the Australian way of life. Here I was, finally, on the very earth where Albert and May, Captain and Maggie, Clara and Pincher, Cubbo, Toby, Jacky, Bobby, Channool, Whackemall, Cocky and Murrially had all lived and worked. I got these much-loved books out of my swag and passed them around amongst the contemporary custodians of that country and their visitors. No one had ever seen or heard of either book.

SIX

The Creative Imagination: Greg Dening

I t is a crisp, clear Canberra morning and Greg Dening, historian and anthropologist, begins a ten-day postgraduate workshop by gathering the twenty chosen scholars in a circle of conversation and telling them that this is what postgraduate education can be: a community where we can expose our vulnerability because there is equality and trust, and where we can gamble because the consequences are not hurtful, except perhaps to our pride. He speaks softly, with a careful, sacred manner. His pauses, his silences, are also eloquent. He has the full attention of the room; we already sense that this is no ordinary academic occasion. Outside, the magpies carol and elegant scribbly gums stake out the flooded valley of the Molonglo that is Lake Burley Griffin.

The academic workshops that Dening and his wife and fellow-historian, Donna Merwick, offered postgraduate students in the humanities and social sciences for the decade that bridged the new millennium were called *Challenges to Perform: The Creative Imagination in the Presentation of Knowledge*. It was my privilege to teach alongside them (and with others) at these events at the Australian National University from 1998 to 2004. I remember hurrying excitedly across campus for the next round of student performances, knowing I had a ring-side seat at the best show in town. It was autumn: leaves and lives were turning and Professor Dening's Exercises were in session.[1]

'Each of you is the expert on your subject,' Greg assures us (we are sceptical of this), 'but no one else wants to know what's in your head' (we recognise this!). So here is the challenge – to engage others, to make connections, to join a world conversation.

Dening gently leads us away from a precious or adversarial sense of originality – as something defined without or against others – towards a robust celebration of intellectual debts and dialogues. Knowledge grows out of conversation, and 'conversation' can be informal, spontaneous, equal, erotic, unpredictable, public, social, civil and unbounded. 'We begin,' he says, 'by plumbing the depths of our own plagiarism.' We begin with admiration.

These are deliberately dangerous words in the modern university – *vulnerability, gamble, celebration, plagiarism, admiration*. I have seen some of Dening's students and colleagues made uneasy by them. Some scholars yearn for a more easily recognisable 'critical culture', and for the heroic cut and thrust – and black and white – of battle. Others contrive their originality by smoothing away their debts.

'Long ago,' Greg wrote in 1994, 'I discovered two things that were important to me and my happiness. I discovered that I didn't feel threatened by the skills and talents of my students (and my readers), and that I had no time to be gladiatorial about knowledge when I so much enjoyed celebrating it.'

Dening was impatient with thinkers who want the last word, and with disciplines that claim a final truth. He was bemused by 'the culture of envy' in academia and the 'blood sport' of debunking. It was not the nature of Dening's criticism to boundary-ride or point-score; rather, it was to rejoice, inspire and imagine. His valedictory book, *Beach Crossings* (2004), glows with this spirit. In his volume of essays and reviews, *Readings/Writings* (1998), Dening introduces us to historian John Stilgoe's evocation of 'loomings', that magical visual experience where the tricks of ocean vastness may bring distant objects – even those beyond and below the horizon – shimmeringly close. Greg wrote many of his books from a desk on the Otway coast overlooking Bass Strait, where he gazed out to sea over the canopy of eucalypts, where he could walk a beach at will and where the loomings of a blue horizon could enchant him. Stilgoe writes in *Alongshore* (1994) that 'seamen and seers can sometimes see over the horizon, beyond the curve of space if not of time.' Dening's gaze seemed to project over that curve, and what he saw shimmered.

Greg criticised as he taught: by indicating further possibilities, by enlarging the subject, by lifting one's eyes to a more distant horizon (or casting them to submarine depths) and then asking what may lie beyond and beneath. Here we approach the experience of his students, forever compelled to look beyond what they might have thought achievable, 'pushed off a cliff and thrown handlines that seemed just out of reach', as one recalled. Historian Clare Wright, who 'did' a short form of the Exercises in 1999, recalls being in Dening's class: 'When Greg told us, his students, his flock, that a good history essay was like an iceberg – the revealed tip belying a massive foundation of knowledge – I knew I wanted to sail to the arctic depths of my intellect.' In the workshop, Clare remembers there was 'Not an academic scaffold in sight. We were free-falling.'[2] Dening always believed that learning requires a little cognitive dissonance. His teaching strategy was to expose his students to exciting and sometimes bewildering freedoms – above all, the freedom to experiment and fail (safely). When I tutored for Dening in 1980, I came to realise just how generous he was to those who chanced their arm – he was determined to reward originality and creative courage, even if it went awry. The only way to fail Professor Dening was not to take a risk.

❧

Greg was born in 1931 beside the Pacific surf in Newcastle. His family moved to Perth, on the Indian Ocean, and then to Melbourne, on the edge of Bass Strait. The son of a sailor who talked him to sleep with stories of the sea, Greg became a scholar of the Pacific, and his intellectual metaphors were drawn from the ocean. 'There is no greater joy for me than to walk a beach,' he later confessed, and he was referring to cultural as well as sandy ones.[3] Australia must have suited him, not just because of its littoral majesty, but because it catered for his sense of the creativity of the margins.

Dening was educated at the Jesuit St Louis School in Perth and then at Xavier College, Melbourne. In 1948, at the age of sixteen, he entered the Society of Jesus (in a class of about twenty) to become a priest. After following the course of studies for novices and scholastics, he completed a history honours degree, followed by a masters in Pacific prehistory at the University of Melbourne and later a PhD in anthropology from Harvard University. Greg was another historian forged at John Mulvaney's campfire for he, too, became a field assistant on Mulvaney's first Australian archaeological dig at Fromm's Landing on the Murray River. Greg called his teacher 'a searcher for time in a timeless land'. The great domed Reading Room of the State Library of Victoria, with its arching balconies of books and the green lights and leather of its radial reading desks, became a second home to Greg, 'a magical place with the heavy silence of a great space: It was a silence you could feel on your shoulders, something like standing on the edge of the Grand Canyon or in the Australian bush.'[4]

Dening was chaplain at the University of Queensland when Pope Paul VI issued his 1968 encyclical *Humanae Vitae* ordering Australian Catholic bishops to preach the rationality of banning birth control. For Dening, the encyclical 'turned the moral face of the Church away from the evils of global poverty, of violence within and between nations, of exploitation of the weak, back to the bedroom'.[5] He privately told the archbishop of Brisbane of his dilemma about preaching on the subject and Dening was instructed to leave the archdiocese immediately. A newspaper photographer pursued him to the airport and a conservative Catholic newspaper published a centrefold article about him under a picture of Judas. He left the priesthood in 1970. Later he would write that he *really* left the priesthood because he had been starved of close friendships and 'because I wanted someone to weep at my funeral'.[6]

Greg returned to Melbourne in 1969 to teach sociology and history at La Trobe University, and in 1971 was appointed the Max Crawford Professor of History at the University of Melbourne. At Dening's interview for the Melbourne chair, the first question came from the vice-chancellor, David Derham: 'Mr Dening, do you think it dangerous to introduce sociology into a university?' And the night before the selection was made, the chair of the panel, John La Nauze, called Greg and asked him: 'Will you be a real historian?'[7]

His university teaching, although utterly secular, was suffused by his Jesuitical wisdom and mystery and inspired by a sense of the revelatory. From his studies of the sacred texts and his struggle to be a scholar who was also a believer, Dening learned that 'truth was in the metaphor'. He later reflected that 'Knowing Abraham and Isaac, David, Isaiah was to be as ethnographic an experience for me as fieldwork in The Marquesas.'[8] His time in the novitiate – an intense closed community of self-conscious ritual and theatre in which every action was subject to reflection – honed that essential ethnographic skill of social alertness.[9] His religious experience later enabled him to analyse the theatre of command and punishment in the mutiny on the *Bounty* in *Mr Bligh's Bad Language* (1992), to evoke the monastic, institutional college life of Cambridge University in the late eighteenth century in *The Death of William Gooch* (1995), to cast an ethnographic eye on the often harsh environment of his old school in *Xavier: A Centenary Portrait* (1978) and *Xavier Portraits* (1993), and to turn a suburban parish history into a celebratory, collective, poetic evocation of modern faith in *Church Alive! Pilgrimages in Faith, 1956–2006* (2006).[10] He remembered how, in 1955, he had to go to 'Hell' to read John Stuart Mill, Alfred North Whitehead and Teilhard de Chardin. Hell was a locked room in the Melbourne seminary where all the forbidden books were kept.[11]

Greg's doctoral dissertation at Harvard, a historical ethnography of the Marquesas Islands in the eastern Pacific, was published in 1980 as *Islands and Beaches: Discourse on a Silent Land: Marquesas 1774–1880*. The book's appearance nine years after Dening's appointment to a chair meant that it was enriched by his years of adventurous teaching and became an essay on historical consciousness as well as a disturbing and moving meditation on culture contact. It was radical in its structural separation of narrative and reflection and was imbued with a playful sense of the disciplinary dispositions of history and anthropology. 'I cannot cope with an anthropology of natives and a history of strangers,' he later wrote. 'I have ambitions to do an anthrohistory of them both.'[12]

During the 1970s, Greg pioneered the teaching of Reflective History, first at La Trobe University and then as Social and Reflective History at Melbourne: he called it 'the joy of my educational career'.[13] In this radical course he taught his students the past 'by first requiring them to describe the present': by inviting them to write an ethnography of some ritual, event or drama in their own society. Thus they soon learned how difficult it was to describe the present and 'that everything they discovered was the subject of reflective discourse by somebody else'.[14] In Greg's hands, history was no mere subject at university; it became a form of consciousness, a definition of humanity, a way of seeing – and changing – the world.

When in 1971 Greg Dening delivered a rationale of his teaching strategy under the title of 'History as a Social System', John La Nauze leaned over to his neighbour Max Crawford and could be heard to mutter: 'We have a viper in our nest.'[15] Dening was critical of the narrowing impact of professionalisation on the teaching of history. He urged a new socialising process in undergraduate teaching, one that would free students from the rigidities of disciplines and enable them to write history as well as read it. He exposed his students to exciting and sometimes bewildering freedoms: freedom from the overlay of others' interpretations, freedom to ransack insights from other disciplines, freedom to experiment. In one small Pacific history honours class in 1978, he challenged his six students to write a book together as their assessment – and we did. It was even eventually published, as *Mission to the South Seas: The Voyage of the* Duff, *1796–99*.[16] He took us to the Mitchell Library in Sydney for a week and we spent each day immersed in the archive and each evening discussing our finds. It was another kind of academic retreat.

A string of major books by Dening swiftly followed *Islands and Beaches*, each more experimental than the last. The most famous was *Mr Bligh's Bad Language: Passion, Power and Theatre on the* Bounty, which won a Victorian Premier's Literary Award and – rather like Eleanor Dark's *The Timeless Land* – was selected in the United States as a Book of the Month by the History Book Club. He sought to 'give back to the past its present', literally 're-presenting' it so that all its possibilities were still there. From the late 1960s, he had become the centre of a school of ethnographic history which came to include Inga Clendinnen, Rhys Isaac, June Philipp, Donna Merwick and Patricia Grimshaw. American anthropologist Clifford Geertz, whose ideas and seminal book *The Interpretation of Cultures* (1973) helped to shape their conversations, later called it 'the Melbourne Group'.[17] Geertz's style of anthropology, which found cultural meaning expressed in public symbols, in words, actions and images that were often captured in the historical record, inspired historians in the 1970s and '80s to 'do ethnography in the archives'.[18]

With intellectual mentors and colleagues such as Clifford Geertz, Marshall Sahlins and Bernard Cohn, Dening became better known outside Australia than within. But, as Dening's influence deepened, some of his contemporaries reserved special vitriol for this gentle man. In 1980 the Deakin University professor Francis West criticised him for being 'multicultural' and 'trendy', for dealing in guilt, for intruding into his analysis, for peddling cultural relativism, for his sympathies with structuralism and postmodernism. West bridled at the implication in *Islands and Beaches* that 'all cultures are equal'.[19] In *The Killing of History* (1994), Keith Windschuttle accused Dening of being one of the murderers of the discipline by blurring history and fiction and preferring theory over facts. It was a gross misreading of a scholar who had a sacred sense of the integrity of the past. But Australians can now see that these attacks prefigured the History Wars of the early twenty-first century, when new scholarship into the violence of Aboriginal frontier experience attracted an angry, conservative backlash. At the end of *Beach Crossings*, Greg (who was not averse to celebrating his 'cliometric' or quantitative moments) said of the fate of the Marquesans: 'I have never counted the dead I have told about in the years 1796–1814.'[20]

Dening's earlier work about the Pacific was suffused with an elegiac sadness about the fate of Islander peoples and the silences he found on their beaches, but his later work became animated by his recognition of the creative continuities of Indigenous cultures.[21] He was committed to overcoming the idea of a 'zero point', that dividing moment 'between a Before, when an indigenous culture was in its pure form, and an After of the encounter, when it was somehow adulterated'.[22] He argued for *process*, for writing history in the present participle, for an ever-unfolding Now. In the 1990s he began to write more about 'deep time' and his Pacific scholarship strengthened in its Australian dimensions, making a contribution – as colleague Bronwen Douglas observed – to reconciliation in Australia.[23] When Greg visited Lake Mungo with Aboriginal custodians in 1999, he felt so connected to the palpable 'timelessness' of the place that he wanted to say it was 'his' land too.[24] In 1990 he wrote: 'Aboriginal history is the history of us all.'[25] He was dedicated to releasing voices from 'the silence of aboriginality' and to writing the kind of history that disturbs the moral lethargy of the present enough to change it. A month before he died, Greg was elated that the Australian Parliament finally issued a formal and meaningful apology to the Stolen Generations.

~

Greg first did the full thirty days of the *Spiritual Exercises* of Ignatius Loyola, the founder of the Society of Jesus, when he was seventeen. Loyola's Exercises are a set of prayers, meditations and mental practices that were first published in 1548. Dening described the book as a slim and sparse text, 'all design and structure, not substance and content'. They shape a retreat into acts of imagination and meditation, whether it be for the full thirty days, which Greg did twice, or the eight-day version he did every year for twenty years. They script an open-ended drama of the soul in which the players had agency and opportunity, but also the security of support and structure. The days followed a rhythm of intensity and ordinariness, of exultation and lethargy, rationality and celebration. There was a progression from uncertainty to decision. Retreats were a time to renew one's fervour.

Every prayer event was preceded by acts of imagination and meditation. In Dening's words, Loyola insisted on 'the careful construction of an ambience that corresponded with the goal of the particular exercise, using darkness or sunlight, closed or open spaces to create a reflectiveness'. One's imagination was primed by this 'composition of place', by this sensual projection into a site of contemplation. A recommended method of evoking these images was to envisage oneself in the scene by successively seeing, smelling, hearing and touching everything in it.

For fifteen minutes the night before, 'points of meditation' were to be prepared. They aimed to define 'the significance of the narrative' that one pondered. 'They were in fact moments of art,' Dening recalled, 'of creative thinking and writing. Often they were performed to others, often listened to as others performed them.' And they were balanced by a fifteen-minute reflection after the meditation, in which one became a critic of one's own theatre of preparation and performance.

In a funny, sad and profound essay called 'Ethnography on My Mind', Dening analysed his earlier life and training as a Jesuit for its enduring imprint on his thinking.[26] For those of us who came to know Greg after he left the Jesuits and the priesthood, this essay was a typically generous gift of himself, a window on how his religious discipline came to inform his history. As one of his students, I was shown my teacher in the making and recognised with delight the truth of his reflection that, in his seventies, Greg was indeed still doing a version of the exercises. He liked to call it his 'academic grandparenting'. Stefan Sippell, a postgraduate scholar who flew from Munich for a workshop, found the professor waiting at the Canberra baggage carousel, holding a card with his name on it. Greg confessed that he saw these extended workshops with doctoral researchers from around the world as 'a secular academic retreat, a sort of intellectual spiritual exercises'. He believed that immersion scholarship could be transformative – of oneself, and also of the world.[27]

◈

'Don't rail against the limits,' Greg urges the assembled doctoral scholars. 'Discover them, play with them, extend them.' As a Jesuit, Dening knew 'what it was like to be totally enclosed by rule and formality'. He had to learn how to make rules enabling, how to use them creatively and mischievously, how to respect them at the same time as transcending them. He had a rule about rules: 'Don't let anybody hide behind the "bad faith" of saying they have to do something in a particular way.'

So the workshop, like Loyola's exercises, is all design and structure at the same time as being frighteningly and excitingly open. The weeks

are governed by a series of rhythms – of alternating staff and student presentations, of programmed mornings and free afternoons, of intensity
and ordinariness, of performance and judgement. There are four themes
(perhaps echoing the four weeks of the full exercises), and each takes two
days, and they come between single days of introduction and conclusion.
Many of the themes focus on the senses, such as seeing, hearing, writing,
reflecting, even dancing. Greg has written that the Jesuits 'had always
believed that physical space, time and the body shaped the spiritual'.[28]
Something like that is at work here: in these two weeks the students transform this 'academic' space with their voices and their bodies.

As the days unfold, Dening is at work in mysterious ways. He is
warm and engaged yet also distant. His manner is – there is only one
word for it – priestly. His pronouncements are enigmatic, his inclination is to gesture to possibilities rather than to lead. This style creates
space and freedom; it leaves his audience, his students (and his readers)
with work to do; it invites a continuing, open conversation. Such mystery can be unsettling, and Greg knows that it can create trauma as well
as exhilaration. And so the community created by this secular academic
retreat – by the very nature of its cohesion and intensity – leaves some
personalities feeling marginal, because they are irritated or puzzled or
unmoved. Perhaps they are suspicious of the fervour.

All participating scholars are expected to give a 'performance' of
fifteen minutes. Here's how Greg described the task:

> These performances will be subject to critical review in the session.
> This review will take into account not just your literary abilities, but
> such performance details as your posture, your voice, your capacity
> to catch the rhythm of your writing, your presence – the sorts of
> things that might be relevant to radio, TV, lecture hall, interview
> appearances. Your ability to perform your piece in exactly 15 min-
> utes, no more than a few seconds over or under, will be especially
> under review.

It is, then, a piece of theatre, a 'moment of art'. You don't 'take a long run up to it', as Greg would say. It is whole in itself. You prepare for it carefully. And then you do it. Risk is at the heart of it. Dening was drawing on a long Jesuit tradition of theatre that believed that 'the best teacher was performance'. His book of essays, *Performances* (1996), elaborated his belief that 'the abiding grace of history' is that 'it is the theatre in which we experience truth'. Academic history had lost its moral force, he believed, because it had been subverted by its own reality effects and had lost its sense of theatre.[29]

The scholars are assigned to groups of five, and each group performs every second morning. These constellations of fifteen-minute performances become the highlight of the workshop and quickly outshine the 'staff' presentations. The degree of experimentation increases as the days pass and the audience's trust and expectations rise. And the individuals within each group begin to work together in creative and surprising ways while preserving their own fifteen minutes of fame. They begin to indulge in 'the careful construction of an ambience' by playing with the senses and doing surprising things with an ordinary room. This crescendo gives the whole workshop the shape of a fine piece of music.

As a student of Dening's in my undergraduate years at Melbourne, I recall a day in 1977 when a group of students studying 'Social and Reflective History' transformed a raked lecture theatre into the sea-swept deck of the *Bounty*. We were no longer audience but sailors under command, absorbed in the action of hauling ropes, hoisting sails and battling Cape Horn, bending our bodies under shouted orders as we strove to bring our wooden ark (with its awkward desks and aisles) to safe harbour. It was a relief to arrive in seductive Tahiti (we were each given a flower), and then a wrench to be put to work again on the open sea, where we were sucked into the maelstrom of the mutiny itself. I remember how Greg looked that day. He could hardly believe the cleverness of his own children.

Social and Reflective History was a remarkable experimental space designed by Dening in the 1970s in which unusual forms of teaching and response could be tried — he offered oral examinations, writing-in-class, lectures by students, writing workshops (these were 'tutorials' *where people actually talked*), collaborative ethnographic fieldwork, immersion in archives. When I took the course, Greg was supported by the brilliant teaching of Pat Grimshaw, herself an inspiring scholar and a pioneer of women's history in Australia. We knew that our teachers were always thinking, always exploring, always pushing the boundaries as they urged us to do. Dening was keen to talk about the scholarly process too, about note-taking, headings, formatting, writing that first sentence and the last, how to survive low moments, 'hitting the wall', creative indexing, copyediting, authorial presence, crossing disciplines. I suspect that Greg's students knew him almost as well as anyone, for this was where he was most revelatory. Students were stunned to find someone ready to talk about these things. And all this from a man whose natural state was meditative silence.

One day in Social and Reflective History Greg lectured to us from his current research — he was writing a history of Xavier College — and we sat and listened in the steeply ranked seats of the old hall to his accounts of discoveries in the archives. He had come across a letter written by a Xavierian serving abroad in the First World War, a letter from a mud-filled dugout to the mother of a dear friend killed by a piece of shrapnel as he cooked breakfast for his mates. It was a letter of utter devotion and love, and of compassion for the woman who would read it. Greg decided to read the letter to us — I guess, so that we could feel the raw emotion of the archive, and so that we would know and always remember that, however playful he encouraged us to be, history is not a game. It was a long letter and Greg read it slowly, his voice faltering. Then he waved his hand apologetically at us and walked out the door. The lecture was just twenty minutes in, and yet it seemed, suddenly, to be over. I suppose Greg didn't know that we sat there in silence for some time, first looking at the door through which he had disappeared and might, for all we knew, suddenly reappear. We gradually, quietly dispersed.

I do not think that the final bit of this 'performance' was scripted. I'm sure that Greg, like us, was deeply moved by the letter, but also perhaps by his presumption to make it public. And by the futility of words, especially words of translation and mediation. He suddenly wanted the original words, the words from the trench, to hang in the air; he did not want to dilute their power. Unscripted though this ending might have been, it could not have been better theatre. Once you engage in performance, you involve the audience, you gamble, and you never quite know how the dice will fall.

At the beginning of his exercises, Dening would say: 'We never learn the truth by being told it, only by experiencing it.' The ritual of performance puts that maxim into practice. And for those who question the possibility of criticism in an environment of such trust and generosity, Dening's answer might be this: 'It is difficult to fool oneself as a performer. We recognise restlessness, boredom, silent disapproval in an audience too easily. We know what we do not achieve in performances.'

In these intellectual spiritual exercises, there is anxiety, discovery, reflection, climax, catharsis – and perhaps even conversion or rejection? And finally, there is celebration. The Exercises are over and we are bound together by them, and changed by them. We know – even those (perhaps especially those) unsettled by Dening know – that we have been working with a great teacher. At the celebratory lunch, speeches are spontaneously made, and Greg indulges us with another ritual. He has a certificate to give each of us. He stands in the middle of our circle and presents it to the first person alphabetically, and that person presents the certificate to the next, and so on. It's a way of acknowledging how much we have learned from one another. And as Greg says before the final lunch: 'The biggest plus of these two weeks could be that you've found a reader, or two or three. The reader is always right.'

Greg's enduring performances are his books. He always believed that 'a book on a shelf' offered him a kind of earthly immortality. Books and archives, 'the erotics of writing and reading', the physicality of paper and text, were crucial to a man for whom history was a craft at once practical and poetic, sensual and philosophical. Greg went to his desk each day to chisel and mould and sculpt; he felt as well as thought his way towards truths. His writing glowed with the physicality of the archive, and his books with the delight of his aesthetic. He encouraged his students to imagine their books in the hands of readers, hopefully being read, of course, but also as objects that would become part of daily material culture, to be carried, loaned, gifted, cared for, talked about. Historians indeed hope that their books might entwine intimately with the lives of their readers and that their histories may sit on bedside tables ready to enter dreams.

All Dening's teaching was directed towards cultivating 'the creative imagination' of his students. Greg's advocacy of the creative imagination was shaped by his engagement with two different worlds; he liked being 'in-between' and this was another of his beaches. On one side was the academy. His foundation lecture, 'History as a Social System', was his challenge to that institutional inheritance, and all his teaching was radical and dangerous in the way it undermined the academic poses of neutrality and dispassion and made explicit the socialisation of disciplinary knowledge.[29] The other world he addressed with the phrase 'the creative imagination' was that of public literary culture. Greg was a writer who loved to read and wanted to be read. He urged his students to be 'open to those other ethnographers of our living experience' – our poets, novelists, comics, cartoonists, film-makers and photographers.[31] He was in awe of Herman Melville's ability to transform the non-fiction of his life into the fictions of his writings.[32] He had us reading novels for our history tutorials, and he loved writers' festivals.

Greg embraced the world of fiction with generosity and excitement, but he was also keenly aware that our literary culture privileges the made-up story over the true one. And it exalts the art of invention over the art of re-presentation. Rhys Isaac, in his magisterial study of the eighteenth-century Virginia planter patriarch Landon Carter, observed that if Carter's diary had been a fictional creation, 'it would have been instantly hailed as a literary classic, and its central character would have been greeted as the invention of genius' – and thus Rhys made a plea for recognition of his protagonist as 'a creative writer overdue for acclaim'.[33] In recent years in Australia we witnessed a vigorous debate about the different and overlapping roles of history and fiction in our literature and public culture, as I explore in Chapter 12 with reference to Inga Clendinnen's response to Kate Grenville's comments about her novel *The Secret River* (2005).

It is sometimes part of the theatre of the fiction writer to present themselves as lone virtuosos. 'Research' is characterised as heroic, a matter of pride but not of faith. Writing is instinctive; creativity is unconscious; insights are personal. The exhilarating freedoms of fiction are contrasted with the dutiful obligations of non-fiction. Mystery, tension, poetry and art seem only to be available to the novelist. These are the very literary codes that Dening challenged and subverted when he advocated 'the creative imagination in the presentation of knowl-edge'. Without making a battle out of it, he quietly subverted all these default contrasts between fiction and non-fiction. Research, he reminded us, is collegial and requires courage; imagination need not be fantasy; freedoms *do* exist in non-fiction; creativity can be collaborative and communal; true stories are entrancing. Not only did he urge his students and colleagues to feel that all the arts of fiction were available to them in writing true stories, but he also aimed to educate the public to a different understanding of the realm of imagination, to see the creativity in the telling of true stories. 'There is much fiction in your non-fiction, I tell [students],' he wrote. 'Actually, I don't let my students call themselves "non-fiction" writers. They shouldn't write "non" anything ... Maybe I don't have a word to replace "non-fiction". But I tell them to see themselves as writers of true stories. Creative writers. Yes, they are creative writers.'[34] 'Be mysterious,' he would urge, echoing Paul Gauguin's advice on translating silences.[35] Be 'experiential', 'entertaining', 'compassionate', 'performative', 'reforming', 'reflective', and – Greg would always say it – 'take risks'.

Like Greg, I am enthralled by the craft of discipline and imagination that is history. Sometimes the 'non' in 'non-fiction' *can* be seen as a denial or a suppression. To call our writing 'non-fiction' seems to deny its creative, imaginative dimensions; it's *not* something, and the something it's not is that wonderful and captivating world of fiction. I am reminded of the simple opposition expressed in a federal department of education question to Australian academics about their publications: 'Is it a piece of research or a creative work?' I bridle at that choice. Historians, like novelists, are producing literary texts that have their own internal demands of consistency, plausibility and integrity, their own organic rationale derived from decisions about where to begin and end, about which characters to foreground, about what relationships to map. In non-fiction writing, this internal, textual, literary dynamic wrestles also with hard external reality. But historians also have some greater freedoms available to them. Some novelists will tell you that writers of non-fiction have a broader canvas to paint on than they do, because truth really is stranger than fiction.[36] Historians can get away with narrating a much wider range of human action because they can show that, astonishingly, it actually happened, whereas credibility can be a narrower and stricter measure when applied to fiction. In real life, people don't behave predictably or consistently, events come from left field, and astonishing coincidences do occur, but an artist of invention might not be able to get away with it. But even when telling true stories, historians have to strive to make them believable.

A historian's finest insights are intuitive as well as rational, holistic as well as particular – and therefore always invitations to debate. As they write, they incite; they expect disagreement and they try to furnish their readers with the grounds for offering it. Footnotes are not defensive displays of pedantry; they are honest expressions of vulnerability, generous signposts to anyone who wants to retrace the path and test the insights, acknowledgements of the collective enterprise that is history. Historians feed off the power of the past, exploiting its potency just as historical novelists do, but historians also constantly discuss the ethics of doing that. To whom are we responsible – to the people in our stories, to our sources, to our informants, to our readers and audiences, to the integrity of the past itself? How do we pay our respects, allow for dissent, accommodate complexity, distinguish between our voice and those of our characters? The professional paraphernalia of history has grown out of these ethical questions.

As Inga Clendinnen observed, historians have a moral contract with the past in the way that many novelists don't. I would add that historians also have a moral contract with each other. How could they even pretend to be brilliant loners when their ethic and their creativity are so collegial? This is another gift of Greg's – to help us be generous in our scholarship, and in our scholarly lives. Every work of history is built upon the labour and insights of others, and if it is good it seeks to display those debts and is no less creative or original for that. Greg's metaphor for such respectful engagement was 'conversation': intimate, civilised, everyday, life-enhancing. History is 'the discipline without a discipline', the one social science that aspires to represent the totality of human experience. 'Discourse is unending,' Greg reminded us. 'Nothing is discovered finally. The moments of understanding stand like sentences in a conversation.' Reflective history makes us participants in the conversation, makes us good conversationalists. Dening acknowledged elaborately and discursively his mentors, his teachers, his colleagues, his students. He wove us gratefully into the tapestry of his knowledge.

In March 2008 there was weeping at Greg's funeral. And there was theatre. At a Requiem Mass in Newman College Chapel at the University of Melbourne celebrating his life, a copy of Ignatius Loyola's *Spiritual Exercises* was placed on a silk pillow on the coffin. Not just any copy, but a rare, precious, ancient, first-edition book on loan from the State Library of Victoria for the occasion, and placed there with ceremony and reverence at the start of the service by Shane Carmody, a student of Greg's and Director of Collections and Access at the library. It was, I think, one of the most beautiful gestures possible, combining Greg's secular and religious lives, and a kind of obeisance by the state to an outstanding intellectual citizen, the gift of a rare book from the very library where Greg's deep reading (and further philosophical transformation) had begun. One of the jewels of the state collection was willingly exposed to the uncertainties of a performance and, for a time, was lost from sight in the incense. The book, appropriately, was laid open. At the end of his 'Challenges to Perform' workshops, Greg would say that although there was celebration, sadness and parting, there was no ending, for the conversation goes on. The pages of the book, the pages of all his books, lie open and inviting.

SEVEN

The Frontier Fallen: Henry Reynolds

'I'M A LOYAL MONARCHIST' says Australian PM . . .
Until then, there's Glenfiddich to enjoy.

S o declared an advertisement for whisky in the English *Guardian* newspaper in October 1995, when Paul Keating was prime minister. The English tabloid media loved to hate the republican 'Lizard of Oz' and indulged in headlines about Keating wanting to 'oust' and 'ditch' the Queen. In English popular culture of the time, an Australian PM who was a monarchist was as unthinkable as life without Glenfiddich. But just nineteen weeks later, loyal monarchist John Howard was elected PM and British whisky drinkers were in shock.

At the time, I was working at the Menzies Centre for Australian Studies at the University of London, where it was our job to explain the peculiarities of Australian history, politics and culture to the British public. Within a few weeks of the March 1996 federal election we felt the outer tremors of Howard's ideological revolution – I was preparing a major conference on *Aboriginal Land Rights: Australia and the Mabo Judgment* to be held at Australia House in April. The High Court's *Mabo* case of 1992 had recognised native title and led to the federal government's *Native Title Act 1993*, and our conference was to bring lawyers,

anthropologists, historians and mining executives to London to explain
the new cultural and business environment in Australia. The conference
had been suggested and largely funded by the Department of Foreign
Affairs and Trade through the Australian High Commission – I had
taken delivery of the brief from the Deputy High Commissioner himself, in his office at Australia House during halftime in the television
coverage of an AFL game.

As the date for the conference drew nearer and the 1996 federal election loomed, the modest sum of DFAT money was transferred, as a
precaution, to the Menzies Centre. Howard swept to power, and the
High Commission was promptly instructed to have nothing to do with
the event, which nevertheless went ahead in its own building. Thus a
conference designed to explain calmly to British business and academic
leaders the nature of the new era in Australian Indigenous politics opened
instead in a climate of crisis. We had unwittingly created an international
forum for the first serious assessment of the new government's direction
in Aboriginal affairs.[1]

The Howard government's swift attack on what it called 'the
Aboriginal industry' and its deliberate fostering of a backlash against
reconciliation created what Aboriginal leader Noel Pearson reported to
the London gathering was a 'deep sense of panic and dismay amongst
Indigenous leaders'. Pearson, a lawyer who played a key role in negotiating the native title legislation, had planned to address the London
conference but the dramatic events in Australia made it impossible for
him to leave home. In his speech, which was read to the Australia House
gathering by Senator Margaret Reynolds and reported in Australia and
Britain, Pearson declared, 'Much has changed since the idea of this conference was first proposed ... It is now likely that the progress made by
the country in forging a legal and philosophical framework for a future
relationship between the colonists and the colonised of Australia,
founded on reconciliation, will be stalled and reversed.' He explained

that 'the country's opportunity to cross the colonial Rubicon with *Mabo* now hangs in the balance.'

The conference audience, which Australian Associated Press identified grandly as 'Britain's opinion leaders', heard anthropologist Deborah Rose explain how 'Big England' was viewed by the Aboriginal people she had worked with in the Northern Territory and how Captain Cook remained an emblematic figure of injustice in their stories.[2] Rose evoked for the London audience the dusty dignity of outdoor courts where, together with the Aboriginal Land Commissioner, she had waded across crocodile-infested rivers to sit in the sand and listen to traditional owners speak of their country. Historian Bain Attwood spoke about the way the *Mabo* judgement was underpinned by the emergence of the new field of knowledge called 'Aboriginal history'.[3] And historian Henry Reynolds powerfully reminded the audience that London was a most appropriate place to hold a conference on Aboriginal land rights.

In the imperial capital were to be found the official Colonial Office records where some of the secrets of the Australian frontier have been unearthed. Those records held the key to understanding why pastoral leases issued to Australian settlers did not extinguish native title, as confirmed by the High Court's *Wik* decision the following year, 1997. Reynolds' research influenced the historical narrative of the High Court in both the *Mabo* and *Wik* judgements, and his examination of the Colonial Office records unearthed significant statements that were made in the late 1840s by Earl Grey, the colonial secretary who was responsible for the pastoral lease. A Colonial Office memorandum from Grey to the NSW governor in 1848, for example, declared that 'leases are not intended to deprive the natives of their former right to hunt over these Districts, or to wander over them in search of subsistence, in the manner to which they have been heretofore accustomed'.[4] Thus it was in 'Big England' that Reynolds' question to our conference really hit home: 'Will Australians of the late twentieth century have less respect for Aboriginal rights than the aristocratic Englishman who ran the Colonial Office 150 years ago?'

The political milestones in Aboriginal affairs in the 1990s included the establishment of the Council for Aboriginal Reconciliation and the final report of the Royal Commission into Aboriginal Deaths in Custody in 1991 and the publication of the Australian Human Rights Commission's *Bringing Them Home* report in 1997. Noel Pearson predicted at the London conference that the ideological differences unleashed by Howard would unfold as a debate over history: 'Those who control the understanding of history can seek to control the present, because they affect peoples' understanding of the truth.' Pearson was eventually to find his own political reconciliation with John Howard – a man he came to respect – but his prophecy proved correct. In the opening years of the new century, a war of words about Australia's frontier history was declared. The History Wars, as we have seen, were part of a conservative backlash against the decades of reform in Aboriginal politics, and they especially took aim at Henry Reynolds, a scholar who, it is often said, 'has changed Australian history – in both senses of that word'.[5]

Henry Reynolds began his path-breaking book *The Other Side of the Frontier* (1981) by recalling a conversation with an old Torres Strait Islander man who recounted how his forebears had scrutinised a sailing ship lying offshore and had seen the Europeans on deck looking back at them using their telescopes, or 'white men's eyes'. At that moment, Reynolds reflected, 'the idea of seeing Australian history from the other side of the frontier sprang into life.'[6] Reynolds' historical consciousness was disturbed by his move in his late twenties from Tasmania (via two years in Europe and Britain) to North Queensland, where he felt that the frontier past 'was still alive'.[7] He encountered the 'fraught context' of Townsville society, a place where to 'talk openly about Aboriginal history was, in itself, a political act'. He experienced his move north from Tasmania to Townsville as a physical shock; he observed every-day racism and felt implicated. It was as if he had arrived in another country – or, as historian Alan Atkinson put it, 'he sounds like a time-traveller visiting another generation.'[8]

Reynolds faced a familiar historiographical dilemma: the creative tension between politics and history, passion and objectivity. On issues of race in northern Queensland, he found there was little light to be glimpsed between the two positions, between the history and the politics. His history, he declared, was 'inescapably political' because it dealt with issues that continue to arouse 'deep passions'.[9] Reynolds and his fellow Queensland historians felt a 'sense of urgency': 'We were self-appointed missionaries who were required to enlighten the public. If we raised our voices we felt that was necessary to shatter once and for all the great Australian silence.'[10] Raising one's voice – challenging the even tone of scholarly neutrality with missionary zeal – was necessary to bring about change, and especially so if that 'neutrality' was revealed to have been unwittingly partisan. The sources of his scholarly awakening were the 'ancestral' gestures of the street and the looks in people's eyes. This was the sense in which Reynolds' work was *inescapably* political: he observed a history at work 'which pressed heavily on the present'. 'I could never completely separate in my mind past and present,' he has reflected.[11]

Such seamlessness is the realm of myth, where the past and present are bonded. Reynolds was dealing in myth as much as history, and in order to overturn it he had to raise his voice, be a missionary, offer something mythic in its place. As the historian Paul A Cohen has put it, historians 'in the process of challenging one mythologised past, inevitably fashion others'.[12] Reynolds' memoir, *Why Weren't We Told?* (1999), with its driving moral question, was shaped by the author's strengthening need to bring 'my professional life into line with my political life'.[13]

When considering how to find a path between the 'two positions' – history as an instrument of reform and history as a process of understanding — Reynolds concluded that 'Those lacking the anchor of complete moral certainty will find themselves uneasily adrift between the two.'[14] *Complete moral certainty*, then, offered itself as an anchorage in a stormy sea. As he pursued his long-term inquiry into the history of race relations, Reynolds increasingly favoured the moral and the political over the academic, and so it could be said that his work became more utilitarian over the years — and perhaps more 'mythic'. Noel Pearson, who admires Reynolds' work and shares his human rights perspective, nevertheless feels that 'more dispassion and less politics' might have enabled his history to be more unifying.[15]

It was this struggle between 'professional standards' and 'political ends' that shaped the kind of historian Reynolds is: empiricist, rational, highly structured, heavily evidenced, reinforcing and repetitive, professionally conservative, accessible to the courts.[16] Reynolds takes every opportunity to assert the empirical ballast of his arguments, and his early prose, especially, was freighted with corroborative evidence. The more radical his 'political ends' became, the more traditional his 'professional standards' needed to be. This was a conscious balancing act. Greg Dening observed that 'Reynolds has always been a "just do it" historian,' and Peter Cochrane considered that he was 'no stylist'.[17] But this *is* his cultivated style — lean, linear, logical — and it is honed out of his engagement with passion, politics and power. It means he has never had much interest in epistemological questions about the nature of history: 'They seem to me to be second division issues, which I am quite happy to let [other] people argue about endlessly,' he has remarked. 'Their fundamental question is "How can we know?" Well, my basic question is "How should we live?"'[18] Reynolds addresses his readers directly and fraternally by embracing them with the 'we' of *Why Weren't We Told?*, the intimate 'our' of *This Whispering in Our Hearts* (1998) and the solidarity of regarding the *other* side of the frontier. His scholarship, as Alan Atkinson observed in 2002, remained

Eurocentric: 'Blacks are vital as subjects but Whites are vital as readers and listeners.'[19] But Reynolds' concept of 'we' and 'our' broadened when he discovered his own likely Aboriginal ancestry, a lineage through a paternal grandmother that had been carefully suppressed as a family secret. For the first time ever, he looked at old family sepia 'snaps' through a magnifying glass – 'and I was amazed at what I saw'. The great historian of the Australian frontier then brought a personal angle to his exploration of the predicament of people of mixed descent in *Nowhere People* (2005).[20]

I am going to look at how the debate about frontier violence erupted at the turn of the millennium and why it often simplified the peculiar character of frontier society and Australian memory. Then I will return to Reynolds, drawing attention to his powerful investment in nationalist legends of Australian history, a quest that has culminated in his advocacy of Aborigines as Anzacs.

In a series of articles in *Quadrant* magazine from 2000 and in a book entitled *The Fabrication of Aboriginal History* in 2002, Keith Windschuttle accused historians, in particular Henry Reynolds, of grossly exaggerating the number of Aborigines killed by Europeans in the occupation of the continent. Soon historians were exhuming bodies from the archives and counting them. What was the nature of the violence between Aborigines and settlers? How many Aboriginal people were shot or poisoned during the European occupation of the continent? Windschuttle was especially critical of the historiography of massacres and of Reynolds' estimate that 20,000 Aboriginal people died in frontier conflict across Australia. Windschuttle argued, for example, that the number of Aboriginal people killed by British settlers in Van Diemen's Land was much less than alleged, could be precisely known, and was 118. He was dismissive of any possessive Aboriginal relationship to land and was keen to argue against the idea of a frontier 'war'. He believed that the historiographical debate was fundamentally about 'the character of the nation and, ultimately, the calibre of civilisation Britain brought to these shores in 1788'. Windschuttle portrayed frontier history as a political conspiracy of left intellectuals seeking to denigrate their own country, and charged a generation of historians with 'misrepresentation, deceit and outright fabrication'.[21]

It was an attack upon the scholarship presumed to underpin 'the adventurism' of the High Court in *Mabo* and *Wik* – and it was also a disturbing allegation against the ethics and practice of a whole academic profession. The media took a strong interest in the revelations of this 'whistleblower'. Historians responded by closely examining not only Windschuttle's work but also their own.[22] Although Windschuttle's allegations of fabrication were soon exposed as ill-founded and his own historical method shown to be deeply flawed, historians across the country took the opportunity to discuss not only Australia's frontier but also the craft of history itself.[23] Windschuttle's articles and books, as well as the responses to them, became prescribed reading in university history courses. Scholars created forums where polemical sparring in the media could be developed in more subtle and considered ways: thus debates, workshops and seminars were organised both inside and outside universities. The National Museum of Australia, which was the subject of one of Windschuttle's attacks, hosted a major conference in 2001 on *Frontier Conflict: The Australian Experience*, to which Windschuttle and Reynolds both contributed.[24] Stuart Macintyre and Anna Clark analysed why Australian history had become such a political battleground in *The History Wars* (2003), and Robert Manne edited a critical collection about Windschuttle's work entitled *Whitewash* (2003). John Connor brought a military perspective to frontier conflict in *Australia's Frontier Wars* (2002), Mark McKenna wrote a regional history that wove the national debate into an investigation of local memory (*Looking for Blackfellas' Point*, 2002), and Bain Attwood offered a profound reflection on the controversy and its implications for historical method in *Telling the Truth about Aboriginal History* (2005). Bain later invited me to join him in organising a conference and editing a book on the impact of Henry Reynolds on Australian history, entitled *Frontier, Race, Nation* (2009). New, impressive work was completed on the historical experience of various Australian frontiers: James Boyce on Van Diemen's Land, Grace Karskens on the Cumberland Plain near Sydney, Tiffany Shellam on King George's Sound in Western Australia, Rebe Taylor on Kangaroo Island, Darrell Lewis on the Victoria River District in the Northern Territory, Libby Connors on south-east Queensland and Tony Roberts on the Gulf Country, to name a handful.[25]

Windschuttle was, of course, just one of many spurs to this research, but the range, depth and gravity of this scholarly response itself disproved his claim that academic history was conspiratorial and monolithic. In retrospect, his provocation can be seen to have played a role in generating a notable surge of original scholarship, and we now have a clearer understanding of the ubiquity, variety and trauma of frontier violence in Australian history. As a result of this work, Reynolds has now revised his controversial 1981 estimate of 20,000 Aboriginal dead upwards to 30,000 and beyond, 'perhaps well beyond'.[26] But as Windschuttle had foreshadowed, the debate was never just about the body count, for it plumbed fundamental disagreements about the nature of history and memory, and also the language and idea of 'war'.[27]

Windschuttle's earlier book, *The Killing of History: How a Discipline Is Being Murdered by Literary Critics and Social Theorists* (1994), expressed his anger and anxiety over the apparent impact of postmodernism, deconstructionism and other forms of 'critical theory' on the discipline of history. His concern – a common one since the 1980s – was that the distinctions between history and fiction were being dissolved and that the past had been deemed unknowable.[28] More fundamentally, Windschuttle's book was a defence of the idea of history as an objective science and a privileged product of Western society. A number of those scholars he chose to attack – Greg Dening, Inga Clendinnen, Paul Carter and Anne Salmond – were amongst those who tried to step outside the imperial, European view of the past in order to embrace a cross-cultural history. Windschuttle was unsettled by the relativism that discarded the notion of unilinear, directional time and placed Indigenous perspectives on equal terms with Western ones. He affirmed his belief that there is such a thing as a singular *history* and not a multiplicity of histories and that, therefore, the history of the world was the story of Westernisation.

In this view, history was not just written by the winners but also helped put Western culture at the top of the social evolutionary ladder; it was one of the gifts of civilisation and one of the tools of invasion. The substitution of history for myth was, then, a triumph of European civilisation that spiritually paved the way for the occupation of the New World. Europeans had a history and were continually *making* it, whereas 'primitive' peoples were the timeless subjects of a different form of analysis, anthropology. In the nineteenth century, history became scientific by being accurate and factual, by revering the official documents of the new nation states, and by championing a discriminating infatuation with 'the primary source'. In the very period of Australia's absorption of its frontier, history defined itself as exclusive of the non-literate. Such a view of history – as the triumph of the West, the end and the means – was destined to breed contempt for any history from 'the other side of the frontier'.[29]

Therefore, when Windschuttle looked at a book by the New Zealand anthropologist Anne Salmond, *Two Worlds: First Meetings between Maoris and Europeans, 1642–1772* (1991), he was dismayed that 'she wants to give Maori opinions of the meaning of their contact with Dutch and English explorers the same status as those of the European visitors'. Windschuttle explained that the European side of the story was not simply 'one more example of the genre of discovery tales' but 'contained within itself the very metanarrative that the Maori perspective lacked'. And scholars who take the 'meta' out of the 'narrative' are, Windschuttle believed, subscribing to 'one of the contemporary era's most potent political forces': 'the revival of tribalism'.[30]

So Windschuttle's argument was partly a campaign for a simpler empiricism, one that privileged counting, figures of authority and legal conventions, and one in which a 'reliable figure' of clandestine violence is achievable. He resented the fact that Indigenous memory and forms of history have been given serious attention by the Western tradition. The stronger the oral evidence of violence amongst Aboriginal people, the clearer it was to him that it was 'mistaken': because Aboriginal knowledge is less scientific, non-literate, and thus emotive and parochial. And mistaken also because, like the Maori, Aboriginal people lack the metanarrative. People who lack the 'metanarrative' are, by definition, the losers: 'they were the objects rather than the agents of history'.[31]

When, as historians, we get close to the 'frontier' – that dangerous site of cultural encounter – we often find it evaporating into intimacy or distance. Early European collectors of Aboriginal artefacts, for example, might be thought to be 'primary sources' on Aboriginal culture because they dealt in the raw material of cross-cultural exchange. And sometimes they were. In his study of ethnographic collectors in South Australia, Philip Jones portrayed the frontier as 'less a line which separated than a zone which unified' and as a source of 'new and potent forms of culture'.[32] But collecting could also be an act of distancing, a way of keeping the frontier at bay, a means of denying the vitality and continuity of the other culture.[33] In other words, the frontier messes mischievously with that conventional division between primary and secondary sources, between contemporary and reminiscent ones, between eyewitnesses and hearsay, between presence and absence. The frontier is a phenomenon supremely designed to undermine the rule of law, and the legal method. So a historical method that applies these distinctions too slavishly is prey to foolish error and serious oversight.

∾

In his 1980 Boyer Lectures entitled *The Spectre of Truganini*, art historian Bernard Smith suggested that Australian culture is haunted by the dispossession and violence done to Aborigines. It is 'a nightmare to be thrust out of mind', he wrote. 'Yet like the traumatic experiences of childhood it continues to haunt our dreams.'[34] Bernard Smith and W E H Stanner (in his earlier series of Boyer Lectures) urged their fellow Australians to interrogate the 'Great Australian Silence' about Aborigines, not only to reveal suppressed facts about the frontier, but also as part of an essential exploration of the white Australian psyche.[35] For the Great Australian Silence was often 'white noise': it sometimes consisted of an obscuring and overlaying din of history-making. But the denial was frequently unconscious, or only half conscious, for it was embedded in metaphor and language and in habits of commemoration. Silences are not just absences, although they can be manifest in that way. Silences are often discernible and palpable; they shape conversation and writing; they are enacted and constructed. We need to pay them as much attention as we pay official white noise.[36] And analysing the uneasy language of conflict helps us discern the emotional and political slippage – the distinctive dissonance – at the heart of the Australian frontier experience.

The euphemisms of the frontier, laconic and sharp, entered the Australian language. Aborigines were 'civilised' or 'dispersed' or 'pacified', white settlers went on a 'spree' and boasted of the 'black crows' they had shot, and the land itself received new names – such as Murdering Creek and the Convincing Ground – that mapped the unofficial violence. The wordplay was conscious and mischievous. 'A quiet tongue' was said to be a qualification for a frontier policeman, and the infamous W H Willshire boasted that it was his carbines that 'were talking English'.[37] These forms of language and description slip in and out of recognising the violence of the frontier. They reveal that many colonists accepted murder in their midst; but they reveal, too, their awareness that it could not be openly discussed. There were good reasons to be silent, especially after the prosecution and execution of seven stockmen convicted of murdering Aboriginal people at Myall Creek in 1838. Describing the organised shooting of Aborigines in Gippsland in the 1840s, F J Meyrick noted that 'these things are kept very secret as the penalty would certainly be hanging.'[38] Even those who were appalled by what was happening found themselves forced into impotence and silence. Meyrick commented in 1846: 'If I could remedy these things I would speak loudly though it cost me all I am worth in the world, but as I cannot I will keep aloof and know nothing and say nothing.'[39]

In the language of conflict there is a constant conflict over language. In 1998 in the Kimberley, I discovered that someone had carefully scratched out three words on a government interpretation sign about Aboriginal–settler relations. One of the words removed was the Bunuba term for white people, *Malngarri*, which acknowledged the existence of a distinct local language; another was the word 'religious', implying an alternative belief system; and the final word scratched out was 'invasion', invoking the possibility of war, sovereignty and land rights. Recognition of Aboriginal culture, religion and country constituted the 'offensive' language of this sign. The Great Australian Silence continues to work in quiet ways.

For over five years in the 1980s I officially ministered to popular anxieties about the changing boundaries between public and private in Australian history. I was employed as field officer for the State Library of Victoria, a job that involved the acquisition of historical manuscripts and pictures for the library's Australiana research collections. It took me into the lounge rooms of Victoria to discuss the future of family papers, and the likely public uses of quite personal pasts. That work exposed me to the politics of the past, to the dilemmas of collection, possession and preservation. It was a time when the political and scholarly revolution in Aboriginal studies was making its mark on the history and commemoration of the Australian frontier. In Victoria, the state's sesquicentenary in 1984–85 prompted the controversial memorialisation of conflict between Aborigines and settlers, even on official plaques. Descendants of pioneering settlers were unsettled, and wondered what historians might find in family papers donated to libraries. The transformation of family history into national heritage could seem, in these circumstances, a dubious honour.

Libraries and museums link people and things to the world of storytelling and scholarship. Donors of archives therefore warily monitor the fashions of research. There is a tense, symbiotic relationship between what they choose to make public and how history is told. Of course, historical records are constantly lost and destroyed without purpose or import – randomly, carelessly and deliberately. But what is kept is kept with purpose, and what is made public has import. And therefore the gaps and silences in the public record can be equally revealing. A fascinating graph might be sketched of the cycles of preservation and destruction and their relationship to the fashions and politics of scholarship.

In the 1970s and '80s there may have been an increase in the burning of early pastoral diaries and letters. As an official collector of such records, I certainly heard stories that this was so. The reasons for such culling could be defensive or constructive. One descendant of both settlers and Aborigines (and a supporter of Indigenous land rights) told me that he had once destroyed a station's records 'to protect people from an explosive political situation' and 'in the hope that it might clear the air for a fairer future'. He described how and where he set the evidence of massacre to flame. He later regretted his action. 'I thought I was doing the right thing at the time. I hope I don't burn in hell for it.'

In the 1990s some farmers feared being 'Mabo-ed', as they put it. 'We've found things,' confessed one Queensland landholder: 'There would be things all over that no way are people going to show anyone. You'd have to be stark raving mad.'[40] In 1997 further hysteria was whipped up following the High Court's *Wik* decision. It's possible that anxieties about this judgement led to the suppression of evidence of another kind, this time evidence not so much of conflict as of sharing and negotiation on the pastoral frontier.

When records are officially preserved, they often leave the locality of their origin, go to the city, become institutionalised and thereby become subject to local suspicion. For anyone schooled in the professional discipline of history, it is a shock to encounter the proud oral culture of rural Australia. Academic historical practice, founded as it was on the craft of documentary scholarship, has often viewed oral tradition with distrust. In a small community, however, oral sources of history are often regarded as the pre-eminent means of access to the local past. History is a possession of the town's elders, the approved custodians of the past, sometimes 'the oldest resident'. Such 'old-timers' have earned the right to pass on and interpret their town's inherited wisdom. Knowledge gains authority from its genealogy. Residents view with scepticism any alternative, outside avenues of access to that past, especially if they are literary, official or urban.[41]

In the year following the *Mabo* judgement, David Roberts explored 'the knowledge' of the Australian country town of Sofala and found a resilient oral tradition of a local massacre (at Bells Falls Gorge), telling of a large number of Aboriginal people who were shot or pushed off a cliff.[42] Such stories survive in many Australian rural communities, as Judith Wright's poem 'Nigger's Leap' attested. Most Sofala residents, reported Roberts, maintained 'that the story is not just a yarn or a myth but a "local knowledge", not requiring the details and tangible proofs that historians use as the foundation of their work.' Although surviving documents tell of the declaration of martial law in late 1824, of reprisal parties sent out against the Aborigines, and of several incidents of multiple murder, no contemporary written evidence precisely confirms the oral tradition. Pages of letters are missing, and official reports were not filed or have not survived.

The community Roberts visited and questioned in 1993 clung to the oral tradition of decisive violence but also seemed averse to discussing Aboriginal association with the area in any detail. Residents declined to recognise registered Aboriginal sites in the region at the same time as they memorialised the place of a remembered massacre. There were stories that, because of fears of land claims, farmers may have destroyed large collections of bones, presumed to be Aboriginal, which they uncovered on their properties. People kept quiet about local discoveries of Aboriginal relics. The proprietor of Sofala's museum declared: 'You tend not to want to find Aboriginal stuff for obvious reasons. You're asking for trouble.' The local massacre may well have happened, and written evidence suggests its likelihood; but the story may also have focused the memory of widespread violence onto one dramatic feature of local topography, concentrating diffuse conflict into a conclusive parable. 'What of the local Aborigines?' asked Roberts at the Royal Hotel. 'They're all killed, mate,' replied the bush storyteller. And so the story of the massacre could have served a similar purpose to the 'last of the tribe' monuments erected across Australia in the late nineteenth and early twentieth centuries. Such forms of commemoration, even where they were sympathetic to Aboriginal people or angry about their suffering, served mostly to reinforce a sense of inevitability about what happened, and gave a misleading sharpness to the notion of frontier.[43]

The sinews of settler memory are palpable and strong, and historians have to wrestle with them. The Australian frontier reveals its character through memory and history-making as much as it does through recorded contemporary experience. We need history because some things cannot be recognised as they happen.

❧

At the heart of the frontier conflict debate – and of the concern with the number of dead – is the language and idea of 'war'. It was a frustration to many colonists that the constant domestic tension and sporadic conflict of the Australian frontier did not fit their image of a war, although they often used that term. In 1913, Western Australians even inscribed the phrase 'Lest We Forget' on a monument to explorers killed by Aborigines.[44] But the experience of settlers was generally not of public violence against a respected foe, but more frequently a private drama of betrayal, fear, suspicion and disdain. 'Deep down,' wrote poet Les Murray in 1975, 'we scorn the Aborigines for not having provided us with the romantic vision of a remembered war.'[45] A proper war would have dignified the settlers' violence, brought it out in the open and allowed them the romance of heroes and campaigns. But 'war' – much as it might have offered psychological relief – was legally and politically unacceptable.

'War' was also culturally imagined elsewhere. In nineteenth and early-twentieth-century Australia, there was a curious conflation of a vision of pastoral peace and a keen anticipation of war. Colonists yearned for the sort of blooding on an international stage that would prove their racial vigour and exorcise their convict inheritance. At the same time as they celebrated the peaceful occupation of their new land and projected sunny images of patrician pastures and woolly flocks, they hungered for war – a real war – that would baptise their nationhood. So denial of war on the Australian frontier underpinned nationalist yearnings. And a powerful silence was cemented at the core of an emerging Australian identity.

'War' is a word that Windschuttle was keen to avoid. It was because he was bending over backwards to hang on to that word 'murder'. He was concerned above all to demonstrate the effective embrace of British law and justice, and so he found it easier to recognise rogue violence ('murder') than conflict over land and resources ('war'). Constant, sporadic and personal violence is less disturbing to the state than political slaughter. 'Massacre' is an ambiguous word because it uncomfortably slips between the categories and could seem more like 'war'; it describes organised, mass killing, yet it is also unequal and illegal. The Myall Creek massacre of 1838 was Windschuttle's favourite example because it was one of the few massacres declared to be murder at the time. He appeared to find civic relief in the insight, already widely established by historians, that most Aborigines were not killed in massacres, but in ones or twos.[46]

Reynolds saw settlers defending newly won land. Windschuttle saw 'legitimate police operations'. Police were 'doing their duty' he told us again and again, clinging innocently to that word. But what *was* their 'duty'? Was it civil or military or something uncomfortably in-between? Did the violence take place within the civic frontier, that is, within the effective embrace of British law and justice, or did the violence take place on 'the other side of the frontier', in a war zone? Or was it neither completely one nor the other? Windschuttle turned away from the most interesting dimensions of frontier history – the gaps between expectation and reality, and between experience and language. It is in these dissonances that we find the distinctive character of the Australian frontier – and the origins of the unease at its heart.

Reynolds was a strange target for Windschuttle because his work embodies empiricism and empire in some of the ways that Windschuttle wanted. As Peter Cochrane has noted in a perceptive critique of Reynolds' work, he piles up his evidence, indulges in 'relentless documentation' and writes with 'a morally charged positivism'. Reynolds resists the Australian nationalist narrative that equates 'self-government' with democracy and fairness, casts imperial restraint on colonists in the most positive terms, and downplays homegrown humanitarianism. His history gives the high moral ground to the common law – which was ignored, defied or misunderstood by settlers – and consequently writes, as one commentator put it, 'the kind of history that the law can take notice of'. Reynolds is therefore particularly infuriating to conservatives, argues Cochrane, because he has defeated them on their own ground.[47]

Critics saw Reynolds' political and historical interest in war, land rights and sovereignty as 'separatist' politics. They argued that the invention of widespread frontier violence, now and in the past, has been in the service of a politics of 'separatism' that aims to isolate Aboriginal people from white society. Separatists of every era, they suggested – from the missionaries of the nineteenth century to the likes of Reynolds today – exaggerate frontier violence to justify protective reserves, land rights or even a separate Aboriginal state. The language of war does make conflict political and it links violence to land and nation. There is therefore a clear political lineage, and one pursued in Reynolds' work, that moves from frontier conflict to war to land rights to sovereignty. But labelling Reynolds a separatist completely misunderstands his work. His oeuvre is daring for the very reason that it attempts nothing less than the integration of Aboriginal history into the great themes of Australian settler nationhood.

Reynolds' analysis of Aboriginal experience had its origins in the dominant white myth – or *legend* – of the frontier. He arrived at university, as he puts it, as 'a radical nationalist in the quite distinctive Australian sense of that term'. Radical nationalism was an influential postwar school of historiography that rebelled against earlier imperial history and traced the growth of a distinctive Australian identity in literature, art and the labour movement, particularly of the late nineteenth century. The writers of the

Bulletin school, especially Henry Lawson, Joseph Furphy and 'Banjo' Paterson, gave it voice. The archetypal historical text of the school was probably Russel Ward's *The Australian Legend* (1958), which celebrated the formation of a unique Australian character on the frontier, especially amongst the 'nomad tribe' of bush workers.

Reynolds' first piece of historical scholarship, as an honours student, focused on the radical nationalist literature of the 1890s. He handled old copies of the *Bulletin* with awe and was 'star-struck' by Lawson and Furphy.[48] He found their larrikin egalitarianism 'both familiar and exciting' and was 'rather breathless' in his celebration of the benign and creative influence of the outback environment: 'This, I felt, was the essence of Australia.'[49] He was 'deeply influenced' by Ward's *The Australian Legend*, which came out the year before Reynolds worked on his honours thesis. This new book honoured the 'noble frontiersman', was informed by a respect for oral culture and a love of the rhythmic ballads of the bush that Reynolds himself adored, and was inspired by radical politics. Years later, Reynolds was to pay tribute to Ward for his 'robust view of history', for his willingness to 'engage the real world and change it'.[50] Perhaps he had found a kindred soul.

Once we become aware of this academic influence upon Reynolds' historical sensibility, we begin to see new meanings in the title he chose for *The Other Side of the Frontier*. It not only refers to a commitment to explore the Aboriginal side of the encounter, but also declares a determination to unveil the dark side of the white frontier experience. *The Other Side* of the noble frontiersman was his racism, violence and misogyny; the other side of the legendary bush virtues was their foundation upon the oppression and exploitation of an invisible people. There was another, forgotten 'nomad tribe' out there (to use Ward's famous phrase for the white pastoral workers). The ubiquitous presence of a black underclass strengthened the egalitarianism of all whites, the use and abuse of Aboriginal women underscored male mateship, and the secrecy of frontier violence enhanced settler solidarity against an interfering government. How could 'a fine, creative historian like Russel Ward' have missed the guns, wondered Reynolds? 'It was as if Russel and I had researched totally different places or had worked on quite distinctive periods of time, such disparate things did we see.'[51]

There was yet another *other side* of the title. Reynolds slowly and unwillingly relinquished his romantic notions about the outback, but he did not relinquish the structure of 'the Australian Legend' itself. Instead, he reversed it. Having unveiled the other side of the noble frontiersman, he went on to activate the other side of the Australian Legend. Reynolds' boldest historical argument was not so much to reveal frontier violence or Aboriginal agency as to bestow the virtues of the golden Australian Legend itself upon the despised blacks whose suffering had fostered it. As historian Ann Curthoys has noted, Reynolds' mission was to discover many of those legendary frontier virtues – egalitarianism, courage, adaptability, pioneering fortitude, laconic humour – amongst the Aboriginal people of Australia.[52] It is in this sense that Reynolds does indeed turn Australian history – or at least the school of history into which he was initiated – 'inside-out'.[53] Reynolds offered us *The Other Side* of *The Australian Legend*, and the two books might indeed be viewed as companion volumes.

The fact that the myth that Reynolds overturned was one to which he had once given himself 'breathlessly' perhaps explains the sense of betrayal that underlies his exasperated cry, 'Why weren't we told?' He was himself seduced by the radical claims of the heroic settler mythology only to find that, in racial respects, it was deeply conservative and oppressive. Humphrey McQueen's *A New Britannia?* (1970) was an earlier, angrier, urban response to the Australian Legend from another scholar brought up within its traditions.

So Reynolds applied the traditional radical nationalist structures and virtues to the Indigenous people of his country. He found black explorers, black bushrangers and black pioneers. And – most radical of all – he cast Aborigines who defended their soil against settlers as 'Anzacs', the revered term for the overseas soldiers of Australia and New Zealand. This was the ultimate turning-inside-out of the Australian frontier.

Reynolds assailed this silence directly by explicitly contrasting the forgotten Aboriginal dead with the revered fallen warriors of Australia's overseas wars.[54] 'All over the continent,' he argued in 1982:

> Aborigines bled as profusely and died as bravely as white soldiers in Australia's twentieth-century wars ... [But] do we make room for the Aboriginal dead on our memorials, cenotaphs, boards of honour and even in the pantheon of national heroes? If they did not die for Australia as such they fell defending their homelands, their sacred sites, their way of life.[55]

'Fell' is an immensely powerful and symbolic word here, as Ken Inglis has noted in his book *Sacred Places* (1998). It is an impressive appropriation of the imperial language of war.[56] And putting a number on the dead enables Reynolds to bring this whole arena of Australian history and memory into the conventions of military commemoration.

Reynolds began his research by enumerating the whites killed by blacks with the aim of demonstrating that 'settlement' was not peaceful but contested and at times uncertain. The numbers of fallen whites became a measure of the challenge of occupation and also established Aborigines as agents and not just victims, as enemies and not just subjects. Then Reynolds took seriously the far more difficult task of estimating black deaths. A conservative estimate of the casualties (20,000) enabled him to compare its significant size with the numbers of Australia's overseas sacrifices. Another reason to count – or at least to try – was to recognise, as our culture does in war, that each individual life lost in such a cause was valiant, a death to be honoured in its uniqueness, another fallen hero without a genuine grave.

Conservative critics mostly misunderstood the sources of Reynolds' historiography and did not perceive that it was an integrative nationalist endeavour.[57] He extended and subverted the radical nationalist story and offered a way of embracing Aboriginal experience within familiar settler tropes. Reynolds' work might be placed in that great tradition of historiography about the Anzac legend – a lineage that invokes C E W Bean, Geoffrey Serle, Bill Gammage, Ken Inglis, Joan Beaumont, Peter Cochrane, Bruce Scates, Marilyn Lake and Peter Stanley amongst others. Many historians have acknowledged frontier conflict and have now travelled to the other side of the frontier, but no one other than Reynolds has so tenaciously championed Aborigines as Anzacs.

We know just how controversial this strategy is from the response to Ken Inglis's suggestion in 1998, at the launch of his book *Sacred Places*, that the Australian War Memorial should represent warlike encounters between black and white. Inglis's proposal came out of his lifelong study of the settlers' culture of commemoration, and in a book steeped in intelligent sympathy for the rituals of war. It wasn't a war, wrote his critics. And even if it was a war, then it wasn't an officially declared war and both sides didn't wear uniforms. And even if it still rated somehow as a real war, then Aborigines were the other side, *and* they were the losers, and victors don't put up monuments to the losers. Aborigines are not Us.[58] Here speaks the real politics of separatism in Australia today.

It is pertinent to remind ourselves of the critical reception of Roger Milliss's book *Waterloo Creek: The Australia Day Massacre of 1838* (1992), a book that Windschuttle incorrectly described as having been 'reviewed with universal favour when it appeared'.[59] Although there was widespread admiration for Milliss's archival tenacity, and the book won several prizes, historians found aspects of the book to be disappointing. By the early 1990s, there was a strong feeling amongst people researching Aboriginal history that a narrow obsession with violence and white guilt ignored the more subtle and complex understandings of the frontier that had since developed. They were keen to discern the sharing and accommodation between black and white cultures as well as the confrontation and violence. Historians became critical of the limitations of massacre history — it was white history, they said, and it diverted attention from intimate and institutional forms of violence. Historians criticised Milliss for contributing to a simplified and uncomplicated morality, for perpetuating a fixation with overt violence, for returning to a concept of a purely oppositional frontier, for overlooking the Aboriginal experience, and for failing to interrogate the silences.[60] Peter Read summed up the situation with these words: '*Waterloo Creek* would have been state-of-the-art in 1970, it would have been in the mainstream in 1980. In 1992 it is dated in conception and analysis.'[61] 'War' is where a complex analysis of frontier encounters and interactions in Australia might begin, not where it should end.

When Noel Pearson gave the W K Hancock Memorial Lecture in 1994, he recalled that 'until very recently there were old people still living at my community who told of massacres of their people on their land.' Aboriginal stockmen mustering at Cape Melville in the 1950s found the bones of their people littering a landscape that is inscribed with names such as Battle Camp, Police Lagoon and Hell's Gate. 'This is not a thing of the distant past,' explained Pearson, 'it is a reality which is still fresh in the minds of their children and grandchildren.'[62] Of frontier violence generally, he reflected that 'it is not the horrific scenes of mass murder that are most appalling here; it is the mundanity and casual parsimony of it all ... Anonymous, extrajudicial, unreported, mundane. Like eradicating vermin. Or inferior beings of human likeness.'[63]

Pearson grew up on Hope Vale mission in Cape York in the late 1960s and '70s and studied history and law at Sydney University. For his history honours thesis in 1986 he researched the world of his elders, the history of the Guugu Yimidhirr people of the Cooktown region who, in 1770, interacted with James Cook while he repaired the *Endeavour*.[64] They gave to the world the word for the hopping marsupial, *gangurru*. Pearson's history of his people, written when he was twenty-one, grew out of his conversations with his grandfather Ngulundhul, Charlie Pearson (1900–86), and other old men and women of the mission community. It was a plea for the importance of the oral tradition in Aboriginal history, so often ignored or misused by white historians to the disappointment of blacks. Astonishingly, when Pearson applied (with the support of his supervisor Jan Kociumbas) to the History Department of Sydney University for permission to quote his informants in Guugu-Yimidhirr as well as English, the department refused because of thesis word-length restrictions.[65]

As 'a third-generation legatee of mission protection', Pearson says he necessarily holds complex perspectives on the history of colonisation: 'Without the Lutherans my people would have perished on the Cooktown frontier.'[66] In his scholarly exploration of the 'historical and spiritual turmoil' which is his inheritance, he found that elders like Dhaluygu (Peter Gibson) did not dwell on the violence but told instead of Aboriginal survival, 'of how they had managed to avoid becoming victims of the new order'.[67] That historical wisdom underpins Pearson's own crusade for recognition of Aboriginal responsibility as well as rights. As 'a Rugby Union–following Lutheran Aboriginal with a love for the literature of England', he seeks to transcend the debilitating white 'tribalism' that prevails between the right and left in Australian politics and culture.[68] So he struggles with the violence of Australia's modern history. For the sake of a successful referendum on recognition, he wishes to avoid 'the fiercely partisan cultural conflicts over the nature of the dispossession which Australians called the History Wars', but he finds that he can't. The endemic forgetfulness of the dominant culture means that 'clearly it is necessary to keep dragging the dead cat out of the cupboard.'[69] 'I hoped to avoid the past,' he wrote in 2014, 'but it is not possible. I hoped to dis-remember the past, but it is not possible.'[70]

EIGHT

Golden Disobedience: Eric Rolls

S oon after *A Million Wild Acres* was published in 1981, I read the book and realised that I had encountered something momentous.[1] It was a history of a forest in northern New South Wales, the Pilliga 'Scrub' (as it was disdainfully known), written by a local farmer, Eric Rolls. It is a regional history like no other, where birds, animals and plants share the stage with humans. I felt as poet Les Murray did when he wrote of Rolls' book that he read and reread it 'with all the delight of one who knows he has at last got hold of a book that is in no way alien to him'.[2] I was living in Melbourne and was moved to write to the author, whom I had not met and could hardly dream of ever meeting, and who seemed to live in an extraordinary, magical and especially dynamic place. It was slightly mystifying because I recalled once as a child in the 1960s being driven through Coonabarabran, and I could remember the vast tracts of the Pilliga Scrub rolling endlessly past the car window. It had not seemed extraordinary, magical and especially dynamic then. Had it changed? Had I changed? Had this man's book opened my eyes? All of the above. I had never before realised how strongly words on a page could animate actuality.

In my mid-twenties and freshly home from my first trip overseas, I therefore wrote a brief letter to Eric Rolls, telling him that *A Million*

Wild Acres was one of a handful of books about Australia that I would like to put in the hands of any visitor to help them understand my country. Now I would make greater claims for it. I think it is the best environmental history yet written of Australia, and I would hope it could be read not just by visitors but by all Australians. Eric was seduced by the vastness, mystery and wildness of the forest beside his farm, and by its 'scented tunnels'. He ended up writing, as he put it, 'the story of a forest which grew up and drove men out'.

I wrote a letter to Eric not because I wanted or expected a reply, but because I had to write it. But he *did* reply. He told me of the work he was doing on his history of the Chinese in Australia (which became *Sojourners*), offering me a brief, vivid snippet of his writing life. I now know that Eric got lots of letters like mine, and that he replied to more than I would have thought possible. I've been looking at his correspondence in the archives.

Eric's papers, mountains of them, are in at least three libraries. He conducted a quiet, constant, private dialogue with his readers in parallel with his public writings and presentations. With such letters, Eric continued his quest to educate his fellow citizens, one by one. And amongst the correspondence you can find testimony from people moved by his books to write to him, even when writing does not always come easily to them. Some people normally unfamiliar with written words are clearly living Eric's words. One wrote in stumbling script of *A Million Wild Acres*: 'This is the first book I have ever read. Thank you for writing it. I enjoyed it so much I am now going to try reading other books.'[3]

Another correspondent wrote at more length and with spelling difficulties:

Dear Eric,

Just a note or a few words, to say how much I liked your two books, A Million Wild Acres, 'They All Ran Wild'. The best I have seen. I will get your other books and read them soon.

I would of liked to been with you, and read all the books and papers, and places you went to-get all the true information. A great bit of work. I do not no how many times I have read 'A Million Wild Acres'. I no I have read 'They All Ran Wild' twice last month.

... I lived all my early life at Pilliga. I will tell you more later. I like reading History of Australia. And you love the Bush, and no all about it.

... If you are ever over this way call in and have a yarn, and stay with your family. We have plenty of room. I will write again to you soon, hope you get some rain. 'And keep writing', all the best.

Yours truly ... [4]

And here are the words of another reader who admitted that (like me) she did not often write fan letters, but in this case could not stop herself: 'I enjoyed your book more than I am capable of expressing. You made the Pilliga come alive on the page and I hope you make trillions ... On nearly every page I found something to exclaim over (mostly I exclaimed how on earth did this man have time to fit in the farming!)'[5]

Eric often wondered that himself. He wrote of the constant battle between words and acres, between the soil as a source of his originality and the farm as a demanding distraction. He knew that the battle to win time for writing was part of the necessary discipline. When I talked to Eric in his seventy-seventh year, he declared that 'unless you feel so intensely about writing that you are prepared to murder anybody who stops you getting to your desk, it's no use thinking of being a writer.'[6]

In his book *Doorways: A Year of the Cumberdeen Diaries* (1989), Eric described his workspace, his desk, as it was at his farm 'Cumberdeen' on Pretty Plains. He always wrote with his back to a broad window, the words in front of him, the acres behind. 'The imagination works better against a blank wall,' he says. But the sun on his back warmed him, reminding him of the outside world he was trying to capture on paper. Of his silky oak desk, he said: 'Everything on it knows its place. Words come to it that I am not expecting.' On that desk were a pile of handwritten notebooks, eleven dictionaries and books of words, and a typed outline of his current book. He added five new pages of writing to the pile each day. Empty blocks of lined A4 paper sat beside him, as did the two fountain pens that had written all his books. In front of him was a large, disconcerting pile of letters that needed answering, and that we now know he would eventually get to. There was also a big splinter of fragrant sandalwood, a tail feather from a swamp pheasant, little soapstone turtles from China, a branding iron and two blocks of mulga.

Let's imagine Eric there at his desk, wrestling with words and acres in the late 1970s as the book he has always wanted to write materialises into chapters – but never fast enough! He described the battle in letters to Sue Ebury, the editor at Thomas Nelson publishers with whom he worked on *A Million Wild Acres* and also to his agent, Tim Curnow.

In October 1974 Eric offered the idea of the book to his publishers and they accepted it immediately and enthusiastically. He told them he hoped that it might be finished in seven months.[7] But two years later the final writing had hardly begun. On the first of June 1976, with years of experience, observation and research behind him, he took a deep breath: 'The frame of the book is already mostly planned – it is only wording to be considered.' Three months later he reported: 'I've got within a fortnight of beginning to write and am getting excited.' Another year later, in September 1977, Eric explained to his publisher that he had not yet signed their contract because he was 'frightened harvest is going to fall on me like a guillotine when there are two chapters still to go. I don't want to let anyone down and enough money has come in to keep me writing until harvest – so I'll just do my damndest and see how far I get.' 'Most days', he added, 'I read about six hours and write for six – if it is not ready on time it won't be for lack of trying.'[8]

But the acres continually interrupted the words. Another year later, in September 1978, he explained:

I lost three precious weeks writing when the lad who was working here burnt himself as he began crop spraying – he is still off work but I'm back to the writing. The tractor we use for odd jobs was burnt completely. I had to finish spraying then do the summer ploughing. It is cruel changing over from writing to farming unexpectedly. And I'd been concentrating so hard I was not even living in this century when it happened.[9]

'One nearly gets torn in halves sometimes trying to lead two lives,' he exclaimed.[10] But 'Without the farm there would have been no book, even if it delayed publication.'[11] Eric believed that contact with the soil preserves a writer's essential sense of the ridiculous. As a farmer, he reflected that 'some years one can look back with considerable self-mockery and realise that if one had done nothing at all one would be much better off.'[12] And Eric was never afraid of getting his hands dirty. Instead of writing a general statement like 'ploughing killed native plants and encouraged weeds', he reported: 'I have had well-worked cultivation paddocks growing dense weeds up to 40 centimetres high. I crawled about them looking for native plants and could not find one.'[13]

In his house, he virtually re-enacted the settlement process he was describing. Just getting the right pioneers into the right places at the right time was a demanding and arduous job. He recalled: 'I lined all the men up against one wall – 37 men – each had a pile of papers, each named, all their years, and then I had the map at the other end of the room. I'd pick up a pile and march the man across the room to his place on the map ... You had to see him getting there.'[14]

A reviewer of the book, the environmental historian and philosopher George Seddon, later described these early chapters of the book as 'like the Book of Genesis, with its endless "And Joktan begat Almodad, and Sheleph and Hazarmaveth, and Jerah". There is a walk-on-walk-off cast of thousands, and the detail is numbing – but this *is* the Pilliga Book of Genesis, and I think the author was right to put it all in.'[15]

In July 1979 Eric reflected on a job nearly complete:

The end of the Pilliga book is in sight, thank God. I'm appalled that it has run so long over time. Each estimate I made seemed certain — I know how much I can do a day. Then what seemed certain plans for the farm would come unstuck and I'd have to do a couple of months hard work. It is hard not to go on writing and leave it. But one has to be practical. If we went broke in the middle of the book it would cost more time than ever. And there is not much leeway on the land now. Fixed costs are enormous and increasing. As much as I love the farm, it will have to be sold. It will not only cost me too much time but too many books. I'm also afraid it will cost me years of my life. It is excruciatingly difficult each time coming back to an unfinished chapter. So much reading has to be done again — days of it.[16]

And on 4 October that year, 1979, he records: 'I've just written the last word of the Pilliga book.'[17]

Three years of intense writing, in the available spaces. But for years before there had been the source material of experience, of life with the soil, of walking and talking the forest, collecting scats to analyse animal hairs, learning the names of plants, mastering in words the craft of the timber-getters. And all that correspondence! Eric's papers spill out with letters requesting and receiving information: To the curator of mammals at the Australian Museum, 'How rare is the rat kangaroo?' and could they possibly, as one old-timer attested, 'be seen hopping about in dozens on a moonlight night'? To the Patent Trade Marks and Design Office in Canberra, 'Can you tell me anything about early patents for barbed wire in Australia?' To the secretary of RAS Kennel Control, 'Can you tell me if there is still a breed of dog known as a staghound?' To the president of the Quirindi and District Historical Society, 'Do you know exactly how the old acetylene lights worked?' To Mrs King of the Tamworth Historical Society, 'Have you any local information about the construction of George Clarke's stock yards at Boggabri — near Barber's Lagoon?'[18]

It is the detail that matters, and it is getting it right that matters, too. 'Much of the game of writing history,' he declares at the start of the book 'is keeping it true.'[19] And keeping it true, for Eric, means not just finding out what happened, but also finding a sense of wonder about it, and understanding it in such detail and with such precision that he can make the story live. Use of the active tense – and his books bristle with it – requires quite specific knowledge. The passive tense, by contrast, allows slippage and can mask ignorance. Rolls' prose is bracing and vivid. 'At times,' he says, 'I can even smell what I'm writing about.'[20] His books won many awards, but he was particularly proud to win the Braille Book of the Year and the Talking Book of the Year, for he often said: 'I write to make people see.' There is also a 'swagger' to his style – and he consciously cultivates it – because it enables him to tell a story with conviction. This careful accretion of authentic organic detail generates the power of his non-fiction. But Eric would have refused that division of fiction and non-fiction. As he put it, 'There's imaginative writing and pedestrian writing, that's all.'[21]

Les Murray celebrated this literary quality in 1982 in a wonderful manifesto called 'Eric Rolls and the Golden Disobedience'. Murray grew up near the great forests of the lower north coast of New South Wales, where his father had been a bullock driver and timber-getter, and he remembered his father's stories of the thickening bush. He therefore seized Rolls' 'prose masterpiece' with a kind of elation because it gave credence and dignity to vernacular experience. Eric's disobedience, explained Murray, was his freedom to sidestep received literary sensibilities, his ability to transcend the conventional boundaries between fiction and non-fiction and between humanity and nature, and his commitment to ecological democracy. In the early '80s that unruliness seemed 'to be available to non-fiction writers in greater measure than to other writers of literary texts'. 'It is even possible,' he continues, 'that the novel, a form we have adopted from elsewhere, may not be the best or only form which extended prose fiction here requires.' Murray was describing an Australian style of landscape writing as 'made up of strings of vivid, minute fact which often curl up in intricate knottings of digression'. Nicolas Rothwell, working in this tradition and honouring it, sees the method as 'a reflection of the bush itself in all its reduplications and its beginning everywhere and nowhere, its undelineated expansiveness'.[22] Murray considered *A Million Wild Acres* to be like an extended, crafted campfire yarn in which everyone has the dignity of a name, and in which the animals and plants have equal status with humans in the making of history: 'It is not purely human history, but ecological history he gives us ... one which interrelates the human and non-human dimensions so intimately.' Murray compared its discursive and laconic tone to the Icelandic sagas.[23] Through his democratic recognition of all life, Rolls enchanted the forest and presented us with a speaking land, a sentient country raucous with sound.

❧

One of the book's heroes is Eric's beloved tree, the white cypress pine (*callitris*), especially the magnificent 'Old Greys' that came to life in open grassland and died in heavy forest. The cypress pine was a kind of brother creature that also lived life passionately. Rolls wrote that 'at pollination time when hundreds of cones go off together with a sharp crack and spurt brown pollen a metre into the air, the whole tree shivers.'[24] 'One does not expect a tree to move in passion.'[25] When Eric died on the last day of October 2007, his family and friends had a coffin made for him by a local carpenter – it was a simple, oblong box with silver handles and was made of white cypress pine from the Pilliga.

When I spoke to Eric seven years before his death, he reflected on the writing of *A Million Wild Acres*:

I began to think that the whole forest seemed to be an animate thing, with voices, and that perhaps I ought to give the trees themselves an identity, and then I thought that's absolute bloody nonsense, you've got a wonderful story to tell, just tell it in a straightforward manner in the best way it can be written. One of the reviews said that the whole book reads as though the trees themselves were telling the story, which delighted me. If I'd tried to do it that way, the book would have been hopeless.[26]

One of Eric's earliest public performances made nature animate. Every Friday afternoon at his kindergarten in Grenfell, his teacher, Miss Postlethwaite, used to tell the class stories. She would do this from her slightly elevated stage, with a mat at her feet. But she was rather dull. So one day five-year-old Eric put up his hand and said, 'Miss Postlethwaite, I'd like to tell a story this afternoon.' She said, 'All right, come out here.' Eric was prepared. It was sowing time on the farm, so he went up the front and pretended he was a grain of wheat. He jiggled down into the ground and buried himself in the earth, pulling the mat over his body. Then the roots grew and the legs stuck out. Then leaves sprouted and the arms waved. The little boy wriggled and danced. As Eric recalled, 'So I grew up, and a header came along and stripped me, and then the sheep went into the paddock and I got eaten.' He started telling stories every Friday afternoon, and adults began to join the gathering, too, making quite an audience. 'I realised that telling stories was a good thing to do if you did it properly.'[27]

Born in western New South Wales in 1923, Eric was five when his father drove north from Grenfell to Narrabri to take up his own farm. Well, it was not really his own farm; the rabbits owned it. The farm was too far from any school Eric could attend so he had to wait until he was seven to begin lessons with Blackfriars Correspondence School. Eric recalled how he 'spent two exciting years with a pack of dogs walking about hunting rabbits into burrows and hollow logs' so that

his father could chop them or dig them out.[28] He slept on the verandah of the wooden homestead, waking at night to watch the play of
moon shadows and in the early morning to see the light come onto
the Nandewar Ranges. Eric later won selection to Fort Street Boys'
High School in Sydney, where, as he recalled, he taught the other kids
how animals reproduced and they taught him how humans did. He
missed the chance to go to university because he got chickenpox just
prior to his exams, and then the Second World War intervened. After
serving in Papua New Guinea he returned to Australia, where he
farmed his own land for forty years on the edges of the Pilliga Scrub.
Eric wrote more than twenty books, as well as hundreds of articles
and essays, mostly in the second half of his life.[29]

As the success of *A Million Wild Acres* both settled and unsettled
his life, he did a stocktake:

> On my sixtieth birthday I happened to be working out how many
> years it would take me to write the next five books: say another three
> years on this one, eighteen months, two years on that, seven years'
> research and writing on the next big one. Then I realised with con-
> siderable shock how old I would be. I decided from then on to work
> words a day every day instead of acres.[30]

The central story of *A Million Wild Acres* is a simple and compelling one, told richly and persuasively. It is, in Eric's words, about the
growing of a forest. His original achievement was to confront and provoke Australians with the idea that in many areas of the country,
landscapes that had once been grassy and open are now densely vege-
tated, that there might be more trees in Australia now than at the time
of European settlement, that forests – which we so readily and roman-
tically see as primeval – could often be the creation of our own act of
settlement. How many trees make a forest, he asked?[31] 'It is not a paradox that the fires that once kept our forests open should now cause

them to grow denser.'[32] Eric brought an observation that was common-place in local lore forcefully into the scientific and historical literature. Many of today's forests, Rolls reminded us, are not remnants of a primeval jungle: 'They do not display the past as it was, they have concentrated it.'[33] Eric portrayed them as different and new; he revealed them to be exaggerated communities of plants and animals, as habitats both volatile and vulnerable. As Les Murray put it, Rolls' work recognised that Europeans arrived in Australia to find a vast parkland, 'a *paysage humanisé* and *moralisé* which the Aborigines had maintained for untold centuries'. The 'wilderness we now value and try to protect', agreed Murray, 'came with us, the invaders. It came in our heads, and it gradually rose out of the ground to meet us.' However that thesis might be challenged in various details and regions, we will not now retreat from the fundamental and enduring truth at the heart of it. Eric offered us not only a scientific insight, but a poetic one, and the two visions are necessarily intertwined.

Ross Gibson, who (with John Cruthers) made the award-winning film *Wild* based on Eric's book, described his history of the Pilliga as an 'unruly tract of local history' and 'a deliberately feral book'.[34] 'Feral' is a fitting adjective for the work of the author of that other landmark book, *They All Ran Wild: The Story of Pests on the Land in Australia* (1969).[35] 'Wild' has often been used to describe nature that is untouched and pristine. But Eric the farmer found 'wild' nature to be feral, mongrel and hybrid, nature stirred up, nature enlivened by human presence and intervention; it was dynamic, historical nature.[36] So the forest that he grew in the pages of his book was 'concentrated' and volatile.

When Eric's editor at Nelson, Sue Ebury, suggested the title 'A Million Wild Acres', Rolls had reservations: 'I'm a bit dubious about another title with wild in it – I am partly civilised,' he replied.[37] Eric's own earlier suggestions had celebrated the novelty of the nature he described: 'Pilliga', 'An Exaggerated Country', 'Unexpected Forests',

'Phoenix Forest' or 'Ungentle Men Unsettled Land'. 'Wildness' fascinated him: the invaders, the cattle, rabbits, foxes, their adaptability and sheer vigour even as they wrought damage – and the feral humans, too, the 'wild men', the 'ungentle' white settlers of Australia. He was impatient with those who disowned such ancestors. 'This book,' he writes in *A Million Wild Acres*, 'is not written by a gentle man.'

A Million Wild Acres challenged the traditional contrasts of European settler thinking about nature. It revolutionised those assumptions that disturbed nature is somehow always lesser nature. Such views brought Eric into conflict with aspects of the green movement. At the same time as recognising the fragility and integrity of native ecosystems, he wanted to acknowledge the creative ecology of invasion. This relish for the fecundity of life and an irrepressible optimism also underpinned Eric's joint advocacy of the causes of nature conservation, on the one hand, and human immigration to Australia on the other. He was always determined to see the creativity of encounter.

When Rolls was writing *A Million Wild Acres*, the conservation battlegrounds in Australia were the rainforests, most notably at Terania Creek in northern New South Wales in 1979.[38] As Rolls acknowledges in his final chapter, woodchipping was also an issue and had become shorthand for indiscriminate forest clearing and exploitation. Rolls considered it a necessary industry committed to unnecessary destruction.[39] So his book was written in the midst of those campaigns, when forests were depicted as timeless and primeval, and human disturbance meant the destruction of trees. He wrote a detailed regional study showing that forests could also be the creation of settlement. He wasn't the first to notice this phenomenon: the anthropologist, naturalist and explorer Alfred Howitt, for example, presented his observations of the increasing density of forests in Gippsland to a scientific audience in 1890.[40] The power of *A Million Wild Acres* was that it gave voice to a myriad of these earlier observers. And Rolls told a multi-causal story of how it had happened in one region, a place he knew intimately. He saw system and pattern and creativity in it. His book attracted little scientific or green criticism for over a decade and a half, awaiting another political context. By the mid to late 1990s, the frontline of conservation battles had moved from the logging of old-growth forests on public land to the clearing of native vegetation for farming on private or leasehold land. In this new context, Rolls' argument about the history of tree density was misinterpreted for political purposes by both farmers and scientists.[41]

There was also continuing scientific and cultural resistance to rec-ognising the significance and sophistication of Aboriginal burning.[42] As Judith Wright wrote in her 1982 review of *A Million Wild Acres*:

> It is as strange to me as to Rolls that some scientists and others still dispute the effect of Aboriginal fire-management, or even that there was such management. Again and again in my own reading of stock-inspectors' reports in the Queensland of the sixties and sev-enties, there is reference to the change in pasture growth and shrub cover which followed the vanishing of the Aborigines and the fierce protectiveness of squatters for their timber fences, huts, yards and vulnerable slow-moving flocks of sheep. But no doubt such evidence is too much that of laymen to be trusted by academic ecologists.[43]

The politics of this issue are so embedded and have such a long history that they are often unconscious.[44] Scientific disdain for Aboriginal ecological knowledge was once racist; now it is sometimes simply anti-humanist. In other words, the same scientific suspicions can apply to settler knowledge – indeed to local knowledge of any kind – because it is human, anecdotal and apparently informal.[45] So the debate about Rolls' work sometimes presents itself as a clash of disciplinary styles, a methodological tension between the sciences and the humanities. The very qualities for which literary scholars and cultural historians cele-brate Rolls' book – its vernacular and organic dimensions, holism and narrative power – can be seen by others to diminish its scientific credentials. But Eric himself continually paid tribute to scientists, and his book *Australia: A Biography* (2000) was dedicated to them.

Eric was never afraid of a dangerous idea. He liked to tell it as he saw it. It got him into trouble, of course. When Pauline Hanson called Aborigines 'cannibals', he responded that she was more savage than any cannibal. When he wrote an article about the damage that cats do to the environment, the *Sun-Herald* reported that they had never had so many letters and phone calls about anything they had ever published, and Eric received violent threats, including one woman who threatened to burn his home and his car and to destroy everything he owned. When researching an essay on the use and abuse of water resources for the *Independent Monthly* in 1992, he told the editor, Max Suich, of how his research had provoked a dark, watery threat: 'I had no idea that things are as serious as they are, or that it will take so long to rectify them, or that there are such murderous forces at work opposing change. It is quite startling to be told "you better pull your punches or you'll end up with concrete shoes". I haven't pulled any punches.'[46] He was just as ready to run the gauntlet of the conservationists as he was the developers or the bureaucrats. He was especially critical if any of them were 'short on history'.[47]

'People,' declared Eric Rolls, 'must always be given hope.'[48] He was an irrepressible optimist. He was prepared to deliver the hard, grim facts when necessary, but he also wanted to inspire action and guide change, and for that, he knew, we do indeed need hope. Historian though he was (as well as poet, farmer, cook and fisherman), Eric also believed that 'tomorrow is more exciting than yesterday'. He had faith in the future, and in the capacity of people to meet it; he was a historian whose history had to serve the future for which he was so hungry.

There was a fearlessness about Eric's work, as well as a swagger. And there is a complexity to *A Million Wild Acres* behind the compelling narrative power. It is a truly original work, yet it speaks directly to so many people; it is unique and path-breaking, yet it also seems to represent an organic integrity and a common vernacular. That is Eric's artistic achievement. That is why readers wrote to him, and why reviewers compared *A Million Wild Acres* to the Book of Genesis, or a campfire yarn, or an Icelandic saga. That is why it is possible for this to be the first book someone might ever read.

NINE

Voyaging South:
Stephen Murray-Smith

When Stephen Murray-Smith voyaged to Antarctica on the *Icebird* in the summer of 1985–86, the third-last summer of his life, he experienced moments of high excitement, profound boredom, homesickness, intellectual challenge, despair, unexpected patriotism and deep professional satisfaction – and he also had this moment . . .

Sailing steadily through a placid sea towards Davis station, the sun low on the horizon as midnight approached, the *Icebird* came up against a great rampart of ice. A silent crowd of passengers and crew on the bridge watched tensely and full of wonder as the ship threaded its way between great bergs that they could almost reach out and touch, and the low sun flooded the parapets and ice floes with 'a golden, refulgent light' so that the shadow of the ship accompanied them along the icebergs. They felt as if a brief window to the sanctuary had been opened for them, and that time and space and ice and light had conspired to allow them to pass. Stephen recalled that the normally noisy mob on board was still and quiet, like 'philistine tourists silenced by the soaring columns of Chartres or Salisbury'. It was, he wrote:

the most moving and beautiful visual experience of my life. We've all stood and admired wonderful prospects, the memory of which stays with us even as it fades. But what happened to me between 9 pm and midnight on 20 January 1986 has trailed clouds of glory about my life ever since, has taught me that it is possible for an atheist to have, in his own way, a transcendental experience, and completed any conversion I needed to humility in the face of the natural world. It was an experience which has not faded. Its joy was tempered only by sadness that those I would most have wished to share it with were not with me.[1]

Stephen was deeply moved by the awe-inspiring beauty of Antarctica – and, by contrast, he was appalled by the recent, ugly mark of humanity on the continent. He found that visiting Antarctica was an emotional roller-coaster: 'If you were constructing a psychological drama in which people were dumped from elation into depression in a very short space of time, you couldn't have done better,' he wrote.[2] Nature and culture had never before seemed in such antipathy.

Antarctica has become, in the words of the American nature writer Barry Lopez, 'a place from which to take the measure of the planet'.[3] It is not only a region of elemental majesty; it is also a global archive, a window on outer space and a scientific laboratory. As well as a wondrous world of ice, it is a political frontier, a social microcosm and a humbling human experiment. It offers us an oblique and revealing perspective on modern history, an icy mirror for the world. To voyage to Antarctica is to go beyond the boundary of one's biology towards a frightening and simplifying purity. 'The home of the blizzard' is, paradoxically, a land of enveloping silence. How does life sustain itself in the face of such awesome indifference?

Space and time take on new dimensions in Antarctica. The clear polar air is famously illusive, and there are few shadows to provide perspective. Light and looming can reveal features beyond the horizon. A man sledging on the ice could lift his gaze and see the party ahead of him projected as an inverted mirage some distance above their heads. A matchbox could assume the size of a barn. The American geologist Laurence McKinley Gould, always seeking rock amidst the endless ice, once identified a huge exposure of boulders ahead of him on the homeward trail, only to find out it was just sledge-dog droppings. Raymond Priestley and his companions found that what appeared to be a dog team travelling towards them on the horizon turned out to be a little scrap of black film paper fluttering near the skirting of their tent.

Time, too, is warped. The extremes of climate and geography, and the distortions of high latitudes and compressed longitudes, make a weird nonsense of the passage of a day. The polar winter – in its sheer generosity of time – recalls for many a childlike innocence. You can feel the 'slope of time'; it has contours, seasons and a geography that resists rationalisation.[4] This is a peculiarity of Antarctic culture: the task-orientation of peasant societies endures there in surprising company with technology and modernity. The time-spirit of the industrial world has struggled to tighten its net around the continent of ice.

In Antarctica, it can feel like time has not only skipped a beat, but has lost the beat altogether. Time there assumes different rhythms. The human generations are annual. There is the deeper pulse of the ice ages, the seamless months of eternal light or night, the transcendent otherworld of a blizzard, the breaking up of the sea ice, the exciting return of the Adélie penguins in spring, the schedule of the summer ships, and the intensity of the 'changeover' of people at Antarctic stations. A century might signify a hundred generations in Antarctica, or just one tick of the glacial clock.

Antarctic history combines the vastly inanimate and the intensely intimate. You find yourself exposed both to elemental majesty and social claustrophobia. In Antarctica, it is dangerous to be alone. It is a continent that often draws people who seek solitude, only to condemn them to an intense human intimacy.

So humans in Antarctica are way outside their biome; they are tiny ecologies of their own, waning heat sources in a vast terrain of ice, doomed always to retreat. Nature is different there and so is history. Down south, each year begins anew with the break-up of the winter ice. Antarctic civilisation lays the workings of history bare. Historian and literary editor Stephen Murray-Smith had a professional interest in the way knowledge is preserved and passed on, how traditions and rituals are created and sustained, and how the sinews of public and private memory are exercised. What, he wondered, prevents human culture from dissipating each year with the sea ice?[5] This chapter explores Murray-Smith's historical consciousness more than his scholarly practice. It is not so much about the writing of history as about historical thinking – and the crucial role that history plays in any functional society, especially at the end of the Earth.

The great southern continent, Australia's cold Gondwanan cousin, was sensed long before it was seen. Just as the classical cartographers intuited Antarctica's presence from arguments of earthly symmetry and elemental equilibrium, so did early voyagers divine the ice continent before they found it: they felt its breath. Antarctica has an aura. I don't just mean its magical otherworldliness, its implacable grandeur, and its capacity to haunt all who have visited it. I also mean that this land over the South Pole, which is covered by a single mineral, actually emanates ice, water and air well beyond its geographical boundaries. It took people a long time to realise that there was not just land down there but a continent, that it was high and dry and covered thickly in ice, that it was very, very cold, much colder than the Arctic, and that it affects the climate of the rest of the world. Time-lapse photography from satellites now reveals to us that Antarctica is like a giant, breathing organism clamped to the base of the globe. Every winter as the southern hemisphere tilts away from the sun, so much sea ice forms that the size of the white continent appears to double, only to shrink again in the summer, like a billowing creature rhythmically expanding and contracting. When the surface of the sea turns to ice, it releases a dense brine that plunges to the ocean depths, and that thrust of salty water to the sea floor is the piston-stroke that drives the engine of ocean circulation, sending cold Antarctic bottom-water northwards, even infiltrating the northern hemisphere. Meanwhile, continental Antarctica, where ice forms kilometres thick on ancient bedrock, is an ice-making machine of prodigious dimensions. Slowly, inexorably, ice moves from the central heights of Antarctica towards the coast, where great chunks are launched as icebergs, some the size of countries, some big and fast enough to sail to the edge of the tropics. There is so much ice in Antarctica that it skews the Earth into a slight pear shape.

On planet Earth today it could be said that we inhabit the Antarctic moment. The last century of world history has seen Antarctica move from the geographical periphery of our consciousness to the centre of our scientific and intellectual concerns. Each year now, tens of thousands of tourists visit a realm that, just a few generations ago, was virtually unknown. The physics and politics of global warming have turned our eyes towards the great southern ice cap because that's where you find 90 per cent of the world's land ice and 70 per cent of the globe's fresh water. Antarctica has become valued as a luminous relic, a clue to lost ages; it enables us to travel through time to the Pleistocene Earth. Thus, it was ice that delivered the sense of urgency we now feel about global warming, because the archive of air it contains revealed that carbon emissions are disturbing the pulse of the planet. Ice cores – especially those deep, long cores from the high domes of Antarctica – are the holy scripts, the sacred scrolls of our age.

When Stephen Murray-Smith sailed south, the heroic era of Antarctic history – the world of Douglas Mawson, Robert Scott and

Ernest Shackleton – seemed far in the past. After the 'Race for the Pole' of the early twentieth century, there was a 'Scramble for Antarctica' that echoed the famous 'Scramble for Africa' amongst European powers in the late nineteenth century. By early 1939 an expedition from Adolf Hitler's Germany had bombed Antarctic ice with hundreds of cast-iron swastikas, each carefully counterbalanced so that it stood upright on the surface. In the early 1940s Britain and Argentina battled over the possession of the Antarctic Peninsula and nearby islands. Stamps, post offices, maps and films were weapons of war. In February 1952 Argentinian soldiers fired machine-guns over the heads of a British geological party trying to land at Hope Bay on the Antarctic Peninsula. In 1946–47, a huge American expedition involving 4000 personnel, a dozen icebreakers and an aircraft carrier lay siege to the ice. In 1950 the USSR announced its renewed interest in Antarctic exploration, occupation and sovereignty. It seemed that the Cold War had found its way to the coldest part of the planet.[6]

But at the height of the Cold War, a remarkable Cold Peace was negotiated. The launching of the Russian spaceship *Sputnik* on 4 October 1957 seemed to many in the West a threatening symbol of escalating superpower rivalry. But in Antarctic skies it was welcomed as the culmination of a huge, cooperative human endeavour. *Sputnik* was the most visible efflorescence of the International Geophysical Year of 1957–58 (known as IGY). IGY was the single biggest cooperative scientific enterprise ever undertaken on Earth, a hugely successful intervention of science into politics, and it was centred on Antarctica. It cut through the increasing cacophony of postwar territorial rivalries down south.

Nearly 30,000 scientists from sixty-six nations took part at locations across the globe, with the aim of studying the poles, the ocean floors and outer space – three regions made newly accessible by technology. During IGY, the summer population in Antarctica reached almost 5000. Free exchange of data between nations was part of the agreement, and there was a constantly expressed intention to put science before politics. For fifty years the main motives for Antarctic work had been national honour and territorial conquest, and scientific work was, in general, of secondary importance. As the Australian Antarctic leader, Phillip Law, said, 'The IGY changed all this.'[7] However, as historian Alessandro Antonello has analysed, even during and after IGY Australia stubbornly adhered to its long-held national interests and did not relinquish efforts to maintain its sovereignty in this southern frontier.[8]

IGY was such a resounding success that it cried out to be institutionalised. Intensive diplomatic activity in the late 1950s culminated in the drafting of an Antarctic Treaty, which set aside territorial claims in the interests of common and peaceful endeavour. Led by Australia, military activity and testing of any kind of weapons were prohibited south of sixty degrees, so this became the first disarmament treaty negotiated during the Cold War. Scientific information was to be shared, and inspections of other nations' bases allowed at any time. On 1 December 1959 the Antarctic Treaty was signed in Washington by the twelve nations that had participated in IGY in Antarctica, including Australia. Science as an international social system had never before revealed itself to be so powerful.[9]

Stephen Murray-Smith sailed south two and a half decades after the treaty was ratified, and at a time when it was coming under increasing pressure. The Antarctic Treaty had not dealt explicitly with resource politics, and from the mid-1970s this began to seem a fundamental and possibly fatal flaw. The twentieth-century world depended on fossil fuels, especially coal and oil, and in 1973 the Organisation of Petroleum Exporting Countries (OPEC) restricted production. Oil and natural gas prices skyrocketed, and exploration for alternative fields quickened. Knowledge of possible offshore oil and natural gas reserves in Antarctica was growing and, by 1980, experts believed that exploratory drilling down south was only a decade away.

From the late 1970s, therefore, there was a significant increase in the number of states acceding to the Antarctic Treaty. Krill and hydrocarbons were the chief riches expected of this icy 'treasure island'. The Malaysian prime minister, Dr Mahathir, declared: 'I have heard that the South Pole is made of gold and I want my share of it.'[10] In 1982 treaty nations initiated negotiations over a Minerals Convention, which aimed not to instigate mining in Antarctica but to set down rules should it ever happen. Many environmentalists believed it was better to have a regime than no regime. Australia, keen to assert its 42 per cent territorial claim to the ice (which was based on exploration led by Douglas Mawson earlier in the century), embarked on a massive building program at its Antarctic bases. The heroic era of romantic and abstract ideals seemed very distant, and in 1985 Stephen arrived in an Australian Antarctica that looked like a building site, where the ice was dusty with cement.

Stephen was not there as a tourist, a seafarer, a historian or an editor; he was there as an emissary of his government. Barry Jones, then minister for science in the Hawke Labor government, had sent him south as a 'ministerial observer'. It was an astute move by Jones to send his friend to Antarctica. As minister, Barry Jones had inherited a building program in full swing and a concentration on the physical possession of the continent that left little room, financially or intellectually, for the science he so wanted to foster. Murray-Smith would be his eyes on the culture of this distant place at a time of critical strategic importance.

Since his return from the Second World War, Stephen had hankered after Antarctica. In 1945, recently back from New Guinea, he wrote from Melbourne to Douglas Mawson inquiring about a place on an expedition to the Antarctic. Mawson explained that the plan to establish a permanent Australian research station on the continent was far from realisation.[11] When, forty years later, Stephen boarded the *Icebird* in late December 1985, he was fulfilling an early dream and had become an official assessor of Mawson's legacy. He had already made himself an experienced voyager of the roaring forties, for he had been an explorer of sorts in his own backyard of Bass Strait. All his favourite holidays played at the edges of the vast southern realm – at Port Fairy, Wilsons Promontory, and especially on uninhabited Erith Island in Bass Strait, where he camped annually with friends and family from 1962. Between 1966 and 1971, in the company of scientific friends, he made several short voyages of discovery amongst those Bass Strait islands, the peaks of submerged mountains on the vast plain that once connected the Australian mainland to Tasmania. They were nunataks in an ocean of meltwater. Landing on them, describing plants and animals, scaling them and investigating their intriguing human history, enabled him to make his own contribution to the literature and science of exploration.[12] Stephen greatly admired all seafarers and lighthouse-keepers; he knew who was behind those guiding beams that swept across the ocean darkness. Murray-Smith may have been a roundtripper, a boffin and – even worse – a ministerial observer, but his Southern Ocean was already storied and peopled, and he settled into the *Icebird* with the relish of a man who loved messing about in boats.

Unpacking his typewriter in his cabin, he was about to renew a favourite form of writing. During the war in New Guinea, he had started a diary 'as an exercise in contemporary history', and afterwards he wrote it out as a way of preparing himself for scholarly study in history.[13] In most issues of *Overland*, the literary journal he founded in 1954, he wrote a thoughtful commentary on intellectual and literary life called 'Swag' because he wanted a personal, human presence in his journal rather than distant, authoritative editorialising. 'Swag' allowed him to be funny, complex and contradictory, to showcase evolving thought, rather than to be definitive. It is this organic concept of intellect that attracted him to the diary format. As he headed south, he felt that 'the story-books of generations were coming alive', and that he was adding to them.

The book he wrote about his voyage was called *Sitting on Penguins: People and Politics in Australian Antarctica* (1988), and it was the confidently opinionated book of an older man. In the judgement of his friend, John McLaren, 'While he may have become grumpier, [Stephen] is one of the few to whom age brought wisdom.'[14] The book was not meant to be 'a study in repose' or 'a disinterested history'. It is an argument with himself as much as others about what Australia was doing in Antarctica. He took the title of his book from an entry in the *ANARE Field Manual* on emergency sources of food. 'Penguins may be killed,' the manual explained, 'by breaking and cutting the neck or by squashing the air out of their lungs by sitting on them for a fairly long period. Penguin stew is very palatable ...' But for Stephen the term 'sitting on penguins' was a powerful metaphor for Australia's giant territorial claim over Antarctica, and it conjured the worrying spectre of a country sitting in a proprietorial, indolent and purely strategic way on the life of Antarctica. It raised the question: Is Australia intellectually and politically investing in Antarctica, or just sitting on it? Murray-Smith's criticisms of the Australian Antarctic Division, some of which were first published as feature articles in *The Australian*, stirred official responses, even while he was still voyaging. 'Don't they see that, behind it all, I respect and believe in our commitments here?' he mused. 'That is the real message of what I've been writing. But I'm buggered if I'll write publicity handouts for a government department.'[15] He believed that all true societies should be involved in a perpetual *apologia*.[16]

As a passenger on a routine resupply ship, Stephen was about to observe what is known as 'the changeover'. The changeover is the most crucial operational exchange in Antarctica, a period of urgent refuelling in every sense, a passing-on of learning and wisdom in a matter of days.

What other societies may do in years, Antarctica has to achieve in hours. Anticipation, experience, memory and history are telescoped into one frenetic moment and become indistinguishable. At Casey, Stephen watched with wonder as 2300 tons of supplies were unloaded efficiently and safely in near-freezing conditions and with good humour by his shipmates: 'We were in danger of not realising that the greatest marvel of all was right under our noses; that we had the privilege of observing, and for many of us taking part in, the major annual resupply of an Antarctic base.' Everyone on board, he noted, suddenly had a place to go and a job to do.

Stephen was an unusually keen and learned observer of this Antarctic ritual. He was an expert on technical education and deeply admired practical intelligence. But he also had an intimate understanding of the logistics. Each year, when re-establishing his own isolated camp in Bass Strait, Stephen masterminded the stores and their stowage, always bringing more than anyone else thought was needed and expecting their help to unload it. So, here at anchorage in Antarctica, in the calm between blizzards, he knew that he was witness to the climax of years of work. It was hair-raising watching it all, but the job was done and done with speed and grace. In spite of himself, Stephen felt a surge of embarrassing patriotism: 'I was moved, very moved. I began to feel well of my own countrymen. All this immense labour, carried out without complaint, without shouting, in good humour, without congratulation. Could anyone else do it as well?'[17]

Murray-Smith was not usually an admirer of bureaucracy. When he was a commando in New Guinea, he was contemptuous of the arrogance and stupidity of the members of the officer class he encountered, and of the way they interfered with the decisions of the men on the spot. His years in the Communist Party had left Stephen disillusioned with the whole formal process of politics and deeply suspicious of ideology and bureaucracy. He had joined the party on his return to

university in 1945 and resigned in 1958 following the revelations of
Stalin's tyranny, the Soviet invasion of Hungary and the execution of
the leader of the Hungarian uprising, Imre Nagy. But Murray-Smith
remained grateful for those years in the party, for they gave expression
to his revolutionary energy, cultivated his international political conscience and helped him strive for the integration of ideas and action.
He felt that membership of the party, together with his marriage into
a Jewish family, had prevented him 'from being just another middle-
aged, middle-class ex-public schoolboy'.[18]

His political drive became directed towards education in the
broadest sense. Through his editorship of *Overland*, which incorporated the socialist journal *The Realist Writer*, Murray-Smith invested
in intelligent popular culture. The magazine carried as its motto an
adapted phrase of the Australian writer Joseph Furphy – 'Temper democratic, bias Australian' – and was established to give voice to the
working class. Stephen always asked his writers to imagine as their
reader the hospital matron at Port Hedland; he invoked her so often
that he wondered if he should offer her a gift subscription. *Overland*
was founded in an era when, as Ken Inglis recalled, recent history honours graduates at Melbourne University asked each other, 'What aspect
of the history of the Australian labour movement are *you* going to work
on?'[19] Stephen's closest friend was Ian Turner, a radical labour historian who, like many of his generation, was encouraged by the writings
of Keith Hancock and Brian Fitzpatrick and the teaching of Manning
Clark to believe that 'in Australia the labour movement has been the
principal initiator of social change.'[20] Turner embraced the radical
nationalist tradition in Australian history, and Murray-Smith fostered
an independent Australian culture through his editorship. Thus
Stephen took to Antarctica pragmatic social democratic ideals, a distrust of authority and bureaucracy, a sympathy for the ordinary worker,
a commitment to international cooperation and the politics of peace

and disarmament, and a belief that good policy must be embedded in a knowledge of local history and culture. His democratic temper left room for educated wisdom and his Australian bias demanded stringent national self-criticism.[21]

Stephen was also drawn to Antarctica by his interest in the social life of isolated communities. He was, after all, the emperor of one. The Tasmanian government had appointed him warden and crown lands bailiff of the Kent Group of Bass Strait islands, and during summers on Erith he had learned all about what he called 'incestuous island patter'. He greatly admired Eleanor Dark's *The Timeless Land*, with its account of 'the establishment *ab initio* of a society which over-ran a continent in a century, and the best documented colonisation in history at that'.[22] The year he went to Antarctica, Stephen had completed a historical study of the three remote communities of Tristan da Cunha, Pitcairn Island and Cape Barren Island (his visit to Tristan da Cunha had involved five weeks on a tramp steamer). Each of these isolated societies, he noted, was democratic in style but dependent on individuals with 'authority of character and vision' (like himself on his own island realm?). His academic and practical interest – with Stephen they were always fused – was in the emergence of a moral order in such communities. And he wanted to know: what is it that caused some communities to self-destruct?[23]

So when Stephen arrived at Australia's Casey station in the summer of 1985–86, he was intrigued to find himself in the middle of a coup.

Casey, one of three Australian stations in eastern Antarctica, had become a dysfunctional community. The previous officer-in-charge (they were known as *oics*) had been isolated by his fellow expeditioners and there had been an 'effective takeover' of the base during winter. Stephen reflected that:

It can happen so easily, it seems. A wrong word here, a suspicion of
too much clubbiness among a few there, a decision to go out biv-
ouacking in the old Antarctic way, then when the weather blows up
a bit a call over the radio to be collected in the search-and-rescue
Hagglund. Suddenly authority has crumbled – the oic's authority
can only be based on his personality, anyway – and the tough guys
are getting up in the mess at dinner time announcing that there will
be a public holiday tomorrow, while the oic eats by himself, shunned
even by his friends, in a corner.[24]

Portraits of the Queen and Lord Casey hanging in the station were
damaged and taken down. There were explosive tensions between scientists and the building workers supplied by the Department of Housing
and Construction. Boffins and builders were not only out of sympathy
with one another, they worked for different institutions and did not
share a mission. Newcomers were 'intimidated by the hard-drinking,
foul-mouthed crew' who gathered in the mess every evening. These
men, it was recorded in the logbook, 'seemed malicious in intent'.[25]
The decision was made to send home all those building workers not
attached to the new wintering party, and to dispatch them on the next
available ship – which happened to be Murray-Smith's *Icebird*. The ship's
volleyball court, where the beer was stored, would be locked. There was
discussion of permanently closing the bar. The troublemakers were split
up amongst cabins. But on the voyage home, Stephen, always politically sympathetic to the worker, grew to respect these 'hard cases' or
'animals', as they had been called. 'I was in the army as a private soldier,' he wrote, 'and I know how they feel.'[26]

But the men Stephen enjoyed talking to on the ship home were
not the same men who had rampaged at Casey. Something strange had
happened to them down there. 'Polar madness', especially in the darkness of mid-winter, is an acknowledged phenomenon. It can erupt
without warning. The cause might be as trivial as the way someone

dresses, or as provocative as being served a glass of chilled urine at dinner. It might just be the sound of your voice. All these vexations have caused conflict in Antarctic communities, especially the usurpation of favourite chairs and the slurping of soup. In the 1950s an Australian had to be kept in a storage room for much of the winter after he had threatened people with a knife. In the 1960s a Soviet scientist killed a colleague with an axe because he was cheating at chess. In 1983 the doctor at Argentina's Almirante Brown station burnt it down to force an evacuation home. But most of the harassment and hurt we don't even know about because if it can be suppressed, it will be. Open conflict is too damaging. On the ice, minor disagreements can easily snowball. The never-ending polar night, the claustrophobia of a small community, the boredom of isolation: such an environment of forced intimacy can make the personal habits of your companions unbearable.

Stephen, the humanist, urged the Antarctic scientists and managers to pay more attention to the people of Antarctica, to their traditions, their history, their culture, their morale. He was also fascinated by the deeper structural tensions that precipitated the Casey crisis. Australia's massive building program, he found, had undermined the old moral order of Antarctic life. First there was the physical impact, which was dramatic. 'Yes,' sighed Stephen, 'we've gone a long way towards buggering up one continent. There's no reason why we shouldn't start on another.' Walking from old Casey to the site of the new station was, he recorded, 'the crossing of a divide between the old way of doing things in Antarctica and the new'. Stepping into the new living quarters under construction, 'the Red Shed':

> caused our mouths to drop open ... Not all the talk we heard on our way down about our building program in Antarctica prepared us for this ... It was all so bewildering in its way, such a treacherous attack on what had been my mental image of Antarctica ... Our foreign observers were as taken aback as I was: what we saw could

only be interpreted one way, as a massive statement by Australia that
it was in Antarctica in a big way, and there to stay.[27]

A senior member of the British Antarctic Survey commented to Murray-Smith: 'You [Australians] do seem to go a bit hard at making your mark. Wander around on shore and try to find the science all this is supposed to serve.' Stephen decided that 'these fantasy buildings we are putting up are for aggression-display, not accommodation for scientists'. He was bemused by the imperial ambitions of his nation: 'A country unable to organise a decent taxi service in its national capital now has an empire.'[28]

As Stephen was surveying Casey, the minister for science, Barry Jones, was admitting at home that Australia's research effort in Antarctica was 'falling behind' that of other nations. Australia was on 'thin ice', admitted the minister, because it had devoted so much of its energy and resources to the building program at the expense of scientific research and logistical support.[29] In 1984, a year after he took over ministerial responsibility for Antarctica, Barry Jones wrote himself a memorandum acknowledging that 'we do face a massive credibility gap in Antarctica, claiming so much (42% of the whole) and performing so little.'[30] In the period of his ministry, 1983–87, only 10 per cent of the Australian Antarctic budget was left for research. By the mid-1980s it was commonly accepted that Australia had slipped in the scientific prestige stakes. 'Once a pre-eminent presence in Antarctica, Australia is now heading for the second division,' wrote Jeffery Rubin in *Time* magazine in 1988.[31]

The problem was not just that the buildings exhausted the budget; they also represented a different philosophy, as Stephen had observed. Glaciologist Ian Allison considered the buildings to be 'almost an aggressive statement that we can conquer the environment'.[32] The new stations used energy inefficiently and were not well designed for waste management. The buildings made scientists a minority on stations and seemed to be monuments to distant managers. Some expeditioners felt they were *too* comfortable, cutting people off from the environment and the ideals that had attracted them to Antarctica, severing any last connections with the heroic era. They discerned an Antarctic culture that was becoming more superficial and less elemental, one that was insulated from responsibilities as well as dangers, where station conversations were less about science and more about maintenance and logistics. As Stephen foresaw, the station itself demanded constant attention. As one biologist noted in 1988, 'With the present system expeditioners can spend the year cleaning, fixing, repairing, painting, burning and rearranging things simply to sustain the station.'[33] Meanwhile, outside, the silence was calling.

Murray-Smith felt he was observing a changeover of a larger kind, the loss of vital continuities of knowledge and tradition. He was moved to ponder the nature of historical consciousness on the ice. Stephen depicted Australians in Antarctica as 'the ultimate existentialists'. He was shocked in the 1980s by the poverty of the Australian Antarctic Division's historical imagination, and by the severity of the annual discontinuity between past and present. He found that working data was lacking for every aspect of Antarctic operations. There were no records of the extent of fast ice in the bays, no easy access to information about ground covered by field parties in earlier years, no way even that a plumber could find out the age of a building, no history books or videos available at the stations, little popular knowledge of even the most famous of Antarctic heroes, and the officer-in-charge's daily logs of activities and achievements were, for a time, officially discontinued. And the logs, even where they did exist, remained unopened, disorganised and therefore practically inaccessible. At the start of every year, at the breaking up of the ice, the accumulation of knowledge began anew.

This is a remarkable portrait of a society without history or memory, frozen not just by temperature and energy gradients but also by a challenging information gradient, a disjunction of time in a place already severed in space. While Stephen marvelled at the technical competence of the changeover, he also wondered about the meaning of it all. In the early 1960s he had unexpectedly become an expert on technical education when government funding for research surged in the Cold War space race: 'I was a beneficiary of *Sputnik* – the Russians had rewarded me after all!' he joked. Murray-Smith was offered a research fellowship to write the history of technical education in Australia, which he completed as a PhD; it was an academic inquiry that built on his radical political activism through an interest in social equity and practical knowledge.[34] In Australian Antarctica of the 1980s he discerned a profound failure of technical education, because he felt that technology had outstripped the politics that had given it birth and had become disconnected from its environmental and social consequences. It was a prime example, he declared, of 'a rogue technology', technology that had got out of hand. He found that people were trained to perform their tasks, but not educated to understand the context in which they were working.[35] Australia was building a vast edifice down south. Where were those 2300 tons going and why? During a heated debate in the ship's bar on his return voyage, Murray-Smith challenged his companions: 'Don't you think ideas and ideals are important? I tell you this, if this country has a future in Antarctica it will be because people have *ideas* about it.'[36]

Something surprising was about to happen in Antarctica. It can be seen, in part, as a triumph of idealism – and Australia was to play a leading role. Tragically, Stephen did not survive to see it happen, for he died suddenly of a heart attack in 1988, two years after his voyage, sitting on the steps of his library at home. His Antarctic book was in press.

Throughout the 1980s, with growing international pressure for a resource regime in Antarctica, treaty nations had moved steadily towards adopting a Convention on the Regulation of Antarctic Mineral Resource Activities (known as CRAMRA). Meanwhile, an alternative vision of the future of the ice had been gathering political momentum. In January 1987, the summer after Stephen's voyage, the international pressure group Greenpeace established a station on Ross Island in Antarctica called World Park Base. It was the first long-term non-governmental base to be established there, and it aimed to document and expose the environmental effects of humans on the ice. Greenpeace photos of the giant rubbish dump at the US station McMurdo swiftly led to a revolution in waste management practices and strengthened international pressure for an environmental protocol.[37]

In 1988, after treaty nations had formally agreed to adopt the Minerals Convention, the Australian government invited community debate on the issue. The Department of the Environment received about 20,000 letters and postcards against signing the convention, and the governing Australian Labor Party began to explore alternatives. Labor parliamentarian Bob Chynoweth went on a roundtrip voyage on the *Icebird* in early 1989, watched the moon rise over Antarctica, and became an influential opponent of the Minerals Convention. Treasurer Paul Keating and the minister for resources, Senator Peter Cook, argued within the government against signing the convention, mostly on the grounds of protecting Australia's economic and sovereignty interests, but increasingly for environmental reasons as well. In early 1989 dramatic spills from oil tankers – the *Exxon Valdez* in the Arctic and the *Bahia Paraiso* in the Antarctic – generated dramatic images of slicked polar seas and suffering wildlife, strengthening the hand of the environmental campaigners. Stephen's book must have helped swing opinion too. *Sitting on Penguins* was published posthumously in 1988 and launched its literate and provocative self into the middle of these debates.

Stephen's intelligent voice was remarkably resonant at just the moment we needed him. In April 1989 the Australian Democrats called on the government not to sign CRAMRA, and on 20 April the French prime minister, Michel Rocard, announced that he would not support it. On 2 May, the leader of the opposition in Australia, John Howard, announced that the Coalition parties would not support mining in Antarctica. A few weeks later, at a Cabinet meeting on 22 May, Prime Minister Bob Hawke committed his government to what he called 'Mission Impossible': to reject CRAMRA and argue for the protection of Antarctica as a nature reserve and province of science.[38]

This was a huge political gamble. Management of the treaty is by consensus, so a single dissenting nation is enough to derail an agreement. By refusing to sign, Australia was committing itself to an international diplomatic mission. Other treaty nations responded to Australia's stance initially with disbelief and then with bitter opposition. Andrew Jackson, a policy manager in the Australian Antarctic Division, recalled that Australia was cast as a spoiler, a nation prepared to walk away from the consensus principle and threaten the stability of the treaty. Hawke's change of mind was firmly and publicly rejected by US president George Bush (senior) and UK prime minister Margaret Thatcher, and it was subject to attack in his own Cabinet.

But, over a period of eighteen months, the Australian government mobilised its best diplomats (one of whom was Brendan Doran, who shared Stephen's cabin on his voyage south) and won formal support, first from France, and then from Italy and Belgium, and gradually built a new consensus against mining and in support of an environmental regime. In mid-1991 President Bush announced that the United States, the last government to hold out against the Australian and French campaign, would finally support the no-mining position. And on 4 October 1991 the Protocol on Environmental Protection to the Antarctic Treaty was signed by the treaty nations in Madrid. It included a ban on mining in Antarctica and put into place comprehensive and legally binding measures to protect the Antarctic environment. The negotiation of the Madrid Protocol was a successful test of the robustness of the Antarctic Treaty and represented a dramatic shift from a resources view to an environmental view of the continent of ice. It was also an impressive measure of Australian influence in Antarctic politics.

In just a few years after Stephen's death in 1988, the white continent had become green.[39] We can read his book as a barometer of the change, recording the growing pressures and concerns. Stephen would have found the increased bureaucracy of the era of the Madrid Protocol infuriating, but he would have welcomed the new priority given to environmental protection, for environmental issues had become increasingly important to him throughout his life. And he would have relished his country's effective and independent stance in world politics. It was proof that Australians were not just sitting on penguins.

In 2002 I had the blessed opportunity to sail south myself, also with the Australian Antarctic Division, and I was delighted to find myself on Stephen's old ship, renamed the *Polar Bird* in 1996 when it passed from German to Norwegian ownership. Stephen sailed on it during one of its first summers in Australian service, and I voyaged in its final summer. I took *Sitting on Penguins* on board with me and lent it to some of my shipmates, most valuably to Senator Peter Cook, who had played a critical role in the Hawke government's re-alignment on Antarctica and who was a wonderful conversationalist about world politics and history. I took pleasure in thinking that Stephen's book had come home, not just to his ship, where it stimulated debate as he would have hoped, but ultimately to the ice itself.

The history of Antarctica testifies to the potency of written words and the seductiveness of books. In those huts of the heroic era, in those transported islands of civilisation on the edge of the ice, in the fug and glow of their interiors, where the blubber stove temporarily kept the cold at bay, where men bunkered down in the long polar winter and prepared industriously for the spring, where meteorological observations were meticulously kept, scientific specimens examined, lectures given, food celebrated, a masculine camaraderie fostered and tensions were mostly suppressed – in those huts, the *Encyclopaedia Britannica* settled all disputes and precious libraries from home fed the mind and spirit. From the beginning of Antarctic society, books got blubbery with beloved use. Imagine what book you would choose to take on a sledging journey ... you had to make a judgement about its weight, both physical and spiritual. Is it light enough to carry but heavy enough to sustain you? Will it offer you 'compressed nourishment' like pemmican? Polar expeditions took vast libraries, not only as a source of vital information, but also as a kind of insulation against the elements. On Ernest Shackleton's expedition of 1908–09, Professor Edgeworth David would read aloud for hours after supper in the winter hut. Sometimes these midnight readings were only stopped by a firm reminder from Shackleton, called out from his cabin in the corner, 'that it was after one o'clock and time all "good" explorers were in bed'.[40]

Books, libraries, journals, letters, notes and emails assumed disproportionate influence in Antarctic history. Words stood out starkly against the snow. Explorers sledged desperately across the ice in the hope of reaching warmth and food and safety, but if they could not save themselves, they aimed to get close enough to be found dead with their diaries. We must wonder how much greater is the power of the written word at the end of the Earth, in an abiotic land with the longest night, a world of black figures on a white background. In a culture of such rapid generational change, it was history – written, spoken and visual – that wove bonds across time and held fragile frontier societies together. To survive Antarctica, you need food, you need warmth, and you need stories.

Murray-Smith argued forcefully that history is not a luxury in Antarctica, declaring: 'We shall lack the essential tool to our understanding of Australian Antarctica until those with the interest and capacity to write its history are found. And not just one history. Preferably several, or at least a history that will provoke a debate.'[41] History down south, he was saying, as in any society, is a practical and spiritual necessity. But especially so in a place without families or normal generations, where no one lives their whole life, and where the coordinates of space and time are warped by extremes. And on a continent claimed by various nations but shared by the world, history carries a special international obligation. It is the fundamental fabric of a common humanity.

TEN

History as Art: Donna Merwick

It is an early morning in 1998 and Donna Merwick sits at a desk that seems suspended between forest and ocean. She is in her writing room, the spare bedroom of a log cabin perched on the seaside slopes of the Otway Ranges in Victoria. The land sweeps away beneath her and the cabin looks out towards the blue horizon of Bass Strait. But the aspect of Donna's writing room is upon the olive green of tall eucalypts and their hanging streamers of bark. In her hand is a pencil, for she always writes with a pencil. In fact she has written all her books with the same pencil – a mechanical pencil with replaceable leads. Next to her she has an eraser, because she writes and rubs out, writes and rubs out, searching in this tactile way for the right phrase. Her husband, Greg, also a writer, is always buying her erasers as a measure of her precision and their shared love of words. She writes on pages of lined paper, leaving the bottom half of each page for notes and references. Only after she has written several pages and the eraser has finished its work will she enter the words on the computer, or 'transfer them to the machine', as she says. Her writing life spans a technological revolution.

On this particular morning she writes: 'He was the only one. He was the only man to have committed suicide in the town's seventeenth-century history.' She keeps going and the words come easily and quickly.

In a single sitting she writes the final words of her most renowned book, *Death of a Notary* (1999), the words that will become its preface. This is often the way. Prefaces tend to fall into shape last. But this sequence also reflects the book she is writing, which begins with the death of a forgotten man and then tracks meaningfully back into his life.

I will return to the notary, but first let's consider how Donna Merwick found such an insignificant seventeenth-century colonist and why she expended so much energy in reconstructing his world. To tell that story involves an excursion through the philosophy of history because Donna writes every sentence in conversation with a century's cast of thinkers about her craft. Thus an inquiry into Donna's writing becomes a journey through the two great challenges to the epistemological foundations of history in the twentieth century.

'Tomorrow will be D Day. Or DM day: Donna Merwick will be arriving.'[1] So wrote Norman Harper, the only teacher of American history at the University of Melbourne in the 1960s. It was July 1969, the month of the moon landing, and Harper was eagerly awaiting the new appointment in his field, fresh from Boston. Harper felt intellectually isolated at Melbourne and, in spite of his welcome, so did Donna in those first months. She found the university 'stuffy and alienating'.[2] She was joining what was then Australia's most prestigious school of history, known as the 'Crawford School' after Professor R M (Max) Crawford, who was about to retire but whose presence still graced the corridors. Crawford (1906–1991) had been appointed to the Melbourne chair of history in 1937, and over three decades had left a strong personal signature on its style of teaching: moral in orientation, civic in responsibility, and reflective about the craft of history.[3] Inga Clendinnen, who was a young lecturer in the department, remembered the formal ritual of tea in the staff room, with historians seated in order

of hierarchy down the table and where new appointments were assessed
on their invited contributions to discussion. The prestige and intense
self-consciousness of the school's culture probably made it forbidding
to newcomers. Another new arrival from America in 1974, Charles
(Chips) Sowerwine, an inspirational historian of France, recalled that
it was 'a Department whose consciousness of its own history and traditions occasionally overwhelmed me'.[4]

Crawford came to embody not just his school but Melbourne more
broadly. In 1964, in his book *The Lucky Country*, Donald Horne contrasted the intellectual sensibilities of Melbourne and Sydney in this
way: 'For one [Melbourne] the Putney debates was required reading;
for the other Plato's account of the trail of Socrates ... For the one,
Professor Max Crawford: for the other Professor John Anderson.' At
Melbourne University, observed Horne, there was 'a feeling that the
English Puritan Revolution was still being fought (if in social terms), a
continuing concern with moral affirmation and sincerity of motives,
and a belief in the implementation of eternal righteousness'.[5] Crawford
accepted this characterisation.

There was a remarkable occasion in 1984 when R M Crawford,
Manning Clark and Geoffrey Blainey addressed a public audience about
their craft of history. Crawford taught Clark and they both taught
Blainey, and the threesome was introduced by Graeme Davison, another
Crawford student. The amphitheatre of the Melbourne University public lecture theatre was crowded that day as this Russian-doll set of local
luminaries unpacked themselves before our eyes. Crawford was
approaching eighty and now rarely appeared in public, Clark was a
celebrity and was writing the final volume of *A History of Australia*, and
Blainey had just created a storm of controversy with his comments on
Asian immigration.[6] The audience had gathered to hear fifty years of
thinking about history, from Crawford's sleepless night on the train
south from Sydney to his interview for the chair at Melbourne in 1936

to Blainey's widely reported speech at the Warrnambool Rotary Club a few weeks before. With reference to Crawford's enduring academic influence, Blainey quipped that rarely had a sleepless night produced so many progeny.

One of those offspring, Stuart Macintyre, a student in the Melbourne School of History in the 1960s and a brilliant interpreter of its traditions, found himself transported by Crawford's speech 'to a lost world of fountain-pens and exercise books, twinsets and Fletcher Jones slacks'. Even the linoleum and wooden benches of the old lecture theatre seemed to materialise around him again. Listening to Crawford's 'precise, almost fastidious delivery', his allusions to classical and contemporary authorities, his reaffirmation of history as a moral drama of necessity and freedom, and his confidence in history as a truly liberal education, Macintyre realised with a start 'how irretrievably lost is that humanist vision. It is as outmoded as his capitalization of History.'[7] Barely a quarter-century had rendered this world lost. Donna Merwick joined it just as it was about to be transformed.

Born in Chicago in 1932, Donna took her undergraduate degree at Mundelein College, a Roman Catholic liberal arts college for women in Chicago, and in 1953 she entered the Order of the Sisters of Charity of the Blessed Virgin Mary. She completed her MA at DePaul University, Chicago, and then her PhD in the department of history at the University of Wisconsin, graduating in 1967. These were the Wisconsin department's 'golden years'; it was an exciting time. Donna came under the influence of Merle Curti, a pioneer of the new social history and of the history of ideas, and even more so of William R Taylor, who had just arrived at Wisconsin and, as Donna remembers, 'really electrified the place for all of us' and who 'always pointed towards the literary quality of historical writing'. Taylor asked students to read Perry Miller, who was a passionate explorer of the history of the American mind and whose inquiry into twentieth-century American imperial power had taken him back to the Puritans of seventeenth-century New England. Miller was also a magnificent writer. This was the intellectual chemistry that, together with other reasons, lured Donna away from her calling as a religious sister – she left the Order in 1968 and embraced the secular devotion of writing history. 'I would try to combine literary style with philosophy and the writing of history. That's what I was always aiming to do, and to try to achieve history as a work of art.'

It was a radical mission at a time when historians were often still anxious about whether they qualified as proper social scientists, and thus were tempted to be more predictive, quantitative and reductive. As well as majoring in intellectual history, Donna studied modern and contemporary philosophy, reading big chunks of Descartes, Liebniz and Spinoza, and some more contemporary thinkers as well: Schlick, Carnap, Austin, Russell, James, Dewey, Heidegger. You didn't just read *about* them; you read *them*, their own original words. It was a strategy that would inform Donna's own teaching. When she came to Australia she was looking for an opportunity to introduce her new antipodean students to the excitement of ideas she had relished at Wisconsin.

The centrepiece of Crawford's School of History was his 'Theory and Method' course, which was taken by final honours students. Historians are inclined to be reticent about explicit theory, and Crawford's predecessor, Ernest Scott, although an admired lecturer and administrator, had dismissed the whole concept of a philosophy of history as 'wubbish' (he had trouble pronouncing 'r's).[8] The great biographer of Captain Cook, J C Beaglehole, regarded the philosophy of history as 'sheer drivel', and many others regarded it with 'huffy professional mistrust'.[9] So Crawford's embrace of theory and philosophy as fundamental in historical training was a notable innovation. But its aims remained modest: to place historical reflection at the heart of disciplinary culture, and to bring to the practice of history 'some tincture of philosophy and criticism'.[10] The teaching of the course, recalled

Crawford, began 'simply and ... amateurishly' with staff and final-year students sitting around a table for an hour a week to talk about history.[11] They were exploring questions together and Crawford's own intellectual journey was part of the gentle drama of the course. Students were expected to discuss how historians explain events and to acquaint themselves with a debate that had persisted since the late nineteenth century about whether or not history was a science.

Historians were familiar with the 'science' of sources but what about the 'science' of explanation? Was history 'scientific' in the sense that it generated general laws about human society? If not, then how could it justify its legitimacy as a scholarly discourse? Early in the course students met the philosophers Benedetto Croce and R G Collingwood, who believed that historians did not recover 'a fixed and finished past' but reconstituted history 'from the inside' by reinhabiting past thoughts. It was an imaginative, creative, humane enterprise. But then students settled in for a long tussle with the philosopher Carl Hempel, who in 1942 argued that historical explanations used general laws like any other branch of scientific inquiry. The contrast was a shock. These were very different conceptions of history – one imaginative and the other positivist, one from the inside and the other outside – and staff and students often found them hard to reconcile. Collingwood and Hempel were argued about in the classroom, the corridor and 'the caf'. John Mulvaney, in his first days at the university after the war, overheard his fellow students debating the merits of Collingwood in the caf and assumed 'that they were supporters of the football team rather than philosophers of history'.[12]

Max Crawford was of a literary bent and had been attracted to history as a storytelling discipline. Looking back, he regretted his lurch after the war towards seeing history as a science: 'I got bogged down in Carl Hempel's "The Function of General Laws in History".' Crawford felt that his development as a historian had been deflected, even warped, in the late 1940s, by the analytical philosophical framework and the obsession with the logic of historical explanation. He finally found resolution of these tensions in what he called 'the old literary interests' and 'the pleasing art of historical narration'. Crawford felt that the virtue of the language of the historian (unlike, say, that of the physicist or the sociologist) was that it was a 'common language' – yet this did not mean that it couldn't be used and studied with scholarly precision. As a Renaissance scholar, he treasured the Italian phrase *precisare e approfondire* – precision and depth – with its coupling of the virtues of thoroughness and imagination. His lifelong theme in the writing of history was the drama of necessity and freedom, 'the exploration, wherever it led one, of the compulsions and pressures as well as the possibilities of choice existing in any given situation'. *Wherever it led one* was the important phrase, for it marked history out from the abstracting social sciences like economics. History was an open-ended and empirical inquiry, committed to plain speech and following real life – wherever it led one.[13]

When the staff member in charge of Theory and Method classes went on leave in 1973, Donna jumped at the opportunity to teach a Theory and Method course on the philosophy of history at Melbourne – and she continued it for two decades. She wanted to take students beyond the analytical philosophical approach that had come to characterise the teaching of the course. But her students, of whom I was one, had to master the traditions first. A full-year course gave her the time to be rigorous as well as liberating: students could blunder in the fog for months before the cloud lifted, revealing a landscape whose outlines were all the more cherished. So there were many autumn weeks of discussions about whether or not history could qualify as a science, and there was much reading of the analytic tradition from Buckle to Popper, the Vienna School of analytical positivists, and Hempel too, of course. As the days rapidly shortened towards winter, Donna set out to release students from the stricture to be scientists by giving them a 'baptism in narrative'.[14] She had us read the work of some of the great narrative historians – Francis Parkman, Henry Adams – and to consider the shape of their prose. How might one analyse the literariness of non-fiction where authors are grappling with evidence as well as story? Where do the stories come from?

We had help from Hayden White's *Metahistory* (1973), where he explores 'the deep structure of the historical imagination' in the nineteenth century and shows how great narrative historians – Jules Michelet, Leopold von Ranke, Alexis de Tocqueville and Jacob Burckhardt – 'emplot' the past. White's important book connected philosophy to history by focusing on the practice, and not just the epistemology, of history. It challenged the 'wilful methodological naiveté' of the historian and wondered whether history's supposed role as a mediator between art and science was predicated on a radical disjunction that may no longer be justified. 'Most contemporary thinkers,' wrote White in 1966, 'do not concur in the conventional historian's assumption that art and science are essentially different ways of comprehending the world.'[15] The publication of *Metahistory* has been seen as the moment when the philosophy of history finally took 'the linguistic turn' that was already sweeping through cultural studies.

Donna, having charted a steady course across a deep and perilous ocean from 'history as science' to 'history (also) as art' now found herself in a storm. And she relished it. It was the most exciting time to be alive, she felt, and the most exhilarating to be a historian! From the 1970s, postmodernist intellectual fashions swept through Western universities, especially amongst literature and anthropology departments, and challenged the reliability of historical knowledge. All 'facts', it was suggested, were intellectual constructions; an independent empirical reality would thus be inaccessible. Fact and fiction blurred playfully, dangerously. The discipline of history, with its moral and civic responsibility to insist on that distinction, was challenged to the core. Eric Hobsbawm observed that it became harder for historians to defend their dedication to 'scientific' procedures of evaluating evidence as anything other than pedantry, especially once the grand 'faith in the possibility of a definitive, positivist scientific truth' had passed.[16] Some historians were angry and defensive; some were concerned about the consequences of extreme relativism and what they saw as an attack on the Enlightenment project of rationality; some were capsized. Donna welcomed the tempest because, as a champion of the literary and artistic dimensions of the writing of history, she saw opportunities in the new wind and harnessed them. Remaining steadfastly at the helm, she tacked tenaciously to new, secure lands she could not otherwise have reached.[17]

Merwick did not regard postmodernism as an optional intellectual fashion, but a historical condition. It was a new set of practices and also a new sensibility. In 1999 she wrote:

> Surely postmodernity is a word invented to cover the sets of conditions within which we now live and that exert pressures on our aesthetic practices – as physicists and business managers, as scientists and architects and novelists. I take my obligation to understand that set of conditions very seriously. I do so because my writing is unavoidably a cultural artefact produced within them. I want it to count.[18]

As David Goodman, one of Donna's students, put it, 'Postmodernism is not some exotic importation, but a part of a set of debates in which we are all implicated.' Goodman was arguing against the polarising effect of 'theory' on history in the 1990s: 'There are still, unfortunately, two cultures in history today,' he wrote. 'The divide is theory.' But 'theory can be enlivening', Goodman went on to suggest. 'It can provoke insights and provide reasons for wanting to study the past in the first place. I for one stayed in history because I had teachers who convinced me that the big questions of social or political or literary theory were all the business of the historian – that historians had to be participants in the debates in the contemporary humanities, not simply breathless reporters of what actually happened back then.'[19]

I stayed in history for the same reason as Goodman, who was a contemporary of mine. A world of exciting ideas was opened up to us by history and we were expected to forge an informed relationship with it. The past was a testing ground for thought. Studying English Literature at the same time, I had felt that I was trying to second-guess some undeclared orthodoxy that defined right and wrong answers and good and bad texts. Consequently, there was an exodus of literary-minded students from English to History at Melbourne University in the mid-1970s. The contextual relativism of history – the belief that the meaning of a text was not pre-ordained but awaited discovery – was exhilarating.

For Donna, the 1970s and '80s were 'decades filled with new ways of thinking about and writing history ... historians, yes, but also anthropologists, literary critics, essayists, philosophers, art historians and those doing cultural studies. There were new ways to think about recovering the past (Michel Foucault, Hayden White), many modes of writing to explore (Geertz, Dening, Greenblatt, Barthes), new understandings of ourselves as gendered human beings (Joan Scott), and new methodologies for grasping colonialism and post-colonialism (Chakrabarty, Said, Peter Hulme).' 'Many historians', she reflected, 'found themselves unsettled by the options these discourses offered. I believed they should be put before the eyes of students.' This was where Donna's philosophy of history course was already heading – from history as science to history as art, from the strictures of logic and proof to the liberation of narrative and experiment. Donna was not defensive or fearful about postmodernism and 'the linguistic turn'. Rather, she argued that 'its strategies are the business of anyone using language. And their implications should be among our bread-and-butter concerns.'[20]

Donna Merwick's teaching of the philosophy of history, although radical, built on the traditions of the Crawford School. Her American PhD supervisor, Merle Curti, was a dear friend and correspondent of Crawford's, who spent a sabbatical at Wisconsin in 1959.[21] Curti and Crawford had both moved from literary to historical studies and both were devoted to the history of ideas. Donna's two key words in her teaching – 'precision' and 'imagination' – happened to echo Crawford's vision of the tightrope of historical analysis. And her close attention to the reading of documents found a sympathetic setting in a school where texts were revered in almost a religious way. Graeme Davison wondered whether the school tended 'to attract people who were deeply imbued with the religious conviction that there was a purpose in the past; that the past could be scrutinised for an understanding of the meaning of existence, the meaning of the human condition?' It was certainly a place, he concluded, where 'the meaning of life was to be discerned by a deep reading of texts' and where if you did well 'you would get a licence to preach', to become a lecturer yourself.[22] The drift of postmodernist theory that informed Donna's new course was itself focused almost religiously on language and texts and, in this sense, reinforced the conservative core of historical practice even as it destabilised the search for truth.

Postmodernism also renewed appreciation of history as a form of literature, an influence acknowledged even by critics of the linguistic turn.[23] For Donna, the adventure of writing – of bold literary experiment – was the challenge of history, and it was a passion she shared with her students. Her American History course handout in 1976 declared:

> It [the course] seeks to achieve a goal based on one premise i.e. that students in history want not only to learn what constitutes excellent historical writing but want also *to learn to write history* themselves. For this reason students are asked to write often and from primary

sources – to come to know themselves as thinkers and writers. The course enables students to 'close the context' around a given document and (hopefully) write about it with precision and imagination.

To learn to write history: they are her own italics, and they declare the creative key to teaching history. Students learn best by doing. Kathleen Fitzpatrick, Crawford's longest and closest colleague remembered how, for her, the study of history came alive when she learned 'from the experience of writing essays from primary sources, instead of compiling them from textbooks, that the study of history is not the mastering of an agreed body of knowledge but a process of discovery'.[24] With the same insight, Donna threw her students in the deep end of writing and made it clear that she was interested in what they would discover. And she expected and allowed them to make mistakes. Some writing assignments were carefully examined but not graded; students were encouraged to write bravely, recklessly, and to take risks. True storytelling was a grave responsibility but it could also be playful and fun.[25] But however bold or experimental, one had to be scholarly and exact. *Precision and imagination*, she had advised.

When I recently showed Donna my copy of her 1976 course handout with those words of advice for undergraduates, she looked at the faded document as a historian might, as if it were by another hand from another land. She read it carefully and with great interest. 'Many history schools, especially in America,' she reflected, 'focus on the precision and make a whole regime of it – and they forget the imagination.' She read out her own words: 'Precision *and* imagination.' She nodded with approbation. 'That's right, that's good!'

❧

In *Death of a Notary*, Donna Merwick describes Adriaen Janse van Ilpendam's home in Albany on the Hudson River of north-east America in the mid-seventeenth century:

On this December afternoon, it will get dark early. The winter outside will bring its quiet into the house. A fire and candles will be
needed. Their limited light will reduce the size of the room. It will
reach to the things, however, that even medieval Netherlanders
owned: a table, a chair, some pieces of furniture for storage. Cabinets
and chests are of all kinds, those specially made for prayer books,
others designed for weapons, *tafelkastjes* or tabletop boxes for family
papers, some boxes in a man's house so small and so many that after
his death they are not even inventoried ... Perhaps the light of his
fire now casts its shadows onto the chest ...[26]

The chest in Janse's house stores the documents that it is his official
duty, as a notary, to hold in custody, 'papers that are the secrets of
scores of burghers and farmers'. It is his job to be privy to community
memory, to moments of formality and intimacy. He is a man of ink
and paper who carefully selects and orders the tools of his trade, the
mixtures for ink, the sand that he uses to blot his pages, and the right
kind of foolscap. Janse represents an almost mystical admiration for
writing and scribing that could be found in pre-modern Europe.[27] He
has employment because 'Men and women want the protection that
written documents provide.'[28] He is a scribe; he takes depositions; he
is 'The Writing Man'.[29] It is his job to record conversations. He draws
up and copies documents, and has to retain copies that he can produce
if required by the courts; he is thus also an archivist. In this role as the
recorder of wills, powers of attorney, transfers of property and small
debts and promises, he becomes a witness to the everyday transactions
of town life. Donna thinks of him 'as being someone like myself, a
historian. He was surrounded by stories, those he listened to and
recorded, the hundreds he archived in a chest or trunk, where they
receded into the past.' She peers into his home and at the walls lit by
the dancing firelight: 'The moving light may also be illuminating folio
pages he would have around the room, sheets pierced at the bottom

and hung on the wall to dry, others that he must have to hand at any moment.'[30]

Donna paints this evocative Dutch interior even though she does not know quite where Janse lived. She uses the rich context of her research, her knowledge of other houses of that time and place, to divine the character of Janse's home. Much of what she knows of Janse, she knows through other people, even though the records are mostly by his own hand. Few documents survive that tell of his own life; there are just a handful of his personal letters and there is only one mention of his wife. It is the shadow the man cast upon his official documents that Donna uses to reveal something of his life and of his death.

Donna first met Adriaen Janse van Ilpendam (1618–1686), or Janse, as she decided to call him, in 1976 when she was in the early stages of her research into the Dutch colony of New Netherland. After leaving Boston and arriving to teach in Melbourne, she had to turn to new projects and new sources for her original research. Colonial America was her subject and since there was already a lot of work being done on the colony of New England, she was attracted to the neglected experience of the less populous and oft-derided Dutch colony. There was a new language to be learned: she enrolled in Dutch language classes at the university. Language would become her message as well as her medium, for language emerged as a key to understanding the everyday civic trauma of invasion. She first met Janse when she was working in the New York Historical Society and noticed that he had signed a conveyance of land in bowdlerised English, using the words 'Note Republic' instead of 'notary public'. 'I do remember laughing,' she writes.[31] Her book might be seen as an act of scholarly penance for that laughter.

The Dutch were a wonder of the seventeenth-century world: coming from a small country that became urban, wealthy and powerful, that flowered economically, culturally and politically, and that was the heart of a global trading empire. The Northern Netherlands gained access to the Asian, Arab, African, Caribbean and American markets through the founding of the United East India Company in 1602 and the West India Company in 1621. Spices, gold, ivory, silk, porcelain and sugar filled the warehouses of Amsterdam.[32] Janse was a native of Delft at a time when the Netherlands were a citadel of the written word, for the Dutch possessed the highest concentration of printing presses and the highest rate of literacy in Europe.[33] He was a servant, trader, schoolmaster and local court secretary who had immigrated to America in the 1640s, married in the early 1650s and became a self-taught notary in 1669 at the age of fifty-one. He made a meagre living through his skills with pen and paper by serving as a notary in Beverwijk, which was later renamed Albany by the British. Beverwijk was a small inland town on the Hudson River that was dependent on the beaver fur trade. Janse became part of the apparatus bringing civility and procedure to the rough frontier of the New World. Notaries tended to be unremarkable but essential 'low-level civil servants'. They were at the same time 'quasi-intellectuals' with a culture of books and writing. There was a legally central role for notaries in Dutch mercantile and colonial culture.

The story Merwick tells is a dark one, not just of half-lit interiors, but of how 'so small a life as Janse's' could become a casualty of England's design for territorial acquisition, military invasion and occupation. For Janse became a notary in the years after the rival colonial power, England, attacked and forced the surrender of New Netherland in 1664. The English introduced a new political regime, a new culture of conquest and a new language. Just as the Dutch had dispossessed the Native Americans, so now were they themselves dispossessed. The seventeenth-century history of Albany, argues Merwick, was not a seamless transition from Dutch to English rule or even 'an evolution'; rather, it was a collision and juxtaposition of two different modes of settlement, understandings of land, and ideas of civic order. The Dutch were enveloped by the English, and their institutions, language and customs slowly

withered away. Notaries, once an essential part of Dutch legal procedures, became inconsequential and archaic. The Writing Man, once a
master of words, now 'can't even spell what he is'.[34]

Janse had incidentally attracted Merwick's attention because he was
the creator of one of her key sources about life in colonial New York.
'All of a sudden the penny dropped,' she recalled during one of our
conversations in 2014.

> I was writing about land, ownership and transference of land and I
> was using this source, a big source of all these documents, made by
> this person, an unknown person as far as I was concerned. I was
> concentrating on what his documents told me about the town and
> the townspeople, and when I finished that work, it dawned on me:
> what about this person who wrote all the documents? I knew how
> to handle that. I knew what to do with all the documents that were
> suddenly *his* written material. Rather than talking about how they
> were used by the town, how we historians can use all these papers,
> where we can reconstruct town change, who was on what street, etc.,
> I would look at the person who is giving us all this material. So I
> decided that I would write about him.
>
> It seems to me, still, that once you make that decision, a whole
> new world opens up for you, doesn't it? Even without the five or six
> personal papers, you could still make a lot of headway just working
> with all of the documents that he dealt with and shaped and formed,
> and once you see each document as evidence of a meeting with var-
> ious people, then it becomes *his* world, and with such documents
> you've got a day by day account of what he is doing and what those
> experiences would have been like. So it unfolded beautifully. He
> provided an opening to a more lucid, luminous, intimate record of
> the town. It was glorious. I just enjoyed writing that book!

Merwick has written four books about the Dutch colonisation of New
Netherland (in present-day New York State) in the seventeenth century.
Each book takes a different angle on this distinctive and neglected early
colonisation of America: *Possessing Albany* (1990), which contrasted

Dutch experiences with those of the English who invaded and took over the province in 1664; *Death of a Notary* (1999), her biographical study of what that invasion meant to a humble notary; *The Shame and the Sorrow* (2006), in which she looks at the foundational dispossession of the Indigenous people by the Dutch; and *Stuyvesant Bound* (2013), her portrait of the last director general of New Netherland, Peter Stuyvesant, and his place in history (this book won the 2015 Hendricks Award in the United States). One can see the influence of being an Australian on Donna's oeuvre as it evolved: her teaching at Melbourne, moving from America to Australia, which sensitised her to the significance of small cultural differences, working with her colleagues in ethnographic history (Dening, Clendinnen, Isaac), the liberation of her time at the Centre for Cross-Cultural Research at the Australian National University from the late 1990s, access to the Dutch East Indies archives at the Menzies Library at the ANU during the same period, and living through the years of intense Australian debates about Aboriginal frontier conflict. Together, her remarkable series of books on New Netherland represent what historian Simon Middleton has called 'one of the most sustained and compelling inquiries into the life and culture of a single colony in colonial American historiography'.[35]

Donna discovered contrasts between English and Dutch lifeways and experiences, and hence in their styles of colonisation. The Dutch, she argued, were amphibious; they were used to occupying and defending the littoral; they were an 'alongshore' people who possessed the land by 'navigating' it and by establishing trade routes along the rivers. The Dutch West India Company offered few incentives for immigration; there was a conscious, even principled focus on trade rather than settlement, and so their relations with Indigenous people were more a matter of contracts than conquest. The Company therefore initially avoided conflict with the Native Americans and aimed to purchase land rather than seize it. The English who followed them were more concerned with the landmass itself, with continental hegemony, and thus possessed and occupied land assertively and more comprehensively. They ordered time differently, buried their dead differently, administered their law differently.[36] By distinguishing the cultures of these two imperial peoples, Merwick showed that the English conquest from 1664 was far more traumatic for the Dutch residents than had been previously recognised. An Australian reader immediately recognises the contrast between the Dutch trading empire, which in the seventeenth century found no economic reason to engage with the west coast ecology and peoples of 'New Holland', and the British, who steadfastly colonised our east coast from the eighteenth century.

Merwick's work was aligned with a historiographical trend to see America as part of an Atlantic world, to escape the Anglocentric view of early New York history and to challenge the assumption that the Dutch impact on the mid-Atlantic was negligible.[37] To do this requires not just travelling back to the seventeenth century with the help of newly available, translated archival sources; it also means analysing the 300-year overlay of English history-making that had rendered the earlier colonists, the Dutch, as comic relics, as the source of quaint folktales, and as a people destined to be overwhelmed like the Native Americans. History, it is said, is generally written by the winners. The Dutch West India Company controlled New Netherland for a relatively short period – from the 1620s to the 1660s. 'With the transfer of sovereignty to the English,' wrote historian Joyce Goodfriend, 'the Dutch and their descendants lost control over how their story would be told to future generations.'[38] In order to see those first Dutch colonists afresh, and to evaluate their distinctive relations with the Indigenous people, Merwick had also to become a historiographer of the English, so as to free herself from their prejudices. Along with Peter Hulme and Greg Dening, Merwick aimed to 'stop equating early America with the future United States', to 'allow the colonial years to be reconstituted as the local geographies and histories they in fact were', and to 'return the past to its present'.[39] For the historian, hindsight can be both a tool and a tyranny, and thus it presents itself as a subject of scholarship in its own right.

∾

On 12 March 1686 Adriaen Janse van Ilpendam hanged himself. It was about seventeen days after he last met with clients. He did not leave a letter. No one recorded where he was buried. In the early modern world, 'self-murderers' were often punished through sanctions applied to the perpetrator's fortune, family or body.[40] Janse had no children, his wife had died in 1683, his influential cousin in Holland also, and his income was in decline. Only his corpse remained to be punished and we don't know where it is. And what of his spirit? By committing self-murder he had condemned his soul to 'the everlasting torments of hell'.[41]

But his papers, his legal records of the town's conversations, remained in that chest left in his house. Somehow the papers survived through hundreds of years. They first passed into the hands of the coroner, Jan van Loon, who only reluctantly surrendered them to the town council eighteen years later. Donna can even identify a moment when van Loon disturbed them.[42] She knows he did because a later document fell into the archive like an artefact out-of-time, one that penetrates deeper layers of an archaeological stratigraphy. The papers are Janse's memorial and his negative image is imprinted upon them, awaiting the historian and the discipline to discern it. Donna began her work 'with a passion to give a kind of resurrection' to him.[43]

Janse's decline was partly due to increasing age, but it was an ageing accelerated by cultural change. We are offered glimpses from court archives of the fate of the old: of 'one of the earliest inhabitants' who was a known character around the town behaving improperly or dangerously, or an old woman losing her mind, or an old man throwing scorching wood about the house, endangering his son. What will become of such

people in this frontier society, however pioneering or respected they
might once have been? 'Winter is a time when cold confers age upon
memories,' writes Merwick. 'The house and the memories will seem
old together. Janse lives with the chests and locked-away places that are
the very models of stored memory and intimacy.' She reminds us that
'dying alone is a fearsome thing.' If such a prospect were not forbidding
enough for Janse, he was further marginalised by the new English legal
procedures. Townspeople had less need of his services and his chests of
documents, and his business dwindled. And compounding his alien-
ation was his loss of power and competence in language, the very
substance of his profession. The English not only changed the words,
they even changed the places where words might be uttered with legal
force. Depositions could no longer be taken down except in court. For
everyone it was 'a time of mangled words and attempted translations',
but for a notary, the very core of his expertise and identity was under
attack. The invasion was a real, subtle and personal entanglement, and
not just military. This is Merwick's message: that for Albany's townspeople in the 1670s and 1680s, humiliation, uncertainty and loss were
everyday and deeply felt, and Janse's suicide was part of the unrecognised
violence of the seventeenth-century North American frontier. [44]

The narrative is a slow-burning drama that builds with intrigue
towards a tragic climax we know is coming. Yet the moment of death
is shocking. And then it is instantly past, all the more so because of its
illegality and religious dread. The momentum of history sweeps on and
Janse is buried by forceful words of forgetting. The true climax of the
book is the way such an incidental death, such a forgotten life, is given
larger meaning by the historian.

Death of a Notary has been celebrated as a 'microhistory' in the tra-
dition of Natalie Zemon Davis's *The Return of Martin Guerre* (1983),
Carlo Ginzburg's *The Cheese and the Worms* (1980), Robert Darnton's
The Great Cat Massacre (1984), Greg Dening's *The Death of William Gooch*

(1995), John Demos' *The Unredeemed Captive* (1994), E P Thompson's *Whigs and Hunters* (1975) or Emmanuel Le Roy Ladurie's *Montaillou* (1978).[45] It is a genre that aims to make the smallest of lives, places and episodes luminous with wider significance, and that investigates popular thought and experience. Whereas Ginzburg and Ladurie worked with inquisitorial documents whose distinguishing characteristic was their immediacy and exceptional richness, the vividness and directness of their captured voices, Merwick was handling much more intractable sources. Her patient, forensic investigation and accretion of hard-won and deeply worked detail is a sustained performance in the art of writing history. As Peter Charles Hoffer wrote in the *Journal of American History*, 'Prize-winning-calibre historical writing such as *Death of a Notary* is more than craft. It is art – what the historian brings to the sources.'[46]

Donna Merwick practises the philosophy of history she preaches. 'If we have the courage,' she writes, 'we put on the market our experiments.'[47] *Death of A Notary* does not mention Foucault or de Certeau or Hayden White or Clifford Geertz in the narrative text, but the history is shaped as a piece of art and is written with the freedom and sense of experimental adventure that Donna feels is the spirit of postmodernism:

> I have received the gift of being able to write in *these times* – these times, if you will, of postmodernity ... I thought, that among other things, I could legitimately be a story-teller. I could find a voice for speaking to readers ... I tried to write with honest respect for my readers. I tried, for example, to meet their ability to discern that a story written of Janse's life would necessarily be constructed, that if the story were in his own hands it would be none the less constructed ... readers are not at all unsettled by a writer who is saying that there is no single or true perspective on a subject.[48]

Postmodernist and postcolonial scholarship enabled her to move away from the nationalist narratives, to find a more plural past, and to free the Dutch colonists of America from the fate of being just an incidental prequel to the future nation. Her history does indeed give the past back its own present. It is even written in the present tense, which requires that the historian tune into the precise past moment and not move backward or forward carelessly.[49] Donna invites us to be 'near-sighted' and to inhabit the intimate interiors she portrays with the loving, glowing detail of the Dutch realist painters of the Golden Age. Following Geertz, she aims for 'thick description', and as Benjamin Schmidt declares, '"thickens" archives that would seem, to a less sensitive reader, hopelessly thin'.[50] The most terse, commonplace record is made to reveal insights. The potential of the historical craft to see a world in a grain of sand is pushed to its limit, as is right for a microhistory.

But finding the elusive notary requires extra discipline. The renowned lives of the famous and the notorious are reliably handed down to us through the years, and some ordinary lives become known and celebrated because they were recorded in eloquent personal testimony or because they were captured by an unexpected moment of public glory. But Janse always remained in the shadows and Donna has dug him out against his inclination. It is that act of 'resurrection' that makes the book so compelling, as we witness the author reading against the grain, not just of the historical record and the judgement of posterity, but also of the desire of the subject.

Merwick is playfully experimental but always with respect for her sources. In *Death of a Notary*, she paints six 'still-life scenes' from the archival records, rendering them as 'canvases' of Dutch realism.[51] She imagines news reports that might have been published if a planned New Netherland news-sheet had come to fruition in the mid-1660s.[52] In the third book of her New Netherland series, *The Shame and the Sorrow*, she asks her readers to consider each chapter in the story as part of a gallery's installation where 'each picture in the exhibit asks for its own set of reflections' – and reminds us that 'I've framed each of the objects, realising that I'm defining the conditions of its representation and your contemplation of it. I hope I have done it faithfully.'[53] Later in the book, she has Peter Stuyvesant listening and nodding as historians discuss him, a tactic reminiscent of Natalie Zemon Davis, who convened an imaginary conversation between herself and her three historical subjects (who never met each other) in *Women on the Edge*.[54] One reviewer of *Death of a Notary* wrote that 'the line between history and fiction will, upon some scholars' close scrutiny, appear to be blurred.'[55] But the line is not blurred; it is always clear even when it is stepped over. Another historian reviewing Merwick's work welcomed her use of 'that much avoided – and too often doubted – device of good historical detective work: speculation.'[56]

Death of a Notary is ultimately a tale about the art and fate of writing. It is a portrait of a man who lived with books and writing, who shaped texts, who archived 'the story-matter' (*verhaelstof*) of the town, and whose professional language ran out of power and use. He lived and died by the word. Janse created documents and, in a profession of the written word, became defined by them and confined with them. He was the guardian of the secrets of others. Legal words were in his custody and they, in turn, had *him* in custody. He was literally serving a sentence.

It seems right that Janse was liberated from his archive – to live again in a book – by a historian at the end of the twentieth century who enthusiastically embraced the linguistic turn in humanist scholarship. In the final decades of the century, historians talked a lot about texts and textuality. Some felt threatened by the potential relativism of it all while others found, to their surprise, that their peculiar obsession with archived texts had become a widely shared, even fashionable, source of fascination across the social sciences. Hayden White helped historians see their own writings as texts shaped by literary strategies, and the work of Clifford Geertz and others suggested that social life itself might be studied as a text.[57] Donna resurrected Janse with utterly conventional respect for the archive and she earned her insights with endless hours of patient and systematic study, but she was also a radical adventurer in the world of ideas, ready for some play. She is honest about that. Donna, a literary historian, a postmodernist student of texts, was attracted to a Writing Man buried and memorialised by words. 'I could disregard history as a medium offering information and, instead, do as a story-teller does, that is, embed the experiences of Adriaen Janse in my own life and thinking in order to "pass it on as *experience* to those listening"' (she is quoting Walter Benjamin).[58] 'Experience' is a key word in her work (and also, significantly, in John Dewey's), and ranks with 'precision' and 'imagination'. The experiences she talks about here are Janse's and her own. Good history, I think she would say, can be about both, but it has to be delicately and carefully done. *Death of a Notary* is literally *two* books. First there is the narrative of 186 pages; then there are the fifty-six pages of prose that constitute the Notes and Reflections. They are both works of art, written to be read. One is more about Janse, the other more about Merwick.

We look back on Janse's story today with another jolt of recognition.[59] We too inhabit a critical period of cultural transition as the digital networked age engulfs us. Robert Darnton declares that the explosion of electronic modes of communication is as revolutionary as the invention of printing with movable type.[60] The book endures and in some ways thrives, but writing – in terms of penmanship, of ink and graphite inscribing paper – is in rapid decline (although Donna retains a firm grip of her pencil). Our relationship to writing is changing in ways we can't yet fathom and information is challenging knowledge. We are reading and uttering in shorter formats. Communication technologies are morphing with speed, and our fingers and thumbs conjure words from machines in new ways. Perhaps we are even beginning to think differently. We can read Janse's story – if we can read in depth at all – as a parable for our time.

ELEVEN

Walking the City: Graeme Davison

In his early twenties, Graeme Davison was walking the back-streets of Melbourne's inner suburb of Richmond in search of its nineteenth-century history when he was apprehended by a policeman. He was photographing houses and carrying an old canvas bag containing two cameras and the hammer and screwdriver he needed to carry out running repairs on his uncle Jack's 1948 Triumph Roadster. As he was gazing at the lanes and cottages, he became aware that he was being followed by a car driven by 'two burly young men'. Suddenly one of the men jumped out, bundled him into the back seat of the car and began to go through the incriminating canvas bag. Graeme was suspected of housebreaking.

'What do you think you're doing?' asked the plain-clothes detective.

'Historical research.'

'And how long have you been on this caper?'[1]

It was 1962 and Graeme was finishing an arts degree at Melbourne University. The first in his family to have a tertiary education, he was doing his honours year in history and relished the chance to investigate, in physical and social detail, the city in which he had grown up. But Graeme was from lower-middle-class Essendon and, as he photographed

Richmond's old buildings in Docker Street, Bridge Road and Lennox Street, he felt he was peering into a different world. He was in search of the historical experience of another class: 'the Victorian working class'.

Although Richmond was named nostalgically for its riverside location and seclusion, and attracted some pioneering gentry to its hill, from the 1860s small local industries moved in and the wide river flat became 'synonymous in public estimation with dirt, disease and poverty'.[2] In the late nineteenth century, Richmond, Collingwood and South Melbourne made up Melbourne's 'inner ring of dismal working-class suburbs', as Graeme later described them. In the unsewered city, they occupied flat terrain where drainage was poor, and where the Yarra River, lined with noxious industries, regularly broke its banks. Factories shared their stench and smoke with low-rent housing. The suburb's newly launched newspaper, the *Richmond Guardian*, boasted in 1859 that Richmond was residential, with owners in their own homes and most with a garden or a yard. As further evidence of the suburb's solidity, the newspaper added: 'Many old inhabitants of the Colony are located in it.'[3]

It was these people that a hundred years later Graeme was seeking, and he looked for them in wood and stone, paper and map, allotment boundaries and council archives. He could even hear echoes of them in the political talk that reverberated around the Town Hall as he worked on the local rate books at an assigned desk. He was determined not to write 'the kind of history that makes heroes of city councillors'. Two years earlier, he had heard a lecture by visiting British historian Asa Briggs, promoting the field of urban history and the work of the famous Chicago School of urban sociology, which promoted a holistic and ecological approach to urban studies and envisaged the city as a social laboratory.[4] An urban neighbourhood was a living experiment that could surprise you. Chicago School scholar Robert E Park (1864–1944) was an indefatigable and proud walker: 'I expect I have covered more ground tramping around in different cities of the world than any other living man,' he boasted.[5] The city was to be systematically investigated at street level, as an ethnographer might. By walking the streets and listening to the local lore, Graeme could reinhabit the original urban scale of the working-class community, the 'walking and talking city' that in the late nineteenth century was overlaid by the 'rail and mail city'.[6] He learned to look up and down for clues to the past in chimneys and drain covers, parapets and paving stones. Amongst the modern homes and shops and the imposing churches on Docker's Hill, he found former livery stables, an old shoe factory, humble wooden houses with mockstone facing, the solid bluestone cottage of a stonemason, and the site of a eucalyptus oil distillery. But the greatest discovery he made was 'the excitement of pursuing history in the field'.[7]

A couple of decades later he was to teach an honours course at Monash University called 'History in the Field', which grew into a masters program in public history in 1988 and later the Institute of Public History. Graeme reflected that 'I find it hard to write or teach with conviction about a city that I have not explored carefully on foot.'[8] In this way he was following not only Robert E Park and Asa Briggs, but also the footsteps of the British socialist historian R H Tawney, who believed that good historians need strong boots. As an explorer of city lanes in search of the past life of another class, of 'how the other half lived', Graeme may have also seen himself as working in the tradition of the great urban social investigators he was later to write about – Sidney and Beatrice Webb, Henry Mayhew, William Stanley Jevons and Oswald Barnett. 'Like them, I was a middle-class outsider seeking entry to a plebeian world I perceived as alien.'[9] Certainly he believed that the contemporary fabric of the city was an archive like any other; indeed, it was 'a palimpsest, a richly textured relic of the ideas, as well as physical transformations, that have shaped the city'.[10] In 1980 he edited a book of historic walks called *Melbourne on Foot*, to which he contributed a walking guide to Richmond.[11]

Graeme Davison speaks of his attachment to the pursuit of history as a 'vocation' and a 'calling'. These terms invoke the total, passionate commitment of the scholar, artist and citizen, and draw on two sources of influence. One is religious: like many other Australian historians, Davison acknowledges a religious upbringing and sees history and religion as 'kindred preoccupations': 'In most societies, storytellers are first cousins to priests, prophets and preachers.'[12] Methodism tutored him in 'the cardinal historical belief in the authority of the Word and the conviction that history is primarily a moral activity'.[13] He wondered if the Crawford School of History at Melbourne University, where he completed his honours thesis on Richmond, tended to attract people who shared a conviction that the meaning of existence might be discerned by a deep reading of texts.[14] And his own chosen inspiration for walking the city was 'the social survey', a practice whose history he found to be imbued with a Christian ethos and grounded in 'a framework of belief and action that was as much theological as scientific'.[15] Not the kind of street activism to attract the attentions of a policeman.

The other dimension of this mystical, intuitive sense of calling was the influence of environment, 'a sense of place'. Although Davison happily acknowledges academic influences – for example, the charismatic teaching of Kathleen Fitzpatrick in his first year at university, the quiet wisdom of his honours supervisor Allan Martin, and of Allan's wife, Jean Martin, a sociologist – he feels ultimately that it was place and family that guided him towards history. 'For me,' he reflects, 'history is a pursuit that is founded on a strong sense of place and on the personal and political questions that arise out of living in that place.' Davison located that sense of place in the Melbourne suburb where he grew up, Essendon, which was neither posh and leafy nor industrial and larrikin, a remarkably self-sufficient pedestrian society in the 1940s, a time before traffic congestion and supermarkets, where allotments had remained vacant since the land boom of the 1880s.[16]

And he further located his sense of place in his Methodist family, especially 'the commanding intellectual influence' of his maternal grandfather, Vic Hewett, a bibliophile, printer by trade and local preacher who bequeathed to Graeme a reverence for books and who took his first grandson for walks, pointing out sites associated with the history of the city. One Sunday afternoon he took him into his study to proudly show off a recent acquisition, an original plan of the first Melbourne land sale in 1837.[17] The boy would become the historian of Marvellous Melbourne, the city made famous – and then humbled – by a land boom.

⁓

Cities were long neglected in Australian cultural studies because nationalist writers and intellectuals looked to the bush as the source of distinctive identity. The city seemed to produce no distinct national type, and the suburb, especially, was disdained as a cultural wasteland and a 'terra nullius of the human spirit', as Graeme summarised the attitude.[18] I understand that attitude well: I grew up in Balwyn.

Balwyn is the middle-class eastern suburb of Melbourne that came to represent all that is complacent and stultifying about suburban life – and all that is terrifying too. The Australian rock group Skyhooks memorialised my suburb in 1974 in a song called 'Balwyn Calling', which told the story of a young man pursued on the phone by a woman from Balwyn. 'Hey, boy, it's Balwyn calling!' A one-night stand was threatening to turn into a life sentence: 'A brick-veneer prison is waiting for you.' The song finished with the injunction: 'Get out of Bal-*wyn*!' My first job was as the postman for my own neighbourhood – I had the largest postal round in the eastern suburbs and I knew every letterbox in every hedge and every dog in every driveway in Balwyn. My red postal bike became a rare conduit of community in that reclusive landscape. Escape did not seem likely.

My experience of Balwyn as a child was of a raw, new suburb privatised into houses on blocks behind hedges and fences, inhabited by nuclear families in the nuclear age. It was the arena for three new engines of social change – the car, the television and the supermarket. The large district of Camberwell, within which Balwyn was situated, had been declared 'dry' in 1928 and so there were no pubs. The civic spaces of the suburb were desolate. Koonung Creek, where dark things could happen, was out of bounds and too far away anyway, and it's now a freeway.[19] An overgrown easement (and it was called just that: 'The Easement') provided my only casual access to 'wild nature', which meant a linear paddock of untamed grass. This was clearly different to 'the Nature Strip', which was the common lawn (expected to be mown) at the front of each home. Public transport was poor; the key to freedom was petrol and the private car, and the yawning double garage began to take pride of place over the front door of newly built homes. That my mother didn't drive left her stranded in this wilderness during the long week, especially as her work as a science teacher had been automatically terminated by the education department upon her marriage. The car shaped the suburb – Victoria's first traffic roundabout was built right near us in 1951, and it was such an innovation in a linear, rectangular streetscape that the whole neighbourhood became known simply as 'The Roundabout'.

When, much later, I read *The Cream Brick Frontier* (1995), a book edited by Graeme Davison, Tony Dingle and Seamus O'Hanlon, I learned with a shock of recognition that perhaps the last fitful expression of the Australian 'pioneer legend' was to be found in places like Balwyn. 'On the fringes of the great cities,' wrote Barbara and Graeme Davison, 'in the years after the depression and the Second World War, a new generation of suburban pioneers did battle with the elements, subduing the land, creating little oases of domestic safety and comfort in a dangerous world.'[20] I hadn't realised how adventurous and exciting my unremarkable childhood was.

Our house was built by my father on a gentle hill of vacant paddocks in 1950. There, in quiet, suburban Melbourne in the late 1950s and '60s, I was growing up in a favoured corner of a first-world nation, a 'lucky country' living off its wool cheques from stolen pastoral lands and busy converting paddocks to suburbs as it quickly became one of the most urban countries in the world. It was true that I had come of age on a suburban frontier. My parents were amongst those who, after the war, built with earnest commitment the homes that signified their return to family and security. Building materials were scarce and skilled labour was in demand. The housing shortage was described as Victoria's most 'acute social problem'. Many homes were built in stages by the owners themselves. At the weekend, across Melbourne's burgeoning outer suburbs, people formed working bees around timber frames and humble small-roomed dwellings. The *Age* ran special articles for these austere and determined homemakers, with helpful titles such as 'Making One Room into Two or Three'. Through the newspaper's 'Small Homes Service', a weekly feature established in 1947, Robin Boyd tutored home-buyers and builders in good taste. My parents were willing allies in Boyd's campaign to fight 'the Australian ugliness' by elevating suburban aesthetics. Architectural modernism, with its emphasis on functionalism and simplicity, provided a creative way to transcend the housing crisis.

The first photographs in our family album show the timber frame rising alone against the sky from the grass on the hill, awaiting its brick veneer. Dad queued up each week at the hardware store for a pound of nails, his building ration in hard times, and sometimes enlisted workmates to collect a quota of nails on his behalf. The house that Dad built was ultimately a work of art, an intellectual statement, with its open plan, tall windows, exposed pine and slate flooring, angled walls, skillion roof, broad eaves and exposed rafters. My mother's genius was to create beauty out of simple, natural elements, whether it be a large rock collected from the countryside for her Australian garden, or a bouquet of native grasses and thistles gathered on a Sunday drive, or a piece of Warrandyte craft pottery (by Phyl Dunn or Reg Preston) selected for the coffee table. When I returned this year to walk the streets of Balwyn, I found that our modernist home had been dramatically 'renovated' in a neo-colonial style. The local heritage study regrets the loss and respectfully describes my father – who was a meteorologist when he built the house – as an 'architect'.[21]

In summer we harvested apricots and blood plums from our backyard fruit trees, and there were daily deliveries of milk and bread by horse and cart well into the 1960s. The library was a bus that came once a week and parked, appropriately enough, in 'Caravan Street'. I keenly remember evening visits in my dressing gown to the crowded aisle of the book bus, and then reading the borrowed books during the next week by our open fire. To fuel that fire, the nature strip fulfilled its destiny every winter when it received a delivery of a ton of mallee roots that had been grubbed out of Victoria's north-western plains to convert them to wheatlands. In summer the mallee visited us in another form: red dust blew hundreds of kilometres from those exposed and eroding paddocks, rusting our drying clothes on the backyard Hills hoist.

Eventually the open fire in our lounge room was replaced by an oil heater – a *space* heater, no less – and we moved from wood to fossil fuel and progressed further into the industrial revolution. In the mid-winter of 1969, aged twelve, I remember warming myself by the dying embers of a mallee root as the TV broadcast images of a Saturn V rocket wreathed in smoke and flame inching its way off the ground at Cape Canaveral and exploding out of Earth's atmosphere towards the Moon. There, in our suburban home in Balwyn, I should have felt vertiginous, for I too was being propelled into the future at high speed on the apex of a demographic explosion and an energy revolution. The year Dad built our house – 1950 – was the year we now identify as the beginning of 'the Great Acceleration', a sudden and dramatic growth of the human enterprise after the Second World War. Population, petrol consumption, loss of species, atmospheric greenhouse gases, fertiliser and water use all skyrocketed from 1950.[22]

This was the world that Graeme Davison tenaciously hauled into the centre of our historical vision. He was himself living in North Balwyn and later moved to neighbouring Mont Albert, which he could still recognise in the 1980s as 'the bastion of white Anglo-Saxon Protestantism its founders had dreamt of back in the land boom of the 1880s'. Graeme found that Mont Albert, like the Balwyn I knew, 'exemplified Lewis Mumford's characterisation of the ruling principle of the Victorian suburb: "We keep ourselves to ourselves."' When ASIO needed a place to hide the Petrovs after their famous defection in the 1950s, 'they chose a house just down the way from us,' reports Graeme, adding: '(At least that's the local story, and who would deprive this sleepy suburb of its one moment of notoriety?)'[23] It's a place you could lose someone in, possibly even yourself.

Graeme had been troubled by A D Hope's 1939 poem 'Australia', which depicted our cities as 'five teeming sores', parasite robber-states draining the nation, and the home of 'second-hand Europeans'. It was typical of a widespread literary disdain for the Australian city. Davison found it strange 'that intellectuals should dismiss the places in which most of their countrymen lived with a sneer', and he wondered: 'Could our cities really be so uninteresting, and was our national ethos really so detached from the suburbs where most of us now lived?'[24]

It was the Bush, often with a capital 'B', that was generally seen as the primary source of Australian identity. Weird to the European eye, the Bush held a mysterious power. It had shaped the settler and was said to have forged new national characteristics – hardness, adaptability, mateship, laconic acceptance – from the elements of its own strange nature, from the dry, spare soils and tough, sclerophyll leaves. Russel

Ward's book *The Australian Legend* (1958) gave historical depth to this idea by tracing the development of a culture of ballad and yarn and an ethos of egalitarianism, pragmatism and anti-authoritarianism from convict days to the semi-nomadic 'tribes' of inland pastoral workers and thence to the nation. Crucial in facilitating the transfer of these popular values from bush to city were the writers of the 'Bushman's Bible', the *Bulletin*, especially Henry Lawson, 'Banjo' Paterson and Joseph Furphy.[25] In Don Watson's meditation on *The Bush* (2014), he recognised that its power is not diminished by the fact that the great majority of Australians live in cities; rather, the bush 'adds an exotic or romantic dimension to the suburban cliché of our existence'.[26] This is the paradox of Australian social and cultural life that Graeme Davison, more than any other scholar, has investigated. He studies not only the rise of the city but the decline of the country town, not only the life of the metropolis but the economy of the hinterland, and not only suburban myths but rural ideals.[27] The City and the Bush are the symbolic opposites of Australian life, and Davison does not separate them. *The Rise and Fall of Marvellous Melbourne* ends with the collapse of the land boom in 1889, followed by strikes, floods, locusts, epidemics and the bank crash – and the consequent rise of the rural ideal. Thus 'urban disillusionment and rural mythmaking were intertwined'. 'At the end of the tragic story of "Marvellous Melbourne",' concludes Davison, 'we are embarked on the brilliant career of the "Australian Legend"'.[28]

Davison's contribution was to reverse the assumed flow of ideas about the Bush, and to discern that 'the Australian Legend' also had an urban context. The Bush ideal, he suggested, 'was not so much a relic of a dying rural folk culture as the literary creation of an alienated urban intelligentsia'.[29] His seminal article in *Historical Studies* had a stunning visual prop: a map of inner-Sydney boarding houses where the *Bulletin* writers lived and worked – city streets Graeme had of course walked. His grandfather Vic Hewett, although born in the bush, had lived almost all his life in the city and had a portrait of Henry Lawson on the wall of his study, and it was from him that the young Graeme received a gift of Lawson's collected verse and short stories. Davison mischievously suggests that it was actually those ironic Australian intellectuals who saw their own cities as provincial who were 'still tied to the apron-strings of Mother England and unable to see what was distinctive in their own urban environment'.[30]

'Australia was born urban and quickly grew suburban,' he argued. It came into being as a European colony 'at the very moment when the suburb was emerging as a solution to the urban ills of the Old World'. The suburb was itself also a kind of colony, a place of refuge, 'and it was shaped, therefore, largely by the logic of avoidance'.[31] So it was *meant* to be safe and boring! American urban historian Lewis Mumford called the suburb 'an innocent world', 'an asylum for the preservation of illusion'.[32] It was expected to be a place that separated home from work, that created 'a kind of temple in which the wife ruled', where classes might be segregated and where one escaped the city's disease and noise to commune with nature.[33] Davison was determined to stay at home as a historian and to study his own ordinary environment, so readily taken for granted. He admired the writings of Inga Clendinnen, Greg Dening, Bill Kent and Rhys Isaac, colleagues 'driven by the desire to inhabit other worlds ... enabling us to feel that nothing human is ultimately strange to us', but his calling was to reveal 'the hidden dimensions of the familiar' and to make history of the railway and cable tram, the spec-built cottage, the electric telegraph, the bell-tower, the brick-veneer house, the Holden station wagon, the refrigerator, the washing machine, the Victa mower, the Mixmaster and the freeway.[34] Davison's work explored the history of the suburban dream, for good and ill, and posited Australia as the first suburban nation.[35] And he saw that, by the end of the twentieth century, economic scarcity and environmental extravagance had made 'the suburban sprawl seem as profligate and dangerous as it once seemed safe and boring'.[36] Yet the suburb had virtues that responded to these new challenges: its inherent independence, security and self-sufficiency created an adaptable living space that was 'capable of being recycled and reused', one where residents could harvest their own rainwater and generate their own electricity. Davison believes that social innovation is to be found in the 'remaking of the middle-distance suburbs'. Where do you find the most interesting things happening? 'You don't go to the edge necessarily, you don't go to the centre. The place to really watch is the middle.'[37]

In 1978, when an honours workshop on writing history was organised by students at the University of Melbourne, each historian was described as representing a school of art: Geoffrey Blainey appeared as 'the landscape artist', Greg Dening as 'the impressionist' and Joy Parnaby as 'the pointillist'. Graeme Davison was introduced as 'the cubist'. Although the title may not have been his choice, it was quite an apt characterisation of his intellectual interests and style. Davison's work constantly wrestles with the logic of modernism.[38] He shares with cubism a strong interest in space, mass and time, and in bringing underlying processes, forces and structures to the fore. He seeks insight into form, nature and system by depicting his subject from a variety of overlapping viewpoints, 'from different angles and in different lights'.[39] In the mid-1970s he was attracted to structuralist thinkers such as Claude Lévi-Strauss and Michel Foucault, and especially to sociological critiques that focused on the class structure of the city. He also developed an enduring enthusiasm for the work of the French historian Fernand Braudel on time, energy and material life. Braudel's influence can be seen in Davison's contributions to the bicentennial 'slice' volume, *Australians 1888*, and in his Australian history of time, *The Unforgiving Minute*. In the 1970s historians were turning away from empirical national narratives, towards 'the idea that the main objective of the human sciences, including history, was to expose the underlying structures, the unseen workings of society'.[40] But Davison resists the abstraction and formalism of cubism, and his belief in human agency is so strong, his narrative skills so powerful and his prose so elegant that his scaffolding rarely shows. In his 1978 talk to students as 'the cubist', he spoke of the structures to be divined by the writer of history and of his conviction that truth, once revealed, would have an elegance and simplicity that was beautiful as well as true. And the example he chose was Watson and Crick's double helix, the graceful, entwining molecular strands of DNA.

In 1982 Graeme left his position at Melbourne University when he was appointed to a chair of history at Australia's first drive-in university, Monash University, about 20 kilometres from the CBD and embedded deep in the city's south-eastern suburban sprawl. His previous university office in Parkville had looked south towards the city skyline and 'the monuments of Marvellous Melbourne', whereas his new view from Monash's Menzies building (known as the Ming Wing) was 'across a flatter terrain of triple-fronted brick veneers, freeways, shopping malls, motels, ten-pin bowling alleys and drive-in cinemas'.[41] On a clear day, 'when the westerlies disperse the inversion layer of auto fumes', he could survey 'a tapestry of cream brick walls, terracotta roofs and dark green foliage that stretches all the way to the mountains and the sea'.[42] Looking down from the Ming Wing, Graeme knew he had the chance to make sense of the city from the outside in instead of from the inside out, as most intellectuals have done.[43] Clayton was a long way from the centre of Melbourne and hard to reach by public transport, but Graeme managed to celebrate it as a centre of another kind – he was now at the demographic heart of his city. He had asked for this: he was in the middle of 'the cream brick frontier' – or, as Pete Seeger's famous song described suburbia, a landscape of 'Little Boxes'.[44]

How was he to discern the logic of the sprawling, inscrutable land-scape laid out before him?[45] Because of the influence of Robert E Park and the Chicago School, Graeme had long been interested in the city as a natural system.[46] Seeing the metropolis as an organism – as having a heart, lungs and arteries, and a capacity for growth and self-regulation – was one of the foundational visions of urban sociology. During and after the First World War, Park had been inspired by his reading of plant and animal ecology, which was then an emerging science. By the 1930s he was exploring ideas such as the web of life, the struggle for existence, competition, freedom, collective action and the biotic base of society as if, at a time of stress and crisis in the Western world, he was searching for the source of social equilibrium.[47] Park was especially interested in the ideas of Frederic Clements, an American botanist who observed that individual plants formed common associations as part of vegetation communities and that those communities themselves acted like superorganisms with patterned life histories. This influential theory of vegetational succession suggested to Park that human com-munities might have a similar organic pattern and that there was a need for a 'human ecology'.

Park was also a devotee of the American anthropologist Franz Boas (1858–1942), whose work rejected scientific racism and the idea that there was an indissoluble link between race and culture. At a time when eugenic ideas were on the rise, a social, historical and environmental approach to the city – seeing it as a great human organism with evolved social structures that responded to environmental factors – combatted racial thinking and provided an open-minded framework for urban anthropology.[48] Walking the neighbourhood, investigating the 'cus-toms, beliefs, social practices, and general conceptions of life' of the urban and migrant poor in their 'natural setting', and doing ethno-graphic fieldwork in the streets of one's own city were not only human ecology in action, but also a contribution to the nature–nurture debate of the period, one that sided decisively with the influence of environment over genetics. Perhaps because of this intellectual influence – and the family inspiration of self-made Methodism – Davison always leaned towards the environmental side of this perennial debate. 'I am not much attracted to biological or mystical notions of blood and inheritance,' he wrote later, in spite of his respect for the elegance of the double helix.[49]

From the Ming Wing, Graeme looked out on a sea of suburbia that was both environment and artefact. Discerning its organic character was one way to plumb its inscrutable logic. Another was to look at its mechanics. The city was a machine as well as a natural system; it had technology as well as an ecology. As the son of a plumber, Graeme had often spent school vacations helping his father on building blocks in the city's new suburbs created by the postwar housing boom. So he had grown up with an inside view of the most basic level of city-building and had listened to the talk of builders and tradesmen who constituted one of 'the great repositories of urban folklore'. He was inclined therefore to study the city's systems, structures and processes, its pistons of change, the motors of urban growth and decay, the driving forces of planning, speculating and building, and the agency of its teams of subcontracting architects, stonemasons, bricklayers, carpenters, plasterers and plumbers.[50] On the publication of *Marvellous Melbourne*, the economic historian John McCarty celebrated it as 'an intricate and elegant piece of clockwork'.[51] Graeme was interested in how a city worked. He mapped its material life, its energy flows, its routines and rhythms, its domestic arithmetic, its patterns of social and geographical mobility, its transport and communication, its invisible architecture, its mechanics, its plumbing.

Seeing the city as a machine as well as an organism revealed its tick as well as its heartbeat. And there are wheels within wheels. What machines would you choose to reveal the inner workings of the city? Davison chose the clock and the car. One seeks to master time, the other to conquer space; one is on your wrist, the other in your garage. Both are personal machines, intimate and elegant accessories of our lives, aligned with our status and style and bringing the industrial revolution home.

Davison's time travel, then, is interesting for his attention to the medium itself. Time, for him, is part of the organisation, fabric and logic of society, one of 'the deep structures, the subterranean rhythms and hidden fault-lines' that historians can overlook.[52] He was propelled into the study of time by the grand collaborative enterprise of Australian historians in the 1980s: a multi-volume bicentennial history with its innovation of 'slicing time'. It was a good metaphor, for the aim of 'slicing' was to cut against the grain of the national narrative and offer richly textured portraits of single years (1788, 1838, 1888 and 1938), thus countering the teleological tendencies of commemorative history. As a co-editor of the 1888 volume, Davison faced the challenge of balancing story and contingency, structure and narrative, within the portrait of a single year. Ethnography offered a compelling model, not only because of its attention to lived experience and its focus on episodes, but also because it used narrative *within* structure, 'as a method of exposition, rather than as an explanatory principle', as Davison put it.[53] Ken Inglis, general editor of the bicentennial history volumes, had a dictum for the writers of the slice volumes: they had to write about people who did not know what was going to happen next.[54]

Graeme's history of 'how Australia learned to tell the time', called *The Unforgiving Minute*, grew out of this bicentennial project. One of its heroes is John Wesley. 'Australia was a child not only of the scientific and industrial revolutions of the eighteenth century,' writes Davison, 'but of the religious and moral revolution known as the Evangelical Revival.'[55] Verses from Rudyard Kipling's famous poem 'If', gilt-framed and printed in illuminated letters, used to hang above the bookcase in Graeme's childhood home:

If you can fill the unforgiving minute

With sixty seconds' worth of distance run,

Yours is the Earth and everything that's in it,

And – which is more – you'll be a Man, my son!

British industrial time was imperial, moral and masculine. When the tick of the sacred 'Timekeeper' (as Governor Phillip's chronometer was reverently called) was brought to the shores of Australia in the late eighteenth century, it brought a competitive, guilt-inducing morality of punctuality, discipline and efficiency. In a classic essay on time, work-discipline, and industrial capitalism, the English historian E P Thompson analysed how, from the late eighteenth century, a new morality of time was imposed through the supervision and division of labour, the introduction of fines, bells, money incentives, preachings and schoolings, the suppression of fairs and sports and the rationalisation even of leisure.[56] Punctuality meant civility and time equalled money. A general diffusion of clocks and watches occurred at just the moment when the industrial revolution demanded a greater synchronisation of labour. Time became a social and economic measure as well as a natural and geographic one. It was a currency to be saved, husbanded, redeemed, and spent wisely. One needed to be thrifty with time and to improve each shining hour. Greenwich Mean Time could indeed be mean.

Graeme's book *Car Wars* (2004) did for space what *The Unforgiving Minute* did for time. He looked under the bonnet of postwar Melbourne, beginning with that moment my parents experienced, of starting life again after the war and rebounding like coiled springs following the long period of depression and compression. The 1930s and early 1940s, as well as bringing tragedy and misery, had been 'a time of deferred hopes and frustrated desires' and now Melburnians turned to the quieter, safer lives of which they had dreamed: 'all the pent-up longings of the war years – sexual, scientific and material – were released.' And the car came to embody and accommodate those dreams of freedom, independence and also of domesticity. The Sunday drive, argues Davison, was quickly supplanting the Sunday church service as 'the favourite celebration of family togetherness'. Cars were 'the biggest, most complicated and most fascinating machines ever to appear in the average household'. In the postwar decades they wrought what the historian of Marvellous Melbourne's nineteenth-century turmoil recognised as perhaps the most dramatic social transformation in the city's social history.[57]

For Davison, the clock had revealed the imperial rhythms of the industrial revolution, the acceleration and synchronisation of everyday life and the moral world of time-discipline; and the car enabled him to interrogate 'the drive-in logic' of the new suburbs and to enter the ubiquitous postwar landscapes of the carport, service station, motel, drive-in theatre and regional shopping centre. It could all be discerned from the Ming Wing: the abandoned site of Australia's largest drive-in theatre where students now park, the extension to Melbourne's first freeway, the road to Melbourne's first motel and first regional drive-in shopping centre (Chadstone), the sawtooth roofs of Holden's Dandenong plant and, closer by, the now-abandoned Nissan factory.[58] Both the clock and the car enabled Davison to further study 'the Faustian logic of modernisation', the way these machines offered such promises of escape only to impose new levels of regulation and surveillance.[59] Graeme reflected: 'I shared, and was myself a beneficiary, of the great modernist dreams of growth and material betterment that came with the 1950s and 1960s, and I have wrestled, as have all my generation, with the dimming of many of those hopes in the 1970s and 80s.'[60]

That word, *generation*: it is there throughout Davison's oeuvre. It is an emblem of his fascination with the social experience of time. For him, a city 'offers the possibility of a larger kind of human community', one that is more diverse than the family, the clan or the village and also more organic and intelligible than the state or the nation. Large and unruly as it is, a city can still have generations, and Davison's two big books on Melbourne – its nineteenth-century rise and fall and its twentieth-century postwar expansion – both focus on periods of conspicuous generational change. *Marvellous Melbourne* was the study of the gold generation, 'who had built a city in their own lifetime and with their own hands', a 'society without grandparents' that, as it aged, came to face the 'baffling' problem of succession when 'the ideals of fathers were cast aside by their sons'.[61] The myth of 'Marvellous Melbourne' had been 'a creation of the lucky gold-rush generation and their spoiled children'. He told it as a tragedy: 'a story of high aspirations and modest hopes defeated by greed and myopia'.[62] *Car Wars*, beginning as it does with the end of the Second World War and the baby boom, maps the growth of a different city and the aspirations of those 'suburban pioneers' in a new era of dreams. As a child of that generation of surprising pioneers, I enter Graeme's story at this point, as one of a number of fortunate but 'restless youth' hoping to get out of Balwyn. Although the parents may have sensed the emptiness of the carscape they created, Davison notes that 'it was not until their spoiled children fled the parental nest for the narrow streets of yesterday's slums that the suburban dream began to lose its allure.'[63] Both *Marvellous Melbourne* and *Car Wars*, then, chart rises and falls in the suburban ideal, scrutinise generation gaps, and analyse moments when the contradictions of the 'Faustian logic' of modernisation could no longer be avoided.

'Generation' as a historical concept is also a consequence of Graeme's commitment to a practical, civic scale of historical practice. It brings to the forefront the issues of succession, legacy, memory, heritage – and ultimately also of belonging.[64] Davison was a pioneer of public history in the 1980s, an academic historian who was ready to champion history wherever it was practised and who constantly worked to keep the academy receptive to outside influences, especially as it was retreating under the weight of managerialism. 'Many of the most exciting developments in history are now occurring outside, or on the fringes, of the universities,' he observed in 1990.[65] He recognised that history was a part of everyday conversation and community identity and that its popular forms were flourishing even as its academic manifestation was shrinking. He was concerned to close the gap between academic history and the general public that he felt had opened up in the earlier era of university expansion. For several years in the 1980s he became the first non-lawyer to chair the Historic Buildings Council of Victoria, and 'heritage' was, for him, a practical issue of governance as well as an intellectual question.[66] He worked actively with archives, historical societies and museums, studied monuments and commemorations, and defended the National Museum of Australia from conservative attacks about its treatment of frontier violence.[67] Davison believes in the civic virtue of history – it is part of the 'citizenship, public responsibility and free public debate' required to make a city work. The metropolitan and civic dimensions of Australian life, rather than the national and local, draw him most strongly.[68]

If you wish to engage with and learn from popular history, and especially if you are interested in generations of memory, then the academic historian has finally to come to terms with family history. Family history and academic history have had an uneasy relationship – one depicted as an antiquarian hobby and the other as a profession – and there can be political discomfort in ideas of identity founded in notions of blood and breeding.[69] Davison reminds us that democratic societies struggled against the idea of inheritance, and that Australian colonists, with their convict origins, had particular reasons to reject it. Australians were inclined to give credit to the influence of environment over heredity, and to the possibility that people could shape their own lives and begin again under a new sun. Yet, in the late twentieth century, ancestry surprisingly re-emerged as 'the basis for new political and social rights and as a core component of personal identity'.[70] As part of his campaign of respect for public history, Davison urged his fellow historians to take seriously the popular surge in genealogy since the 1970s — as 'an intriguing sociological phenomenon' that reveals much about our relationship to the past, but also as a way of understanding patterns of lineage and kinship in Australian society. 'From the vantage point of the professional historian,' wrote Graeme, 'the average family history may appear not only trivial but almost inscrutable. It seems plotless, disconnected, unselective ... only if we give as much weight to the idea of heredity as liberals customarily give to the influence of environment will we begin to understand its continuing appeal.'[71] Heredity was finally claiming him, but the true test would be to write his own family history.

Graeme Davison begins his book *Lost Relations: Fortunes of My Family in Australia's Golden Age*, with a sixty-nine-word story, 'The Great-Aunt's Story'. It was told to Graeme by his mother, who heard it from her father, who heard it from his great-aunt. So it is with family stories: they have a pedigree. The story tells of Great-Aunt Jane's arrival, aged eighteen, by ship with her mother and seven siblings, in Port Phillip in 1850 'before the gold rush'. She remembers climbing down the ship's ladder, landing at Sandridge, and walking three miles across the swamp to spend their first night at the Globe Inn in Swanston Street. In the story, honed down the years, every detail means something, as does every omission.

Davison 'tells the story behind Jane's story, the one she must have known but did not tell, or perhaps did not even think worth the telling'.[72] These delicate words begin the task of plumbing the mystery of families and of intergenerational knowledge and influence. What did Jane know but not tell or not think worth telling? And how can we recover that lost context and those lost relations? Are they lost because they are forgotten, suppressed, hidden, overlooked, or taken for granted, or perhaps because they were so beloved that there were no words for them? We feel we are best known by our families, yet families lose intimate knowledge with shocking speed. In *Lost Relations*, Graeme confronts his most intractable source: his own family.

It is there in the title: *my* family. Not *a* family, not *any* family, but *my* family. Davison's purpose is to examine his relationship to these people and what that means. He rises to the challenge of his 1978 talk and examines the meaning of that entrancing structure, the double helix. His own DNA, his own biological and cultural lineage, is brought under scrutiny. And so the second beginning to the book takes place in an English country churchyard, where Graeme and his sister contemplate the grave of their great-great-great grandfather, John Hewett, a yeoman farmer from Hampshire. As Graeme stands by the grave, he feels the historian's curiosity about this villager, prematurely dead, whose widow and eight children would voyage to Port Phillip a decade later. But this man John Hewett was also his ancestor, linked to him in some mysterious way, physically and culturally, and therefore more significant than any other in the churchyard. What are those links and how do they persist, even when knowledge of them is lost?

That grave must have been a great rediscovery, a completing of the circle as the great-great-great grandchild, an Australian, makes the pilgrimage back to the source, arrives in the village of thatched cottages, steps through the lychgate, finds the tilting gravestone and reads the lichen-encrusted epitaph to his forebear. It seems romantic and ancestral and we can almost see the parting mists of time. Davison even quotes Thomas Gray's famous 'Elegy Written in a Country Churchyard'. But John Hewett died only a century before Graeme was born, and John's eldest daughter, Jane – the great-aunt – died just a dozen years before the author's birth. These are not great gaps of time, yet so much knowledge – so much beloved, treasured knowledge of face and voice, personality and philosophy, sense of humour and way of life, and even the reason why one would cross the world – is lost. How can this be? How can families, of all social institutions, allow this to happen?

Davison's book of family history is a profound and practical intervention in intergenerational memory, working intelligently against the gradient of loss. He avoided family history most of his life, partly because he was not attracted to biological notions of inheritance, and partly out of professional wariness. Graeme finally 'succumbed' to the appeal of family history, not only because he 'wanted to better understand who I am' but also in order to 'think more concretely about the relationship between the familial and communal pasts'.[75] In other words, the book was a search for identity, as all family history fundamentally is, but it was also a reflective exploration of family history as a method – and what better case study could there be than one's own family? But it is more than that. If a historian wants to examine the mystery of the relationship between generations, and if he wants to do it in a personal and contextual way, then he has no choice about where he must go.

The native Algonquin people of the Arctic have a story about a woman and her baby who were left alone in a winter camp and had just one small fishhook with which to catch food. The mother could easily rig a fishing line, but she had no bait, nothing with which to catch the fish. What was she to do? She took a knife and cut a strip from her own thigh.[74] Davison has done the same thing: he has gone fishing with the worm of his own flesh.

Family history is so often forced to reconstruct from the outside in, from the bare recorded outlines of birth, marriage and death. Davison explained that 'little remains in writing of the Hewetts' own words. So I have had to reconstruct their story through the words of others, listen for clues to their thoughts in the voices of people like them, and try to put myself in the situations they faced.' He confessed it is a risky business, pushing the boundaries of what we can know or rightly guess, a risk the trained historian knows well. But with his own family the risk was greater, the intuitive leap so much more righteous and seductive. Davison deliberately put himself in this danger, and enjoyed making fun of his own moral sensibilities. Might his great-great-grandmother have been a prostitute, and if so, why might her distant descendant be disconcerted? Should he be relieved by his discovery that she was not? For a time Davison believed he had discovered that his great-great-grandfather was convicted in the colony for drunkenness, blasphemy, Sabbath-breaking and 'having his person exposed', and Graeme did not know 'whether to feel pleased or sorry' when he finally confirmed it was someone else. 'Why should this matter to me?' he wondered. It seemed that he would have to 'acknowledge the obstinate influence of heredity on my sense of identity'.[75]

He found himself unearthing carefully created silences. 'The Great-Aunt's Story' did not name the ship on which she came because the captain and surgeon of the *Culloden* were quickly engulfed in scandal in Port Phillip and thus it became a ship of shame. Most emigrants identified with the ship on which they arrived, but the Hewetts' story buried theirs. Graeme was also 'a little embarrassed' to find an ancestor who had a spell in Maitland Gaol, and then he wondered why the dread of bad blood should persist in contemporary culture.[76] A further moral problem was posed by another discovery: on Christmas Day 1882, his great-grandmother was unwittingly responsible for a fire that engulfed her sister's home in Williamstown and killed another sister. It was a horrific tragedy, never spoken of. Should that silence be violated, and what are the competing responsibilities of the historian and the family member – and why might they sometimes be at odds?

As the older Davison sought his family, he sometimes encountered his younger scholarly self, a step ahead of him but looking in a different direction. So he researched Henry Mayhew's sensational articles

on the London needlewomen of 1849 before he knew that he had an
ancestor amongst them. He became the historian of Marvellous
Melbourne before he knew that four of his great-grandparents arrived
there on the eve of the 1880s land boom. And what about those explo-
rations on foot in his early twenties in suburban Richmond, where he
felt he was peering across the gulf of class into a different world? Fifty
years later he found that it was in those same streets that his great-
great-great-grandmother Jane Hewett had lived, together with her
daughter Jane, the great-aunt whose story of arrival begins *Lost Relations*.
Graeme, loitering with his canvas bag, had been photographing humble cottages in Lennox Street just like Jane's. It was here that his
founding colonial relations had lived from the end of the 1850s, the
decade that began with their arrival in Port Phillip on a ship on the
brink of mutiny, the threat of which compelled the passengers to clam-
ber down the ship's ladder without their baggage in the dark and to be
rowed ashore, where they huddled together on the beach for warmth,
waiting till dawn before commencing their long and well-remembered
walk to Swanston Street and their new life. By 1859 the mother of the
family was living in Lennox Street and was therefore one of the 'old
inhabitants of the Colony' reported that year by the *Richmond Guardian*
to be living in the neighbourhood. Graeme's research had unexpectedly come full circle. For years he had led urban heritage walks past
the site of his ancestral colonial home. What kind of intuitive inheritance – what uncanny kind of 'calling' – is at work here?

With his long interest in how the past is in the present, Graeme
was always going to find himself examining its most personal and intimate legacies. His upbringing in the self-improving world of Methodism
perhaps also inclined him towards an interrogation of the balance in
our souls between nature and nurture. In his quest to understand how
things 'pass mysteriously from generation to generation', Davison does
finally concede some power to blood and physical inheritance, but he

also traces influences that have more to do with culture, pattern and tradition, and with talents, values and foibles. Like Tolstoy, Davison is interested in the 'common characteristics that bind good families across generations'.

I felt so deeply and personally drawn into this moving saga of another family that I often woke at 3 a.m. after reading *Lost Relations*. It was not just that my own family also looks back to bold and mysterious acts of emigration from Britain, to voyages by sea during which lives were reinvented, to the pitching of a tent on a central Victorian goldfield in the 1850s, and to family pilgrimages back to the 'pummelled' landscapes of alluvial mining. It was also that Davison offers a haunting and complex portrait of fate. Perhaps in the early hours I could consider the lives and fates of these people in a dream-like state, for that is another level of comprehension and empathy.

Fate – which we might define as the unpredictable chemistry of nature and nurture, of necessity and freedom – generally eludes our analysis, but perhaps its workings can be glimpsed if we take an intimate and historical view of generations. Graeme is able to illuminate the lives of his ancestors so well because of his own scholarly work and that of his students and colleagues: it was his school of history that pioneered Australian understandings of the city, charted social and geographical mobility in the colonies, investigated the lives of outcasts and drifters, the emigrant's gamble, the hopes of the gold generation and their children, the drift from the bush to the city, the rise of the suburb, and revolutions in time, energy and material life. These forces and flows move through the family history and we see individuals caught up in them and sometimes exerting their will upon them. When Graeme uses the word 'fortunes' in the subtitle of *Lost Relations*, he is drawing on a gold-rush term to invoke life's game of chance and circumstance. These people, *his* people, made decisions, and they were fateful ones. And only the passing of time – across generations – enables us to see how. Fate and fortune are not the same as luck. They allow us some agency in the vortex of history, even if it is not always conscious. They provide the basis for moral storytelling, itself a way of finding agency in a seemingly chaotic world. There are consequences to individual action that can play out across centuries, and social responsibilities and physical legacies that echo down the years. We begin to understand that the ancestral past lurks within us.

TWELVE

History and Fiction: Inga Clendinnen

In 2007 I gave a first-year English lecture at the Australian National University on Peter Carey's novel *True History of the Kelly Gang* (2000). Near the end of the lecture, a big man in a Kelly helmet burst into the lecture theatre brandishing a gun and shouting, 'I'm not fiction!' He grabbed me by the scruff of the neck and dragged me out, my arms flailing and my papers scattering from the lectern.

I was almost as stunned as the students, but not quite. 'Ned Kelly' was my good friend and fellow scholar Darrell Lewis, who I had happened to bump into on campus that morning.[1] Darrell, a great admirer of Ned's, possessed a full replica of the armour and occasionally wore it at ceremonial events with impressive effect – although people had begun to notice that he and Ned were never in the same room at the same time. Anyway, that morning I had mentioned to Darrell that I would be giving this lecture and wouldn't it be fun if Ned interrupted it? He said that unfortunately he had another commitment, so when a man burst into the back of the theatre, shouting, I was surprised. That, and the fact that Darrell roughed me up as he dragged me out, *and* that he really does dislike Carey's fictionalisation of his hero, made it a pretty convincing intervention. The realistic wooden gun must have got very close to causing a security lockdown, though.

I was invited to present the lecture to give historical context to the setting of the novel. The last thing I wanted to do for students of literature was to commentate on the way the novel departs from known facts. Of course it does. I was much more interested in the independent power of the fiction, the game that Carey was playing with 'truth', and the role of history in stimulating the author's imagination. I was interested in the responsibilities a novelist takes on when they portray a real historical person or event and reimagine them freely. Historian Inga Clendinnen argued in *The History Question* (2006) that novelists don't have a moral contract with the past in the way that historians do. But she also recalled Peter Carey winning her heart at the Brisbane Writers' Festival when he responded to relentless historical questioning about his novel by sinking in his chair and saying, 'I made it up.'[2]

But the thing is, he didn't. Peter Carey carried Ned Kelly's Jerilderie Letter around for years, fascinated by its intensity, and his book is not only a reworking of a real historical person, it is also a conscious extrapolation of a real historical document. The stakes are high. I think Carey, because he trades in the power of a well-known past, invited and expected commentary on historical grounds as well as on literary ones. He expected us to evaluate the authenticity of the voice and his ability to get inside the famous helmet. He was playing with a past that he knows we know – indeed, our independent knowledge of the 'true' history provides the grounds for his game. I don't think he could have written that novel until Ian Jones had written his biography of Ned Kelly, and equally, we cannot now write the history of the Kelly Outbreak without learning from the extraordinary ventriloquism of the novel.[3] This is the intriguing dance between history and fiction.

Historians and novelists do not constitute inviolable, impermeable categories of writers. Historians write fiction and novelists write history: Judith Wright, Thomas Keneally, Drusilla Modjeska, Roger McDonald, Helen Garner, Barry Hill, Tony Birch, Shirley Hazzard,

David Malouf, Peter Cochrane, Anna Funder, Ross Gibson, Delia Falconer, Peter Stanley, Alexis Wright and Richard Flanagan, just to name a handful. Novelists adopt the devices of non-fiction in their novels; historians tell stories with mystery, imagination and style. They are all creative artists who are conscious of something significant when they change genres and, thankfully, they often reflect upon it.

In 2005, following the publication of Kate Grenville's novel *The Secret River*, she and Inga Clendinnen had a passionate public conversation about the relations between history and fiction. It aroused some bitter feelings, especially in Grenville. Sadly, the debate (and the way it was reported in the media) concealed the sympathy and symbiosis that generally exists between history and fiction. I think we can make sense of the tensions that animated that debate by seeing how Grenville unwittingly stumbled into the middle of an issue that goes to the heart of the craft of history. For Inga Clendinnen, in particular, reflections on the differences between history and fiction had long shaped her understanding of the peculiar moral responsibility of historical scholarship and the limits of empathy in writing about the past.

History and fiction have often played complementary roles in shaping debates about dispossession and cross-cultural violence in Australia over the past century. From the 1930s, fiction led the way in imagining the other side of the Australian frontier. As we saw in Chapter 1, the novelist Eleanor Dark was well ahead of Australia's historians in realising that the big story about the British colonisation at Port Jackson was the encounter between settlers and Aborigines. By the 1970s historians were catching up with Dark's imaginative leap – Henry Reynolds, Lyndall Ryan, Raymond Evans, Peter Read and others were investigating the Aboriginal experience of British colonisation. And one of the first and best frontier histories to be written was by a poet, Judith Wright. In

Chapter 5 I explored how the political context of Wright's campaigning for Aboriginal land rights drew from her a different kind of writing: a scholarly history, *The Cry for the Dead* (1981). Henry Reynolds' *The Other Side of the Frontier* was published in the same year. Over the next twenty years, historians would transform our understanding of Australia's forgotten war.

By the late 1990s frontier conflict had become accepted in Australian historiography and a conservative backlash sought to discredit a generation of research. Critics initiated a fight over footnotes and tried to count the precise number of Aboriginal and settler dead on the frontier, as if it decided the ethics of the issue. As if such a count could ever be certain or definitive in any case; as if history was just about discrete gobbets of fact. It was the moral vacuum created by this critique that invited, indeed demanded, works such as Mark McKenna's *Looking for Blackfellas' Point* (2002), Inga Clendinnen's *Dancing with Strangers* (2003) and Kate Grenville's *The Secret River* (2005), all published in the early 2000s, and all stories that aimed to remind us of the intimacy and familiarity of the frontier, of its visceral, violent reality, and also of its alternative human possibilities. These three books, two of history, one of fiction, sought to enlarge our capacity for compassion, to win back ground for tolerance and understanding.[4]

Grenville's commentary on her novel addressed this context directly. 'The voice of debate might stimulate the brain,' she declared in 2005, 'the dry voice of "facts" might make us comfortable, even relaxed. It takes the voice of fiction to get the feet walking in a new direction.'[5] I think that Grenville's phrase 'the dry voice of "facts"' referred not to history generally but quite specifically to the aridity of the 'counting the dead' debate, and her words 'comfortable, even relaxed' gestured to Prime Minister John Howard's refrain about how he hoped Australians would feel about their past. And it's likely that Grenville's hope that fiction might 'get the feet walking in a new direction' alluded to the Walk for Reconciliation across Sydney Harbour Bridge in 2000, when she locked gazes with an Aboriginal woman and suddenly had to know how implicated her own ancestor was in frontier bloodshed. Her hunger for a new direction in the adversarial political debate was widely shared – and the solution she offered was 'the oblique voice of fiction'.[6]

The Secret River drew inspiration from the life of Grenville's great-great-great-grandfather, Solomon Wiseman, a convict transported to New South Wales in 1806 who later settled on the Hawkesbury River. The novel culminates in a massacre of Aboriginal people in which William Thornhill (the character based on Wiseman) was an aggressor. In a later memoir about the writing of the novel called *Searching for the Secret River* (2008), Grenville explained how it began life as 'a non-fiction book', perhaps a 'biography' or 'a portrait of his times'. Her memoir tells of this journey, of 'looking for my own sliver of that history'.

Much of the first half of the memoir shares with the reader the excitement of trying to tell a true story – of wanting to know 'the real man', cherishing 'the actual phrases he used', and trying to constrain a novelist's inclination to make things up. Grenville wondered how to give her book 'richness and life without compromising [its] factual basis' and she struggled with 'telling the unvarnished story as truthfully as I could'. These are the delights and challenges of the historian: how to reveal things that her protagonists didn't know and 'the difficulty of establishing even the simplest fact'. Grenville reflected that 'Human beings were slipperier than the ones I was familiar with on the page: the creatures of fiction. This was the muddle of real life.'[7] When she discovered a portrait of her ancestor, she found it confronting: 'He was standing at a table, looking directly at me ... And the face – big, powerful, pronounced chin, tight-held mouth. The force of his will! He came right out of the picture, dominating, unyielding ... It was a spooky feeling to be looking him right in the face. Almost more real than I could handle. He frightened me.'[8]

Almost more real than I could handle. They are telling words, for Grenville then recounted how she gradually succumbed to the rising tide of fiction, at first fighting it determinedly, then yielding to it with relief. First, in the face of the inscrutability of the archive, she gratefully realised that 'I didn't have to approach the past in a forensic frame of mind. I could *experience* the past – as if it were happening here and now.' She began to relax the strictures of period and place: 'These things didn't happen to Wiseman, of course,' she writes, 'but they'd happened only ten years earlier and a few kilometres from where they *could* have happened to him.' And when drawing on a historical source from an entirely different period she reassured herself, 'Something told me that nothing had changed all that much.' She welcomed the flooding revelations of intuitive insight: 'Suddenly I was claustrophobic ... At this moment I was absolutely certain – as sure as if I'd seen it with my own eyes – that there'd been trouble here on this quiet bend of the river.' Her search for a specific history of her ancestor was gradually taken over by a larger story 'of what happened when white met black on the edge of settlement across the country'.[9]

For help, Grenville turned gratefully to historians. At this stage, she was still trying to write non-fiction: 'It was a tale that drew its power from the fact that it was real,' she explained; 'interposing a layer of invention would defeat my aim.' But here she encountered another problem, a fatal one. She found that her attempts to write non-fiction tended to be boring, the unvarnished story dull: 'I could either write a truthful book that would be so dull as to be unreadable, or I could write a made-up book that might be read but not believed.' Her memoir, then, is an account of a defeat. As she moved steadily away from real people in actual context, she remembered that intimidating image of her ancestor and imagined him watching her 'sardonically'. She silently apologised to him and decided not to meet his eye as she wrote him into fiction.[10]

This was also a story of an escape into freedom. Once she decided that she really could abandon non-fiction, Grenville confessed that 'I was feeling the relief of a kid who's been told the maths homework had been cancelled.' She stopped *analysing* and allowed herself 'to go back into the unconscious'.[11] She embraced the confidence of 'knowing' and discarded the uncertainty of not knowing. 'The historians' whose work she drew upon remained collective and anonymous; even their books were not distinct, but 'pile up' on her desk. Inspiring fiction writers were named, her publisher was named and allowed a personality, but 'the historians' were a strange breed of distant workers, busy, nameless and communal.

The memoir created an appealing drama around a difficult search for an elusive historical figure. But Solomon Wiseman was sufficiently well known to warrant a biographical entry in the second volume of the *Australian Dictionary of Biography*, which was published in 1967. So, when Grenville described her research in the Mitchell Library and learned with relief about the crime for which Solomon was transported (theft), she was celebrating a discovery that had been on the public record for over thirty years. When she visited London and sought his birth date, *that* too was already well known. When she found crucial facts in the Old Bailey Session Papers and exclaimed, 'If it was so easy to discover, why had no one tried before?', she overlooked those historians who had tried before, and with success. So the memoir centred on the author's experience of research and turned its back on public research by others – on published historical scholarship. This omission heightened the memoir's drama of a personal, unmediated relationship with the past and enabled Grenville to focus on the silences in her own family's story. But it curiously bypassed the insights of a whole genre of literature.

In an essay for the *Monthly* when the novel was released, Grenville explained that Australians growing up in the 1960s were told they 'had no real history: no kings and queens, no invasions, no wars. Except that we did, of course. We'd had an invasion and a war, one that lasted a hundred years or so.' She argued that the dry, bland words of historical documents had obscured these dramatic events. 'It all sounds perfectly reasonable, until you tear through the screen of words and see what's behind it. This is where fiction in Australia, can come in.'[12] She admired Thea Astley's novel *A Kindness Cup* (1974) – a 'cautionary fable' inspired by an 'actual incident', where settler violence to Aborigines was pictured vividly. Grenville described the way a novelist can enable us to get beyond the bland words and 'think of the pictures', imagining the 'violence eyeball to eyeball'. Grenville saw herself as contributing to the History Wars and was braced for 'the backlash' to her novel from people who would find its content confronting.[13] But the criticism was to come from an unexpected direction.

To Grenville's frustration, she found herself questioned about history and fiction rather than frontier violence. And to her surprise, she found herself criticised by the very historians she might have expected to share her political quest, especially the two (Clendinnen and McKenna) whose books had been shaped by the same public conversation.[14] She expressed dismay and a sense of betrayal. In an interview with Grenville in August 2011, Miriam Cosic described Grenville as 'blindsided' and quoted her saying:

> It was the year when Keith Windschuttle and the massacre denialists were in full throat, the people who said, 'Nothing happened, they all just died of measles, isn't it sad.' And when my book came out, I had all my answers for those people. I'd done a lot of research – Henry Reynolds is a mine of fantastic information about it. And then it [the criticism] didn't come from them. It came from people who, I would have thought, politically are on the same side.[15]

The media is inclined to present a discussion as a 'spat'. A potentially rich debate was easily reduced to a narrow, literal dispute about whether or not Grenville said that her novel was history. Criticism by historians of Grenville's remarks about her novel were soon simplified, even by some historians, as sorties in another kind of history war – a 'turf war'.[16] Misleading oppositions were generated between scholarship and imagination, truth and fiction, and history and feeling.

'History' turned out to be a rather mischievous and elusive word in the debate. I accept that Grenville never intended to claim her novel as a work of history, although I don't think that was ever the issue. And I don't agree with Clendinnen that novelists 'have been doing their best to bump historians off the track'.[17] However, I do believe that Grenville was legitimately embarked upon a historical quest, much as Eleanor Dark and Judith Wright were, and that she found herself drawn into public conversations about the past, history and sometimes even 'History' in ways that she encouraged and felt were an important dimension and contribution of her novel. And why shouldn't she? Grenville didn't shrug her shoulders like Peter Carey and say that she had made it up. 'I haven't made it up,' she explained, 'I just put a novelist's flesh on the bones of the documents.' She wanted to talk about the past, and about the influence of the past in the present, and she 'wanted the book to be based at every point on whatever historical veracity I could find'. 'I've taken the skeleton out of the cupboard,' Grenville declared. She 'felt very passionately that the book is probably as close as we are going to get to what it was actually like'.[18] Now *there* is an invitation to a historical debate.

Furthermore, as historian Sarah Pinto has observed, Grenville 'articulated what amounts to an historical methodology'[19], which is to gain access to the past through re-enactment, experience and empathy, and by 'going back into the unconscious'.[20] 'I didn't have to approach the past in a forensic frame of mind. I could *experience* the past – as if it were happening here and now,' wrote Grenville.[21] One of the unstintingly generous dimensions of Grenville's work is her commitment to

explaining what she does, whether in terms of telling stories or researching the past.[22] It is these explanations, verbal and written, that draw
comment from people who research and use the past in different ways.
Perhaps because her historical methodology is so personal and intuitive, commentaries on the method could feel like a personal attack.

'Fiction' as a genre was less scrutinised in this debate than was
'history'. Perhaps it was because Grenville's social realist style of fiction – with its earnest, psychologically transparent relationship to the
past – is rather close to the orientation of traditional history. But many
novelists don't work with history in such a direct and transparent way,
and they allow more room for the power of fiction itself to dramatise
silences and uncertainty, to transform and morph reality, and to resist
narrative closure.[23] Peter Carey's shrug was convincing for the very reason that the magic realism of his novels conjures a relationship to the
past that is playful and irreverent. In a rich and thoughtful contribution to the debate, novelist James Bradley felt that Clendinnen 'comes
close' to assuming that novelists who tackle historical subjects are drawn
to those subjects purely by a desire to recreate the past. He worried that
such a view fosters 'the notion of historical fiction as something closer
to fictional documentary than fiction in any sense' – and Bradley thus
concluded that it was fiction and not history whose cultural authority
might be in decline.[24]

A year before the controversy broke, historian Iain McCalman predicted it. 'One of the unexpected casualties of our current History Wars,'
he wrote in 2004, 'may be a forced cooling of relations between fiction
and history writing.'[25] McCalman penned those regretful words as the
author of a stylish, bestselling scholarly history that had been referred
to as a 'novel'. *The Seven Ordeals of Count Cagliostro* (2003) was no more
a novel than *The Secret River* was a history.[26] But it was clear that the
genres were eliding in exhilarating and dangerous ways. The 'linguistic
turn' in cultural studies in the 1970s and 1980s, argued McCalman, cast

doubt on the capacity of historians to find 'the bedrock of reality out-side the text'. Conservative empiricism launched the History Wars into this crisis of expertise.

An earlier controversy had prepared the ground for media expectations of 'warfare' between opposing camps of 'history' and 'fiction'. In 1995, Helen Demidenko's novel, *The Hand that Signed the Paper*, which won the *Australian*/Vogel Literary Award and the Miles Franklin Literary Award, raised serious and deeply felt concerns about its fictional treatment of the Ukrainian famine and the Holocaust. The public debate was intense, for the novel was quickly seen as history. This perception was fuelled by Demidenko's use of her novel, in speeches and media interviews, as a platform for historical commentary. On these occasions, she drew upon the gravity and authenticity of her own Ukrainian ancestry and family stories. It was later revealed that Helen Demidenko was actually Helen Darville, and her parents were British. The celebration of the literary stature of the book raised the issue of what responsibilities to historical truth are carried by an author of fiction who mobilises the power of such a dark, disturbing and recent past. Defenders of the book argued that it was illegitimate to subject a novel to historical criticism and that such critics were insensitive to fiction and its distinctive art. In response, Robert Manne in his book *The Culture of Forgetting*, analysed the way these accusations of 'political correctness' shaded into dismissals of 'historical correctness' and even cast doubt upon the accessibility of any reliable historical truth. Writing as someone for whom the Holocaust lay 'at the very heart of [his] being' and who had studied history in the hope of understanding it, Manne felt that the public celebration of the novel revealed a divorce in Australian culture between literary and human values.[27] The Demidenko affair thus moulded the terrain for later debates. Media expectations of the opposition of history and fiction were firmly established, and trenches were already dug into the landscape, ready to be occupied when the new war broke out.

Grenville had expected and wanted a debate with the conservative critics of frontier conflict. But the targets of conservatives at that time were historians, and the debate was about the precise, grounded, evidenced truths of history. In order to be a combatant on that ground, you needed time, place and specificity, just as Judith Wright had found in the battle over land rights in the 1970s. Grenville's 'oblique voice of fiction' offered a new direction precisely because it was *oblique*. It was not a work of logic and argument, and it was never going to attract the counting-the-dead conservative critique because it didn't deal in contextual, documented truth. By 'pillaging' the past, as she put it, and by moving incidents out of time and place, Grenville distilled a parable. 'This is a story about all settlers, and settler psyche, in all places, throughout the colonial period,' historian Grace Karskens said of Grenville's novel.[28] *The Secret River* was taken intravenously by its reading public and was, I think, a timely, powerful public intervention in exactly the way Grenville must have hoped.

But Grenville's method, which contrasted with that of Eleanor Dark's contextual historical fiction, left her outside the political debate, to her clear frustration. In her public commentaries, she seemed to want it both ways – to wield the oblique power of fiction *and* the cachet of a researched past. She wanted to join the game of history but to play by different rules. It's not surprising or unreasonable, then, that historians would voice opinions about her historical methodology, as set out in her interviews and memoir, especially at a moment in public culture when they constantly had to defend their craft and explain the sources and methods of good history.[29] Thus Grenville unwittingly found herself in the middle of a debate that goes to the heart of the discipline of history, that matters very much in public affairs, and that is fundamentally not about her.

Inga Clendinnen had been practising her critique of Grenville's style of emotional empathy for at least a quarter of a century before *The Secret River* was published. Writing in praise of English historian E P Thompson in *Historical Studies* in 1979, Clendinnen warned against the 'attempt to simulate the complexity of reality by projecting one's own common-sense interpretations to lend flesh to the skeletal record, in the eerie conviction that the people of the past are simply ourselves tricked out in fancy dress'.[30] It was a metaphor that Greg Dening also often used: 'The most unhistorical thing we can do is to imagine that the past is us in funny clothes,' he wrote.[31] The unreflective flow of empathy can inhibit understanding. American historian and educationist Sam Wineburg, in his aptly titled *Historical Thinking and Other Unnatural Acts*, found that historical thinking goes against the grain of how we ordinarily think. He warned against 'the seduction of coming to know people in the past by relying on the dimensions of our "lived experience"'. Like Clendinnen and Dening, Wineburg argued that the discipline of history is required to help us discover what we cannot instinctively feel or see.[32]

In her final year at school in Geelong, Inga had been captivated by Max Crawford's book *The Renaissance and Other Essays*. She wryly remembered its 'vision of the past having once really been alive' as 'a well-kept secret in the writings of most historians'.[33] At Melbourne University she discovered the astonishing existence of the man himself, lecturing to her 'in the delicate, elegant flesh'. She reflected later that when she first joined Crawford's School of History as a tutor, her chosen field of study was 'the men and women of the History Department', for she 'was a girl from the provinces, and they were my Paris'.[34] Then in the late 1960s she was propelled into another exciting milieu when she became one of the daring appointments of the founding professor of history at the new La Trobe University, Allan Martin. At La Trobe, where she taught Spanish-American history, Clendinnen fell into the circle of ethnographic historians that included Dening, Rhys Isaac and Donna Merwick.

The distinctive approach of this Melbourne Group centred on the determination to get inside episodes of past experience by attending especially to recorded action, by stripping back the overlay of interpretation to recover and reconstruct the raw theatre of past behaviour, and by using systematic intellectual procedures to work against the assumptions of empathy and intuition. Dening wrote of how the eyes of the past 'sometimes see things they did not expect to see. I think we can sometimes see through them to something else.'[35] Clendinnen's analysis of the spearing of Governor Phillip in *Dancing with Strangers* is a classic example of this method of 'double vision'. As a member of that Group, Clendinnen had long thought about the intellectual discipline required to cross 'the gulf between sources and past reality'.[36] To underestimate or deny that gulf, to be innocent about it, to be anything but humble in the face of what we have lost of the complex past, was to be vulnerable to error.

Clendinnen reflected that she was herself 'cured of residual faith in the utility of empathy' by her sustained study of Aztecs and their confronting culture of human sacrifice. The killing performances that distinguished the Aztec empire in the early sixteenth century took place at central blood-stained shrines in the elegant city of Tenochtitlan, where hundreds of people were publicly killed every year as sacrificial victims to the Sun God. These captives from imperial wars were ritually prepared for death, led to the high shrine and then forced back over the killing stone, where a priest drove a flint blade into their chests and ripped out the still-pulsing heart, raising it to the sun. Writing in 1991 in *Aztecs: An Interpretation*, Clendinnen found her curiosity sickened at 'the terrible matter-of-factness', the bureaucratic calculation of these brutalities, 'the combination of violence with apparent impersonality', and she felt haunted by those other victims who, in her own century, had filed to their deaths.[37]

She found that, if she were to penetrate the Aztec world of the imagination, she had to keep her own imagination 'on a very short

leash'. In 1995, she was propelled by the Demidenko affair – and especially Robert Manne's *The Culture of Forgetting* – into a study of the
literature of the Holocaust.[38] The resulting book, *Reading the Holocaust*
(1998), was an effort to overcome her bewilderment about such horror.
'I felt guilt about my bafflement because I suspected its origins: that it
arose because my reading of the Holocaust had been no more than
dutiful; that I had refused full imaginative engagement.'

What is the nature of the full historical imagination she envisaged?
In what was a sustained meditation on the historical method, Clendinnen analysed not only the Holocaust but also her bafflement. She
was 'invaded by a paralysis, a chilled inertia in the face of what seemed
an impenetrable monotony of suffering, an impenetrable monotony
of cruelties'. She 'could not frame the kinds of questions that would
let me make the human connections – connections with both perpe-
trators and victims – which lie at the root of all purposeful inquiry'.
She had felt this paralysis before, in her study of the Aztecs, but she
found that the horror roused by the Holocaust 'was more intimate,
more inchoate, and more comprehensively disabling'.[39] To make sense
of this, she introduces the legend of the Gorgon.

A Gorgon was a terrible creature of ancient Greek mythology whose
glance turned everything to stone. Perseus was able to slay the Gorgon
Medusa by holding her reflection in his polished shield and cutting off
her head. Clendinnen uses this legend as a metaphor for the Holocaust
and the difficulty of looking full in the face of its horror. For many
scholars, she explains, the Holocaust remains a unique event in world
history and one that is 'morally and intellectually baffling', 'unthinkable'.[40] Clendinnen's aim is to 'dispel "the Gorgon effect" – the sickening
of imagination and curiosity and the draining of the will which afflicts
so many of us when we try to look squarely at the persons and processes
implicated in the Holocaust'. She believes that 'If we are to see the
Gorgon sufficiently steadily to destroy it, we cannot afford to be blinded

by reverence or abashed into silence or deflected into a search for reas-
suring myths.'[41] So the question she poses is this: what kind of steady,
systematic scrutiny, what kind of moral intelligence, might enable us
to hold this terrible thing in our contemplation? Her answer is the craft
of history.

She believes that the Holocaust 'is potentially understandable' and
that it is imperative that we make this intellectual effort, for 'perplexity
is an indulgence we cannot afford'. She rejects the conclusions of many
scholars that the Nazis occupy an unknowable realm of evil and that
Nazi leaders such as Hitler, Eichmann, Speer, Stangl and Hoess can be
simply categorised as 'monsters', as 'inhuman' and therefore beyond the
reach of our understanding. That is to be petrified by the gaze of the
Gorgon. She will not be daunted by 'a sense of trespass' into the sacred
territory of survivor testimony. And nor will she accept that the Holocaust
was unique, because it would then 'risk falling out of history'.
Understanding a Nazi, she insists, 'is not qualitatively different from the
problems of understanding any other human being'. She insists that the
members of the Hamburg Reserve Police Battalion 101, who perpetrated
massacres in Poland and Russia, were 'ordinary men'. 'If these men were
ordinary after all, that recognition does nothing to diminish the horror
of their actions. It increases it.'[42] To understand is not to justify or to
excuse. It is not about refusing to judge.

How, then, does the craft of history help us to understand the other,
even of such an alien kind? Here Clendinnen explores a 'major mystery'. The quest for understanding must begin with sympathy, with 'the
recognition of a shareable human condition' – but the test must not be
whether or not we can identify with our subject. Clendinnen is ada-
mant about the limits of identification: 'In my view understanding does
not require anything so heroic as "identification", which is at best a
slapdash procedure and too often a misleading one. Extrapolations from
our own experiences and their associated emotions will not take us far

in comprehending people of different cultures, or even of different generations and genders within our own culture.' Recognising 'likeness' in others can be constraining – it can paralyse rather than liberate the imagination. Particularly misleading can be intuitive flashes of empathy, 'because they are untestable and may simply be wrong'.[43]

Instead, historians have to work in another way. Clendinnen exalts the high moral task of history but describes its methods as laborious and unglamorous, always working close to the ground with 'muddy actuality'. The historian, she argues, uses the kind of techniques we use every day for the evaluation of gossip: 'the piecing together of contexts, the establishing of sequences of actions, the inferring of the likely intentions behind those actions from our knowledge of the individuals involved and our general stock of knowledge about human motivations'. What distinguishes 'the scrupulous retrievals and analyses of "good history"' from 'the lightning flash of intuition' is that they are 'at all points open to scrutiny, criticism and correction'.[44] One of her tools of historical analysis is 'thick description', an approach championed by the American anthropologist Clifford Geertz, whose interpretation of human behaviour as symbolic action appealed to social historians in the 1970s. Geertz's anthropology argued that meaning was not locked away inside people's heads but was embodied in publicly available symbols (words, actions, images). Thus anthropologists (and historians) did not require the miracle of empathy but, rather, the rigorous, interpretive, ethnographic analysis of those systems of symbols – or 'thick description'.[45] One of the chief virtues of this approach, in Clendinnen's view, is that it 'reduces the role of untestable "intuition" by making the business of interpreting actions a public affair; it inhibits the casual offloading of our own expectations onto unlike others'.[46]

So this is the 'major mystery' of understanding as she defines it: we may begin with sympathy but we have to employ an armoury of techniques that work against the grain of empathy and intuition. And especially so if we are trying to understand Nazi leaders, 'men who typically concealed their subjectivities from others and often from themselves' – in such circumstances 'only the patient burrowings, the slow-motion assessments and retrievals, and the fastidious rule-bound interpretations of the historian will serve'.[47]

This kind of discipline is important because we need to prevent the Holocaust, or any past, from being forgotten, trivialised or deformed. 'Historians take the large liberty of speaking for the dead, but we take this liberty under the rule of the discipline, and the rule is strict,' declares Clendinnen. It is a heavy and solemn burden. It means that the quest to understand past action is public, contestable and communal. For Inga, 'the relentless critique of sources' is 'the central organising narrative for all serious historians'. The artistic opportunity for historians is to deploy the reader's critical imagination alongside theirs in the interrogation of evidence. She argues that this is what we find in 'good historical writing today: writing whereby the reader is brought into a constructed, controlled, directed engagement with the texts, and is invited to join the writer's search for their meanings.' We each have our favourites, she says. Hers at that time were Peter Brown, E P Thompson, Robert Darnton and Greg Dening.[48]

In the early 1990s Clendinnen was hijacked by serious illness and, in her hospital bed, she found herself turning to fiction. 'Through giving me access to the inner thoughts and secret actions of closed others, fiction has taught me most of what I know, or think I know, about life,' she confessed in *Reading the Holocaust*.[49] She had long been an avid reader of novels: Joseph Conrad's *Heart of Darkness* drew her back again and again.[50] Trapped in a noisy shared hospital ward and metal bed with a rubber sheet, waiting for a liver transplant, she wrote to escape: 'Now for the first time I felt the desire to write fiction. I wanted to feel I could change this inexorable place, these lonely shapeless deaths, even in imagination: fiction as defiance of exigency.'[51] Clendinnen 'discovered that fiction can make its own claims to truth ... Fiction began to offer a balm for the obstinate opacities, the jagged inadequacies of memory.'[52] After the transplant operation, she experienced hallucinations, which were 'like ancient flints' deep inside her that had worked their way to the light. 'I was beginning to suspect, after my drug-induced thrashings and wallowings, that we are fictions too.'[53] Her research was circling back in haunting ways: 'Everyone commented on the irony of me specialising in Aztecs taking living organs out and then me getting a living organ installed.'[54] She wrote more stories. Her memoir of this period of her life, *Tiger's Eye*, can be seen to share something with Grenville's memoir, *Searching for the Secret River*, in that they both wrestle in a personal way with the relationship between history and fiction.

In 1999 Inga Clendinnen gave the ABC Boyer Lectures and turned finally to her own country's past, a subject she had avoided for over thirty years (thus following a similar trajectory as Robert Manne, whose reading also moved from the Holocaust to Aboriginal Australia at about the same time). The lectures, entitled *True Stories*, were stimulated in part by John Howard's 'partisan opportunism' in the uses of history and his denunciation of 'black armband' historians. Clendinnen offered a close analysis of 'a cornucopia of true stories' of European and Aboriginal encounters and argued that the study of history can encourage civic virtue and provide 'useable truths'. But she also rejected the idea that history's true purpose is patriotic or integrative. Historians, she believed, have a greater responsibility to the past than they do to the present or future.[55]

Her next book revealed her willingness to travel (with scholarly discipline) into a past moment for a present purpose. *Dancing with Strangers* (2003) was a study of the first years of British settlement at Port Jackson and portrayed a 'springtime of trust' at the beginning of Australia's history of race relations. Once again we are taken to that iconic moment of encounter on Australia's eastern shore in the late eighteenth century. It is a rereading of anthropologist W E H Stanner's 1963 interpretation of those first years, where he believed that 'the history of indifference' between colonists and Aborigines began.[56] Clendinnen, by contrast, elaborates those early interactions with the positive metaphor of 'dancing', which evokes intimacy, sympathy and engagement as well as strangeness. Her book can be seen as an intervention in the History Wars because it brought a focus on hope, innocence and idealism at first contact, thus offering a historical source of reconciliation. She was writing in the years when Prime Minister Howard led a retreat from what Clendinnen described as 'the innocent enthusiasm for Aboriginal rights' that characterised the 1990s. In 2004, for example, she protested against federal government attacks on the Aboriginal and Torres Strait Islander Legal Services for endangering 'a delicate, promising, essential enterprise in trans-cultural understanding and, in the process, any developing hope that white law might be able to deliver useful justice to Aboriginal Australians'.[57] In making that argument she invoked the first years of cultural encounter at Sydney Cove.

Three days after the arrival of the First Fleet at Port Jackson, Lieutenant Bradley described an encounter with Aborigines where 'these people mixed with ours and all hands danced together'.[58] Clendinnen describes Bradley's watercolour painting of the event as whites and blacks 'dancing hand in hand like children at a picnic'.[59] But it was never quite that innocent. Grace Karskens has drawn our attention to the 'red coats' – the British soldiers – who were nearby, watching, as indeed were the Aboriginal warriors.[60] Literary scholar Deirdre Coleman accused Clendinnen of 'incurable romanticism', of using an outmoded and reactionary sensibility of the Enlightenment – that of chivalry – 'to gloss the wrongs of colonisation'.[61] Rachel Fensham, a dance scholar and a student of Dening's, offered a cross-cultural ethnography of dance in which she contrasted the constricted jig of the sailor's hornpipe, a regimen of

British naval training, with the dynamic, amplifying gestures and collective authority of Aboriginal dancing. Clendinnen's confidence that the British initiated the dancing was thus challenged by a postcolonial reading that admitted 'two kinds of sovereignty'.[62] I can imagine Inga delighting in these critiques, with their close cultural readings of art, action and ritual.

In *Dancing with Strangers*, Eleanor Dark's Bennilong reappears on the shoreline as a rather different Baneelon. As a professional historian, Clendinnen confessed that she knew the history of Australia 'as I know Chekhov's or Tolstoy's or Nabokov's Russia: from novels'.[63] *The Timeless Land*, she told me, was not one of those admired novels, but she shares Dark's timeframe (as did Stanner), and when Clendinnen called the Aborigines who encountered the British at Port Jackson 'the Australians', she made an imaginative leap not unlike Eleanor Dark's. The term had also been used of Aboriginal people by Marjorie Barnard and Flora Eldershaw in *Phillip of Australia* (1938). When Clendinnen first heard of Grenville's novel about the early colony, she welcomed it as a 'sympathetic reconstruction' and said she 'would like to think it will extinguish the history wars, to a degree'.[64] As she wrote in *Tiger's Eye*, 'Only fiction can redress the existential ambiguities which stalk the real world.'[65] But she also observed: 'Fiction also affords the pleasure of the effortless penetration of fellow humans who are in the real world chronically enigmatic.'[66]

In 2009 historian Grace Karskens revisited Sydney's foundation in her wonderful book *The Colony*, which analyses a whole generation of encounter and settlement. In Karskens' history, the British are the Berriwalgal, and Aboriginal people are shown to successfully make an enduring place for themselves in Sydney from its beginning. Karskens explained that she wanted 'to continue Clendinnen's and Grenville's project of re-examining and rethinking early colonial race relations'. Thus Karskens included the novelist in her historiography. The story of settlers pushing into new country up the isolated reaches of the Hawkesbury River had long fascinated local historians and novelists, as Karskens explained: '[Eleanor] Dark's protagonist Andrew Prentice recovers his humanity on the river; Grenville's William Thornhill discovers the depths of his inhumanity.'[67]

Like Grenville and Clendinnen, Karskens aims to look unflinchingly at the violence of the past. But whereas Grenville's goal in *The Secret River* is primarily to dramatise the violence – so that the reader may experience it – the burden of the historian is to try to explain it in broader social terms. 'How do we explain such brutality?' asks Karskens. 'Is it possible to explain it? Is there any logical explanation, any way of grasping it, making it part of the "known"? Or are sickening acts like this somehow beyond the pale, hanging repellent, unexplainable, in a separate dimension to history?' She argues, with Clendinnen, that it is possible to 'stare the Medusa down' by *historicising* the murders of the frontier, 'not in order to justify or excuse them, but to understand how such a thing could have happened'. In doing so, atrocities might be recognised as more than acts of personal evil, as symptoms of social and cultural history.[68]

So Karskens reveals that 'the "secret river" had in fact been long familiar'. The specificity and particularity of the Hawkesbury and of the war on the Cumberland Plain – time, place and chronology – matter very much in Karskens' search for understanding: 'One story will not do for all.' And as with Judith Wright's historical reconstruction of the Wadja, the silences become part of the narrative of *The Colony*: 'When the details get sketchy, when I am spinning thin threads of interpretation between scanty sources, I will tell you.'[69] As a historian, Karskens is dedicated to that quest to retrieve the unique particularity of past experience and to 'recreate as fully as possible the past's own present', to see it as a time, like our own, when choices existed and the future was not determined.[70] This is not just in order to understand the real complexity of the past, but also because such specificity gives us a purchase on the future. As Rhys Isaac put it:

> History is the most particularizing of the social sciences; it must stand tall to remind the others of the power of contingency in human life ... [historians] have a responsibility ... to proclaim the deep truth that the world is what it is because of the particular sequences of what has been done. This is not just a ... scholars' debate; it is an affirmation of the possibilities of changing the disposition of things ... The shape of the world to come remains to be made by human action in circumstances that can never be foretold.[71]

Ross Gibson is another historian who has recently returned to that enigmatic period of cross-cultural conversation in eastern Australia in the late eighteenth century, in his book *26 Views of the Starburst World* (2012). In writing of Lieutenant William Dawes and his encounters with the Eora at Port Jackson, Gibson chose a literary form – non-fiction – 'that avoids the lures of fellow feeling'. He has also experimented with fiction as a stage for uncertainty and distance – as in his *The Summer Exercises* (2008) – but in *26 Views* he was searching for more space for speculation and inconclusiveness. 'So this book,' he wrote, 'is meant to help you knock your analytical thinking against your intuitive rumination.'[72] What he needed, as he sought the form of his writing, was 'a means for accommodating doubt, for understanding that mystery and the *inability to understand* are strong parts of what Dawes began to record in his notes.' Gibson honours two Dawes-inspired novels by Jane Rogers and Kate Grenville and the way they encourage the reader 'to empathise with distinctive characters', but for his purpose he needed 'a form that *works with* rather than *works away* the estrangement that the notebooks show not only between two cultures but also between the present and the past'.[73] His deliberately fragmentary and dispersed non-fiction rebels against the individualism and conclusiveness of the classically styled novel and strives for access to environmental or communal mentalities 'that reach beyond the bounds of single, sovereign subjects'. Gibson's project also involves a search for a form of writing that is 'at odds with the assertive and individualistic urges of colonialism'. He thus has political as well as literary reasons for wanting to free himself from the deterministic tendencies of the realist historical novel, whose emergence was coincident with colonialism and was so influential on the writing of history in the nineteenth century.[74] History and fiction are not easily teased apart, in life or art.

Barbara Kingsolver, novelist and essayist, wrote: 'I love fiction, strangely enough, for how true it is.'[75] Eric Rolls, poet and historian, reflected that 'Much of the game of writing history is keeping it true.'[76] Barry Lopez, writer of non-fiction and fiction, wrote that truth 'is something alive and unpronounceable. Story creates an atmosphere in which it becomes discernible as a pattern.'[77] Novelist Alex Miller, trained in history, wrote that 'History and fiction may seem to be sibling rivals for the truth sometimes, but they are essentially complementary in their civilising project.'[78] James Bradley also sees them as 'not opposed, but complementary, one a mapping of the real, of what was, the other a mapping of the subconscious, of the way we understand the real, and of the way we understand ourselves'.[79]

British novelist Pat Barker, who has fictionalised real, historical individuals, argued (like Grenville) that fiction allowed her to 'slow down' the experience of horror so that she and her readers could think about it as it happened.[80] In *Dancing with Strangers*, Clendinnen also 'does some things in slow motion' and the technique can be seen at work in her analysis of the spearing of the governor.[81] Historian Tiffany Shellam, in her ethnographic history of King George's Sound, *Shaking Hands on the Fringe* (2009), also slows down the cultural encounters she describes so that we can perceive coincident action on the edge of vision.[82] Kim Scott's award-winning novel *That Deadman Dance* (2010), explores the same history of encounter in the same place and is inspired by years of extensive documentary research and family storytelling. Scott, who is one of a community of Wirlomin Noongar people descended from coastal country to the east of Albany, appreciates Shellam as a fellow artist: 'I think she sounds most of all like a novelist when she writes: "more time on imagining people's motivations is a worthwhile activity; we see possibilities and choices rather than inevitabilities."' 'Oh yes,' declares Scott, 'that was my concern, researching a novel: not what was, but what might have been, and even what might yet be …'[83] Mary Anne Jebb, who reviewed the novel and the history together for *Aboriginal History*, explained how they 'emerge out of different writing traditions' and both 'slow down the frontier to imagine its smaller elements'. 'They explore the edges of historical imagination in a way that will help to keep Australian history alive.'[84]

Here we listen to historians and novelists wrestling with truth. They are, as Miller, Bradley and Jebb insist, on a common campaign, and they each influence the other much more than either will professionally say. Often they will guide and inspire each other further into their distinct enquiries; sometimes their purposes will collide; sometimes a writer will change genres for political or artistic purpose. Both require what Inga Clendinnen called 'full imaginative engagement' – but of quite different kinds. Novelists are free to 'pillage' the past, but it is the historian's civic and moral duty to insist on context.

There is much common ground between history and fiction. They are a tag team, sometimes taking turns, sometimes working in tandem, to deepen our understanding and extend our imagination. History doesn't own truth, and fiction doesn't own imagination, but sometimes the differences between history and fiction are very important indeed. And it is incumbent on historians – on those who choose at certain moments to write history – to insist and reflect on the distinction.

Sometimes those important explanations have been misinterpreted as defending territory.

Whereas Clendinnen sees a gulf between history and fiction, I see an intriguing dance around a shifting, essential line. The good historian, like the top tennis player, plays the edges and hits down that line. History's commitment to evidence that can be revisited, to a journey of discovery that can be retraced and challenged, increases the writer's artistic opportunities exponentially. Historians always have at least two stories to tell: what we think happened, and how we know what we think happened. So the 'non' in our 'non-fiction' signifies an edge that can sharpen our prose and heighten our sense of danger and wonder. It also acknowledges that there are things we don't and can't know. Silence, uncertainty and inconclusiveness become central to the narrative.

The art and science of history is in keeping it true – true not to some internal consistency of the created text, or true to a personal insight or feeling, or true to gathered facts, but rigorously, contextually, imaginatively and verifiably true to a reality beyond the text. The whole discipline of history and its community of scholarship strive to enable a kind of thinking that goes beyond and often against intuition, so that the strangeness of the past may, to some extent, be recovered.

The necessary and creative tension between history and fiction is not a turf war. The past is all we have. The present is but a breath, and the future doesn't exist except as a projection of the past. The past – the full sum of human experience – is all we have on which to base our hopes and plans, and from which to draw our conversations, ideas and stories. When asked, 'Do you draw your characters from life?', Eleanor Dark responded in exasperation, 'In Heaven's name, what else is there to draw them from?'[85] History and fiction journey together and separately into that past; they are sometimes uneasy partners, but they are also magnetically drawn to one another in the quest for deeper understanding.

THIRTEEN

The Feel of the Past: Grace Karskens

In 1992 the first issue of the Australian journal *Public History Review* was published in Sydney. At the time, I was practising and teaching public history in Melbourne and I snapped the journal up, delighted to see 'public history' – then still regarded askance by many academics – given its own space and voice. There were many good articles in that first issue, but the one that spoke most directly to me was by a Sydney public historian called Grace Karskens, entitled 'Public History – Academic History: The Common Ground'.[1] Ah, we needed that article! Public history had emerged strongly as a new field of professional practice and academic teaching in the 1980s, and here was a thoughtful reflection from the frontier. Grace's article was confident of the scholarly integrity of public history and of the equality and potential creativity of its relationship with academia. It was also honest about the peculiar pressures of doing public history and began with 'select excerpts from the diary of a public historian':

February 1985

My first job as a consulting historian. I research the history and architectural development of Admiralty House at Kirribilli for an archaeologist in about six days. A visit to the site reveals the ruins of the early twentieth century garden, the vistas to sea, the mass of fretting stonework.

March 1985

Clambered around an old stone bridge in overgrown paddocks at Cherrybrook. Is this part of the original Great North Road, built in 1830? Is it really the oldest extant bridge on the mainland? How will it survive when surrounded by new houses?

May 1985

Concord Heritage Study. I fill in one form for each of one thousand houses in Concord. They all start looking the same. As I walk the long footpaths all day, photographing, lace curtains twitch. One lady comes out to tell me I look so suspicious she was going to ring the police.

July 1986

The Public Works Department wants me to research and write about the Conservatorium of Music. I read through five million archive boxes and produce a short essay setting out the significance of the building through its role in the establishment of high versus low culture and the way this is expressed in its architectural design and details. The architects are unimpressed and the Government Architect remarks that my piece is 'a bit journalistic.' All they really wanted to know was the interior paint colour schemes and maybe a time-line.

December 1986

After six months of nothing, Holroyd Council suddenly wants action on its history project. The Town Clerk demands that I come in and sign the contract on Christmas Eve. It is hot. The traffic is unbelievable. I get lost. When I get there I have to make an impassioned speech about professional historians having to be paid regularly, not right at the end because they eat, have mortgages and pay tax like normal people. The Town Clerk mulls on this, then alters the contract and we sign. I do not yet know what I am in for.

June 1987

I have a fantasy of combining work, holiday and family. We all spend two days at Jenolan Caves while I research the buildings. The kids think the caves are boring. They like snakes and ladders and packets of chips in the bar much better. As I whiz past in the ranger's vehicle, I avert my gaze from Richard, standing forlornly in the freezing cold holding a little girl on each side.

August 1987

The Lands Department plans to establish walking tracks along surviving bits of Cox's Road, the first road over the Blue Mountains. I agree to do an historical and archaeological survey which involves field work from Emu Plains to Bathurst. I find I must be tactful and pleasant when trailing around after Cox's Road. Obsessed surveyors walk along obscure cow paths over paddocks in the middle of nowhere, claiming to be able to 'feel' the road. A mad rush to get the report finished on time ...

October 1989

The history and archaeology of George St North in Sydney's Rocks involves photographing gutters, outlets, roadway and drains. I look up at one stage to find myself surrounded by curious tourists. One asks in an American accent, 'What exactly are you doing?' I tell them.

February 1991

One of my interviewees has written on the bottom of her release form, 'My Auntie and I enjoyed what you wrote.' I count this amongst the most pleasing comments I have ever received.

March 1991

Holroyd: A Social History of Western Sydney is launched. O Happy Day.[2]

These excerpts establish a clear pattern: the public historian lives an exciting and stressful life of competing pressures, defending professional status yet also reaching adventurously beyond the discipline, feeling marginal yet curiously useful.

In Melbourne in the same decade I was working as a public historian, too. Selected excerpts from my diary read like this:

June 1982

My first job as a consulting historian. I am a postgraduate student and the only person to express interest in a two-month job as a 'Historian' advising the National Museum of Victoria and its neighbour, the Science Museum of Victoria, on their first joint exhibition as a new amalgamated institution, the Museum of Victoria. To be called 'The Story of Victoria', it will open in 1984 to mark the 150th anniversary of the foundation of the Port Phillip District of NSW. I convene a meeting of the two museum directors, who find working with one another (not to mention a historian) quite novel. I find getting paid to do history quite novel.

October 1983

I am employed as Field Officer for the State Library of Victoria. Best job ever! It is called the 'cup of tea' job because I visit people who are interested in donating old diaries, letters, pictures and photos to the library's Australiana research collections. I come to know every back road in Victoria, and quite a few attics and old barns too.

March 1985

I work with the Italian Historical Society of Victoria on a joint exhibition with the library about 'Victoria's Italians'. Their enthusiasm is infectious and inspiring and they are clearly moved to see their story embraced by the state library. Every morning I put a fresh bouquet of red and white carnations with green leaves at the exhibition entrance and watch as Italian grandparents visit the library for the first time and delightedly find themselves in the old photos on display.

September 1987

A man with crazy eyes is in my office telling me that the end of the world is nigh. He wants to give his old newspaper collection to the state library which he seems to believe will survive the apocalypse. I edge towards the door.

February 1989

I am appointed Historian in the Department of Conservation, Forests and Lands and my first task is to research the history of the forested mountain country east of Melbourne as part of a heritage survey for the Land Conservation Council. I have to learn fast and often on foot, and work in a team surveying hundreds of sites and relics, looking for old waterwheels and quartz batteries among the tree-ferns. Sometimes mysterious stonework lies beneath the leaf litter of the giant, beautiful mountain ash. My 18-month-old daughter proves to be particularly good at forest archaeology.

May 1989

Our survey team meets a bunch of miners in a pub in the mountain town of Jamieson and barely survives a rigorous examination on local history and conservation politics. These men know every unworked and abandoned gold seam in the ranges — and they *don't want no heritage orders.*

October 1989

Our heritage report is submitted, together with my environmental history of the forests. Cultural values become part of the case for a Yarra Ranges National Park. I give my boots a celebratory scrub — and avoid the Jamieson pub.

The American term 'public history' gained currency in Australia in the 1980s to describe the types of work that these diaries evoke. Grace Karskens' 1992 article argued that the public historian aimed to bring together the often separate worlds of academic and popular history — without compromising scholarly standards and without losing that wider audience. 'As the go-betweens,' she observed, 'public historians are hit with all the misconceptions, prejudices, ignorance, in short the dysfunction arising from the longstanding separation of scholarly history from the community.'[3] But they are amply rewarded with new skills, a direct engagement with the material past, and people who read and often enjoy their work.

How did this gulf arise? In Australia after the Second World War, there was a dramatic expansion of tertiary education and the number of academic historians grew in three decades from less than twenty to over 500.[4] By the end of the 1950s, according to John La Nauze, who was then professor of history at the University of Melbourne, Australian history had been redeemed by the universities. And he had no doubt who it had been rescued from: the local amateurs and enthusiasts, the 'antiquarians', as he called them, who 'still pursue their hobby, at once so interesting and so harmless'.[5] History had become truly professional and academic by developing a science of the document, and Australian academic historians looked to the university cultures of Britain and Europe (and later America) as the source of their discipline, rather than to their own backyard. Newly appointed professors traced their intellectual lineage back to Oxford and Cambridge and thereby to the influential German school of history.[6] For La Nauze and many other academic historians in those years after the war, becoming professional meant becoming international, institutional, urban, exclusive, detached and scientific. Above all, it meant recognising university standards and style, and distancing oneself, often disdainfully, from the kinds of history practised outside the academy.

'Public history' moved into that yawning gap, and even its name seemed to suggest that history originated in the universities and was only later made public.[7] By the 1970s, the period of university expansion was over and gradually there appeared to be more jobs for trained historians outside the academy than in it. But it was the intellectual and practical challenges of public history that excited and drew many of us – there was fieldwork, teamwork and often greater support for writing than could be found in academia, where research was often seen to compete with teaching. In championing the new field, Karskens appreciated the 'variety, diversity and flexibility' of the work, although she confessed that she had 'perhaps played down the long hours spent at the desk'. The public historian had the prospect of reaching new audiences and influencing policy, of shaping landscapes, archives and collections. And for anyone interested in the philosophy and practice of history, it was exhilarating. You were always marginal, always required to explain your craft. As Karskens put it, you were a 'conduit' for popular history and scholarly history to enter into dialogue. The foundations of your expertise could never be taken for granted: 'History has to be constantly asserted, defended and defined.'[8]

But the really distinctive quality of much public history, Karskens argued, lay in its attachment to real places. 'Public historians', she wrote, 'often find themselves looking at sites, areas or subjects which are off-beat, distant, or so ubiquitous that they have been ignored' – and, as a result, one is forced to challenge neat theories or 'to explain what at first may seem inexplicable, meaningless'. For Grace Karskens (as for Graeme Davison), pounding the pavements of the city (and filling out those forms on a thousand houses in Concord, where she almost drew the attention of police, as Graeme had done in Richmond), made her think more deeply about suburbia and why historians had so often dismissed or disdained it.[9] In her commissioned history of the municipality of Holroyd, a tract of western Sydney suburbs, 'the history of ordinary people in their little houses' became her subject.[10]

In her 'diary of a public historian' Grace wrote that she hardly knew what she had taken on with the Holroyd history – and surely the municipal council hardly knew what they had taken on either. They had employed a tenacious and original researcher who was determined to make their municipality the site of an illuminating history of

Australian settlement, one that would truly meet its goal to 'tell the richly varied stories of everyday life'.[11] Grace had grown up in a brand-new brick-veneer house in neighbouring Baulkham Hills in the 1960s, the daughter of Dutch migrants making a new life after the war, and she remembers playing alongside Toongabbie Creek, which was then a mysterious, meandering watercourse with an occasional great sandstone overhang and shady black-soil banks. Around the age of twelve, Grace read Eleanor Dark's *The Timeless Land*, and the power of its prose helped her to think about those overhangs and begin to imagine that they had been the living places of Aboriginal people.[12] She was 'fascinated by the idea that our little creek might run into a river and then to the sea, but had no idea that this was true', and her many day-long expeditions along its course revealed it just to wind on forever. She wanted to connect that creek, that suburban life, to something bigger.[13]

When taking on Holroyd, she decided that 'the more traditional style of local history' would not do, with its focus on great (and there-fore wealthy) men and its tale of inevitable progress. For historians and architects in thrall to the legacy of a few stately houses, 'the past' was the imagined charms of the gentry or the 'history of a well-ordered community' and rarely the story of ordinary folk or of experiences of poverty, disadvantage and discrimination. But Karskens wanted to know who lived in the timber or fibro cottages, the poultry farms and market gardens, what had brought them there and what sort of society they had made. Women naturally moved to the centre of her story. Many of the people she asked to interview were at first taken aback. 'Why do you want to talk to me?' they said. 'We don't know anything about his-tory ... we weren't important people.' But soon they found themselves in this new history of Holroyd. The book, launched on that 'Happy Day' in March 1991, was a warm and vital portrait of a changing com-munity, and it also made the case for a different kind of local history, one woven out of memories, languages, habits and outlooks, the lifetime experiences passed from generation to generation. Without attention to this 'intangible heritage', argued Karskens, history would 'remain the rather dry and inhospitable preserve of the "buffs"; or the unfamiliar other-world peopled by distant, prominent figures; or the simple projection of the present backwards over time; or the creation of a picturesque, respectable, peaceful past that never was'.[14]

At the end of a hot day in the summer of '79, Grace was driving through the 'forgotten valley' of the Macdonald River, a northern tributary of the Hawkesbury, when she got talking with two women swimming in the river. They told her of an old convict road high on the ridge, long abandoned, its massive stonework still visible in the bush. The romantic story of the old road sank deep and stayed with Grace. When she started an MA in historical archaeology at the University of Sydney (following completion of a history degree), she decided to investigate the road, known as the Great North Road, which was built by convict labour between 1826 and 1836. The road – 240 kilometres of it – had been constructed to connect Sydney with the Hunter Valley. For five years from 1980 to 1985, Grace went in search of its surviving features and found original retaining walls, wharves, culverts, bridges and buttresses both abandoned in the bush and around and under modern roads. Alongside her research in the documentary record, she studied the archaeological evidence in the bush, pursuing the remnants of the road down dale and up hill, where her old Volkswagen finally died amongst the rocky outcrops of Mount Manning.[15] Some of the features of the road are awesome: buttressed stone walls stand up to thirteen metres high, made of interlocking blocks of different sizes held together without mortar, and some of the formations, quarries and cuttings are massive. She had to master the details of road engineering and later to convince a posse of male engineers that she knew what she was talking about when it came to culverts and drains – so she gave a talk about the road's construction to the Institution of Engineers and wrote for their *Transactions*.[16]

Those stone structures, so grand and surprising in the bush today, are the most extensive and visible record of the work of the convict gangs, and encoded within them is information not just about the building of the road, but also about the working patterns and conditions of convicts in gangs, and thus about the nature of convict society itself in this gaol without walls. Convict road gangs were traditionally viewed as inefficient and ineffective ways to get work done, yet these towering stone walls in difficult terrain speak of skill and perseverance, even perhaps of pride. How did a bunch of twice- or thrice-convicted men – the 'refuse of the colony' – manage to construct some of the most ambitious and impressive engineering of the colonial period? Teaching a stone to talk is a metaphor for the impossible, yet Grace identified six broad patterns of surviving masonry and discerned the ways in which the size, shape and arrangement of the mute stones were actually surveyors' signatures and clues to the politics of forced labour, the lives of overseers, and the skills – or not – of the convict men themselves.[17]

There was another convict road (also mentioned in her diary of a public historian) that won Grace's attention in the 1980s. It was Cox's Road, celebrated as the first road over the Blue Mountains and symbolising the colony's release from the coastal plain into the golden pastures of the interior – and in 1987 it was Grace's job to record and analyse its surviving features as a bicentennial project.[18] With surveyors, she walked it from the Nepean River at Emu Plains to the cow paddocks approaching Bathurst, 'hunting for the lost road, rescuing the fragments out of time with photographs and maps and measurements, writing them together again'.[19] Beside the modern highway, she found old road surfaces smoothed from solid rock, some deeply scored by carriage wheels, corridors of trees that signalled the line of the old thoroughfare, and sockets cut into the stone where great logs were fitted to support the decking of timber ramps that spanned the gorges.

Because of its symbolic importance in the breaking of 'the barrier', Cox's Road has been weighted with history and myth: as heritage conservationist Siobhan Lavelle has shown, it was a tale that grew in the telling.[20] The legend of Blaxland, Wentworth and Lawson, who allegedly achieved the 'first crossing' of the Blue Mountains in 1813, gathered force with the years, even though they were not the first to do so. Eleanor Dark enjoyed making fun of this pretension in her provocatively titled novel *No Barrier* (1953), which showed Aboriginal people and escaped convicts moving freely across the blue plateau.[21] But 'the dauntless three' did open the way for the road, which was surveyed by George William Evans in 1813 and built under the direction of William Cox in 1814–15. It has often been feted as an engineering triumph, a highway forging into the west and opening the way for expansion and the colony's future. But Grace found that the archaeological evidence told otherwise: Cox's Road had none of the majesty of the Great North Road but was a simple track, made in haste and with crude techniques.

The road has also been commemorated as a heroic site of oppressed convict labour. In 2005, a Road Builders Memorial was unveiled at Katoomba that features convicts with their legs and arms shackled in irons, their faces contorted in agony as they heave great boulders, supervised by a grinning soldier swilling rum with two Aboriginal men watching in the background. But Grace's later research – when she returned to speak about the road at its bicentenary – revealed that the convicts working for Cox were not shackled in irons or flogged but were working for their freedom. Emancipation at the end of the job was part of their contract. They were generally older men on life sentences, probably already living independently as tradesmen, labourers or small farmers in the Hawkesbury/Nepean area, and they were chosen because they were (as Cox described them) accustomed to field labour and inured to 'the fatigue of hard work and sleeping on the ground'. Many of the men went on living in the district after the road was built, became well-known local identities and are buried in local cemeteries. Only two out of more than fifty men involved in the building of the road moved over the mountains. Many of those working on Cox's Road were already married or in de facto relationships and had children. Many more married after the road was completed, so Grace argues that, with its promise of emancipation, 'the road itself was a vector for marriage'! And she can't resist adding: 'Clearly Cox's men ... do not entirely fit Russel Ward's model of convicts as the forerunners of the white nomad tribes.'[22]

Symbolism distorted how the road has been remembered, and symbolism was there at its birth too. It was built to serve Governor Macquarie's need to demonstrate to his superiors in Britain that he was facilitating colonial progress and inland expansion. But, as New South Wales was still a penal colony, the road could not become a highway; it must remain deliberately difficult and primitive to hinder escape. From her Great North Road work, Grace was already familiar with what a feat of 'magnificent engineering' might look like in the early nineteenth century, and Cox's Road was not that. It was something different – still impressive, but for other reasons: as a road to freedom for the men working on it, who with their wives and partners looked forward to returning, liberated, to their own farms.

Karskens enjoys tilting at legends and undermining stereotypes with careful scholarship. But she also appreciates the power of *mythos* and believes historians are obliged to enliven and complicate myths, not so much to demolish them as to turn them over and explore their underside. So she asks of the mountain crossing legends: 'Can they be about rivers and pebbly fords, mysterious plateaux and the lore of cattle, the true drivers of expansion? Can Aboriginal people be explorers and travellers as well as people who were dispossessed? Can convicts be more than nameless, faceless, powerless slaves in chains? Can they be husbands and fathers, pathfinders, workers and settlers? Can lovers, wives, children and intimacy play key roles in the making of this colony?'[23]

Grace's report on Cox's Road, published in 1988, prompted 'some disquiet': a letter arrived from the Blue Mountains Historical Society protesting her account of Cox's convict workers because it failed to include chains and floggings.[24] Why has this view of the early colony as a brutal gaol been so persistent in the face of the evidence? Why have Australians appeared to need their shore to be fatal, and their convict ancestors to be victims? Grace was now on a road herself, to investigating and overturning that stubborn misconception.

By some miracle of time travel, we find ourselves in Sydney in the year 1800. The colony is barely a decade old but already there is a distinct neighbourhood of convict huts and houses clustered on a headland of sandstone outcrops just west of the cove where ships are anchored, known as The Rocks. That is where we, too, have been 'transported' and now we are peering in through the curtained glass window of a rubble stone house with plastered walls, shingle roof, chimney and hearth. As our eyes adjust to the interior light, we see a family – mother, father and children – sitting at a table sharing a meal. Their table is spread with a tablecloth and set with good-quality edged-ware, with a blue-rimmed, rather deep-welled dinner plate and a matching bread and butter plate for each person. There are also lidded tureens and large meat platters. The walls of the room are tinted pink and are hung with pictures and ceramic plaques inscribed with religious exhortations. We can also see trunks full of clothing and linen, baskets and bags of laundry, a canvas cot for a child, a chest of drawers, fabric pieces to be made up as dresses or petticoats; there are umbrellas and muskets, a kettle and tea caddy. We are regarding a convict household.[25]

This domestic scene of a convict or ex-convict family in their own home – using quality edged-ware and matching plates no less – comes as a shock to visitors from the twenty-first century who are so familiar with the images of tyranny and slavery that dominate films and books about Australia's convict beginnings. In the middle of The Rocks today, that stereotype is perpetuated by a sandstone sculpture of a representative convict who inevitably wears a leg-iron. Grace Karskens, who has transported us to this window in the convict home (and who even knows what's cooking in the kitchen), says that when she tells stories of early Sydney and The Rocks, the first question she is asked is, 'What about the convicts in the jails, the barracks, or the gangs?' That is, where are the real convicts? She reminds us that in early Sydney, there were no barracks for the first thirty-odd years and the only people in the gaol were those who had committed crimes since arriving in the colony. 'It was the household, not the gaol or the gang that was fundamental to both the society and economy of early Sydney.'[26]

The view we are given through the window in The Rocks *is* a kind of miracle, but it is magic worked by long, hard work with earth and paper. In 1986, the same year Karskens was reading through the 'five million archive boxes' about the Conservatorium of Music, she became a consultant for a historical study of a site in Cumberland and Gloucester Streets in the heart of The Rocks. As a teenager, she had made the pilgrimage 'into Town' from her home in western Sydney to visit the place that had been ardently defended against developers in the early '70s and then promoted as the 'birthplace of a nation'. In 1986, when one of the circles of life brought her back there, this time in a professional capacity, she was astonished to find that there was no comprehensive history of this famous place. An idea was thus lodged in her mind and, four years later, she began doctoral research on the early convict community on the headland. In 1997 it became a prize-winning book: *The Rocks: Life in Early Sydney*.[27]

It's a history in the active tense, an ethnographic portrait of people doing things, where the fragrance of baking bread mixes with the stench of offal, and the sounds of raucous street life intrude upon quiet moments of domestic intimacy. The study employed the historical-demographic methods of the new social history of the 1960s and '70s, building an analysis of 1290 Rocks residents and almost 300 households from the original notebooks for the 1822 Muster and then pursuing each of them in the 1828 census. In 1822, only a fifth of the Rocks' residents had arrived free, and half of those had followed a convict spouse to the colony. A third of the population were children.[28] Grace knows where they all lived and how they got about. Everyone has a name: she is so familiar with these folk that she dreamed of them. The historical archaeologist lurks behind every sentence, and material culture is present in the story as both precious surviving evidence and the everyday texture of a lost world. Complexity is never sacrificed to argument; it *is* the argument. Her history is driven by a determination to give these people dignity, or as E P Thompson memorably put it, to rescue them from the condescension of posterity. Thompson's work was clearly an inspiration, as were James Deetz and Henry Glassie on material culture, John Hirst and Alan Atkinson on colonial history, Richard Waterhouse's pioneering scholarship on popular culture, and Rhys Isaac and Greg Dening on cultural theatre and performance. Donna Merwick's *Possessing Albany* offered a model.[29]

The view through the window became possible because, in the course of Grace's research into the historic neighbourhood, she found herself back at the same Cumberland and Gloucester Street site she had studied in 1986, this time as the project historian in an intensive archaeological excavation of the two half-city blocks. For twenty weeks in 1994, over 400 volunteers, led by a team of archaeologists directed by Richard Mackay (of Godden Mackay Pty Ltd), dug and sifted the earth where forty-two dwellings, shops and hotels once stood. The many layers and the maze of broken walls, pits and foundations yielded more than 750,000 artefacts, each carefully recorded and analysed. The site furnished an extraordinary and often beautiful material record of urban life. Small (and large) things forgotten came to light: pretty ceramics, coloured shards of glass, clay pipes (of course!), broken plates, bones and shells, building materials, toys, and even a Japanese figurine and a nail-cleaner shaped like a fish. There was intense public interest in this 'buried treasure' and in 1994 more than 10,000 visitors were attracted to the 'Big Dig' (as it became known) by the glamour and earthy mystery of the outdoor detective work, and by 'that sense of *connectedness* with the past, the immediacy of the physical, the tactile dimension'.[30]

Objects have an aura: they are tangible and immediate and make us feel in direct touch with a past world. And this is not just a sensory illusion, for objects are as much expressions of who people are as the words that historians value so highly. The great American folklorist Henry Glassie, who came to history through an interest in 'sombre old barns and merry round pots', regretted in 1982 that 'some professional historians feel the land, its fields, houses, and buried broken crockery, cannot serve truly as documents.' They feel that artefacts are suspect, and oral storytelling too, for only the written word is valued. Thus, laments Glassie, 'the historian's story retains its dreary elitist bias, since few of the past's people wrote and most of them were tied to an upper-class minority.' And writing captures a peculiar kind of bias, he argued. When we attend only to written words, 'history erupts as a chronicle of anguish, since it is not a happy, balanced person who burns his night out blackening pages in solitude, creating the documents historians use to compose the past as a series of crises met by prosperous men.' It is a startling insight and an effective provocation for us to pay attention also to the material world. For while we fixate on documents, 'beyond, around us, spreads the vast and democratic handmade history book of the landscape'.[31]

Historical archaeology is founded on that passion for the revelatory potential of landscapes and objects. In 1977, Glassie's friend, the American archaeologist James Deetz, wrote an influential little book called *In Small Things Forgotten: An Archaeology of Early American Life*.[32] He argued that 'we know far more about the philosophical underpinnings of Puritanism than we do about what its practitioners consumed at countless meals.'[33] The French historian Fernand Braudel felt that if he could travel back to Voltaire's time, they could talk easily about philosophy but 'all the details of material life, even his personal hygiene, would shock us'.[34] Material culture offers insights into commonplace life, and its evidence is vital where we are dealing with people who could not read or write. Glassie, in his remarkable study of *Folk Housing in Middle Virginia* (1975), which was full of his beautifully drawn plans of homes, said of his Virginians: 'They left no writing, but they did leave all those houses.'[35] And Deetz went so far as to say that 'Material culture may be the most objective source of information we have concerning America's past.' For these scholars, the stubborn independent otherness of the artefact elevates it as evidence. Deetz finished his book with this decree on behalf of humanity: 'Don't read what we have written; look at what we have done.'[36]

This defiant declaration alludes to a curious competition between words and things in historical archaeology, as if words are too malleable, too subjective, too powerful to be trusted. Just as historians can be ignorant about objects, so are historical archaeologists often suspicious of words. This wariness of the written record stalks the discipline of historical archaeology and has sometimes hampered its collaboration with history. It has resulted in a strange neglect of words even when they are available to make sense of objects and sites. It is a peculiar reticence in a discipline whose very distinctiveness as a type of archaeology is its relationship to literacy. Historical archaeology distinguished itself from 'prehistoric archaeology' through studying literate societies (even though many people in them couldn't read). The material culture of the colonising Europeans was 'historical' and that of the Indigenous (before 'contact') was 'prehistoric'.[37] An unfortunate result of this bifurcation was an early neglect of post-contact Aboriginal archaeology.[38] The discipline has largely moved beyond these awkward definitions, but at the heart of historical archaeology there remains a relationship with writing – and therefore with historians, who often study the same people and places through documents and words. As Karskens put it, 'Historical archaeology, in its true sense, is a discipline which broaches the gulf between things and words.'[39]

But historical archaeology, which emerged as a discipline in Australia in alliance with the heritage conservation movement in the late 1960s, remained slow to integrate documentary evidence – partly from a desire to be distinct from 'history', and possibly also from the early influence of prehistoric archaeologists on its practice. By the mid-1980s the first reviews of the field appeared and they were critical of its preoccupation with description and lists over contextual analysis – one of the discipline's pioneers, Graham Connah, declared there was too much 'stamp collecting' and not enough 'problem-oriented research'.[40] With aspirations to be a science, there was a preference for collecting, recording and counting things *en masse*, a retreat to statistical anonymity at the expense of retrieving the specific cultural context of artefacts through documentary research where possible. Analysing and graphing a scatter of window glass was more archaeological and congenial than reading the diary of the building's occupant.[41] And such was the lure of fieldwork that even archaeologists themselves showed a surprising lack of interest in artefacts already in collections.[42] Why ransack museum cabinets when you can dig up new objects yourself, thus enacting the profession's essential rite of passage? As for those museums, when they got around to displaying excavated artefacts they often did so by recreating the theatre of excavation rather than the original social context of the object itself – thus trapping us forever on the surface, in the wonder of discovery. So the separation of archaeology and history, words and things, often began at the dig and continued all the way to museum cabinets and exhibitions – and thus historical archaeology was prevented from making the impact on narratives that it should.[43]

Grace Karskens observed all that and was determined to change it. From the 1990s her work began to emerge as a compelling alternative model of historical archaeology, one that integrated not only archaeology and history but also collection and social research. Trained both as historian and archaeologist, she argued in two directions: that historians should pay more attention to the material world and that historical archaeologists should integrate history. Her archaeological imagination compels her to get inside the feel of the past – how it looked, sounded, felt and smelt. She takes seriously the challenge of art historian Bernard Smith to seek 'a more balanced, a more archaeological, a more humanist view of our history', and to tune into the 'sensuous enjoyment of material things'.[44] When she wrote *Holroyd* she had to understand what it was like to work in a hot, humid and dusty cotton spinning mill, or in a brickworks amidst 'the endless clanking of pressed bricks being stacked by hand for the kiln', and when she pursued the Great North Road through the bush she described the dressing, facing and matching of stones as well as the blasting, breaking and carting of rubble.[45] When she had the chance to return to The Rocks, she did so as part of what was, surprisingly, a radical innovation in urban archaeology: the appointment from the beginning of a historian who was an established expert on the social history of the place, and who could also bring the intimate research of family historians into the mix. Historical archaeology in Australia had been good at excavating and recording, but what had been missing, argued Karskens, 'was a sophisticated and broad cultural context in which to place archaeological evidence'.[46] She had the temerity to declare that 'we cannot simply "dig up the past". Artefacts do not "speak" for themselves.'[47]

The Big Dig was driven, of course, by archaeological method and traditional post-excavation analysis. The development of the site itself was studied in detail so that archaeological context could be reconstructed accurately, and all artefact types were separately analysed – ceramics, bone, glass, metals, building materials, pollen, soils and macrobotanical remains. Karskens developed key research questions for the site and partly dismantled those boundaries introduced between artefact types so that she could 'see across them' and discern the relationships between them, and also between the artefacts and the people who made and used them. Thus people known from the documents entered the stories of the site. There was the butcher and hotelier, George Cribb, who was arrested in 1812 for attempting to smuggle rum (charges not proven) and who may have been an illegal distiller of alcohol: was that terracotta vessel found discarded down his well 180 years later the incriminating still?[48] Or Margaret Byrne, pipe-smoking mother of seven, whose sewing equipment including lace-making pins 'slipped and fell through the floorboards, collecting gradually under her house, together with the marbles her children had played with, twenty-five in all'. Karskens tells what happened to those children too, their fates so bound up with their material inheritance that descendants still live in the area to this day.[49] These and many other poignant human stories, generated by objects and sites, were told in the Cumberland/Gloucester Streets interpretative volume, which Karskens then rewrote for a general audience and published in 1999 as *Inside the Rocks: The Archaeology of a Neighbourhood*.

Resistance amongst historical archaeologists remained. Partly it was their disciplinary insistence that artefacts *must* be allowed to speak for themselves before they are overwhelmed by the cacophony of recorded words. But there was also a distrust of the power of good writing and the seduction of human stories. And then there was outright academic blindness: in 1998 Graham Connah declared the discipline in 'crisis' at the very moment when environmental and heritage legislation had stimulated new perspectives and publications from a series of collaborations launched largely outside universities, of which the Big Dig was a fine example.[50] Connah overlooked other important integrations of history and archaeology that were current or imminent: Alan Mayne and Tim Murray's collaboration on the excavation of a site in Little Lonsdale Street in Melbourne, Susan Lawrence's studies of the archaeology of whaling and the goldfields, and Jane Lydon's work on the Chinese community in The Rocks. It was mystifying that Connah should call for historical archaeology 'to reach a wider audience' yet discount the very projects in his own country that were then generating energetic engagement with the public. It was as if projects that involved historians *and* consultants made the work both less archaeological and less academic. This was the old divide between public history and academic history that Grace had addressed in the 1980s; she was still championing 'the common ground'. Together with consultant archaeologist Richard Mackay, she replied cheerfully and robustly to Connah's sense of crisis, rejecting his 'rather narrow version of historical archaeology as a fading "scholarly discipline" anchored in academia' and calling instead for 'a culture which reflects the inevitable interdependence of academia and consulting practice'. Instead of a crisis, they described a 'most exciting and fruitful phase', a creative awakening.[51]

Their critique also addressed historical archaeology's unease with social history. For Connah, historians were a problem because they either neglected archaeology or – if they did take notice – threatened its purity. He warned that 'Important though historical sources are, in the end our task as archaeologists should be to ask archaeological questions of archaeological data.'[52] It was as if questions from other disciplines would corrupt or dilute historical archaeology – or deny 'archaeology's unique epistemological potential', as another scholar feared.[53] In response, Mackay and Karskens regretted that 'Archaeologists seemed shy of reaching out into "wider questions" for fear that they might be "historical"; or quite simply "not what we do".[54] They felt that the Big Dig and other new collaborations were, by contrast, a sign that 'historical archaeology in Australia has at last become "historical" through a new engagement with history.'

The past *is* a foreign country, Grace reminds us. We have to learn to see its difference — and archaeological evidence has the power to do that, to shock us if only we allow it. That view through the window into a convict household in The Rocks was prompted by material evidence, and led to large insights about early colonisation. It revealed a lively consumer culture amongst people we thought were degraded prisoners, amongst families who spent more on fabrics, buttons and bobbing than on rum.[55] They were interested in domesticity, cleanliness and comfort, in refinement at the table, yet their culture was also violent and communal, and the curtained window where we stand looks out onto a slaughteryard.[56] The archaeology of convict households only makes sense, argues Karskens, if we think of early Sydney not as a gaol but as a colony.

She was building on the insights of one of the most important books written about Australian history in the late twentieth century: John Hirst's *Convict Society and its Enemies* (1983). As Hirst explains in his opening words, the book records a conversion. He set out to answer the question of how a penal colony had changed into a free society. But his research revealed that it was the wrong question: for this 'was not a society which had to become free; its freedoms were well established from the earliest times'. 'In New South Wales,' argued Hirst, 'convicts were treated, not according to their crimes, but to their usefulness', and the early governors were overwhelmingly concerned 'not with penal discipline but with survival and economic development'.[57] No bar was placed on the economic activities of convicts; many enjoyed normal legal rights, and their children were born free. It was only later, following the Bigge Report on NSW in 1822, that greater regulation, severity and brutality

were introduced via a road-gang system and a network of distant penal
stations. Karskens says Hirst's work 'turned the traditional view of early
NSW society on its head'.[58]

In order to understand the early colony, we have to 'dissolve the
view', as Grace puts it, and travel back through the archaeological layers
of time and experience – through the late-nineteenth-century hindsight
of convict shame, around the misrepresentations of the enemies of trans-
portation, and beneath the changes wrought on the convict system in
the 1820s and '30s and the later industrialisation of colonial society – to
retrieve a preindustrial yet opportunistically commercial settler world
that was there at the foundation of British colonisation. The archaeology confirmed that there was no sharp break between the 'convict' and
the 'free', or between a more preindustrial way of life and a modernising
industrialised one; the transitions in material life were slow and took
place over decades. A Sydney historian is more likely than, say, a
Melbourne historian to glimpse this colonial world before it was overwhelmed by industrialism, for the city of sandstone has this earlier layer
of immigrant society to plumb. And the 'small things forgotten', retrieved
from the earth of The Rocks and studied beside the equally precious
words from the time, are remarkably revealing of the creative assemblage
of economies and sensibilities, 'new and old, compatible and contradictory', that made up Australia's earliest urban community. Karskens
wanted to rescue that foundation period, those first thirty-odd years,
from being dismissed as a grim period of stasis and waiting, just a 'primitive prelude' to the national story.[59]

At the Cumberland and Gloucester Street site, archaeologists found
amongst discarded shards a piece of Chinese porcelain that they believe
was flaked at its edges by Aboriginal hands.[60] The porcelain flake, discarded by whites and worked by blacks, lay on the interface between

natural topsoil and introduced loams; it penetrated the horizon of 1788. It was an artefact that told of cultural encounter, overlap and exchange. Not only had Aboriginal people lived in that place for tens of thousands of years; they stayed on there – and made the Sydney of the invaders their town too. This deeper continuity of the city's history – which gave the lie to another 'primitive prelude' – became a powerful theme of Karskens' remarkable book *The Colony* (2009). Writing in *The Monthly*, Alan Atkinson welcomed this big book where 'every page is startling for the mass of human and geographical detail, and for the extraordinary freshness of the argument. It propels Karskens straight to the first rank of Australian historians.'[61]

An urban Aboriginal presence was long considered to be a late historical development. Inhabitants of a 'timeless land' were not expected to adapt; the British alone carried the burden and promise of 'history' on this distant shore, its metre measured by the sacred Timekeeper they carried on board their ship with wings.[62] When Aboriginal people adapted, the colonists were blind to it, or regarded it as a loss of 'authenticity'. Yet Aboriginal people drew on their long history of change to respond to the calamity of invasion. 'Aboriginal people did not survive by staying the same,' argues archaeologist and historian Paul Irish, who studied with Karskens.[63] *The Colony* tells the story of Sydney the Eora town, where Aboriginal people have lived ever since Bennelong, his family and friends 'came in' in late 1790.[64] They made themselves at home; they knew everyone and were the gossips of the town; they wove themselves into the urban fabric: 'They acted as if they owned the place.'[65] 'What is striking about the earliest urban Aboriginal people', argues Karskens, 'is the way they so quickly forged new lives among the invaders in the growing port town, in ways which were nonetheless compatible with their customary habits and laws.'[66] Her work joined that of Heather Goodall and Alison Cadzow, Peter Read and Dennis Foley, Maria Nugent, Paul Irish and other scholars who have collaborated with

Aboriginal people to explain their long, hidden history in the heart of our oldest city, from its very beginnings.[67]

Joseph Banks, in his *Endeavour* journal of 1770, described gazing over Botany Bay at night and seeing scores of small lights dancing on the dark waters, and realising that each was a fishing *nowie*, a simple bark canoe steered by an Aboriginal woman.[68] In *The Colony*, Karskens gives us this image of the lights at night – a powerful, entrancing, mysterious glimpse of habitation and industry on the eastern shore of Australia in 1770 – and she uses it to entice us into complex thinking about culture, gender and history. It is one of many enigmatic and sparkling threads that weave their way through the book, but let's follow this one to get a sense of the author's purpose.

We are invited to look more closely at the bark canoe or nowie. The Eora were saltwater people, fish and shellfish were a major part of their diet, they excelled in fishing, swimming and diving, they could manoeuvre these narrow, unstable little canoes skilfully even in a big surf, and it was women who were best at it. Those twinkling lights at night were the fires lit within each bark canoe for warmth and cooking. The fires were kindled on little clay pads, and the strange red bubbled scars on the lower backs of fishing women were caused by the daily proximity of the fires. They knelt with straight backs, their bottoms on their heels and their knees pressed against the sides of the nowie to give them control and stability. Some had infants at their breasts or on their shoulders and older children at the front, and their singing carried on the sea breeze. Grace directs our attention to the background of early paintings of Sydney's shoreline, and there they are: the women sitting in their nowies.[69]

It was a woman's world out there on the water in these delicate bark canoes. Each Eora woman had the top two joints of her little finger removed as an infant, as a sign of status, but possibly also to help their fishing. It was women alone who used hooks and lines and they fashioned their distinctive fish hooks from turban shells. Thus Karskens makes us look closely at the object, the pearly, crescent-shaped fish hook, and what it meant. *Burra*, as the hooks were called, only came into use on the south-east coast between 1200 and 500 years ago. Archaeologist Paul Irish reminds us that the British assumed that they were recording timeless tradition, but they were 'in fact witnessing the latest incarnation of an ever-changing way of life': the flotilla of nowies was 'using a relatively recent fishing technology in areas that were once dry land'.[70]

The hooks and lines made fish of deeper waters available, so the women could range further in their canoes, extending their independent world. Aboriginal women 'dominated the waters of the harbours, and the coastlines in between', and they did most of the food gathering. Drawing on anthropological studies as well as historical accounts, Karskens argues that women's fishing, made possible by the pearly burra, was linked to gender politics and the balance of power over food. The development of hook-and-line fishing enabled women to catch more fish for themselves and their children, and moderated the social and ritual dominance of the men. Those twinkling lights that Joseph Banks saw – those independent, floating households – were canny interventions in the social and sexual economy, for the fires were kindled to cook the fish as they were hauled out, and 'women ate their fill and fed their children before they returned to the shores' to feed their men. So we are led from the dancing lights to the world of the canoe to the shell hooks to deep-time archaeological history to eighteenth-century Indigenous gender politics – and then to biography.

Barangaroo was an Eora woman, a Cammeragal, who the British found striking and a little frightening. Karskens explains that other Eora women politely agreed to put on clothes, but Barangaroo refused. 'All she ever wore, even at the governor's table, was a slim bone through her nose.' And when the British invited her to watch a convict flogging,

Barangaroo was disgusted and furious, and tried to wrest the whip from the flogger's hands. She was about forty in 1790, had lost a husband and two children to smallpox and she now had a new, younger husband: the ambitious Bennelong. Why was she so unhappy that her man was consorting with the newcomers? Why did she seek to sabotage these relations? Was she just cranky or feisty, as some assumed, or could she see the threat that the British posed to the power of women in Indigenous life? The colonisers came with alternative sources of food and were determined to deal officially with men. For Barangaroo and other strong, senior Eora women, living with the British and relying on their food would mean dependence on men, white and black. The status and self-esteem of Eora women, so bound up with the economy of fishing and the world of the canoe, would be in jeopardy.[71]

Karskens deftly uses the burra to hook further themes. For example, there was a time in April and May of 1789, when few nowie were seen on the water. The smallpox epidemic was wreaking havoc amongst Aboriginal people on the coast, and there were pustule-covered bodies on the shorelines. And it was likely that women were the hardest hit. By early June, some canoes were back. As we saw in Chapter 1, Karskens discerns what 'must have been a reduced and much-altered society: far fewer old people, fewer mature women, proportionately more young men and youths'. The individuals with whom the British would parley were already marked out – they were men, they were young and they were survivors of smallpox.[72]

So in just this one thread of story and analysis, we can see Grace's archaeological imagination at work; we are introduced to the nowie and the burra and to their place in society and economy; we are made to look more carefully at paintings of the period, at the action offstage and offshore. Her ethnographic eye discerns the eloquence of gestures caught miraculously in the historical record. The sensory world of the past is brought vividly before us – the fires burning at the backs of the women, the water-oriented world of early Sydney, the politics and personalities of known individuals, the horror of smallpox. And the big ideas grow organically from the intimate detail: the colonists arrived in a beloved landscape that was already spiritual and political; the urban history of Aboriginal people goes right back to the foundation of Sydney; colonial history is also Indigenous history and we need to learn to read the peripheral vision of the sources.

I am reminded of the sociological breadth of Rhys Isaac's *The Transformation of Virginia*, which itself grew out of such loving engagement with the material past.[73] And the way Grace uses art not just as illustration but as argument and text is reminiscent of Tim Bonyhady's *The Colonial Earth*.[74] Of course, one also thinks of Inga Clendinnen's *Dancing with Strangers*, a kind of companion work that focuses on the first four years of the colony.[75] But Karskens, by extending her analysis to a whole generation, explores those very questions left hanging at the end of Clendinnen's book. Grace shares with Alan Atkinson a close attentiveness to social texture, language and voices, and with John Hirst an interest in the strong continuities of the colonial project. One more comparison we might make is with another notable recent work of colonial history, James Boyce's *Van Diemen's Land*.[76] Boyce and Karskens both do environmental history without necessarily separating or signalling it. It is fully and seamlessly integrated so that Indigenous history, environmental history and colonial history are indistinguishable and intertwined. A further appealing dimension of the book is its natural and generous acknowledgement of the rich scholarly context within which it sits. As Karskens puts it, 'This book has its roots deep in a great mountain of existing research, thinking and histories. Historians work collectively, within a wider community of scholars.'[77] So the book is, very satisfyingly, a historiography as well as a history.

Grace's voice is original and distinctive. Her attention to social and environmental detail and her teasing out of startling vignettes gives her

prose a magical glow. This is more than a style; it seems to me to deliberately create a space within which emotions, dreams, senses and hopes
might be given proper play as forces of history that are just as powerful
as politics, law and economics. Perhaps we might call this a kind of
'magical realism'. Grace, who tells true stories, might be wary of this
label, but let's hear how literary scholar Matthew Strecher defines magic
realism: it is, he declares, 'what happens when a highly detailed, realistic setting is invaded by something "too strange to believe"'.[78] Good
history is often like that.

Perhaps Greg Dening, another inspiration for Karskens' work,
might have called it 'the poetics of history'. Dening, by the way, was
happy to be called, on one occasion, a magical realist. In a 1991 essay
called 'A Poetic for Histories', Greg wrote that 'Poetics are the relationships we have with the texts that suffuse our lives.' He went on to argue
for an understanding of history as not only a discipline or technique of
inquiry but also as a human characteristic, as 'the vernacular of our cultural and social systems'. 'We all make histories endlessly,' Greg argued.
'It is our human condition to make histories. No sooner is the present
gone in the blink of an eye than we make sense of it as past. We tell
stories about it. We interpret the meaning of gestures made, of words
spoken, of actions done. We make a narrative of the past in our mind,
in our conversations.'[79]

I sense that some of the power of Grace's prose and analysis derives
from her vocational commitment to public history, from her dedicated
engagement with history as a human characteristic, from her intellectual curiosity in history as not just a product of the academy but as also
the vernacular of our cultural and social systems. Her inquiries have
arisen from a public hunger for history, from council commissions,
from heritage processes and battles, from environmental threats and
assessments, from the stimulus of real places and sensuous things, and
from a desire to make sense of how the past is in the present – in other

words, from the poetics of history, as Dening put it, from 'the relationships we have with the texts that suffuse our lives'. If Grace's book is a historiography as well as a history, then her historiography extends to all the ways we tell stories about the past including the contours of memory, and it embraces all the incidental and accidental evidence caught by culture and nature.

So Grace has more than fulfilled the promise of her own 1992 article in finding common ground between public history and academic history. We might have wondered, in the 1980s and 1990s, what the new sensibilities of public historians might do to our scholarship, and we might have wished that public history was not just applying history but also revolutionising it. Here in *The Colony* we have the finest realisation of our hopes.

FOURTEEN

Dr Deep Time: Mike Smith

Crouched in the red sand, handling a stone artefact with an arc of blue desert sky above him, Mike Smith is at home. He is a connoisseur of deserts and has a discerning eye for the distinctive character of Australia's Red Centre. Smith is an archaeologist who has revolutionised our understanding of the human history of Central Australia. His great work, *The Archaeology of Australia's Deserts* (2013), is one of the most important books about Australia's ancient human history since John Mulvaney's *The Prehistory of Australia* (1969). That earlier ground-breaking work was published when modern Australians finally realised that they had usurped a continent with a deep human past. Suddenly the newcomers found themselves gazing into a dizzying abyss: the 'Timeless Land' was actually replete with time. How were they to comprehend this inheritance? Smith, who possesses the wit and wisdom of a Time Lord and is known affectionately as 'Dr Deep Time' by colleagues at the National Museum of Australia, has made it his quest to understand those Australian depths, both stratigraphic and philosophical.

Mike Smith's career unfolded during the 1970s and '80s, when settler Australia was coming to grips with this time revolution. In 1989, together with Rhys Jones and Bert Roberts, he excavated an Arnhem

Land site called Malakanunja II (Madjedbebe) and obtained the earliest evidence of the human occupation of Australia, dated at 50,000 to
55,000 years ago, now more likely around 60,000. As historian Billy
Griffiths put it, 'What they discovered in twelve days of hot, sweaty
digging made headlines around the world.'[1] But it was to be Mike's
investigation of a remarkable rock-shelter in western Central Australia
that would represent his greatest archaeological breakthrough. In the
early 1980s he wanted to test the generally accepted belief that Central
Australia had been occupied by people only after the last ice age. There
was evidence of human occupation extending back 25,000 to 30,000
years in almost all the ecological zones of the continent – but what
about its arid core? Had the desert really not been settled until after the
peak aridity of the ice age had passed? The earliest evidence of people
in that region was then no older than 10,000 years, so this did seem a
possible scenario.[2] To test it, Mike needed a site that would make full
use of his stratigraphic skills and surgical precision, a site that would
give him a window into past climates, geomorphic processes and cultural systems. He searched for it for years.

At the beginning of the 1980s Mike was appointed field archaeologist at the Northern Territory Museum in Darwin, and his 'amazing
brief' was to engage in the field survey and excavation of Aboriginal
and Macassan sites in the Northern Territory. By 1982 he was keen to
move his base to Alice Springs, for the Red Centre had got in his blood.
The desk he inherited had a pile of slips of paper in a drawer, and one
of the newspaper clippings noted the existence of a large cave near
Mount Winter in the Cleland Hills. The clipping reported that rock
art specialist Robert Edwards and his Aboriginal guide, Timothy
Jugadai Tjungurrayi (c. 1920–1988), had located a shelter in 1969.
Further details of the find had slipped from memory, so the scrap of
paper in the desk was a vital clue. But Smith recalled that 'it took a
lot of time to work out quite how to get out there and also where to

go.' Finally, with the help of the Central Australian historian Dick Kimber and the rock art scholar Grahame Walsh, Smith was able to get to the remote Cleland Hills, a beautiful, dissected red sandstone escarpment in spinifex, desert oak and sand ridge country. The Cleland Hills are one of a series of small rocky ranges laced with shade and water that are strung across the vast 'inland sea', one range visible from the other on the horizon, 'like an archipelago of islands'.³

It was 3 August 1986, and they had just one morning to search sixteen kilometres of the range for the great hollow of a cave. Kimber walked south and Smith walked north. In the searing sun, Mike walked and walked. Finally he came around a corner of the outcrop and saw something:

> I could see these shadows at the base of an escarpment and it looked like it could be something quite big. So I walked over and there was this absolutely huge rock shelter, I mean enormous! A big opera shell structure. I have not seen anything like it since; it is absolutely the most remarkable site. I knew that was the site, it matched the description. It was the site that would warm any archaeologist's heart. I knew this was a site that would give me a good sequence.⁴

Mike could see a scatter of chipped stone artefacts, broken grinding stones, and pieces of worked wood across the floor and a frieze of paintings along the rear wall. He especially eyed the earthen floor of the shelter – the promising flux of sediment that would be his time machine. Dick Kimber recorded that 'A short time later I met Mike. He was elated. He had found the cave.'⁵

Mike Smith arrived in Australia from Blackpool, England, in 1961, aged six, the son of Ten-pound Poms. Soon his father's work took young Mike for a few months during his primary school years to remote Ceduna, the last major settlement before crossing the Nullarbor Plain, with a population that was mainly Greek and Aboriginal. In this town of sand and cinder-block houses, Mike remembers collecting lizards and playing in rusty cars. He began to develop a taste for arid Australia: 'the smell of the country, that light, the sense of openness and adventure'. Although Smith knows Australia as few do, he has never lost his British accent and has been known to treat it humorously as a 'speech impediment'.

In late primary school he made a conscious decision to pursue a career in archaeology. He had corresponded with staff at the South Australian Museum about his reptiles, and by the age of fifteen he was asking to join a museum dig at Roonka on the Lower Murray, and then one led by Hungarian émigré Alexander Gallus at Koonalda Cave in the Nullarbor. Carrying buckets at dig sites enabled him to meet the well-known archaeologist Rhys Jones, 'a very inspirational man' who was happy to 'talk to a kid'. By the time Mike came to the Australian National University in 1974 to study archaeology with John Mulvaney, he already had substantial field experience and was 'hooked on Australian work'. When I interviewed Mike for the National Library of Australia in 2012, he recalled the excitement of this period: 'There were new discoveries every six months or so. And this combined with my own personal exploration of the continent. I was interested in geography; I was interested in the structure of a continent. And archaeology was my means of travel as much as anything else.'

Ceduna had played a part in seducing him to aridity, but so too had visits to the South Australian Museum, where Mike gazed, fascinated, at 'those older museum displays of Arrernte ceremonial costumes: the big, conical, feather-down headdresses with the feathers glued on with blood'. They seemed to depict a society that was not just exotic but totally alien, and yet the setting was his own continental backyard, that great alluring heart of desert that was part of the geographical imagination of South Australians. He glimpsed the mysterious world captured in *Songs of Central Australia* by the anthropologist T G H Strehlow, and in the writings of Baldwin Spencer and Frank Gillen. Mike realised that 'there was a rich, exotic Aboriginal cultural and political system out there. Central Australia is where I wanted to be.'

In the quarter-century following the rediscovery of Puritjarra in 1986, the remote rock-shelter was to occupy much of Smith's archaeological attention. After Lake Mungo, Puritjarra is the single most important archaeological site in the Australian desert – not simply because of its intrinsic values but because of the time invested in its analysis. Thanks to Mike's enduring commitment, it is one of the best documented and dated sites in the whole of Australia. Puritjarra deepened the chronology of human history in the centre of the continent from 10,000 to 35,000 years, a period at least as long as modern humans have occupied Western Europe. Modern Australians began at last to realise that they were the inheritors of a human saga of global significance, a drama in which people survived ice-age cold droughts in the Central Australian deserts and managed to sustain civilisation in the face of massive climate change. When Smith stands in his trench at Puritjarra, he knows he is shoulder deep in a Quaternary desert and that the walls of his pit span 100,000 years of desert history. And when he looks up and gazes at the shelter's sandstone roof, his imagination travels back a further 360 million years, for that roof is the hollowed-out form of an ancient dune, the cast of an even older desert.[6] Puritjarra is a palimpsest, a place that Australians should revere.

Smith's book on *The Archaeology of Australia's Deserts* uses Puritjarra to tell the story of all Australia's arid lands. It explains and analyses the social and environmental history of the largest area of desert in the southern hemisphere. Australia's arid zone has a variety of deserts with great natural diversity; it is a vast region of drylands, dune fields, stony plains, ephemeral rivers, salt lakes and desert uplands, all quite different to the deserts of southern Africa, South America or North Africa. Mike's insights come from a lifelong commitment to understanding this unique region: he worked on an outback sheep station as a roustabout, hiked and drove the country as a field archaeologist, walked with a string of camels through remote country west of Lake Mackay and in the Simpson Desert, and dug carefully into desert sands. He sees himself as 'holding the region up to the light like a gemstone, turning it around and watching its personality refracted in different ways'.

Smith's work is notable for its thorough absorption, acknowledgement and encapsulation of all the scholarship that precedes it. He sees himself as of the generation of archaeologists who picked up the baton from John Mulvaney and Rhys Jones and completed the basic archaeological exploration of the continent: 'In terms of finding the corners of the room, that was a job that my generation finished, completed.' He is part of the first generation of Australian-trained archaeologists yet also amongst the last to have travelled and worked with Aboriginal people who grew up in the bush without major contact with Europeans. He was a student of Mulvaney's and, like John, is a cultural historian as well as an archaeologist. Both men see archaeology, with its palaeo-environmental data and its science of stratigraphy, as ultimately a humanities discipline.

Although Smith helped establish some of our oldest dates of human occupation, he believes that the best way to demolish the 'timeless' metaphor that stalks ancient Australia is to piece together a complex, contoured history of social and environmental change from the first arrival of people in Australia to the present. A nuanced narrative of change through millennia ultimately conveys depth better than dates can. Therefore Smith works across time in both directions – from the ancient past forwards and from the ethnographic and historical present backwards.

In deep time Smith connects Australians to the human exodus from Africa, and in recent millennia he proposes an Australian history of constant social change. But a narrative of cultural transformation can deliver findings that are politically unpalatable to a polity determined to equate rights and authenticity with cultural continuity. When British colonists encountered Australia's Indigenous peoples, most of the learning was done by the invaded. Bennelong stands as a brilliant example. It was not just because of the power relationship; it was also because Aboriginal peoples were used to change and encounter, and they were at home. They lived in a land with hundreds of languages, where travel involved cultural sensitivity, ritual and exchange, and where the Dreaming sanctioned a constant, adaptive renaissance. Customs and ceremonies that Europeans labelled ancient, primordial and timeless were often new, dynamic and creative. Smith concludes that the foraging landscapes of Central Australia that Ernest Giles described in 1872 and the elaborate ritual and ceremonial life recorded by Spencer and Gillen in 1896 'appear to be products of historical changes within the last millennium'.[7] It turns out that the classic ethnographies of a 'timeless' people actually described desert societies that had survived and been transformed by an environmental roller-coaster and which, at the moment of contact, were undergoing accelerating cultural change.

The American archaeologist Richard Gould, who did important work at the Puntutjarpa rock-shelter in the Western Desert in the late 1960s, is quoted on the back cover of *The Archaeology of Australia's Deserts*. He declares the book 'A "must" for anyone seriously interested in Australian cultural history'. Note that Gould does not modify his description of the field with words such as 'archaeology' or 'prehistory' or 'Aboriginal'. I think there is a kind of coming of age of a settler nation in being able to say that a new book in archaeology is, quite simply, a landmark work in Australian cultural history.

∾

In 1996, reflecting on the Australian time revolution, archaeologist Denis Byrne wrote a brilliant essay for the journal *Aboriginal History* in which he meditated on what it means for a settler nation to embrace as its own the past of a culture it once rejected as a savage anachronism. Byrne analysed the way the discourse of depth – which is such an appropriate and seductive metaphor – has sometimes inadvertently led to archaeology's disconnection from the living Aboriginal present and to an essentialism of a timeless, traditional Aboriginal past. He argued that 'If archaeology were to cease concerning itself with the nation's desire for depth, it might rise, as it were, to the surface.' By 'surface', he meant the relatively horizontal (post-1788) terrain 'where duration is measured in terms of generations rather than millennia'. Such practice would cease to locate real Aboriginality in the pre-colonial past, and would refuse the obsession with cultural purity. Writing almost two decades ago, Byrne could not have foreseen how quickly this apparent binary might be transcended and how effectively the depths and the surface might be united.[8]

Smith is so enamoured of stratigraphy that he got a grave-digger's certificate through TAFE to learn the ins and outs of timber shoring, but he has also sifted the 'surface' of his beloved deserts at the scale of generations as well as millennia. As part of his commitment to understanding Puritjarra holistically, he has written a modern history of the movements of people in its region since colonisation. *Peopling the Cleland Hills* (2005) is a history of the frontier that has swirled around Puritjarra, drawn from documents, memories and conversations-in-place. Smith believes it is important to retain a feeling for the contemporary cultural landscape in which his archaeological sites are embedded, and so he uses Puritjarra as a place from which to view the modern social exchange and disruption generated across Kukatja country by the European invasion.

In his writing of colonial history he sifts documents and memories instead of sediments. The history of the Australian desert, Smith points out, differs from other parts of the colonial frontier. Rather than the coastal pattern of 'dispossession and dispersal', the arrival of Europeans in Central Australia 'set in motion a chain migration of desert people into the settled districts that took several generations to run its course'. In the 1950s and '60s government patrols in western Central Australia were still looking for 'smokes' to identify Aboriginal inhabitants, just as James Cook had done when sailing along the east coast in 1770. In the late 1950s, 170 years after British colonisation at Port Jackson, there were Aboriginal people living in western Central Australia who had never laid eyes on a white person and who were still supporting themselves on or near traditional lands. In the 1960s a Pintupi man who saw a white man for the first time recalled that 'he glowed like white quartz.'[9]

Jeremy Long, who was a government patrol officer in the region in the 1950s and '60s, has criticised the 'white Australian folklore' about Aboriginal dispossession ('that can be traced back to Governor Macquarie's day') which declares that Aboriginal people were found in those deserts because they had been driven out of more productive and well-watered areas, seeking refuge in the arid interior. The folklore was wrong. Aboriginal people who were found by government parties in western Central Australia, some as recently as the 1980s, were there because it was their home. And they did not helplessly 'drift' into settlements. Rather, they left their hunting ranges out of curiosity and in order to exploit new resources of food, water and tobacco at pastoral and mission stations, mining camps, depots and townships. Tjintjiwarra, a Matuntara woman who moved to Hermannsburg Mission probably in the 1920s, left when the drought broke in 1930, declaring, 'Too much soup! Too much Jesus!'[10] The pull of the homelands remained so strong that many hoped to return, and some did.[11] When Pintupi man Tjapaltjarri walked out of the Gibson Desert with his family group in 1984, he was following a consistent pattern of smokes in a southerly direction – and the people he met were his relatives. Smith reflects that these small dramas were probably played out across the region: a family moves back into country and one night they hear 'an unfamiliar voice beyond the firelight'.[12]

Dick Kimber's experience and research have been crucial to our understanding of society and biography in Central Australia. He travelled with Pintupi men through their country in the 1970s, learning about his friends' desire to return, and recording how they respectfully greeted ancestors with fire, sang the country into life again and used the land in practical ways. He watched as a small group of Pintupi men dug into the sand to drink from the seeping waters of Ilypili spring, and how careful they were not to disturb the ancestral creator Ice-Man. The oldest people told him their memories of the 'foot-walk' days prior to contact and of their nostalgia for a time without ill-health: 'No pills, Tjakamarra.' But Kimber also observed openness to change – and 'a continuum of remarkable acceptances, questionings and adjustments to the present times'.[13]

In the Cleland Hills, Smith's focus was on the neighbouring but less well-known diaspora of the Kukatja, who were on the move by the late 1880s. The prospect from the Puritjarra rock-shelter during the nineteenth and early twentieth centuries reveals large-scale movements of peoples, white and black, back and forth, ebbing and flowing, east and west. The stalling of the pastoral frontier slowed the invasion and allowed a cross-frontier traffic to develop, helping to maintain the traditions and identity of the Kukatja.[14] Smith's archaeological imagination anchors his history deeply in one place, right back to the age of the Ice-Man, and gives him an inside, earthed perspective on the modern, shifting frontier. 'I aimed to fix the locality and allow people and events to become the variables,' he writes. Looking out from the shelter, he enables us to behold events as they play across the broader landscape, occasionally leaving a local residue. Although his focus is the last century and a half, there are tens of thousands of years of history implied in his gaze. Rather than following large-scale events themselves, pursuing them off-stage as it were, Mike keeps us grounded in place and we see them flicker past or feel the ripple of their distant impact.

Anthropologist Deborah Rose has analysed how, in settler societies, the frontier is constructed as a disjunction between wholly different kinds of time and thus imagined 'as a rolling Year Zero that is carried across the land cutting an ontological swathe between "timeless" land and historicised land'. However Rose finds that in much of northern and Central Australia 'Year Zero' remains in suspension: the frontier may have arrived 'but the rest of the story has not yet followed along behind'.[15] This rather different frontier is revealed by Smith's view from Puritjarra: one in which black and white cultures moved both ways across a shared and contested landscape, where the desert frontier emerges as a vast zone of flux and encounter rather than as an imperial, progressive and transformative line. There is a kind of Aboriginal patience in this earthed archaeological view, this steady, embedded watchfulness over particular country. It is a perspective in which proper pre-eminence is given to place over time.

Naming people changes the kind of history we write. There is an impressive act of respect in the tenacity with which Smith traces and portrays individuals and families. Instead of being subsumed in the usual anonymity of frontier history, Aboriginal people appear in the narrative as individuals and as members of families over generations. When the European explorer Ernest Giles came to the Cleland Hills in 1872, he commented on the scarcity of water and the ubiquity of Aboriginal burning. In a passage probably given classical resonance by his ghost writer, Giles observed that 'the natives were about, burning, burning, ever burning; one would think they were of the fabled salamander race, and lived on fire instead of water.'[16] Using documentary records, Smith has travelled back to that moment and surmised the identity of some of the people holding those firesticks. He is even able to show that, more than a hundred years after Giles, some of the descendants of the nineteenth-century firestick farmers were (and still are) there. In 1985, on Mike's first field trip in the Cleland Hills area, he travelled with John Multa, whose great-grandmother, Taluka Nungarrayi, watched Giles move through the area.[17]

We can sense in *Peopling the Cleland Hills*, more explicitly than in any of Smith's other work, how intimately and even spiritually he has come to identify with the desert and its modern people. This is the source of a powerful poetic vision that illuminates his science and connects his writing with the grand tradition of Australian desert literature of which he is keenly conscious: Ernest Giles, Baldwin Spencer, Frank Gillen, J W Gregory, C T Madigan, T G H Strehlow, H H Finlayson, Francis Ratcliffe, Deborah Rose, Barry Hill, Darrell Lewis, Nicolas Rothwell, R G Kimber.

Smith has worked with three generations of the Multa and Tjukadai families and has thus himself been drawn into regional history. By following several generations of Kukatja families he is able to conclude that people were 'remarkably tenacious in maintaining the religious and social links binding individuals to specific places'. But he reflects that 'eventually, you outrun your data.' He recalls the pleasure of having desert blokes from Haasts Bluff down to Canberra for a meal: 'And usually I would probe Douglas Multa for a little bit of information, family history stuff. On one occasion I was saying, "That uncle, what was his name?" And he said, "Look him up in that book." Meaning my book. At this point I've gone full circle.'

Mike Smith begins and ends *The Archaeology of Australia's Deserts* with the Arrernte ceremonies performed for Baldwin Spencer and Frank Gillen in the summer of 1896, those 'exotic' rituals that first fascinated him as a boy. He calls the ceremonies 'a watershed event in anthropological literature, a profound intellectual exchange between elite members of two very different societies'. He explains at the end of the book that he has tried to approach the 1896 ceremony from the other side, 'reconstructing the long history that shaped the world of the Arrernte elders sitting across the ceremonial ground' from the observing Europeans.[18] And in his colonial history of Cleland Hills, he argues the great importance of Hermannsburg Aboriginal Mission (established by Lutherans in the MacDonnell Ranges in 1877) as 'one of the few places on the Australian colonial frontier where there was such sustained intellectual engagement between Aboriginal people and Europeans over several generations', a dynamism distilled in figures of national stature such as Albert Namatjira and T G H Strehlow. The mission was 'an intellectual conduit by which Aboriginal perceptions and knowledge entered European thought'.[19] Smith hopes his own scholarship might contribute to that dialogue. Reflecting in 2013 on his big archaeological book, he said: 'This is a rich history. It is something that sits next to the Dreaming. It doesn't displace it, it doesn't replace it, but it's a rich history here, it's something to be proud of ... It's been my privilege to work on this history, but in a sense it has also been my gift.'

When Europeans and North Americans look for cultural beginnings, they tend to assume that humans and their civilisations are products of the Holocene (the period since the last ice age) and that we are all children of this recent spring of creativity in the history of the world. In the deep histories produced by the transatlantic hegemony, we are presented with a relentlessly northern and icy version of the Pleistocene, where the great ice sheets eradicated life, and 'civilisation' did not commence until after the great thaw began 13,000 years ago. North American historian Daniel Smail has written with great insight about 'deep history', but he makes two assumptions an Australian scholar would argue with: that 'civilisation' is a term associated with agriculture, and that 50,000 years is a possible horizon for modern humanity.[20] Aboriginal Australia shatters those assumptions.

In greater Australia at the last glacial maximum, we did not have an ice age so much as a *dust age*. And the history of Aboriginal people takes us back, if not into the ice then certainly into the dust, through periods of temperature change of 5°C and more, such as those we might also face in coming generations. An Australian history of the world includes the experience of people surviving cold droughts in the Central Australian deserts from 30,000 years ago, and the sustaining of human civilisation in the face of massive sea-level rises and temperature changes. Our growing understanding of anthropogenic climate change urgently requires deep-time historical analyses, century-scale histories of science and philosophy, and studies of human and social resilience from both the ancient past and the unfolding present. We need meaningful histories of the truly *longue durée* that enable us to see our own fossil-fuel society in proper perspective, and to see ourselves not just as a civilisation but as a species. Australia, with its unusually long human history, unique ecology and compressed colonial revolution, offers striking parables for a world facing transformative social and environmental change.

Epilogue

As I was finishing this book, a powerful object returned to Australia for the first time in two and a half centuries. It is a beautiful Aboriginal shield of red mangrove wood, warm and rough-hewn. 'This is the one all the elders talk about,' says Dharawal man Michael Ingrey. 'The one that Cook took …' The shield was owned by a Gweagal warrior who had stood on the beach at Botany Bay and watched a British ship sail towards him. It was 28 April 1770 and the ship was the *Endeavour*, captained by James Cook. Forty years afterwards, Aboriginal descendants remembered that some of their forebears 'thought the ship was a large bird'. But as the strange vision came closer they realised that 'it was a large canoe with people on board'. The British hoped to land and search for water, but the Gweagal families on shore and those fishing nearby seemed at first to ignore the ship, to the astonishment of the newcomers. It was as if the strangers floated in a different dimension.[1]

But when the sailors tried to take the longboat ashore, two warriors opposed them. Cook discharged a warning shot with his musket, and one of the Aboriginal men threw a stone towards the landing party. Cook fired again, injuring one of the warriors, who then 'lay hold of a shield' to defend himself. As the British came ashore, the Gweagal men threw two spears and Cook fired a third time. As the Australians withdrew from the beach, they left the shield behind. It was picked up by Cook's party, taken onto the *Endeavour* and eventually became a part of the collection of the British Museum in London. 'All they seem'd to want was for us to be gone,' wrote Cook.[2]

In late 2015 the shield was brought back to Australia as the centrepiece of an exhibition called *Encounters* at the National Museum of Australia in Canberra. I gazed at it through glass, and through time. It had returned briefly to its homeland. You can still see the small hole in the centre of it that Joseph Banks noted and recorded in his journal in 1770. Was it a spy-hole for the warrior holding it or had the shield earlier been 'pierced through with a single-pointed lance', as Banks thought? Or, as many elders believe today, was it caused by a bullet from Cook's gun? The shield is an emblem of encounter and it embodies conflict, collection, dispossession, resistance – and now reconciliation.

On the evening *Encounters* opened in Canberra, on 2 December 2015, representatives from twenty-seven Aboriginal communities around the continent gathered with other Australians and visitors from London in the courtyard of the National Museum, against the backdrop of delicate gums and under a beautiful dusk sky. The gentle sounds of many Aboriginal languages could be heard at the centre of the capital that night. As the sun set behind the building and the inland air cooled, the Martu mob from the Western Desert gathered more closely around the glowing coals of their courtyard campfire. Then the ceremonies began. One of the speeches was by June Oscar AO, a Bunuba woman from the Kimberley, who spoke in one breath of the grief and the triumph of the history of encounter. They could not be separated, these stories of loss and survival, of destruction and creativity, she said. Oscar believes 'we can break the linear confines of history, so our lessons of justice transcend the bounds of time.' She was finding hope in the face of pain, and expressing an Aboriginal sense of time, an understanding of change that is also cyclical.[3]

The Gweagal shield's circle of homecoming – from a violent encounter on an Australian beach in the eighteenth century to the centre of the British Empire and then back again to form the heart of an exhibition about shared history – was Bennelong's journey too. It also parallels the arc of this book's narrative. These chapters travel from the timeless land to a land deep with time, from Bennelong as a tragic figure to Bennelong the survivor, from imperial history to Indigenous history, from the cave with the invented name (Jerrikellimi) to the cave in Kukatja country with 35,000 years of habitation (Puritjarra). Eleanor Dark looked out from her cave and wanted to tell a story of her land from the inside out – and over the following generations that story emerged, turning Australian history upside-down as well. The story of the land is no longer told as a footnote to empire and it no longer begins with 'a blank space on the map', as Professor Ernest Scott put it in *A Short History of Australia* in 1916. Scott's history finished with 'a new name on the map' – *Anzac* – the colonists' national apotheosis on the other side of the world.[4]

Australia at that time was seen as a new, transplanted society with a short and derivative history, a planned, peaceful and successful off-shoot of imperial Britain. History and culture of stature came from abroad. Professional history had its beginnings in the nineteenth century in northern-hemisphere archives and universities and was closely aligned with the rise of the nation state; therefore it was seen to develop in Australia only in late colonial society and in tandem with the consolidation of the new Commonwealth of Australia. Aborigines, as non-literate, non-urban and non-national, could have no 'history' and did not constitute a 'civilisation' – thus they could find no place in the national polity or the national story. Australian history was first taught at university as the subject of the last lecture of a British history course and only flowered fully in the mid-twentieth century. As late as 1959, Professor John La Nauze could depict the history of Aboriginal people as a 'melancholy anthropological footnote'.[5]

But in the half-century that followed, Australians discovered that the New World was actually the Old, and that the true 'nomads' were the colonisers. The nation continent was reimagined as a jigsaw of bio-regional countries, which had for so long been its state. The biological cringe about 'monotonous gums', 'songless birds' and 'fossil animals' was replaced by a deep historical narrative about the continent's south-ern organic genesis.[6] Australian history became as much about ecological, social and technological discontinuities as about the political stability and continuity for which the European settlers first celebrated it. British colonisation was seen as both an invasion and an awesome social exper-iment; there was dancing with strangers and there was war. Historians ventured to the other side of the frontier and peered back at the 'white men's eyes', and Aboriginal people were compelled – and some chose – to cross the beach in the other direction. In remote parts of Australia, the Indigenous inhabitants became the custodians of white history as well as black, because they stayed on country while the whites moved away.[7] In the coastal cities Aboriginal people were found to have always been part of Australia's modern urban history. Indigenous scholars stud-ied the nation's unending frontier and the intense colonial revolution into which they had been thrown. 'The gradual surfacing of the very history that had allegedly been "vanquished",' observed Mark McKenna, 'would come to represent the most significant shift in historical con-sciousness in twentieth-century Australia.' From that moment, McKenna came to believe (as had Greg Dening) that 'there was no history of Australia that was non-Indigenous.'[8] All these insights, with their com-pelling new narratives, have emerged since I was in primary school.

In the mid-1980s the young historian Noel Pearson sat with the old men of his community on the verandah of the Old People's Home at Hope Vale and yarned about language, mission life, history, customs, hunting, birds, animals, plants, the weather, the past, the present, the future, Christianity, the church, politics and land rights.[9] Ten years later and two years after *Mabo*, Pearson gave the W K Hancock Memorial Lecture to the Australian Academy of the Humanities and, declaring that 'the truth must be sought', he honoured the craft of history because of its 'ability to explain present inequalities in terms of past injustice'.[10] Marcia Langton, another historian and a student of John Mulvaney's, felt that the formal study of history brought 'a terrible burden' for an Aboriginal person. It had for so long been used as a weapon against her. But she also asked the question: 'Without history, how would we believe in the idea of Australia?'[11]

History is essential to meaning and identity and it is a powerful disciplinary tool in the search for truth. But its greatest virtue is uncompromising complexity. As we study the past it changes before our eyes, affected by our gaze and eluding definitive capture, like the electrons that orbit a nucleus. No matter how practised we are at history, it always humbles us. No matter how often we visit the past, it always surprises us. The art of time travel is to maintain critical poise and grace in this dizzy space. There is a further hazard: we never return to exactly the same present from which we left, for time cycles on remorselessly even when we seek to defy it. And in the course of our quest we find that we, too, have changed.

Acknowledgements

I hope this book conveys the collegiality of writing and researching history and the strong sense of collaborative inquiry that informs the discipline. My sincere gratitude goes to the subjects of these chapters for the inspiration of their writing and teaching, and in many cases for conversation and friendship. My intellectual debts to these great writers are revealed through the portraits. I have met them all except for Eleanor Dark – and in her case I was made welcome in her home, where I was privileged to work in her writing studio at 'Varuna' in the Blue Mountains. I am grateful to Varuna (The Writers' House, Katoomba) for a residential fellowship that stimulated my interest in Dark's work, and I thank Peter Bishop and Vera Costello for making it possible. I was also fortunate to meet and talk with Mick and Jill Dark and to give the inaugural Mick Dark Lecture in Katoomba in 2007. Mark O'Flynn kindly guided me to the Darks' cave in November 2014.

I am deeply indebted to my fellow historians, in Australia and around the world, for the stimulus of their work and the model of their citizenship. As well as the historians I've portrayed here, I am grateful to Alessandro Antonello, Alan Atkinson, David Armitage, Bain Attwood, Alison Bashford, Tim Bonyhady, Tom Brooking, Jane Carruthers,

Michael Cathcart, Dipesh Chakrabarty, David Christian, Ann Curthoys, Jim Davidson, Bronwen Douglas, Kirsty Douglas, Moira Fahy, Tim Flannery, Meredith Fletcher, David Garrioch, Andrea Gaynor, Heather Goodall, David Goodman, Billy Griffiths, Pat Grimshaw, Brigid Hains, Christine Hansen, Barry Hill, Katie Holmes, Ken Inglis, Rani Kerin, Dick Kimber, Steve Kinnane, Shino Konishi, Marilyn Lake, Jane Lennon, Darrell Lewis, David Lowenthal, Stuart Macintyre, Iain McCalman, Mark McKenna, Christof Mauch, Joy McCann, Gregg Mitman, Cameron Muir, Chris O'Brien, Emily O'Gorman, Stephen Pyne, Peter Read, Libby Robin, Tim Rowse, Tiffany Shellam, Stefan Sippell, Dan Smail, Peter Stanley, Rebe Taylor, Stuart Ward, Richard Waterhouse and Clare Wright.

I feel lucky to work in a stimulating and supportive school of history at the Australian National University and I thank all my colleagues and students, especially Malcolm Allbrook, Gemma Betros, Frank Bongiorno, Nicholas Brown, Alex Cook, Doug Craig, Diane Erceg, Karen Fox, Pat Jalland, Rebecca Jones, Daniel May, Ann McGrath, Melanie Nolan, Maria Nugent, Jayne Regan, Alex Roginski, Carolyn Strange, Martin Thomas, Chris Wallace and Angela Woollacott. As chair of the editorial board of the *Australian Dictionary of Biography*, I am privileged to witness the depth of biographical scholarship in Australia and to work with the general editor, Melanie Nolan.

Many people have generously assisted me with references, information, practical assistance and stimulating discussion. I especially thank John Arnold, Geoffrey Bolton, John Cashmere, Michael Davis, Delia Falconer, Anne Faris, Kate Grenville, Kate Griffiths, David Hansen, Marcus Haward, Bernadette Hince, John Hirst, Paul Irish, Brian Matthews, Meredith McKinney, Tony Marshall, Philip Mead, Alison Pouliot, Joe Powell, Tony Press, Deborah Rose, Barry Smith, Will Steffen, John Thompson and Patrick Troy. My thanks to the staff of the National Library of Australia (and its wonderful Petherick Room), the Mitchell Library of the State Library of NSW, and the State Library of Victoria. The National Museum of Australia is an essential part of my work in Canberra and I thank its staff and director, Mat Trinca, for their support for research and scholarship.

Publishers and editors have encouraged my writing and shaped my thinking in the course of this inquiry, and I especially thank Peter Browne of *Inside Story*, Morag Fraser of *Eureka Street*, Brigid Hains of *Aeon*, Phillipa McGuinness of NewSouth Publishing, Peter Rose of the *Australian Book Review* and Julianne Schultz of *Griffith Review*. I am also grateful to those who invited early versions of these portraits: Bain Attwood and Stephen Foster, John Dargavel, Elaine van Kempen, Anthony Low, Camilla Nelson and Christine de Matos, Stuart Macintyre and Deborah Gare, Doug Munro and John Reid, and Mark Peel. I was fortunate to work closely with Bain Attwood in editing a book about Henry Reynolds and with Tim Bonyhady in editing a book about John Mulvaney and I learned a great deal from them both. Mark McKenna has generously encouraged this work with enthusiasm, scholarship and good conversation. Special thanks to Stuart Macintyre, who has cultivated the field of Australian historiography for decades.

It has been a pleasure working with the impressive and talented staff at Black Inc. My publisher Chris Feik fostered this book from its beginnings with intelligent questioning and thoughtful support. His strong commitment meant a great deal to me. Jo Rosenberg is a brilliant senior editor and helped to make this a better book. It was great fun working with her.

Malcolm and Jane Calder, Guy Fitzhardinge and Mandy Martin, Charlie and Christian Menzies-Wilson, Steve Morton and Faye Alexander, Richard Nelson and Debbie Miller, Alan and Margaret Platt, Mike Smith and Manik Datar, and Angela and Grahame Smith have constantly engaged me in exhilarating discussions about art, science, books and ideas.

I am grateful to John Mulvaney, Donna Merwick, Graeme Davison, Inga Clendinnen, Grace Karskens and Mike Smith for comments on the chapters about their work and to Alessandro Antonello, Bain Attwood, David Goodman, Stuart Macintyre, Mark McKenna and Libby Robin for reading draft chapters. Billy Griffiths has read every word and I have benefited immeasurably from his perceptive insights and literary judgement.

My family has always encouraged me in my writing and helped to make it feel like a natural part of our life together. I feel blessed to have their love and support. My heartfelt thanks go to Libby, Kate and Brent, and Billy and Emily.

My mother, Kathleen Wembridge (1921–2008), introduced me to Eleanor Dark and Judith Wright, and my father, Raymond Griffiths (1923–2011), shared my admiration for Eric Rolls and Greg Dening. A science teacher and an engineer, they encouraged my study of history and enjoyed reading and talking about all the writers portrayed here.

This book celebrates reading and Australian writing. In that quest I've had treasured companions who are always happy to go time-travelling (as well as just travelling), and whose wisdom, conversation and sense of adventure are a constant inspiration. This book is dedicated to them: Michael, Julie, Mardie and Dominic Landvogt.

Tom Griffiths
April 2016, Canberra

Endnotes

Prologue

1 Fernand Braudel, *The Mediterranean and the Mediterranean World in the Age of Philip II* (trans. Siân Reynolds), 2 vols, New York: Harper and Row, 1972–74.

2 Emmanuel Le Roy Ladurie, *Montaillou: Cathars and Catholics in a French Village, 1294–1324*, London: Scolar Press, 1978.

3 Marc Bloch, *Strange Defeat: A Statement of Evidence Written in 1940*, London: Oxford University Press, 1949; Marc Bloch, *The Historian's Craft*, Manchester: Manchester University Press, 1954; Carole Fink, *Marc Bloch: A Life in History*, Cambridge: Cambridge University Press, 1989, pp. 286–90.

4 Graeme Davison, *The Use and Abuse of Australian History*, Sydney: Allen & Unwin, 2000.

5 Hugh Stretton, 'Ideas for Australia', Unpublished paper presented at the National Ideas Summit, Melbourne, 1990.

6 Carolyn Walker Bynum, 'Wonder', American Historical Association Presidential Address, 1996, *American Historical Review*, 102 (1), February 1997, pp. 1–17; Richard White, *Remembering Ahanagran: A History of Stories*, Seattle and London: University of Washington Press, 2004, p. 13.

7 Fernand Braudel, *The Identity of France: Volume 1, History and Environment* (trans. Siân Reynolds), London: Fontana Press, 1989, pp. 85–103.

8 Emmanuel Le Roy Ladurie, *The Mind and Method of the Historian*, Brighton: Harvester, 1981, pp. 174 f.

9 Fernand Braudel, 'History and the Social Sciences: The *Longue Durée*', in his *On History* (trans. Sarah Matthews), London: Weidenfeld and Nicolson, 1980, pp. 25–54; and his Preface to *The Mediterranean*.

10 Bloch, *The Historian's Craft*, pp. 27–8; Braudel, 'History and the Social Sciences', p. 47.

11 Jeremy Popkin, 'Ego-histoire Down Under: Australian Historian-autobiographers', *Australian Historical Studies*, 38 (129), 2007, pp. 106–23; David Goodman, 'The Promise of History', *AHA Bulletin*, 78/79, December 1994–April 1995, pp. 43–7.

12   This was the question Marnie Hughes-Warrington was constantly asked (and welcomed) when she wrote her book *Fifty Key Thinkers on History*, 3rd edition, Oxford and New York: Routledge, 2015, pp. xv–xvi. Hughes-Warrington, an Australian scholar, did not include a single Australian in her collection.

13   Brian Greene, 'Fabric of the Universe', *Free Library Podcast*, 29 February 2012.

14   Stephen Hawking, *A Brief History of Time*, London: Bantam, 1988, pp. 37–9, 163, chapter 9.

15   David Christian, 'The Longest *Durée*: A History of the Last 15 Billion Years', *Australian Historical Association Bulletin*, 59–60 (August–November 1989), pp. 27–36, 'The Case for "Big History"', *Journal of World History* 2 (2), 1991, pp. 223–38; *Maps of Time: An Introduction to Big History*, Berkeley: University of California Press, 2004.

16   John Lewis Gaddis, *The Landscape of History: How Historians Map the Past*, Oxford: Oxford University Press, 2002, p. 71.

17   Gaddis, *The Landscape of History*, pp. 30–1.

18   David Lowenthal, *The Past Is a Foreign Country*, Cambridge: Cambridge University Press, 1985, p. 20.

19   Gaddis, *The Landscape of History*, p. 22.

20   Jules Michelet, quoted in Carolyn Steedman, *Dust*, Manchester: Manchester University Press, 2001, p. 27. See also Hayden White, *Metahistory: The Historical Imagination in Nineteenth-Century Europe*, Baltimore: John Hopkins University Press, 1973, pp. 149–62.

21   Mark McKenna, *An Eye for Eternity: The Life of Manning Clark*, Melbourne: The Miegunyah Press, 2011, p. 468. Manning Clark, *A Historian's Apprenticeship*, Melbourne: Melbourne University Press, 1992.

22   Quoted by Bloch in *The Historian's Craft*, p. 43.

23   W K Hancock, *Professing History*, Sydney: Sydney University Press, 1976, pp. 20–1.

ONE   The Timeless Land: Eleanor Dark

1   For most of this chapter I have followed the spelling of Bennilong's name in Dark's novel. In the final stages of the chapter, where I refer to recent historiography, I have spelt his name 'Bennelong' (which is also the spelling observed by Dark in her 1966 *Australian Dictionary of Biography* entry).

2   This is Graeme Davison's characterisation of the novel in *The Unforgiving Minute: How Australians Learned to Tell the Time*, Melbourne: Oxford University Press, 1993, p. 7.

3   Eleanor Dark, *The Timeless Land*, Sydney: Angus & Robertson, 1980 edition, pp. 151, 179–80, 406.

4   Dark, *The Timeless Land*, pp. 49–50.

5   Dark, *The Timeless Land*, p. 57.

6   Dark, *The Timeless Land*, p. 334.

7   Marivic Wyndham, *'A World-Proof Life': Eleanor Dark, a Writer in Her Times, 1901–1985*, Sydney: UTSePress, 2007, pp. 195–6.

8   James Bradley, Response to Clendinnen, Quarterly Essay 24, Black Inc., Melbourne, 2006, pp. 72–6.

9   'The Timeless Land', rough typed copy, Box 5, Eleanor Dark Papers, MLMSS
        4545, Mitchell Library, Sydney.

10   Drusilla Modjeska, 'Hammer at Destiny: A Study of Eleanor Dark, Novelist and
        Social Critic', BA (Hons) thesis, Australian National University, 1973; *Exiles at
        Home: Australian Women Writers, 1925–1945*, Sydney: Sirius Books, 1984; Barbara
        Brooks and Judith Clark, *Eleanor Dark: A Writer's Life*, Sydney: Macmillan, 1998;
        Marivic Wyndham, *'A World-Proof Life'*, 2007.

11   For example, Modjeska recognised *The Timeless Land* as 'a pioneering work of
        research in Australian history', but her focus remained on the way the trilogy
        enabled an expansion of the social critique Dark ventured in her earlier novels:
        Drusilla Modjeska, 'Hammer at Destiny', footnote 6, p. 80.

12   Dorothy Fitzpatrick to Eleanor Dark, 2 December 1941, MLMSS 4545,
        Box 29/4.

13   Brooks and Clark, *Eleanor Dark*, p. 66.

14   Letter from Jean Devanny, 1945, quoted in Brooks and Clark, p. 218: "'[S]tuck in that
        beautiful home on top of a mountain,' Jean Devanny wrote, 'She is in the clouds.'"

15   Dark, *The Timeless Land*, p. 118.

16   Manning Clark, *The Quest for Grace*, Melbourne: Penguin, 1991, p. 162.

17   Eleanor Dark, diary, 2 August 1940, MLMSS 4545, Box 21.

18   Brooks and Clark, p. 203.

19   Marie B Byles, 'Mount Hay – A Bee-Line from the Nepean', *Sydney Bushwalker*,
        72, December 1940, p. 9.

20   Eleanor Dark, diary, 29 May 1940, MLMSS 4545, Box 21.

21   Eleanor Dark, diary, 14 October 1941, MLMSS 4545, Box 21.

22   Brooks and Clark, p. 219; Wyndham, chapter 5.

23   Brooks and Clark, p. 345.

24   For Eric's medical appointments diary, see Brooks and Clark, p. 237.

25   Eleanor Dark to James Putnam, 8 September 1941, MLMSS 4545, Box 25.

26   Modjeska, *Exiles at Home*, pp. 238–40.

27   Eleanor Dark, diary, 3 January 1938, MLMSS 4545, Box 21.

28   Eleanor Dark, diary, 2 January 1938, MLMSS 4545, Box 21.

29   I am grateful to Blue Mountains poet and author Mark O'Flynn for guiding me to
        the cave and for passing on the Bay of Pigs legend.

30   Eleanor Dark, diary, 5 and 7 August 1938, MLMSS 4545, Box 21.

31   Dark to Margaret Kent Hughes, 29 September 1947, quoted in Brooks and Clark,
        p. 314.

32   Eleanor Dark, diary, 5 August 1940, MLMSS 4545, Box 21.

33   Eric Lowe, 'Novelist with World Audience', *Australasian Book News and Library
        Journal*, September 1946, quoted in Brooks and Clark, p. 213.

34   Quoted in Brooks and Clark, p. 213, drawing on Alan Gill, 'Dark Family
        Secret No Longer', *Heritage Conservation News*, 6 (1), December 1990,
        p. 11.

35   Brooks and Clark, p. 186; Barbara Brooks, 'Introduction to Eleanor Dark', *Storm
        of Time*, Sydney: HarperCollins, 2002, p. vii.

36   Quoted in Brooks and Clark, p. 347.

37   Eleanor Dark, diary entries for May–July 1937, MLMSS 4545, Box 21.

38 Quoted in Brooks and Clark, p. 193.

39 Eleanor Dark, diary, 27 January 1939, MLMSS 4545, Box 21. The day I read this entry I went to town in morning & worked at Mitchell. Lunch in gardens, Mitchell in afternoon.

40 Marjorie Barnard to Miles Franklin, 10 March 1937, in Carole Ferrier (ed.), *As Good As a Yarn With You: Letters Between Miles Franklin, Katherine Susannah Prichard, Jean Devanny, Marjorie Barnard, Flora Eldershaw and Eleanor Dark*, Cambridge: Cambridge University Press, 1992, p. 38.

41 Quoted in Brooks and Clark, p. 263.

42 Percival Serle to Eleanor Dark, 23 January and 5 February 1949, MLMSS 4545, Box 30.

43 Archaeologist Rhys Jones used this phrase, 'the edge of the trees', and it inspired a sculpture and soundscape outside the Museum of Sydney: 'The newcomers struggling through the surf were met on the beaches by other men looking at them from the edge of the trees. Thus the same landscape perceived by the newcomers as alien, hostile, or having no coherent form, was to the indigenous people their home, a familiar place, the inspiration of dreams.' Rhys Jones, 'Ordering the Landscape', in I. Donaldson and T. Donaldson (eds.), *Seeing the First Australians*, Sydney: Allen & Unwin, 1985, p. 185.

44 Hassoldt Davis, 'Out of Australia', *The Nation*, New York, undated clipping, p. 316, Eleanor Dark Papers, NLA, MS 4998, Folder 2.

45 Dorothy Canfield, *The Bookman*, New York, 28 September 1941.

46 Mark McKenna, *An Eye for Eternity: The Life of Manning Clark*, Melbourne: Miegunyah Press, 2011, pp. 232–3, 252.

47 Clark, *Quest for Grace*, pp. 161–2.

48 Clark's publisher, Peter Ryan, was another student in those early lectures and recalled that Clark's picture of the early years of British settlement was drawn largely from Dark's novel: Peter Ryan, 'Manning Clark', *Quadrant*, September–October 1993, pp. 9–22.

49 Clark to Dark, 22 August 1963, Eleanor Dark Papers, NLA, MS 4998, Binder No. 3, Item 318.

50 Manning Clark, diary, 13 May 1976. I am grateful to Mark McKenna for supplying this reference.

51 Manning Clark, telegram to Eleanor Dark, 5 September 1980, MLMSS 4545, Box 30.

52 Andrew Shrylock and Daniel Lord Smail, *Deep History: The Architecture of Past and Present*, Berkeley: University of California Press, 2011, Introduction.

53 Quoted in Brooks and Clark, p. 220.

54 Quoted by A K Thomson, *Understanding the Novel: The Timeless Land*, Brisbane: Jacaranda Press, 1966, p. 7, which is in turn quoted by J J Healy, *Literature and the Aborigine in Australia 1770–1975*, Sydney: St Martin's Press, 1978, pp. 174–6.

55 Brooks and Clark, p. 350. For draft prologue, see MLMSS 4545 Box 5 and for Eleanor Dark to Curtis Brown, 19 November 1940, and Collins to Dark, 29 November 1940, see Box 22.

56 Sydney Ure Smith to Eleanor Dark, 2 April 1944, MLMSS 4545, Box 29/1.

57 Eleanor Dark, 'The Conquest of Nature', undated typescript, MLMSS 4545, Box 10.

58 Grace Karskens, *The Colony: A History of Early Sydney*, Sydney: Allen & Unwin, 2009, pp. 371–8 (quote on p. 378).

59 Bennelong's real daughter died in infancy. Dark imagines she survived.

60 Quoted in Eleanor Dark, *No Barrier*, Sydney: Collins, 1953, p. 239.

61 Marcia Langton, 'They Made a Solitude and Called it Peace', in Rachel Perkins and Marcia Langton (eds.), *First Australians: An Illustrated History*, Melbourne: SBS/Miegunyah Press, 2008, p. 28.

62 See Tom Griffiths, *Hunters and Collectors: The Antiquarian Imagination in Australia*, Melbourne: Cambridge University Press, 1996, chapters 3 and 4.

63 Dorothy Fitzpatrick to Eleanor Dark, 2 December 1941, MLMSS 4545, Box 29/4.

64 Eleanor Dark, 'Bennelong (1764–1813)', *Australian Dictionary of Biography*, National Centre of Biography, Australian National University, http://adb.anu.edu.au/biography/bennelong-1769/text1979, published first in hardcopy 1966 (accessed online 29 May 2015).

65 Inga Clendinnen, *Dancing with Strangers*, Melbourne: Text, 2003, p. 272. I'm grateful to Inga for a conversation about Dark at the Sydney Writers' Festival, May 2007.

66 Langton, 'They Made a Solitude ...', p. 28.

67 Keith Vincent Smith, *Bennelong: The Coming in of the Eora, Sydney Cove 1788–1792*, Sydney: Kangaroo Press, 2001; Kate Fullagar, 'Woollarawarre Bennelong: Rethinking the Tragic Narrative' (pp. 3–6) and 'Bennelong in Britain' (pp. 31–51), Emma Dortins, 'The Many Truths of Bennelong's Tragedy' (pp. 53–75), and Keith Vincent Smith, 'Bennelong Among his People' (pp. 7–30), in *Aboriginal History*, volume 33, Sydney: UTSePress, 2009.

68 Karskens, *The Colony*, pp. 422, 425.

69 Smith, 'Bennelong Among his People', p. 7.

70 Dortins, 'The Many Truths of Bennelong's Tragedy', pp. 53–5.

71 Wyndham, 'A World-Proof Life', p. 186. Wyndham does acknowledge, however, that Dark 'brought a fresh and imaginative approach to the writing of Australian history' (p. 181).

TWO   The Journey to Monaro: Keith Hancock

1 Quoted on the back cover of Jim Davidson, *A Three-Cornered Life: The Historian W K Hancock*, Sydney: UNSW Press, 2010.

2 'You see my work in the past has been what you might call global – Commonwealth history ... So after being global, I want to be local and cultivate my own garden,' in Robert Lehane, 'Fresh Fields May Prove Greener', undated newscutting [1967] in the Hancock Papers ('Discovering Monaro' files), MS 2886, National Library of Australia.

3 Hancock, 'Discovering Monaro: Progress Report', Cooma, 5 May 1969, Hancock Papers, Noel Butlin Archive, ANU, Canberra. This chapter draws on my contribution to a conference convened by Anthony Low at ANU to mark the centenary of Hancock's birth in 1998, and published as 'Comment: Tuscan Dreaming' in D A Low (ed.) *Keith Hancock: The Legacies of an Historian*, Melbourne: Melbourne University Press, 2001, pp. 237–48, a revised version of which was published as 'Discovering Hancock: The Journey to Monaro' in *Journal*

of Australian Studies, 62, 1999, pp. 171–81.

4   W K Hancock, *Discovering Monaro: A Study of Man's Impact on His Environment*,
     Cambridge: Cambridge University Press, 1972, p. 12.

5   Deryck Schreuder, 'History's Page – Australia as a Post-Colonial Society', in
     Schreuder (ed.), *The Humanities and a Creative Nation: Jubilee Essays*, Canberra:
     Australian Academy of the Humanities, 1995, p. 11.

6   W K Hancock, *Professing History*, Sydney: Sydney University Press, 1976,
     p. 68; Lehane, 'Fresh Fields May Prove Greener'; Interview with Robin Gollan,
     Canberra, 11 August 1998.

7   W K Hancock, *Country and Calling*, London: Faber and Faber, 1954, p. 246.

8   W K Hancock, *Australia*, London: Ernest Benn, 1930, p. 233.

9   Hancock, *Country and Calling*, p. 239.

10   Hancock, *Professing History*, p. 27.

11   Julian Thomas, 'Keith Hancock: Professing the Profession', in Stuart Macintyre
     and Julian Thomas (eds.), *The Discovery of Australian History, 1890–1939*,
     Melbourne: Melbourne University Press, 1995, pp. 146–57.

12   Hancock, *Professing History*, pp. 2, 6.

13   Manning Clark, *Bulletin*, 8 July 1972, pp. 45–6.

14   Oskar Spate, *Canberra Times*, no date [1972], W K Hancock Book Review File,
     NLA.

15   Hancock invoked Stretton in his 'Work-in-Prospect Seminar', History, Research
     School of Social Sciences, 7 March 1968, entitled 'Discovering Monaro – First
     Sight of a Seven Years' Task', Hancock Papers, NLA.

16   Hancock, *Discovering Monaro*, pp. 145–7; Jim Davidson, *A Three-Cornered Life*,
     pp. 464–5; Deirdre Slattery, 'Baldur Byles: A Forester Above the Treeline', in Brett J
     Stubbs, Jane Lennon, Alison Specht and John Taylor (eds.) *Australia's Ever-changing
     Forests VI: Proceedings of the Eighth National Conference on Australian Forest History*,
     Canberra: Australian Forest History Society, 2012, pp. 1–20.

17   Podocarpus [Baldur Byles], 'Snow Gum – The Tree', quoted in Hancock,
     Discovering Monaro, pp. 190–1.

18   Hancock makes the links between these three in his *South Australia's Lifeline*,
     Public lecture delivered at the University of Adelaide, Adelaide, 1983, pp. 16–17.

19   Les Murray, 'Eric Rolls and the Golden Disobedience', in his *Persistence in Folly*,
     Sydney: Angus & Robertson, 1984, pp. 149–67.

20   See, for example, the *Australia's Ever-Changing Forests* series, published by the
     Australian Forest History Society since 1988.

21   Hancock, *Country and Calling*, p. 243.

22   Hancock, *Country and Calling*, p. 245.

23   See Hancock, Book Review File, NLA.

24   The incomplete manuscript of *Country and Calling* exists in fifteen notebooks
     which form part of the Hancock Papers held in the Institute of Commonwealth
     Studies Library, Russell Square, London.

25   Hancock, *Country and Calling*, p. 241. The omitted sections of the autobiography
     relating to Hancock's skirmish with the ANU are to be found in Notebook 13,
     pp. 28–32, and Notebook 14, pp. 33–46. For an excellent account of the
     foundation (and later) years of the university, see S G Foster and Margaret M

Varghese, *The Making of the Australian National University, 1946–1996*, Sydney: Allen & Unwin, 1996.

26   He criticised the attitude that 'Canberra had merely to whistle': Notebook 13, p. 31.

27   Hancock to Colin Badger, 30 January 1947, Hancock Papers, P96/23, Noel Butlin Centre, ANU. Hancock mentions his prospects of employment at 'a post-graduate University in Canberra' as early as 1941 (Hancock to Herbert Burton, 26 May 1941), and in another letter to Badger (17 January 1943), he asks him 'to spy out the land for me as my employment agency', but warns (as Copland was to discover) that he would be 'exacting about terms'.

28   Notebook 13, pp. 30–1, ICS Library, London.

29   Davidson, *A Three-Cornered Life*, pp. 232–58.

30   Quoted by Neville Meaney in Hancock Book Review File, NLA.

31   Hancock to Badger, 30 January 1947, Hancock Papers, Butlin Archive.

32   I owe this insight to Geoffrey Bolton.

33   For Theaden's frank comments to Copland, see Foster and Varghese, *The Making*, p. 46. Hancock's concerns are expressed in his letter to Badger, 30 January 1947, Butlin Archive.

34   Notebook 13, p. 13, ICS Library, London.

35   Hancock, *Country and Calling*, p. 223.

36   Hancock, *Country and Calling*, p. 70; Hancock, *Attempting History*, Canberra: ANU Press, 1969, pp. 23–7.

37   Hancock to Badger, 23 March 1955, Butlin Archive; Interview with Robin Gollan.

38   Michael Roe to Libby Robin, 31 July 1998. Roe also made the point about Hancock's positivism.

39   The British scientist and novelist C P Snow argued in 1959 that there was a debilitating split in the intellectual life of Western society between the two cultures of the sciences and the humanities: *The Two Cultures and the Scientific Revolution*, Cambridge: Cambridge University Press, 1959.

40   Alan Barnard (ed.), *The Simple Fleece: Studies in the Australian Wool Industry*, Melbourne: Melbourne University Press and ANU, 1962; H J Frith and G Sawer (eds.), *The Murray Waters: Man, Nature and a River System*, Sydney: Angus & Robertson, 1974; N G Butlin (ed.), *The Impact of Port Botany*, Canberra: ANU Press, 1976; Dan Coward, *Out of Sight: Sydney's Environmental History*, Canberra: Department of Economic History, ANU, 1988.

41   Sir Douglas Wright joked about the book in these terms with H C Coombs: Foster and Varghese, *The Making*, p. 127.

42   Hancock, *Country and Calling*, p. 129.

43   Ian Britain, *Once an Australian*, Oxford and Melbourne: Oxford University Press, 1997.

44   Hancock, *Country and Calling*, chapter 3; Hancock, *Ricasoli and the Risorgimento in Tuscany*, London: Faber & Gwyer, 1926.

45   Hancock, *Professing History*, pp. 71–2.

46   Hancock, *Country and Calling*, p. 95.

47   Quoted in Robert Lehane, 'Fresh Fields May Prove Greener'.

48   W K Hancock, *Economists, Ecologists and Historians* (The Edward Shann Memorial Lecture in Economics), Perth: University of Western Australia, 1974, p. 18.

49   Hancock, *Professing History*, p. 71.

50   Ros Pesman, 'Hancock and Italy', in D A Low (ed.), *Keith Hancock: The Legacies of an Historian*, Melbourne: Melbourne University Press, 2001, pp. 22–32.

51   Mark McKenna, *Looking for Blackfellas' Point: An Australian History of Place*, Sydney: UNSW Press, 2002, pp. 37, 74.

52   Hancock, *Discovering Monaro*, p. 112.

53   Christine Hansen, 'Telling Absence: Aboriginal Social History and the National Museum of Australia', PhD thesis, ANU, 2009. See also Michael Young (comp.), *Aboriginal People of the Monaro: A Documentary History*, Sydney: Department of Environment and Conservation, 2005.

54   Marc Bloch, *Strange Defeat: A Statement of Evidence Written in 1940*, London: Oxford University Press, 1949, pp. 2, 140.

55   W K Hancock, 'Italian Metayage', in *Politics in Pitcairn and other Essays*, London: MacMillan, 1947, pp. 140, 142.

56   Hancock, *Professing History*, pp. 70–1, 127, 121 (footnote 1), 160, 163.

57   Davidson, *A Three-Cornered Life*, p. 465.

58   Hancock, *Discovering Monaro*, p. 121, 126.

59   Stephen Dovers, 'Still Discovering Monaro: Perceptions of Landscape', in Dovers (ed.), *Australian Environmental History: Essays and Cases*, Melbourne: Oxford University Press, 1994, pp. 119–40.

60   Hancock, *Discovering Monaro*, p. 163.

61   Hancock, *Discovering Monaro*, p. 163.

62   Some of these oppositions are drawn from Wendell Berry, 'The Conservation of Nature and the Preservation of Humanity', in *Another Turn of the Crank: Essays by Wendell Berry*, Washington: Counterpoint, 1995, pp. 71–2.

63   Hancock, *Economists, Ecologists and Historians*, p. 17.

THREE   Entering the Stone Circle: John Mulvaney

1   Aubrey Burl, *A Guide to the Stone Circles of Britain, Ireland and Brittany*, New Haven: Yale University Press, 1995, pp. 72–4. This chapter draws on my earlier writing on Mulvaney and his career: see chapters 3 and 4 of *Hunters and Collectors: The Antiquarian Imagination in Australia*, Cambridge: Cambridge University Press, 1996; 'In Search of Australian Antiquity' in Tim Bonyhady and Tom Griffiths (eds.), *Prehistory to Politics: John Mulvaney, the Humanities and the Public Intellectual*, Melbourne: Melbourne University Press, 1996, pp. 42–62; and my foreword to John Mulvaney, *Digging Up a Past*, Sydney: UNSW Press, 2011.

2   Alastair Service and Jean Bradberry, *A Guide to the Megaliths of Europe*, quoted in www.rollrightstones.co.uk/index.php/stones/ (accessed October 2015).

3   D J Mulvaney, 'Archaeological Retrospect 9', *Antiquity*, 60, 1986, pp. 96–107.

4   I am indebted to Billy Griffiths for this and other references and insights from his 'Deep Time Dreaming: Uncovering Ancient Australia', unpublished PhD thesis, University of Sydney, 2017. The original reference is D J Mulvaney, 'A note taken in 1948', undated draft in correspondence (Manning Clark), Mulvaney Papers, National Library of Australia, MS9615/1/66 (Box 8).

5   See Jon Rhodes, *Cage of Ghosts*, Canberra: National Library of Australia, 2007.

6   Robin Hill, *The Corner: A Naturalist's Journeys in South-Eastern Australia*,
     Melbourne: Lansdowne, 1970, p. 180.

7   Martin Thomas, *The Artificial Horizon: Imagining the Blue Mountains*, Melbourne:
     Melbourne University Press, 2004, pp. 287–90; Grace Karskens,
     The Colony: A History of Early Sydney, Sydney: Allen & Unwin, 2009, pp. 546–7.

8   Maggie Walter, 'Listen to the Stories in the Land', *Mercury* (Hobart), 5 January
     2015, pp. 16–17.

9   For example, in 1936 the International Commission for the Study of Fossil
     Man (which reported to the International Geological Congress) requested
     reviews of evidence of human antiquity from several Australian states. The
     Sub-Commission for Victoria, consisting of D J Mahony, B Baragwanath,
     Frederic Wood Jones and A S Kenyon, submitted a twelve-page analysis
     of artefacts, bones and skulls, and concluded that 'it must be regarded as
     reasonably certain that man has not a geological history in Victoria'. A copy of
     the Sub-Commission's report is in a file labelled 'Antiquity of Man' held in the
     'Indigenous Cultures' section of Museum Victoria.

10   D J Mulvaney, *Prehistory and Heritage: The Writings of John Mulvaney*, Canberra:
     Department of Prehistory, Australian National University, 1990, p. 149.

11   C F Kurtze to S Mitchell, 3 July 1961, Mitchell Papers, Canberra: Australian
     Institute of Aboriginal and Torres Strait Islander Studies.

12   H M Hale and N B Tindale, 'Notes on Some Human Remains in the Lower
     Murray Valley, South Australia', *Records of the South Australian Museum*, 4, 1930,
     pp. 145–218.

13   F D McCarthy, 'The Lapstone Creek Excavation: Two Culture Periods Revealed
     in Eastern New South Wales', *Records of the Australian Museum*, 22, 1948,
     pp. 1–34.

14   A S Kenyon, 'The Camping Places of the Aboriginals of South Eastern Australia',
     Paper read to the Historical Society of Victoria, 1911, Kenyon Papers, State
     Library of Victoria, Box 9/3 (vi).

15   See, for example, S Mitchell to C P Mountford, 9 January 1959, Mitchell Papers.

16   T Murray and J P White, 'Cambridge in the Bush?', *World Archaeology*, vol. 13,
     1981, pp. 255–63.

17   D J Mulvaney, 'Why Dig Up the Past?', *Twentieth Century*, 6 (3), Autumn 1952,
     pp. 27–40.

18   Mulvaney, 'Archaeological Retrospect 9', p. 98.

19   John Mulvaney and Bernie Joyce, 'Archaeological and Geomorphological
     Investigations on Mt Moffat Station, Queensland, Australia', *Proceedings of the
     Prehistoric Society*, 31, 1965, pp. 147–212. Kenniff Cave eventually provided
     evidence of occupation through 19,000 years.

20   Mulvaney, 'Archaeological Retrospect 9', pp. 100, 102.

21   D J Mulvaney, 'A New Time Machine', *Twentieth Century*, 8, Spring 1952,
     pp. 16–23, especially pp. 21–3. I am grateful to Billy Griffiths for this reference.

22   Acknowledgements, John Mulvaney with Alison Petch and Howard Morphy
     (eds.), *From the Frontier: Outback Letters to Baldwin Spencer*, Sydney: Allen &
     Unwin, 2000.

23   Bain Attwood, 'Writing the Aboriginal Past: An Interview with John Mulvaney',

Overland, 114, May 1989, p. 8.

24 D J Mulvaney, 'Prehistory from Antipodean Perspectives', *Proceedings of the Prehistoric Society*, 37, 1971, p. 245.

25 Johannes Fabian, *Time and the Other: How Anthropology Makes Its Object*, New York: Columbia University Press, 1983, p. 29.

26 Mulvaney, *Digging Up a Past*, p. 292.

27 Bain Attwood, 'Making History, Imagining Aborigines and Australia' in Bonyhady and Griffiths (eds.), *Prehistory to Politics*, pp. 98–116.

28 D J Mulvaney, *The Prehistory of Australia*, London: Thames & Hudson, 1969, p. 12.

29 Bonyhady and Griffiths (ed.), *Prehistory to Politics*.

FOUR   The Magpie: Geoffrey Blainey

1 Geoffrey Blainey, 'Geoffrey Blainey', in R M Crawford, Manning Clark and Geoffrey Blainey, *Making History*, Melbourne: McPhee Gribble and Penguin, 1985, p. 75.

2 This chapter is a revised and updated version of my contribution to a symposium about Blainey's work in November 2000: 'Light Green, Dark Green', in Deborah Gare, Geoffrey Bolton, Stuart Macintyre and Tom Stannage (eds.), *The Fuss That Never Ended: The Life and Work of Geoffrey Blainey*, Melbourne: Melbourne University Press, 2003, pp. 53–66.

3 Stuart Macintyre and Anna Clark, *The History Wars*, Melbourne: Melbourne University Press, 2003, chapter 5: 'The historian betrayed'; Graeme Davison, 'Half a Determinist: Blainey and the Mechanics of History', in Gare, Bolton, Macintyre and Stannage (eds.), *The Fuss That Never Ended*, pp. 15–27; Mark Thomas, 'Geoffrey Blainey', *Canberra Bulletin of Public Administration*, 13 (2), Winter 1986, pp. 95–9.

4 Geoffrey Blainey, 'Antidotes for History', in John A Moses (ed.), *Historical Disciplines and Culture in Australasia: An Assessment*, St Lucia: University of Queensland Press, 1979, pp. 82–100 (revised version of an address given in Hobart in 1968).

5 Foreword to Genseric (Bill) Parker, *Forest to Farming: Gembrook, An Early History*, Box Hill South: JDP Consultancy, 1995.

6 Graham Pizzey and (illustrator) Frank Knight, *The Graham Pizzey and Frank Knight Field Guide to the Birds of Australia*, Sydney: Angus & Robertson, 1997, p. 462.

7 Geoffrey Blainey, 'A Genius to the Fingertips', introduction to Blainey (ed.), *Henry Lawson*, Melbourne: Text, 2002, pp. xi–xii, xxxi; Geoffrey Blainey, *Black Kettle and Full Moon: Daily Life in a Vanished Australia*, Melbourne: Viking, 2003.

8 Geoffrey Blainey, 'Tasmania! Tasmania! The Birth of a Book', *Tasmanian Historical Studies*, 13, 2008, pp. 3–13; Bridget Griffen-Foley, 'The Steven Seagal Factor: The Corporate Histories', in Gare, Bolton, Macintyre and Stannage (eds.), *The Fuss That Never Ended*, p. 80.

9 Sir Samuel Wadham, *Selected Addresses*, with a biographical study by Geoffrey Blainey, Melbourne: Melbourne University Press, 1956, p. 1, 11–15.

10 Geoffrey Blainey, *The Story of Australia's People: The Rise and Fall of Ancient Australia*, Melbourne: Penguin, 2015, 'Preface'.

11   Geoffrey Blainey, *A Short History of the World*, Melbourne: Viking, 2000, p. vii.

12   Stephen J. Pyne, *Burning Bush: A Fire History of Australia*, Allen & Unwin, Sydney, 1992. In the book's bibliographic essay, Pyne recommends (especially to Americans): 'Above all Geoffrey Blainey's major books – *The Tyranny of Distance*, *Triumph of the Nomads*, *A Land Half Won*, and *The Rush That Never Ended* – are not to be missed, probably the most graceful and fascinating entrée imaginable into Australian history.' (p. 495)

13   Stuart Macintyre, *A Concise History of Australia*, Cambridge: Cambridge University Press, 1999, pp. 1–16.

14   Eric Rolls, *Australia: A Biography*, Brisbane: University of Queensland Press, 2000.

15   Geoffrey Blainey, *This Land Is All Horizons: Australian Fears and Visions*, Sydney: ABC Books, 2001.

16   David Christian, 'It's a Small World', *Sydney Morning Herald*, 4 November 2000, *Spectrum*, p. 5.

17   David Malouf, *A Spirit of Play: The Making of Australian Consciousness*, Sydney: ABC Books, 1998.

18   Blainey, *The Tyranny of Distance*, p. 72.

19   Malouf, *A Spirit of Play*, p. 8.

20   Geoffrey Blainey, *Triumph of the Nomads*, revised edition, Sydney: Pan Macmillan, 1982, pp. 253–4.

21   Blainey, *A Short History of the World*, pp. 32–3.

22   He might have identified with J A Froude, a literate British visitor to Australia whom Blainey described as disliking 'what he called "liberal revolutionary sensationalism"'. See Geoffrey Blainey (ed.), *Oceana: The Tempestuous Voyage of J. A. Froude, 1884 and 1885* [1886], Sydney: Methuen Haynes, 1985, p. viii.

23   Blainey acknowledges that it's not a simple contrast: 'Many who favour a return to Nature are pessimistic towards the short-term future of their civilisation but, believing that they hold the ultimate panacea, are optimistic towards the long-term future': Geoffrey Blainey, *The Great Seesaw: A New View of the Western World, 1750–2000*, South Melbourne: Macmillan, 1988, p. 3.

24   Blainey, *Seesaw*, pp. 2–3.

25   Blainey, 'Geoffrey Blainey' in *Making History*, p. 72.

26   Blainey, *Seesaw*, p. 224.

27   Blainey, *Seesaw*, p. 1.

28   Blainey, *Seesaw*, p. 176.

29   Blainey, *Seesaw*, pp. 55, 79; Blainey, *This Land Is All Horizons*, pp. 58–9; Geoffrey Blainey, *A Shorter History of Australia*, Melbourne: William Heinemann Australia, 1994, chapter 16.

30   Blainey, *Seesaw*, pp. 186–7.

31   Blainey, *A Shorter History of Australia*, p. 214.

32   Libby Robin, *Defending the Little Desert: The Rise of Ecological Consciousness in Australia*, Melbourne: Melbourne University Press, 1998, p. 145.

33   Robin, *Little Desert*, pp. 146–9; Tom Griffiths, *Secrets of the Forest*, Sydney: Allen & Unwin, 1992, pp. 63–6.

34   Murray Bookchin, *Re-enchanting Humanity*, London: Cassell, 1995.

35   Simon Schama, *Landscape and Memory*, London: HarperCollins, 1995, p. 13.

36   John MacKenzie, 'Empire and the Ecological Apocalypse: The Historiography of the Imperial Environment', in Tom Griffiths and Libby Robin (eds.), *Ecology and Empire: Environmental History of Settler Societies*, Edinburgh: Keele University Press, 1997, p. 220.

37   MacKenzie, 'Empire and the Ecological Apocalypse', p. 220.

38   Geoffrey Bolton, 'Sunny, Happy and Stormy Australia', *Australian Book Review*, 63, August 1984, p. 31, and Don Watson in 'The Friendly Historian', *Australian Book Review*, 47, December 1982–January 1983, pp. 9–10, discerned a 'Panglossian character' to Blainey's history.

39   'The Quality of Life in Australia' (1990), in Geoffrey Blainey, *Eye on Australia*, Melbourne: Information Australia, 1991, pp. 268–70.

40   Tim Rowse, unpublished early draft of 'Triumph of the Colonists', in Deborah Gare, Geoffrey Bolton, Stuart Macintyre and Tom Stannage (eds.), *The Fuss That Never Ended: The Life and Work of Geoffrey Blainey*, Melbourne: Melbourne University Press, 2003, pp. 39–52.

41   Geoffrey Blainey, 'A Nascent Spectre of Black-White Cleavage', *Sydney Morning Herald*, 10 November 1993.

42   Geoffrey Blainey, 'The Black Armband View of History' (1993), [including a section on 'A scoreboard of ecology'], in his *In Our Time: The Issues and the People of our Century*, Melbourne: Information Australia, 1999, pp. 3–14; 'Drawing up a Balance Sheet of Our History', *Quadrant*, July–August 1993, pp. 10–15.

43   Geoffrey Blainey, 'A Great Tidal Wave', *BHP Journal*, 2, 1981, reproduced in *Eye on Australia*, pp. 8–16.

44   Geoffrey Blainey, 'Three Cheers for the Little Nation That Could', *Australian*, 13 November 2000.

45   H C Coombs, *Matching Ecological and Economic Realities*, Occasional Publication no. 9, Melbourne: Australian Conservation Foundation, June 1972.

46   Blainey, *Seesaw*, p. 4.

47   Blainey, *Black Kettle and Full Moon*, p. 434.

48   Geoffrey Blainey, *A Short History of the Twentieth Century*, Melbourne: Viking, 2005, p. 415; John McNeill, *Something New Under the Sun: An Environmental History of the Twentieth Century*, London: Allen Lane, 2000.

49   See my 'Weather and Mind Games: Why Can't We Talk About Climate Change?', *Griffith Review*, 41, July 2013, pp. 246–65.

50   Mandy Martin, Jane Carruthers, Guy Fitzhardinge, Tom Griffiths and Peter Haynes, *Inflows: The Channel Country*, Canberra: Mandy Martin/Goanna Print, 2001; Libby Robin, Chris Dickman and Mandy Martin (eds.), *Desert Channels: The Impulse to Conserve*, Melbourne: CSIRO Publishing, 2010.

FIVE   The Cry for the Dead: Judith Wright

1   An earlier version of this chapter was published as 'Truth and Fiction: Judith Wright as Historian' (La Trobe University Essay), *Australian Book Review*, no. 283, August 2006, pp. 25–30.

2   Judith Wright, 'The Broken Links' (1981), in her *Born of the Conquerors*, Canberra: Aboriginal Studies Press, 1991, pp. 29–30.

3   Judith Wright, *Half a Lifetime*, Melbourne: Text Publishing, 1999, p. 165.

4   Wright, *Half a Lifetime*, p. 158.

5   Judith Wright to Michael Symons, 23 February 1978, Folder 247, Box 33, Judith Wright Papers, MS 5781, National Library of Australia.

6   Judith Wright, *The Generations of Men*, Melbourne: Oxford University Press, 1959, p. 7.

7   Mary Durack, *Kings in Grass Castles*, London: Constable & Co., 1959; Margaret Kiddle, *Men of Yesterday*, Melbourne: Melbourne University Press, 1961; Elyne Mitchell, *Chauvel Country*, South Melbourne: Macmillan, 1983; Mary Bennett, *Christison of Lammermoor*, London: Alston Rivers Ltd, 1927; Alice Duncan-Kemp, *Our Sandhill Country*, Sydney: Angus & Robertson, 1934; Barbara York Main, *Between Wodjil and Tor*, Brisbane and Perth: Jacaranda and Landfall Presses, 1967. Graeme Davison studies some of these women writers of 'patriarchal history' in 'Ancestors: The Broken Lineage of Family History', *The Use and Abuse of Australian History*, Sydney: Allen & Unwin, 2000, chapter 5.

8   Hazel de Berg interview tape with Judith Wright, NLA, Tape 924 (Copy in Judith Wright Papers, Folder 246, Box 33).

9   Wright, *The Generations of Men*, p. 92.

10   Wright, *The Generations of Men*, pp. 162–3.

11   Judith married Jack McKinney (1891–1966) in 1962; their daughter Meredith was born in 1950.

12   Judith Wright, 'Patrick White and the Story of Australia', in *Going on Talking*, Springwood: Butterfly Books, 1992, p. 52.

13   Judith Wright to Shirley Walker, 10 August 1975, in Judith Wright Papers, NLA, Folder 246, Box 33.

14   Judith Wright McKinney, 'The Writer and the Crisis', *Language: A Literary Journal*, 1 (1), April–May, 1952, pp. 4–6.

15   See also Tim Bonyhady, 'Judith Wright Tribute: Art and Activism', *Ecopolitics*, 1 (1), December 2000.

16   Judith Wright to A L Rowse, 6 April 1982, Judith Wright Papers, NLA, Folder 228, Box 30.

17   Judith's poem was one of the inspirations for Geoffrey Blomfield's detailed history of massacres in the region of the Hastings, Manning and Macleay Rivers, *Baal Belbora: The End of the Dancing*, Sydney: Alternative Publishing Cooperative, 1981. Blomfield, a local grazier, described his bias as 'offensively Aboriginal' and suffered discrimination in his community as a consequence of his research and writing. He describes some of the campaign against him in his *A Dog's Hind Leg: Of Litigation, Lawyers, Louts and Liars*, Armidale: Geoffrey Blomfield, 1990 (kindly drawn to my attention by Barbara Holloway). Judith Wright commented that 'Geoff's book has aroused the bitterest feelings in the New England district, even now – removing the Cover-up is like taking the scab off an unhealed wound.' (Judith Wright to Grace Bartram, 2 November 1982, Box 30, Folder 227.) Grace Bartram wrote a novel inspired by the story of Darkie Point (or Head), entitled *Darker Grows My Valley*, Sydney: Macmillan, 1981.

18   Quoted in Tim Rowse, *Obliged to Be Difficult: Nugget Coombs' Legacy in Indigenous Affairs*, Melbourne: Cambridge University Press, 2000, p. 176. See Judith Wright,

We Call For A Treaty, Sydney: Collins/Fontana, 1985.

19   See Philip Mead, *Networked Language: Culture and History in Australian Poetry*, Melbourne: Australian Scholarly Publishing, 2008, chapter 4: 'Homelessness'.

20   Judith Wright, *The Cry for the Dead*, Melbourne: Oxford University Press, 1981, p. 3.

21   Quoted in Stephen Downes, 'Judith Wright, Indignant Poet', *Age*, 5 June 1981.

22   Wright, *The Cry for the Dead*, p. 4.

23   Veronica Brady, *South of My Days: A Biography of Judith Wright*, Sydney: Angus & Robertson, 1998, pp. 381–2.

24   Judith Wright to Leonard Webb, 22 November 1977, quoted in Brady, *South Of My Days*, p. 381.

25   Judith Wright to Leonard Webb, 4 November 1977, quoted in Brady, *South Of My Days*, pp. 381–2.

26   See H G Barnard, 'Observations on the Disappearance and Probable Cause, of Many of our Native Birds in Central Queensland', *The Queensland Naturalist*, 9 (1), February 1934, pp. 3–7, a source also used by Wright.

27   Discussion with Meredith McKinney, March 2005.

28   Michael Roe, 'The Other Side of the Frontier', *Island Magazine*, no. 11, June 1982, pp. 2–4.

29   Roe, 'The Other Side of the Frontier', pp. 2–4.

30   Inga Clendinnen, 'Reading Mr Robinson', in Morag Fraser (ed.), *Seams of Light: Best Antipodean Essays*, Sydney: Allen & Unwin, 1998, pp. 58–78.

31   *The Cry for the Dead*, p. 152. This period remains unscrutinised in *The Generations of Men*, p. 42.

32   Davison, *The Use and Abuse of Australian History*, p. 95.

33   Wright, *The Cry for the Dead*, pp. 26–7.

34   Wright, *The Cry for the Dead*, p. 23.

35   Wright, *The Cry for the Dead*, p. 195.

36   Judith Wright to Frank Eyre, 6 May 1980, Judith Wright Papers, NLA, Box 9, Folder 71.

37   Wright, *The Cry for the Dead*, p. 5.

38   Henry Nix, 'The Brigalow', in Stephen Dovers (ed.), *Australian Environmental History: Essays and Cases*, Melbourne: Oxford University Press, 1994, pp. 198–233.

39   T B Millar, 'A Phase of Tragedy', *Canberra Times*, 12 June 1982.

40   Edmund Campion, 'The Land Which Fought Back for its Tribes', *Bulletin*, 15 December 1981.

41   Randolph Stow, 'Irrupting into the Inland', *Times Literary Supplement*, 15 October 1982. This honour is more usually granted to W K Hancock's *Discovering Monaro*, Cambridge University Press, Cambridge, 1972.

42   Terry Coleman, 'Australian Squatters and Others', *Guardian*, 1 August 1982. For an example of his own scholarship, see Terry Coleman, *The Railway Navvies: A History of the Men Who Made the Railways*, London: Hutchinson & Co., 1965.

43   Keith Windschuttle, 'The Break-Up of Australia', *Quadrant*, 44 (9), 2000, pp. 8–18; Keith Windschuttle, 'The Myths of Frontier Massacres in Australian History', Parts 1–3, *Quadrant*, 44 (10–12), 2000, pp. 8–21, 17–24, 6–20.

44   The histories of the Henry and Wright families intertwined. James Henry's father was born at Clermont in 1881, and his father's mother was Emily Bell, who was

born at Keefit on the Namoi River in 1852. The Bells were cousins of Charles Dutton, a significant settler and friend of Albert Wright's, who is featured in *The Cry for the Dead*. James Henry's mother was Mrs Norma Douglas Henry of London, a friend of Judith's Aunt Weeta and a teacher of French for many years at New England Girls' School in Armidale (where Judith boarded). Mrs Henry had spent many happy holidays at Springfield, and she also wrote to Judith in the year or so following the publication of *The Cry for the Dead*.

45 James Douglas Henry to Judith Wright, 7 March 1983, Judith Wright Papers, NLA, Box 30, Folder 228. See also James Douglas Henry to Judith Wright, 26 January 1983, Box 30, Folder 229. Another fellow-descendant of the pastoral frontier who wrote to Judith (from Armidale) of the murderous past explained that his own great-great-great-grandfather had been tried for the wanton killing of two Aborigines. He reported that *The Cry for the Dead* had disturbed people; when he told friends about it, they greeted him with 'a loud silence'. But he was himself grateful for the directness of the message. 'It seems we can't say we are sorry for what our forebears did; I can't see why we have such difficulty; Joan and I have to constantly apologise for ours. You are lucky your mob were such a nice lot.' Harold ——? to Judith Wright, 1 August 1982, Box 30, Folder 227.

46 Wright, 'The Broken Links', p. 30.

47 Discussion with Meredith McKinney, March 2005.

48 Axel Clark, 'Lest We Forget Them', *Sydney Morning Herald*, 30 January 1982.

49 Judith Wright, 'Two Dreamtimes' (1973), *Collected Poems*, Sydney: HarperCollins, 1995, pp. 315–18.

50 Wright, 'Two Dreamtimes'.

51 James Norton, MLC, quoted in Wright, *The Cry for the Dead*, p. 274.

52 Wright, *The Cry for the Dead*, p. 279.

53 Frank Eyre to Judith Wright, 28 April 1980, Judith Wright Papers, NLA, Box 9, Folder 71.

54 T B Millar, 'A Phase of Tragedy'.

SIX   **The Creative Imagination: Greg Dening**

1   This chapter draws on my notes from these workshops and my 'Professor Dening's Exercises', *Dialogue* (Academy of the Social Sciences in Australia), no. 21, 2002, pp. 25–9, and 'History and the Creative Imagination' (The Inaugural Greg Dening Memorial Lecture), *History Australia*, 6 (2), 2009, pp. 74.1–74.16.

2   Clare Wright, 'On Being a Performing Historian', presentation in celebration of the work of Greg Dening, University of Melbourne, 11 December 2008, typescript kindly made available by the author.

3   Greg Dening, *Readings/Writings*, Carlton, Vic.: Melbourne University Press, 1998, p. 91.

4   Greg Dening, *Beach Crossings: Voyaging across Times, Cultures and Self*, Carlton, Vic.: Melbourne University Press, 2004, p. 168.

5   Dening, *Beach Crossings*, pp. 111–12.

6   Dening, *Performances*, p. 11.

7   Greg Dening, 'The Art and Science of Claptrap: Reflections on Reflective History',

Fourth Year Seminar paper, Monash University, 14 May 1991, p. 12.

8 Dening, *Beach Crossings*, p. 102.

9 Dening, *Performances*, pp. 27–8.

10 Greg Dening, *Mr Bligh's Bad Language: Passion, Power and Theatre on the* Bounty, Cambridge: Cambridge University Press, 1992; *The Death of William Gooch: A History's Anthropology*, Carlton, Vic.: Melbourne University Press, 1995; *Xavier: A Centenary Portrait*, Kew, Vic.: Old Xaverians Association, 1978; *Xavier Portraits*, with Doug Kennedy, Kew, Vic.: Old Xaverians Association, 1993; *Church Alive!: Pilgrimages in Faith, 1956–2006*, Sydney: UNSW Press, 2006.

11 Dening, *Beach Crossings*, p. 100; Dening, *Performances*, pp. 7–8.

12 Greg Dening, 'Writing, Rewriting the Beach', *Rethinking History*, 2 (2), 1998, p. 170.

13 Greg Dening, *The* Bounty: *An Ethnographic History*, Parkville, Vic.: University of Melbourne, Department of History, 1988, p. 97.

14 Dening, 'Writing, Rewriting the Beach', p. 146.

15 Greg Dening, 'The Art and Science of Claptrap'; Greg Dening, 'History as a Social System', *Historical Studies*, 15 (61), 1973, pp. 673–85.

16 M Cathcart, T Griffiths, G Houghton, V Ancheschi, L Watts and D Goodman, *Mission to the South Seas: The Voyage of the* Duff, *1796–1799*, Parkville, Vic.: University of Melbourne, Department of History, 1990 (Melbourne University History monographs, no. 11).

17 Clifford Geertz, *The Interpretation of Cultures*, New York: Basic Books, 1973; Clifford Geertz, 'History and Anthropology', *New Literary History*, 21 (2), winter 1990, pp. 321–5.

18 Robert Darnton, 'Anthropology, History, and Clifford Geertz', *Anthropology Today*, 4 (4), August 1988, p. 33.

19 Francis West, 'Multi-cultural Wisdom for the Intellectual Trendies', *Age*, 27 September 1980. See the positive reply by Alan Frost, 'Writer Sought Striking Insights', Letter to the editor, *Age*, 4 October 1980. For another caustic review, see James Griffin, 'A Hall of Funny Mirrors', *Australian*, 8–9 June, 1996.

20 Dening, *Beach Crossings*, p. 345. For one of Greg's 'cliometric moments', see his *Mr Bligh's Bad Language*, pp. 62–3.

21 Bronwen Douglas, 'Greg Dening: Wayfinder in the Presents of the Past', *Journal of Pacific History*, 43 (3), 2008, pp. 359–66.

22 Dening, *Beach Crossings*, p. 51.

23 Douglas, 'Greg Dening: Wayfinder in the Presents of the Past'.

24 Dening, *Beach Crossings*, pp. 52–4.

25 Greg Dening, 'The History of Us All' [Review of Peter Read's biography of Charles Perkins], *Australian Society*, December 1990, pp. 42–3.

26 Greg Dening, 'Ethnography on My Mind', in his *Performances*, Carlton, Vic.: Melbourne University Press, 1996, pp. 5–30. See also Ivan Brady's interview with Greg in Donna Merwick (ed.), *Dangerous Liaisons: Essays in Honour of Greg Dening*, Melbourne: History Department, University of Melbourne, 1994.

27 Dening, 'Ethnography on My Mind', pp. 5–30; Dening, 'Some Beaches are Never Crossed: Foundation and Future Reflections on the History Institute, Victoria', *Rostrum*, December 2001, p. 35. On Greg's life and work, see also Douglas, 'Greg Dening: Wayfinder in the Presents of the Past'; Dipesh Chakrabarty, 'An Imaginative

and Original Historian', *Age*, 9 April 2008; and Stefan Sippell, 'Ozeanien ist
ein Kontinent ohne Kontinent' [Oceania is a Continent without a Continent],
Süddeutsche Zeitung, 113, 16 May 2008, p. 16. I have drawn on my 'Obituary: Greg
Dening (1931–2008)', *History Workshop Journal*, 67, 2008. Katerina Teaiwa, a Pacific
Islands scholar and student of the Dening workshops, danced in Greg's memory at
ANU in August 2008.

28   Dening, *Beach Crossings*, p. 104.

29   Greg Dening, *Performances*, pp. 19–20, 126–7.

30   Dening, 'History as a Social System', pp. 673–85.

31   Dening, *Readings/Writings*, p. 211.

32   Dening, 'Writing, Rewriting the Beach', pp. 146–7.

33   Rhys Isaac, *Landon Carter's Uneasy Kingdom: Revolution and Rebellion on a
Virginia Plantation*, New York: Oxford University Press, 2004, p. xxi.

34   Dening, *Beach Crossings*, pp. 263–4.

35   Dening, 'Writing, Rewriting the Beach', p. 145.

36   Conversation with the novelist Marion Halligan during one of Greg Dening's
Challenges to Perform workshops, where she was a presenter. See also her
'Where Truth Lies', *Meanjin*, 64 (1–2), 2005, pp. 95–100.

SEVEN   The Frontier Fallen: Henry Reynolds

1   For further reflections on teaching Australian Studies at the Menzies Centre at
this time, see my 'Playing the Professional Australian', *Meanjin*, 63 (3), 2004,
pp. 166–74.

2   See Deborah Rose, 'The Saga of Captain Cook: Remembrance and Morality',
in Bain Attwood and Fiona Magowan (eds.), *Telling Stories: Indigenous History
and Memory in Australia and New Zealand*, Sydney: Allen & Unwin, 2001,
pp. 61–79.

3   See Bain Attwood (ed.) *In the Age of Mabo: History, Aborigines and Australia*,
Sydney: Allen & Unwin, 1996.

4   Cited in Henry Reynolds and Jamie Dalziel, 'Aborigines and Pastoral Leases –
Imperial and Colonial Policy 1826–1855', *UNSW Law Journal*, 19 (2), 1996,
pp. 315–77, at p. 357, and critically discussed in Jonathan Fulcher, 'The *Wik*
Judgment, Pastoral Leases and Colonial Office Policy and Intention in NSW in
the 1840s', *Australian Journal of Legal History*, 4, 1998, pp. 35–56. The essay by
Reynolds and Dalziel is the published version of Appendix 15 of the *Wik Peoples'
Outline of Argument* placed before the High Court.

5   Bain Attwood and Tom Griffiths, 'Frontier, Race, Nation', in Attwood and
Griffiths (eds.) *Frontier, Race, Nation: Henry Reynolds and Australian History*,
Melbourne: Australian Scholarly Publishing, 2009, p. 3. I am indebted to Bain
Attwood for conversations about Reynolds' work. In parts of this chapter I have
drawn on my contribution to our joint introduction, 'Frontier, Race, Nation',
in Attwood and Griffiths (eds.), *Frontier, Race, Nation*, pp. 40–51.

6   Henry Reynolds, *The Other Side of the Frontier: An Interpretation of the
Aboriginal Response to the Invasion and Settlement of Australia*, Townsville:
History Department, James Cook University, 1981, pp. 2–3. See Bain Attwood,

'"Distance" and Settler Australia's Black History', in Mark Salber Phillips et al. (eds.), *Rethinking Historical Difference*, London: Palgrave, 2013, pp. 207-23.

7   Henry Reynolds, 'History from the Frontier', in Bain Attwood (ed.), *Boundaries of the Past*, Melbourne: The History Institute, Victoria, 1990, p. 22.

8   Alan Atkinson, 'Henry Reynolds, Self and Audience', in Attwood and Griffiths (eds.) *Frontier, Race, Nation*, p. 356.

9   Reynolds, *The Other Side of the Frontier*, p. 1; Henry Reynolds, *Why Weren't We Told? A Personal Search for the Truth about Our History*, Melbourne: Viking, 1999, p. 124.

10   Reynolds, *Why Weren't We Told?*, pp. 40, 95.

11   Reynolds, *Why Weren't We Told?*, pp. 3, 124.

12   Paul A Cohen, *History in Three Keys: The Boxers as Event, Experience and Myth*, New York: Columbia University Press, 1997, p. 213. I am grateful to Bain Attwood for this reference.

13   Reynolds, *Why Weren't We Told?*, p. 79.

14   Henry Reynolds, 'Aboriginal–European Contact History: Problems and Issues', *Journal of Australian Studies*, 3, 1978, p. 64.

15   Noel Pearson, *A Rightful Place: Race, Recognition and a More Complete Commonwealth*, Quarterly Essay 55, Melbourne: Black Inc., 2014, p. 14.

16   Bain Attwood, drawing on the work of New Zealand historian Andrew Sharp, calls this 'juridical history' in '*The Law of the Land* or the Law of the Land?: History, Law and Narrative in a Settler Society', *History Compass*, 2, 2004, pp. 1–30. See also Bain Attwood, 'Returning to the Past: The South Australian Colonisation Commission, the Colonial Office and Aboriginal Title', *Journal of Legal History*, 34 (1), 2013, pp. 50–82.

17   Greg Dening, 'Past Imperfect', *The Australian Review of Books*, April 1998, p. 4; Cochrane, 'Hunting not Travelling', *Eureka Street*, 8 (8), 1998, p. 33.

18   Justine Ferrari, 'Truth be Known, Postmodernism is History', *Australian*, 27 May 2006.

19   Alan Atkinson, *The Commonwealth of Speech: An Argument about Australia's Past, Present and Future*, Melbourne: Australian Scholarly Publishing, 2002, p. 37.

20   Henry Reynolds, *Nowhere People*, Melbourne: Viking, 2005, especially Prologue and Postscript.

21   Keith Windschuttle, 'The Break-Up of Australia', *Quadrant*, 44 (9), 2000, pp. 8–18; 'The Myths of Frontier Massacres in Australian History', Parts 1–3, *Quadrant*, 44 (10–12), 2000, pp. 8–21, 17–24, 6–20; 'The Historian as Prophet and Redeemer', *Quadrant*, 46 (12), 2002, pp. 9–18; *The Fabrication of Aboriginal History, Vol. 1: Van Diemen's Land 1803–1847*, Sydney: Macleay Press, 2002; 'Chapter 11: Mabo and the Fabrication of Aboriginal History', http://samuelgriffith.org.au/docs/vol15/v15chap11.pdf (accessed 4 December 2015); 'White Settlement in Australia: Violent Conquest or Benign Colonisation?', Debate staged by RMIT University, 5 March 2003, *Melbourne Historical Journal*, 31 (1), 2003, pp. 1–10.

22   For a sample of immediate responses, see Henry Reynolds, 'From Armband to Blindfold', *The Australian Review of Books*, 6 (2), 2001, pp. 8–9, 26; Lyndall Ryan, 'Postcolonialism and the Historian', *Australian Historical Association Bulletin*,

92, 2001, pp. 31–7; Raymond Evans and Bill Thorpe, 'Indigenocide and the Massacre of Aboriginal History', *Overland*, 163, 2001, pp. 21–39; Richard Hall, 'Windschuttle's Myths', in Peter Craven (ed.), *The Best Australian Essays 2001*, Melbourne: Black Inc., 2001, pp. 117–30.

23 See, for example, Pat Grimshaw, 'The Fabrication of a Benign Colonisation? Keith Windschuttle on History', *Australian Historical Studies*, 35 (123), 2004, pp. 122–9; Stuart Macintyre, 'History, Politics and the Philosophy of History', *Australian Historical Studies*, 35 (123), 2004, pp. 130–6; David Walker, 'Strange Reading: Keith Windschuttle on Race, Asia and White Australia', *Australian Historical Studies*, 37 (128), 2006, pp. 108–22.

24 I am grateful to Bain Attwood and Stephen Foster for inviting me to speak and write on this subject for the conference they organised at the National Museum of Australia in 2001: see Bain Attwood and S G Foster (eds.), *Frontier Conflict: The Australian Experience*, Canberra: National Museum of Australia Press, 2003. My chapter entitled 'The Language of Conflict' was republished as 'The Frontier Fallen', *Eureka Street*, 13 (2), March 2003, pp. 24–30.

25 James Boyce, *Van Diemen's Land*, Melbourne: Black Inc., 2008; Grace Karskens, *The Colony: A History of Early Sydney*, Sydney: Allen & Unwin, 2009; Tiffany Shellam, *Shaking Hands on the Fringe: Negotiating the Aboriginal World at King George's Sound*, Perth: UWA Press, 2009; Rebe Taylor, *Unearthed: The Aboriginal Tasmanians of Kangaroo Island*, Adelaide: Wakefield Press, 2002; Darrell Lewis, *A Wild History: Life and Death on the Victoria River Frontier*, Melbourne: Monash University Press, 2012; Libby Connors, *Warrior: A Legendary Leader's Dramatic Life and Violent Death on the Colonial Frontier*, Sydney: Allen & Unwin, 2015; Tony Roberts, *Frontier Justice: A History of the Gulf Country to 1900*, St Lucia: University of Queensland Press, 2005.

26 Henry Reynolds, *Forgotten War*, Sydney: NewSouth, 2013, p. 134.

27 Attwood and Foster (eds.), *Frontier Conflict: The Australian Experience*.

28 Keith Windschuttle, *The Killing of History: How Literary Critics and Social Theorists Are Murdering Our Past*, San Francisco: Encounter Books, 1996.

29 Windschuttle, *The Killing of History*, pp. 304–13; Georg G Iggers, *Historiography in the Twentieth Century: From Scientific Objectivity to the Postmodern Challenge*, Hanover and London: Wesleyan University Press, 1997, 'Introduction'; Greg Dening, *Performances*, Melbourne: Melbourne University Press, 1996, pp. 35–63.

30 Windschuttle, *The Killing of History*, pp. 305–8; Anne Salmond, *Two Worlds: First Meetings between Maori and Europeans, 1642–1772*, Auckland: Viking, 1991.

31 Keith Windschuttle, 'How Not to Run a Museum', *Quadrant*, 15 (9), 2001, p. 16.

32 Philip G Jones, '"A Box of Native Things": Ethnographic Collectors and the South Australian Museum, 1830s–1930s', PhD thesis, University of Adelaide, 1996. See also Jones, *Ochre and Rust*, Adelaide: Wakefield Press, 2002.

33 Tom Griffiths, *Hunters and Collectors: The Antiquarian Imagination in Australia*, Melbourne: Cambridge University Press, 1996, Part 1.

34 Bernard Smith, *The Spectre of Truganini*, Sydney: ABC Boyer Lectures, 1980, p. 17.

35 W E H Stanner, *After the Dreaming*, Sydney: ABC Boyer Lectures, 1969, and Stanner, '"The History of Indifference Thus Begins"', *Aboriginal History*, vol. 1, 1977, pp. 3–26.

36 These themes are explored in my *Hunters and Collectors*, esp. chapters 5 and 7.

37 Evans and Thorpe, 'Indigenocide and the Massacre of Aboriginal History', p. 31; D J Mulvaney, *Encounters in Place: Outsiders and Aboriginal Australians 1606–1985*, St Lucia: University of Queensland Press, 1989, p. 129; Amanda Nettelbeck and Robert Foster, *In the Name of the Law: William Willshire and the Policing of the Australian Frontier*, Adelaide: Wakefield Press, 2007.

38 F J Meyrick, *Life in the Bush (1840–1847)*, London and Melbourne: Nelson, 1939, p. 136.

39 Meyrick, *Life in the Bush*, p. 137.

40 Anna King Murdoch, 'A Woman's Long Memories Call upon a Darker Past', *Age*, 13 September 1993.

41 Tom Griffiths, *Beechworth: An Australian Country Town and Its Past*, Melbourne: Greenhouse, 1987.

42 David Roberts, 'Bells Falls Massacre and Bathurst's History of Violence: Local Tradition and Australian Historiography', *Australian Historical Studies*, 26 (105) 1995, pp. 615–33.

43 Bain Attwood analyses the workings of memory on the frontier (and Roberts' study) in *Telling the Truth about Aboriginal History*, Sydney: Allen & Unwin, 2005, chapter 9.

44 Rae Frances and Bruce Scates, 'Honouring the Aboriginal Dead', *Arena*, 86, 1989, pp. 32–51; Bruce Scates, 'A Monument to Murder: Celebrating the Conquest of Aboriginal Australia', in Lenore Layman and Tom Stannage (eds.), *Celebrations in Western Australian History*, special issue of *Studies in Western Australian History*, 10, Nedlands: Centre for Western Australian History, University of Western Australia, 1989, pp. 21–31.

45 Les Murray, *Sydney Morning Herald*, 25 January 1975, quoted in Ken Inglis, *Sacred Places: War Memorials in the Australian Landscape*, Melbourne: Melbourne University Press, 1998, pp. 447–8.

46 Windschuttle, 'The Myths of Frontier Massacres in Australian History', Parts 1–3.

47 Peter Cochrane, 'Hunting not Travelling', pp. 32–40. For a thoughtful and critical review of Reynolds' *This Whispering in Our Hearts* (1998), see Philip Jones, 'Cries and Whispers', *Adelaide Review*, July 1998.

48 Henry Reynolds, 'Class, Race, Nation', in Attwood and Griffiths (eds.), *Frontier, Race, Nation*, pp. 370–1.

49 Reynolds, *Why Weren't We Told?*, pp. 20, 127.

50 Henry Reynolds, Russel Ward Annual Lecture, Armidale, 3 October 1991 [notes], Reynolds Papers, Series 15, box 38, folder 41, National Library of Australia.

51 Reynolds, *Why Weren't We Told?*, pp. 130–3. See Graeme Davison on Russel Ward in his 'Rethinking the Australian Legend', *Australian Historical Studies*, 43 (3), 2012, pp. 429–51.

52 Ann Curthoys, 'Rewriting Australian History: Including Aboriginal Resistance', *Arena*, 62, 1983, pp. 96–108.

53 Henry Reynolds, 'New Introduction' to *The Other Side of the Frontier*, Sydney: University of New South Wales Press, 2006, p. 4.

54 Reynolds, 'New Introduction', p. 10.

55 Reynolds, *The Other Side of the Frontier*, Melbourne: Penguin, 1982, p. 201.

56   Inglis, *Sacred Places,* p. 448.

57   This point has also been made by Dipesh Chakrabarty, who has contrasted
      Reynolds' position to that of Frantz Fanon. See his discussion in 'Reconciliation
      and Its Historiography: Some Preliminary Thoughts', *UTS Review*, 7 (1), 2001,
      pp. 7, 11–12.

58   The Governor-General, Sir William Deane, launched *Sacred Places* and was
      attributed with Inglis's views in some reports of the book launch: Claire Harvey,
      'Black Wars Forgotten: Deane' and 'Veterans Condemn Black War Memorial',
      Australian, 18 November 1998, pp. 1, 2; Helen McCabe, 'Governor-General
      Pushes Memorials for Aborigines', *Courier-Mail*, 18 November 1998, p. 2;
      Glen St. J Barclay, 'The Politics of War ... and a Memorial', *Courier-Mail*,
      20 November 1998, p. 15; Editorial, 'Taking Sides in Neutrality', *Daily
      Telegraph*, 19 November 1998, p. 10; Letter, 'No Views on Black Memorial',
      Daily Telegraph, 19 November 1998, p. 12; Michael Duffy, 'A G-G Running
      Off at the Mouth', *Daily Telegraph*, 21 November 1998, p. 10; Letter, 'An
      Ideal Role for Government House', *Canberra Times*, 23 November 1998, p. 8;
      Letter, 'Governor-General Has No Comment', *Canberra Times*, 24 November
      1998, p. 8; Henry Reynolds, 'Lest We Forget', *Age*, 27 November, 1998; Letter,
      'Keep Politics Out of War Memorial', *Age*, 2 December 1998; Ken Inglis,
      'Media Amnesia', *Eureka Street*, 9 (1), 1999, p. 10; Sir William Deane, 'Abiding
      Memories', *Eureka Street*, 9 (1), 1999, pp. 11–12. See also Ken Inglis, 'The Fogs
      of War', *Weekend Australian*, 1–2 January 2000, p. 26.

59   Windschuttle, 'The Myths of Frontier Massacres in Australian History', Part 1,
      p. 16.

60   Peter Read, 'Unearthing the Past Is Not Enough', *Island*, 52, 1992, pp. 49–53;
      Marian Aveling, 'The Waterloo of White Guilt', *Australian Book Review*, 139,
      1992, pp. 6–7; Gillian Cowlishaw, 'Review Article', *Australian Journal of
      Anthropology*, 4 (1), 1993, pp. 62–7; Adam Shoemaker, 'Exorcising Old Ghosts',
      Australian, 14–15 March, 1992, p. 36; Stuart Macintyre, 'Founding Moments',
      London Review of Books, 11 March 1993, pp. 12–13; Lyndall Ryan, *Australian
      Historical Studies*, 25, 1992, pp. 330–1; Bain Attwood, 'Massacre: Our Absence
      from Our Past', *Overland*, 128, 1992, pp. 83–5.

61   Read, 'Unearthing the Past Is Not Enough', pp. 49–53.

62   Noel Pearson, 'Mabo and the Humanities: Shifting Frontiers', 1994 W K Hancock
      Memorial Lecture, in Derek Schreuder (ed.), *The Humanities and a Creative
      Nation: Jubilee Essays*, Papers from the Academy Symposium, November 1995,
      Australian Academy of the Humanities, Canberra, 1995, p. 51.

63   Pearson, *A Rightful Place*, pp. 20–1, 28.

64   Noel Pearson, 'Ngamu-Ngaadyarr, Muuri-Bunggaga and Midha Mini in Guugu
      Yimidhirr History [Dingoes, Sheep and Mr Muni in Guugu Yimidhirr History],
      Hope Vale Lutheran Mission (1900–1950)', History Honours Thesis 1986
      published in Jan Kociumbas (ed.) *Maps, Dreams, History: Race and Representation
      in Australia*, Sydney Studies in History no. 8, Sydney: Department of History,
      University of History, 1998, pp. 131–228.

65   Jan Kociumbas, 'Introduction' to *Maps, Dreams, History*, p. 60.

66   Pearson, *A Rightful Place*, pp. 24, 26.

67   Pearson, 'Ngamu-Ngaadyarr, Muuri-Bunggaga and Midha Mini in Guugu
      Yimidhirr History', p. 134.
68   Noel Pearson, 'White Guilt, Victimhood and the Quest for a Radical Centre',
      Griffith Review, 16, May 2007; Noel Pearson, *Up from the Mission: Selected
      Writings*, Melbourne: Black Inc., 2009, pp. 348–9.
69   Noel Pearson, 'Mabo and the Humanities: Shifting Frontiers', p. 52.
70   Pearson, *A Rightful Place*, p. 16.

EIGHT   Golden Disobedience: Eric Rolls

1   This is an amended version of an essay first published in J Dargavel, D Hart and
      B Libbis (eds.) *The Perfumed Pineries*, Australian Forest History Society, Canberra,
      2001, pp. 184–94, which later appeared as an introduction to the thirtieth
      anniversary edition of Eric Rolls, *A Million Wild Acres*, Sydney: Hale & Iremonger,
      2011, pp. xi–xxii.
2   Les Murray, 'Eric Rolls and the Golden Disobedience', in his *A Working Forest:
      Selected Prose*, Sydney: Duffy and Snellgrove, 1997, p. 158.
3   Interview with Eric Rolls conducted by Tom Griffiths, Newcastle, 19 February
      2000.
4   K.C., Letter to Eric Rolls, 3 November, 1989, in Rolls Papers, MS 1719/83,
      Mitchell Library (ML), Box 37D.
5   L.A., Letter to Eric Rolls, c. 1995, Rolls Papers (ML), Box 37E (69).
6   Interview with Rolls, 19 February 2000.
7   Eric Rolls, Letter to Anne Godden, Publisher, Thomas Nelson (Australia) Ltd,
      11 October 1974, Rolls Papers, National Library of Australia (NLA), MS 7027,
      Box 10, Folder 67.
8   Eric Rolls, Letters to Sue Ebury and Tim Curnow, 1976–1980, Rolls Papers
      (NLA), Box 1, Folder 2.
9   Rolls to Sue Ebury, 12 September 1978, Rolls Papers (NLA), Box 1, Folder 2.
10   Rolls to Ebury, 21 February 1978, Rolls Papers (NLA), Box 1, Folder 2.
11   Eric Rolls, Letters to Sue Ebury and Tim Curnow.
12   Rolls to Ebury, 12 September 1978, Rolls Papers (NLA), Box 1, Folder 2.
13   Eric Rolls, 'The Farming of a New Planet', typescript, Rolls Papers (ML),
      Box 37A.
14   Interview with Rolls, 19 February, 2000.
15   George Seddon, 'Dynamics of Change', *Overland*, 87, May 1982, pp. 55–60 at p. 59.
16   Rolls to Ebury, 12 July 1979, Rolls Papers (NLA).
17   Eric Rolls, Letters to Sue Ebury and Tim Curnow, 197680, Rolls Papers (NLA),
      Box 1, Folder 2.
18   Rolls, Letters requesting information, 197380, Rolls Papers (NLA), Box 1 Folder 3.
19   Rolls, *A Million Wild Acres*, Melbourne: Nelson, 1981, p. vii.
20   Interview with Rolls, 19 February 2000.
21   Script of Don Featherstone's film (from his *Masterpiece* series) about Eric Rolls,
      Celebration of the Senses, Rolls Papers (ML), Box 37B.
22   Nicolas Rothwell, 'What Lies Beyond Us', Eric Rolls Memorial Lecture, National
      Library of Australia, 22 October 2014, broadcast on ABC Radio National 'Big Ideas',

6 November 2014, www.abc.net.au/radionational/programs/bigideas/what-lies-beyond-us3f/5853506. Rothwell describes Murray's essay as 'a vital manifesto'.

23 Murray, 'Eric Rolls and the Golden Disobedience', pp. 156–7.

24 Eric Rolls, 'Perfumed Pines: The Exploiter and the Exploited', in Dargavel, Hart and Libbis (eds.), *The Perfumed Pineries*, p. 196.

25 Rolls, *A Million Wild Acres*, p. 269

26 Interview with Rolls, 19 February 2000.

27 Interview with Rolls, 19 February 2000.

28 Eric Rolls, 'Before the Bitumen', MS submitted to *The Sydney Review* on 21 July 1989, Rolls Papers (ML), Box 37A.

29 Tom Griffiths, 'Eric Charles Rolls (1923–2007): He Worked with Words and the Land', *Sydney Morning Herald*, 7 November 2007.

30 Eric Rolls, *Doorways: A Year of the Cumberdeen Diaries*, Sydney: Angus & Robertson, 1989, p. 11.

31 See Tom Griffiths, 'How Many Trees Make a Forest? Cultural Debates About Vegetation Change in Australia', *Australian Journal of Botany*, 50 (4), 2002, pp. 375–89.

32 Rolls, *A Million Wild Acres*, p. 248.

33 Rolls, *A Million Wild Acres*, p. 399.

34 Ross Gibson, 'Enchanted Country', *World Literature Today*, 67 (3), 1993, pp. 471–6.

35 Eric Rolls, *They All Ran Wild: The Story of Pests on the Land in Australia*, Sydney: Angus & Robertson, 1969.

36 R Gibson and J Cruthers, 'WILD – Outline for a Film' [1990] in Rolls Papers (ML), Box 37A (69).

37 Rolls, Letters to Sue Ebury and Tim Curnow.

38 John Dargavel, *Fashioning Australia's Forests*, Oxford: Oxford University Press, 1995, pp. 184–5.

39 Rolls, *A Million Wild Acres*, p. 402.

40 Alfred Howitt, 'The Eucalypts of Gippsland', *Transactions of the Royal Society of Victoria*, 2, 1890, pp. 811–20.

41 See for example D G Ryan, J R Ryan and B J Starr, *The Australian Landscape — Observations of Explorers and Early Settlers*, Wagga Wagga: Murrumbidgee Catchment Management Committee, 1995, an undiscriminating report sponsored by the NSW Farmers' Association that strategically linked *A Million Wild Acres* to modern debates about tree clearing and controlled burning. The report was used by opponents of vegetation clearing control regulations, especially those introduced in NSW in August 1995. Ryan, Ryan and Starr were criticised by J S Benson and P A Redpath, who also sought to discount Rolls' book because of the legitimacy and support his Pilliga story could be seen to give to the recent clearing of native vegetation: 'The Nature of Pre-European Native Vegetation in South-Eastern Australia', *Cunninghamia*, 5 (2), 1997, pp. 283–328.

42 For example, David Horton, *The Pure State of Nature: Sacred Cows, Destructive Myths and the Environment*, Sydney: Allen & Unwin, 2000.

43 Judith Wright, 'A Chronicle of White Settlement', *Island Magazine*, 12, 1982, pp. 44–5.

44 Tom Griffiths, *Hunters and Collectors: The Antiquarian Imagination in Australia*, Melbourne: Cambridge University Press, 1996.

45 For a local correction of Benson and Redpath see J R Whitehead, 'A Discussion Paper on Human Impacts on the Vegetation of the Coonabarabran Shire', in Coonabarabran Shire Council, *Vegetation Management Plan, Vol. 3: Appendices*, Coonabarabran: Shire Council, 2000.

46 Rolls, Letter to Max Suich, 6 October 1992, Rolls Papers (ML), Box 26 (69).

47 Eric Rolls, 'Questioning a Few Fervent Opinions', *Island*, 53, 1992, pp. 26–31.

48 Eric Rolls, Letter to Don Garden, 19 December 1992, Rolls Papers (ML), Box 37A.

NINE   Voyaging South: Stephen Murray-Smith

1 Stephen Murray-Smith, *Sitting on Penguins: People and Politics in Australian Antarctica*, Sydney: Hutchinson Australia, 1988, pp. 163–5.

2 Murray-Smith, *Sitting on Penguins*, pp. 100–1.

3 Barry Lopez, 'The Gift of Good Land', *Antarctic Journal*, 27 (2), June 1992, pp. 1–5.

4 'Slope of time' is Barry Lopez's beautiful phrase in *Arctic Dreams: Imagination and Desire in a Northern Landscape*, London: Picador, 1987, p. 172.

5 This chapter draws on my book *Slicing the Silence: Voyaging to Antarctica*, Sydney: UNSW Press, 2007, especially Chapter 12, 'The Changeover'. Another version of it was delivered as the 2007 Stephen Murray-Smith Memorial Lecture and published as 'The Cultural Challenge of Antarctica' in *La Trobe Journal*, 82, Spring 2008, pp. 5–18.

6 Peter J Beck, 'A Cold War: Britain, Argentina and Antarctica', *History Today*, 37, 1987, pp. 16–23; Klaus Dodds, *Pink Ice: Britain and the South Atlantic Empire*, London and New York: I B Tauris Publishers, 2002, Chapter 4.

7 Phillip Law, *Australia and the Antarctic*, The John Murtagh Macrossan Memorial Lectures (1960), St Lucia: University of Queensland Press, 1962, p. 21.

8 Alessandro Antonello, 'Australia, the International Geophysical Year, and the 1959 Antarctic Treaty', *Australian Journal of Politics and History*, 59 (4), 2013, pp. 532–46.

9 Rob Hall and Marie Kawaja, 'Australia and the Negotiation of the Antarctic Treaty', in Marcus Haward and Tom Griffiths (eds.) *Australia and the Antarctic Treaty System*, Sydney: UNSW Press, 2011, pp. 68–96.

10 Peter J Beck, 'Antarctica Enters the 1990s', *Applied Geography*, 10, 1990, pp. 247–63, at p. 251.

11 John McLaren, *Free Radicals: Of the Left in Postwar Melbourne*, Melbourne: Australian Scholarly Publishing, 2003, pp. 48, 350.

12 Stephen Murray-Smith with Jack Jones and M A Marginson, 'South West Island, and Other Investigations in the Kent Group', *Victorian Naturalist*, 87 (12), 1970, pp. 343–70.

13 Response to a military interviewer in 1944, quoted in McLaren, *Free Radicals*, pp. 48, 350.

14 McLaren, *Free Radicals*, p. 330.

15 Murray-Smith, *Sitting on Penguins*, p. 195.

16   Stephen Murray-Smith, *Indirections: A Literary Biography*, Townsville: Foundation for Australian Literary Studies, James Cook University of North Queensland, 1981, p. 60.

17   Murray-Smith, *Sitting on Penguins*, p. 113.

18   Murray-Smith, *Indirections*, p. 14.

19   Ken Inglis, 'John Mulvaney's Universities', in Tim Bonyhady and Tom Griffiths (eds.), *Prehistory to Politics: John Mulvaney, the Humanities and the Public Intellectual*, Melbourne: Melbourne University Press, 1996, p. 26.

20   Ian Turner, *Industrial Labour and Politics*, Canberra: ANU Press, 1965, p. xx, quoted in Inglis, 'John Mulvaney's Universities', p. 27.

21   Ken Inglis, 'Murray-Smith, Stephen (1922–1988)', *Australian Dictionary of Biography*, National Centre of Biography, Australian National University, http://adb.anu.edu.au/biography/murray-smith-stephen-14885/text26075, published first in hardcopy 2012 (accessed online September 2015); John McLaren, 'Stephen Murray-Smith: His Legacy', *La Trobe Journal*, 82, Spring 2008, pp. 19–26. See also Jim Davidson, 'Stephen's Vector', *Overland*, 216, Spring 2014, https://overland.org.au/previous-issues/issue-216/feature-jim-davidson/ (accessed October 2015).

22   Stephen Murray-Smith, 'Darkness at Dawn', *Australian Book Review*, 2 (11), September 1963, p. 178.

23   Stephen Murray-Smith, 'Three Islands: A Case Study in Survival', in Imelda Palmer (ed.), *Melbourne Studies in Education 1986*, Melbourne: Melbourne University Press, 1986, pp 209–24.

24   Stephen Murray-Smith, *Sitting on Penguins*, Sydney: Hutchinson Australia, 1988, p. 105.

25   Barry Martin, 'Casey Station, Antarctica – Report of the 1986 Officer-In-Charge', internal report, Australian Antarctic Division (AAD), Commonwealth of Australia, p. 17 (AAD Library, Kingston, Tasmania).

26   Murray-Smith, *Sitting on Penguins*, p. 234.

27   Murray-Smith, *Sitting on Penguins*, pp. 91–2.

28   Murray-Smith, *Sitting on Penguins*, p. 116.

29   Editorial, 'Australia on Thin Ice', *Canberra Times*, 5 January 1986; Editorial, 'Thin Ice', *West Australian*, 31 December 1985; 'Australia is Falling Behind in Antarctic', *The Examiner*, 31 December 1985; Jane Ford, 'Lack of Research Could Freeze Us Out of Antarctic Treaty', *Australian*, 13 January 1986.

30   The 1984 memorandum is quoted in Barry Jones, 'Getting Antarctica on the Domestic and Global Agenda', Second Annual Phillip Law Lecture, Hobart, 2003 (AAD Library).

31   Jeffery Rubin, 'White Australia', *Time*, 30 May 1988.

32   Quoted in Keith Scott, 'A Presence First, and Science Comes Later', *Canberra Times*, 22 March 1989.

33   Graham Robertson, 'Report on the Biology Program at Mawson' [1988], internal report, Australian Antarctic Division (AAD), Commonwealth of Australia, 1989, p. 37 (AAD Library).

34   Stephen Murray-Smith, 'Recollections', in Ann Curthoys, A W Martin and Tim Rowse (ed.) *Australians from 1939*, Sydney: Fairfax, Syme and Weldon Associates, 1987, pp. 422–31; McLaren, *Free Radicals*, p. 230.

35 Stephen Murray-Smith, *Behind the Mask: Technical Education Yesterday and Today*, The 1987 Beanland Lecture, Melbourne: Footscray Institute of Technology, 1987, pp. 11, 18.

36 Murray-Smith, *Sitting on Penguins*, p. 125.

37 John May, *Greenpeace Book on Antarctica: A New View of the Southern Continent*, London: Dorling Kindersley, 1988.

38 For a brilliant analysis of this period of Australian Antarctic politics, see Andrew Jackson and Peter Boyce, 'Mining and "World Park Antarctica", 1982–1991', in Haward and Griffiths (eds.), *Australia and the Antarctic Treaty System*, pp. 243–73. See also Tim Bowden, *The Silence Calling: Australians in Antarctica 1947–1997: The ANARE Jubilee History*, Sydney: Allen & Unwin, 1997, pp. 410–15.

39 However, ecological thinking about Antarctic space and place had been growing since the 1960s: see Alessandro Antonello, 'The Greening of Antarctica: Science, Politics and Diplomacy, 1959–1980', PhD thesis, Australian National University, 2014.

40 Raymond Priestley, 'The Professor', Paper given in Cambridge [c. 1921], Priestley Papers, Scrapbook relating to T W E David, MS 507, Scott Polar Research Institute, Cambridge.

41 Murray-Smith, *Sitting on Penguins*, pp. 229–30.

TEN History as Art: Donna Merwick

1 Quoted in David Goodman and Donna Merwick, 'American History at Melbourne: A Conversation', chapter 10 of Fay Anderson and Stuart Macintyre (eds.), *The Life of the Past: The Discipline of History at the University of Melbourne*, Melbourne: The Department of History, University of Melbourne, 2006, p. 284.

2 Throughout this chapter I have drawn on a series of conversations with Donna during 2013 and 2014. The unreferenced quotes that follow in this chapter are from those interviews.

3 On the Crawford School, see Stuart Macintyre, 'The Making of a School', Introduction to R M Crawford, Manning Clark and Geoffrey Blainey, *Making History*, Melbourne: McPhee Gribble/Penguin Books, 1985, and Stuart Macintyre and Peter McPhee (eds.), *Max Crawford's School of History*, Proceedings of a symposium held at the University of Melbourne, 14 December 1998, Melbourne: History Department, University of Melbourne, 2000.

4 Charles Sowerwine, 'Modern European History in the Antipodes', in Anderson and Macintyre (eds.), *The Life of the Past*, p. 223.

5 Donald Horne, *The Lucky Country*, Melbourne: Penguin, 1964, p. 231.

6 Crawford, Clark and Blainey, *Making History*.

7 Macintyre, 'The Making of a School', p. 3.

8 Kathleen Fitzpatrick on Scott, quoted in Susan Davies, 'Kathleen Fitzpatrick: Sculptor with Words', in Macintyre and Thomas (eds.) *The Discovery of Australian History, 1890–1939*, Melbourne: Melbourne University Press, 1995, p. 168.

9 Arthur Burns et al., 'R M Crawford: Some Reminiscences', *Historical Studies*, 15, October 1971, pp. 7–21.

10 This is a quote of Crawford's taken from a footnote in Gibbon's *Decline and Fall*

of the Roman Empire: R M Crawford, 'The School of Prudence, or Inaccuracy and Incoherence in Describing Chaos', *Historical Studies*, 15, October 1971, pp. 27–42, at p. 31.

11   Crawford, 'The School of Prudence', p. 31.

12   D J Mulvaney, 'R M Crawford: Some Reminiscences', *Historical Studies*, 15, October 1971, pp. 12–14.

13   'R M Crawford', in R M Crawford, Manning Clark and Geoffrey Blainey, *Making History*, pp. 48–51. See also Crawford, 'The School of Prudence'. For an excellent analysis of Crawford's intellectual turmoil over positivism, see Robert Dare, 'Crawford on Theory and Methods of History', in Macintyre and McPhee (eds.), *Max Crawford's School of History*, pp. 13–39.

14   This is Robert Dare's phrase from his essay, 'Theory and Method', Chapter 13 of Anderson and Macintyre (eds.), *The Life of the Past*, p. 348. Dare was working with the course materials from the year I was enrolled in Philosophy of History, 1978.

15   This quote is from White's article, 'The Burden of History', *History and Theory*, 5 (2), 1966, pp. 111–39, which anticipated the argument of *Metahistory: The Historical Imagination in Nineteenth-Century Europe*, Baltimore: John Hopkins University Press, 1973.

16   Eric Hobsbawm, *On History*, London: Weidenfeld and Nicolson, 1997, p. 272.

17   William Cronon uses a yachting metaphor to explain his struggle with postmodernism in 'A Place for Stories: Nature, History and Narrative', *The Journal of American History*, 78 (4), March 1992, pp. 1347–76.

18   Donna Merwick, 'Postmodernity and the Release of the Creative Imagination', [paper presented to a postgraduate workshop in 1999], in Ann Curthoys and Ann McGrath (eds.) *Writing Histories: Imagination and Narration*, Melbourne: Monash Publications in History, 2000, p. 22.

19   David Goodman, 'The Promise of History', *AHA Bulletin*, 78/79, December 1994–April 1995, pp. 43–7.

20   Goodman and Merwick, 'American History at Melbourne: A Conversation', pp. 285–7.

21   Donna Merwick, 'Crawford and Merle Curti: Their Friendship and Their Correspondence', in Macintyre and McPhee (eds.), *Max Crawford's School of History*, pp. 79–87.

22   Graeme Davison, 'Comment', in Macintyre and McPhee (eds.), *Max Crawford's School of History*, pp. 70–1.

23   For example, see Richard J Evans, *In Defence of History*, London: Granta Books, 2000, pp. 244–9.

24   Kathleen Fitzpatrick, 'A Cloistered Life', in Patricia Grimshaw and Lynne Strahan, *The Half-Open Door: Sixteen Modern Australian Women Look at Professional Life and Achievement*, Sydney: Hale & Iremonger, 1982, pp. 118–33, at p. 122.

25   This was my own experience of Donna's teaching in 1976 (American History) and 1978 (Philosophy of History), and I am also drawing on Robert Dare's excellent summary of Donna's style in his 'Theory and Method'.

26   Donna Merwick, *Death of a Notary: Conquest and Change in Colonial New York*, Ithaca and London: Cornell University Press, 1999, p. 167.

27   Benjamin Schmidt, 'Going Dutch', *Reviews in American History*, 28 (2), June 2000, pp. 187–94.

28   Merwick, *Death of a Notary*, p. 112.

29   Donna Merwick, 'The Writing Man: The Shrinking World of the "Note Republic" in Dutch Albany', *Halve Maen* (New York City), 69 (4), Winter 1996, pp. 57–66.

30   Merwick, *Death of a Notary*, pp. xv, 168.

31   Merwick, *Death of a Notary*, p. 183.

32   Ruud Priem et al., *Dutch Masters from the Rijksmuseum, Amsterdam*, Melbourne: National Gallery of Victoria, 2005, pp. xxvi–xxxix ('The Golden Age').

33   Schmidt, 'Going Dutch'.

34   Merwick, 'The Writing Man', pp. 57–66.

35   Simon Middleton, Review of *Stuyvesant Bound*, in *Reviews in History*, November 2013, review no. 1511, www.history.ac.uk/reviews/review/1511.

36   Donna Merwick, *The Shame and the Sorrow: Dutch-Amerindian Encounters in New Netherland*, Philadelphia: University of Pennsylvania Press, 2006; Joyce D Goodfriend, 'Righting/Writing Dutch Colonial History', *New York History*, January 1999, pp. 5–28; Richard Middleton and Anne Lombard, *Colonial America: A History to 1763*, Chichester: Wiley-Blackwell, 2011, Chapter 5, Part 2.

37   Goodfriend, 'Righting/Writing Dutch Colonial History'.

38   Goodfriend, 'Righting/Writing Dutch Colonial History'.

39   Merwick, *Stuyvesant Bound*, p. 158.

40   Terri L Snyder, 'What Historians Talk About When They Talk About Suicide: The View From Early Modern British North America', *History Compass*, 5 (2), 2007, pp. 658–74.

41   Merwick, *Death of a Notary*, p. 174.

42   Merwick, *Death of a Notary*, p. 178.

43   Merwick, 'Writing the Microhistory of a Small Dutch Community', p. 88.

44   Merwick, *Death of a Notary*, pp. 172–3, 164; Donna Merwick, 'Comments and Response', *The William and Mary Quarterly*, Third Series, 51 (4), October 1994, pp. 736–9.

45   For example, Peter McPhee, 'Sparkle in Microhistory', *Australian Book Review*, September 2002, pp. 50–1; John Demos, 'When Manhattan Became British', *The Washington Post*, 27 June 1999, B8, and Natalie Zemon Davis on the back cover of *Death of a Notary*: 'Here, in Donna Merwick's deft hands, is microhistory at its best.'

46   Peter Charles Hoffer, *The Journal of American History*, 87 (4), March 2001, pp. 1465–6.

47   Merwick, 'Postmodernity and the Release of the Creative Imagination', p. 24.

48   Merwick, 'Postmodernity and the Release of the Creative Imagination', pp. 25–6.

49   David Goodman and Mike McDonnell, 'Interview with Donna Merwick', *The Australasian Journal of American Studies*, 34 (1), July 2015, pp. 60–83, at p. 80.

50   Schmidt, 'Going Dutch'.

51   Merwick, *Death of a Notary*, p. 105.

52   Merwick, *Death of a Notary*, pp. 130–1.

53   Merwick, *The Shame and the Sorrow*, p. 3.

54   Merwick, *The Shame and the Sorrow*, p. 260–1; Natalie Zemon Davis, *Women on*

the Edge: Three Seventeenth-Century Lives, Cambridge, Massachusetts: Harvard University Press, 1995, Prologue.

55   Cathy Matson, Review of Death of a Notary, in The American Historical Review, 105 (4), 2000, p. 1295.

56   Schmidt, 'Going Dutch'.

57   Goodman, 'The Promise of History'.

58   Merwick, 'Postmodernity and the Release of the Creative Imagination', p. 24.

59   Richard J Cox, 'The Information Age and History: Looking Backward to See Us', Ubiquity, 30, 26 September 2000; Elizabeth Yakel, Review of Death of a Notary in The American Archivist, 63 (2), Fall/Winter 2000, pp. 392–4.

60   Robert Darnton, The Case for Books: Past, Present, Future, New York: Public Affairs, 2009.

ELEVEN   Walking the City: Graeme Davison

1   Graeme Davison, 'My Heritage Trail', in Anna Clark and Paul Ashton (eds.), Australian History Now, Sydney: New South, 2013, pp. 181–2; Graeme Davison, 'Preface to Second Edition', The Rise and Fall of Marvellous Melbourne, Melbourne: Melbourne University Press, 2004, p. ix.

2   Davison, The Rise and Fall of Marvellous Melbourne, p. 150.

3   The newspaper is quoted in Graeme Davison, 'Richmond', in Davison (ed.), Melbourne on Foot: 15 Walks through Historic Melbourne, Adelaide: Rigby, 1980, p. 85.

4   Asa Briggs, Historians and the Study of Cities, George Judah Cohen Memorial Lecture, Sydney: University of Sydney, 1960; Graeme Davison, History as a Vocation, Lecture on the occasion of his retirement from the School of Historical Studies, 23 November 2005, Clayton: Monash University, 2006, pp. 6–7.

5   Winifred Raushenbush, Robert E Park: Biography of a Sociologist, Durham NC: Duke University Press, 1979, preface.

6   Davison, Marvellous Melbourne, 1979, p. 9.

7   This paragraph draws on Davison, 'Richmond', and 'Sense of Place', in Bain Attwood (ed.), Boundaries of the Past, Melbourne: The History Institute, Victoria, 1990, pp. 32–3.

8   Davison, 'Sense of Place', p. 33.

9   Graeme Davison, Lost Relations: Fortunes of My Family in Australia's Golden Age, Sydney: Allen & Unwin, 2015, p. 50.

10   Graeme Davison, 'The View From the Palisade Hotel', Meanjin, 65 (2), 2006, pp. 97–8.

11   Graeme later helped to create Melbourne's Golden Mile, a marked walking path through the city's main streets that was modelled on Boston's Freedom Trail.

12   Davison, History as a Vocation, p. 4.

13   Davison, 'Sense of Place', p. 31.

14   Graeme Davison, 'Comment', in Stuart Macintyre and Peter McPhee (eds.), Max Crawford's School of History, Proceedings of a symposium held at the University of Melbourne, 14 December 1998, Melbourne: History Department, University of Melbourne, 2000, pp. 70–1.

15   Graeme Davison, 'The Social Survey and the Puzzle of Australian Sociology',

Australian Historical Studies, 34 (121), 2003, pp. 139–62.

16   Graeme Davison, *Car Wars: How the Car Won our Hearts and Conquered our Cities*, Sydney: Allen & Unwin, 2004, pp. 74–7.

17   Davison, 'Sense of Place', pp. 31–2, *History as a Vocation*, p. 5; 'My Heritage Trail', p. 181.

18   Davison, 'The View from the Palisade Hotel', p. 100.

19   For more about Koonung Creek in the memories of suburban children, see Carla Pascoe, *Spaces Imagined, Places Remembered: Childhood in 1950s Australia*, Newcastle upon Tyne: Cambridge Scholars Publishing, 2011, chapter 3.

20   Barbara Davison and Graeme Davison, 'Suburban Pioneers', in Graeme Davison, Tony Dingle and Seamus O'Hanlon (eds.), *The Cream-Brick Frontier: Histories of Australian Suburbia*, Clayton: Monash Publications in History No. 19, 1995, p. 43.

21   Built Heritage Pty Ltd, *Balwyn and Balwyn North Heritage Study (Incorporating Deepdene and Greythorn)*, Draft report prepared for the City of Booroondara, Emerald, June 2013, p. 127.

22   Will Steffen, Paul J Crutzen and John McNeill, 'The Anthropocene: Are Humans Now Overwhelming the Great Forces of Nature?', *Ambio*, 36 (8), December 2007, pp. 614–21.

23   Graeme Davison, 'The Habit of Commemoration and the Revival of Anzac Day', *ACH: Australian Cultural History*, 23, 2003, pp. 73–4.

24   Davison, *History as a Vocation*, p. 6.

25   Russel Ward, *The Australian Legend*, Melbourne: Oxford University Press, 1958.

26   Don Watson, *The Bush: Travels in the Heart of Australia*, Melbourne: Hamish Hamilton, 2014, p. 94.

27   Graeme Davison, 'Fatal Attraction? The Lure of Technology and the Decline of Rural Australia, 1890–2000', *Tasmanian Historical Studies*, 9 (1), 2003, pp. 40–55; Graeme Davison, 'The Exodists: Miles Franklin, Jill Roe and the "Drift to the Metropolis"', *History Australia*, 2 (2), 2005; Graeme Davison and Marc Brodie (eds.), *Struggle Country: The Rural Ideal in Twentieth Century Australia*, Melbourne: Monash University ePress, 2005.

28   Davison, *Marvellous Melbourne*, 1979, pp. 247–57.

29   Graeme Davison, 'Sydney and the Bush: An Urban Context for the Australian Legend', *Historical Studies*, 18 (71), October 1978, pp. 191–209; Davison, *History as a Vocation*, p. 6.

30   Davison, 'Preface to Second Edition', *Marvellous Melbourne*, p. vii.

31   Graeme Davison, 'The Past and Future of the Australian Suburb', *Australian Planner*, 31, 1993, pp. 63–9.

32   Lewis Mumford, *The City in History*, London: Penguin, 1966, pp. 563.

33   Davison, 'The Past and Future of the Australian Suburb', pp. 63–9.

34   Davison, 'Preface to Second Edition', *Marvellous Melbourne*, pp. vi–vii.

35   Graeme Davison, 'Australia: The First Suburban Nation?', *Journal of Urban History*, 22 (1), November 1995, pp. 40–74.

36   Graeme Davison, 'The Past and Future of the Australian Suburb'; Graeme Davison, 'The Suburban Idea and its Enemies', *Journal of Urban History*, xx (x), 2013, pp. 1–19.

37   Graeme Davison, 'Why We Shouldn't Give Up On Suburbs', *Future Tense*, ABC

Radio National, 27 May 2013, www.abc.net.au/radionational/programs/futuretense/
future-cities/4715824 (accessed 12 August 2015). See also Patrick Troy, 'Saving Our
Cities With Suburbs', *Griffith Review*, 2, Summer 2003–04, pp. 115–27.

38   See also Graeme's history of his own university, Monash, which begins with the
      launch of the Russian satellite, Sputnik, and traces the trajectory of the postwar
      university as a modernist project: Graeme Davison and Kate Murphy, *University
      Unlimited: The Monash Story*, Sydney: Allen & Unwin, 2012, and Graeme
      Davison, 'Founding Monash: The University and the Promise of Modernity',
      Victorian Historical Journal, 80 (1), June 2009, pp. 91–114.

39   Davison, *History as a Vocation*, p. 9.

40   Graeme Davison, 'Slicing Australian History: Reflections on the Bicentennial
      History Project', *The New Zealand Journal of History*, 16 (1), April 1982, p. 5.

41   Davison, *History as a Vocation*, p. 14.

42   Davison, *Car Wars*, p. 81; Graeme Davison and Tony Dingle, 'Introduction:
      The View from the Ming Wing', in Davison, Dingle and Seamus O'Hanlon (eds.),
      The Cream-Brick Frontier, p. 2.

43   Davison, *Car Wars*, p. xvii.

44   Davison, 'The Past and Future of the Australian Suburb', p. 68.

45   Davison, *History as a Vocation*, pp. 11, 15.

46   Graeme Davison, 'The City as a Natural System: Ideas of Urban Society in Early
      Nineteenth Century Britain', in Derek Fraser and Anthony Sutcliffe (eds.),
      The Pursuit of Urban History, London: Edward Arnold, 1983, pp. 349–70.

47   Winifred Raushenbush, *Robert E Park*, pp. 159–64.

48   Barbara Ballis Lal, *The Romance of Culture in an Urban Civilisation: Robert E Park
      on Race and Ethnic Relations in Cities*, London and New York: Routledge, 1990,
      pp. 1, 69.

49   Davison, *Lost Relations*, p. 4.

50   Davison, *Marvellous Melbourne*, 1979, pp. 79, 86–9.

51   John McCarty, 'Melbourne, Ballarat, Sydney, Perth: The New City Histories',
      Historical Studies, 19 (74), April 1980, p. 1.

52   Davison, *History as a Vocation*, p. 13.

53   Davison, 'Slicing Australian History' and 'What Happened to History?', *Historical
      Studies*, 20 (79), October 1982, pp. 294–301. The bicentennial history project
      absorbed the creative energies and scholarly focus of our best Australian historians
      for almost a decade. The published volumes were a critical success, but sales of
      the series were a seventh of what had been hoped, in part because their release
      coincided with the 1987 stock market crash. Over the years it has been rare
      to see these books and their contents cited, perhaps because of their beautiful,
      leather-bound gravitas. The slice volumes remain an interesting anomaly in the
      landscape of Australian history – a billabong, a purposeful diversion from the
      main stream, now cut off from the currents of historiography. Two recent fine
      surveys of Australian historiography completely bypass them. It is time, I think, to
      reintegrate the bicentennial history project into Australian historiography. As well
      as addressing the gulf between academic and popular history, it played a neglected
      role in enabling Australian historians to engage collaboratively with major
      international debates in the discipline.

54 Janet McCalman, 'Translating Social Inquiry into the Art of History', *Tasmanian Historical Studies*, 5 (1), 1995–96, pp. 4–15, at p. 6.

55 Graeme Davison, *The Unforgiving Minute: How Australia Learned to Tell the Time*, Melbourne: Oxford University Press, 1993, p. 13.

56 E P Thompson, 'Time, Work-discipline, and Industrial Capitalism', *Past and Present*, 38, December 1967, pp. 56–97.

57 Davison, *Car Wars*, p. 1, 10, 57, 26.

58 Davison, *Car Wars*, p. 108, chapter 4, p.81.

59 Davison, *History as a Vocation*, p. 15.

60 Davison, *Car Wars*, p. xiv.

61 *Marvellous Melbourne*, 1979, p. 95; see also Graeme Davison, 'Old People in a Young Society: Towards a History of Ageing in Australia', *Lincoln Papers in Gerontology*, 22, Melbourne: La Trobe University, November 1993, p. 9.

62 Davison, 'Preface to Second Edition', *Marvellous Melbourne*, p. vi.

63 Davison, *Car Wars*, pp. 109–10.

64 For Davison's strengthening interest in the theme of belonging, see his 'Rethinking the Australian Legend', 43 (3), 2012, pp. 429–51, and 'Fifty Years of Victorian Local History', *Victorian Historical Journal*, 84 (1), June 2013, pp. 120–38, especially pp. 132–6.

65 Davison, 'Sense of Place', p. 30.

66 Graeme Davison, *What Makes a Building Historic?*, Melbourne: Historic Buildings Council, 1980.

67 For example, see Graeme Davison, *The Use and Abuse of Australian History*, Sydney: Allen & Unwin, 2000; Davison, 'The Habit of Commemoration and the Revival of Anzac Day'; Graeme Davison, 'Conflict in the Museum', in Bain Attwood and S G Foster (eds.), *Frontier Conflict: The Australian Experience*, Canberra: National Museum of Australia Press, 2003, pp. 201–14.

68 Davison, *History as a Vocation*, p. 10.

69 Davison, *The Use and Abuse of Australian History*, p. 90.

70 Davison, *Lost Relations*, pp. 106–9.

71 Davison, *The Use and Abuse of Australian History*, p. 84.

72 Davison, *Lost Relations*, p. xii.

73 Davison, *Lost Relations*, p. xiii.

74 The story was recorded by Ernest Thompson Seton and retold in Annie Dillard, *The Writing Life*, London: Pan Books, 1990, pp. 12–13.

75 Davison, *Lost Relations*, pp. 49–50, 55, 96–7.

76 Davison, *Lost Relations*, pp. 99, 106.

TWELVE   History and Fiction: Inga Clendinnen

1 See Darrell Lewis, *A Wild History: Life and Death on the Victoria River Frontier*, Melbourne: Monash University Publishing, 2012, and *Where is Dr Leichhardt?* Melbourne: Monash University Publishing, 2013.

2 Inga Clendinnen, *The History Question: Who Owns the Past?* Quarterly Essay 23, Melbourne: Black Inc., 2006, p. 32. A version of this chapter was published as 'The Intriguing Dance of History and Fiction' in a special issue of *TEXT* edited by

Camilla Nelson and Christine de Matos, 28, April 2015.

3   Peter Carey, *True History of the Kelly Gang*, St Lucia, Qld: University of Queensland Press, 2000; Ian Jones, *Ned Kelly: A Short Life*, Port Melbourne: Lothian, 1995.

4   Mark McKenna, *Looking for Blackfellas' Point: An Australian History of Place*, Sydney: UNSW Press, 2002; Inga Clendinnen, *Dancing with Strangers*, Melbourne: Text Publishing, 2003; Kate Grenville, *The Secret River*, Melbourne: Text Publishing, 2006. For a further historian's critique, see John Hirst, 'How Sorry Can We Be?', in *Sense and Nonsense in Australian History*, Melbourne: Black Inc., 2005.

5   Grenville, 'Comment', *The Monthly*, October 2005, pp. 16–8.

6   Grenville, 'Comment, *The Monthly*. Grenville also presented this argument as part of her Inaugural Thea Astley Lecture at the Byron Bay Writers' Festival on 5 August 2005, published as 'Saying the Unsayable', in Susan Sheridan and Paul Genoni (eds.) *Thea Astley's Fictional Worlds*, Newcastle upon Tyne: Cambridge Scholars Press, 2006, pp. 176–81. For more on Astley's historical fiction and for thoughtful reflections on the Grenville debate, see Susan Sheridan, 'Historical Novels Challenging the National Story', *History Australia*, 8 (2), 2011, pp. 7–20.

7   Kate Grenville, *Searching for the Secret River*, Melbourne: Text Publishing, 2008, p. 84.

8   Grenville, *Searching*, p. 93.

9   Grenville, *Searching*, p. 47, 119, 64, 104, 120.

10   Grenville, *Searching*, p. 146, 154, 185, 188.

11   Grenville, *Searching*, p. 165, 217.

12   Kate Grenville, 'Comment', *The Monthly*.

13   Quoted in Jane Sullivan, 'Skeletons Are Out', *Age*, 2 July 2005.

14   Inga Clendinnen, *The History Question*, and Mark McKenna, 'Writing the Past', *Australian Financial Review*, 16 December 2005, 'Review' section, pp. 1–2, 8, revised and republished in Drusilla Modjeska (ed.), *The Best Australian Essays 2006*, Melbourne: Black Inc., 2006, pp. 96–110. Kate Grenville's responses were published on her website under 'Facts and Fiction', http://kategrenville.com/node/75 (accessed 12 September 2014, removed in 2015). Compare historian Keith Vincent Smith's sympathetic reading of Grenville's *The Lieutenant* in 'On Fact and Fiction', *Weekend Australian*, 1–2 November 2008, Review, p. 2. For some other media reports of the debate, see Miriam Cosic, 'A History in Fiction', *Australian*, 27 August 2011, Stella Clarke, 'Still Not Settled', *The Australian Literary Review*, 1 October 2008, pp. 3–4, and Deborah Hope, 'Novel Approach to History', *Weekend Australian Review*, 16 June 2007.

15   Quoted in Cosic, 'A History in Fiction'.

16   See, for example, Paul Ashton and Paula Hamilton, *History at the Crossroads: Australians and the Past*, Halstead Press, Sydney, 2007, pp. 21–3. Ashton and Hamilton, both historians and academic teachers of public history, conclude (p. 23): 'It is not, however, surprising that some people had drifted away from the work of those history scholars who showed disdain for wide audience appeal and "powerful popular writing" while issuing permits for permissible pasts.'

17   Clendinnen, *The History Question*, p. 16.

18   All quotes from Jane Sullivan, 'Skeletons Are Out'.

19   Sarah Pinto, 'History, Fiction and *The Secret River*', in Sue Kossew (ed.), *Lighting*

Dark Places: Essays on Kate Grenville, Amsterdam and New York: Rodopi, 2010, p. 185.

20   The last phrase is from Grenville, *Searching for the Secret River*, p. 217. Sue Kossew, in her introduction to *Lighting Dark Places*, describes empathy as 'a keystone of [Grenville's] oeuvre: her approach seems always driven by a desire to understand what she herself may have done or thought, had she been one of her chosen characters' (p. xi). Grenville illustrates her historical method in 'Comment', *The Monthly*.

21   Grenville, *Searching for the Secret River*, p. 47.

22   See Kate Grenville, *The Writing Book: A Practical Guide for Fiction Writers*, Sydney: Allen & Unwin, 2010; Kate Grenville and Sue Woolfe, *Making Stories: How Ten Australian Novels Were Written*, Sydney: Allen & Unwin, 2001; and Grenville, *Searching for the Secret River*.

23   Delia Falconer, 'Review of *Searching for the Secret River*', *Age*, 1 September 2006.

24   James Bradley, 'Response to Clendinnen', Quarterly Essay 24, 2006, pp. 75–6.

25   Iain McCalman, 'Flirting with Fiction', in Stuart Macintyre (ed.), *The Historian's Conscience: Australian Historians on the Ethics of History*, Melbourne: Melbourne University Press, 2004, pp. 151–61.

26   Iain McCalman, *The Seven Ordeals of Count Cagliostro: The Greatest Enchanter of the Eighteenth Century*, Sydney: Harper Perennial, 2003.

27   Robert Manne, *The Culture of Forgetting: Helen Demidenko and the Holocaust*, Melbourne: Text Publishing, 1996, pp. 105–6.

28   Grace Karskens, *The Colony: A History of Early Sydney*, Sydney: Allen & Unwin, 2009, pp. 13–14.

29   An excellent long perspective on disciplinary debates about history and fiction is provided by Ann Curthoys and John Docker in *Is History Fiction?*, Sydney: UNSW Press, 2006.

30   Inga Clendinnen, 'Understanding the Heathen at Home: E P Thompson and his School', *Historical Studies*, 18 (72), April 1979, pp. 435–41.

31   Greg Dening, *Readings/Writings*, Melbourne: Melbourne University Press, 1998, p. 209.

32   Sam Wineburg, *Historical Thinking and Other Unnatural Acts: Charting the Future of Teaching the Past*, Philadelphia: Temple University Press, 2001, chapter 1.

33   Interview with Inga Clendinnen by Robin Hughes for the Australian Biography Project, 8 November 2000, www.australianbiography.gov.au/subjects/clendinnen/intertext13.html (accessed August 2015).

34   Inga Clendinnen, 'Crawford and the Moral Imperative: A Response to Bob Dare's Paper', in Stuart Macintyre and Peter McPhee (eds.), *Max Crawford's School of History*, Proceedings of a symposium held at the University of Melbourne, 14 December 1998, Melbourne: History Department, University of Melbourne, 2000, p. 41.

35   Greg Dening, 'Writing, Rewriting the Beach', *Rethinking History*, 2 (2), 1998, p. 172.

36   Clendinnen, 'Understanding the Heathen at Home', p. 435.

37   Inga Clendinnen, *Aztecs: An Interpretation*, Cambridge: Cambridge University Press, 1991, pp. 87–90.

38 Clendinnen explains the influence of Robert Manne's book *The Culture of Forgetting* at the beginning of *Reading the Holocaust*, pp. 4–6.

39 Clendinnen, *Reading the Holocaust*, pp. 3–4.

40 Clendinnen, *Reading the Holocaust*, p. 7.

41 Clendinnen, *Reading the Holocaust*, p. 205.

42 Clendinnen, *Reading the Holocaust*, pp. 7–8, 25, 20, 130, 153–4.

43 Clendinnen, *Reading the Holocaust*, pp. 24, 104.

44 Clendinnen, *Reading the Holocaust*, pp. 24, 130.

45 Clifford Geertz, *The Interpretation of Cultures*, New York: Basic Books, 1973, pp. 3–30; William H Sewell Jr., *Logics of History: Social Theory and Social Transformation*, Chicago and London: University of Chicago Press, 2005, pp. 179–81.

46 Clendinnen, *Reading the Holocaust*, pp. 137–8.

47 Clendinnen, *Reading the Holocaust*, p. 203.

48 Clendinnen, *Reading the Holocaust*, pp. 204, 198–9, 202.

49 Clendinnen, *Reading the Holocaust*, p. 191.

50 Inga Clendinnen, 'Preempting Postcolonial Critique: Europeans in the *Heart of Darkness*', *Common Knowledge*, 13 (1), 2007, pp. 1–17.

51 Inga Clendinnen, *Tiger's Eye: A Memoir*, Melbourne: Text Publishing, 2000, p. 77.

51 Clendinnen, *Tiger's Eye*, p. 77.

53 Clendinnen, *Tiger's Eye*, pp. 189–91.

54 Interview with Inga Clendinnen by Robin Hughes.

55 Inga Clendinnen, *True Stories*, Sydney: ABC Boyer Lectures, 1999; Inga Clendinnen, 'History Here: A View from Outside', The NSW Premier's History Awards Address 2003, Sydney: NSW Government, 2003.

56 W E H Stanner, 'The History of Indifference Thus Begins' (originally published 1963), *Aboriginal History*, 1, 1977, pp. 3–26.

57 Inga Clendinnen, 'Aborigines Headed for Little Justice in Legal Services Reform', *Sydney Morning Herald*, 6 July 2004.

58 William Bradley, *A Voyage to New South Wales: The Journal of Lieutenant William Bradley RN of HMS Sirius 1786–1792*, Sydney: Trustees of the Public Library of NSW in association with Ure Smith, 1969, p. 67.

59 Clendinnen, *Dancing with Strangers*, p. 9.

60 Karskens, *The Colony*, p. 50.

61 Deirdre Coleman, 'Inscrutable History or Incurable Romanticism?', *HEAT*, 8, 2004, pp. 201–13.

62 Rachel Fensham, 'On "Dancing with Strangers": Rechoreographing British and Indigenous Sovereignty in the Colonial Encounter', *The Journal of the Anthropological Study of Human Movement*, 14 (3), spring 2007, http://jashm.press.illinois.edu/14.3/fensham.html (accessed August 2015).

63 Clendinnen, *Tiger's Eye*, p. 192.

64 Quoted in Sullivan, 'Skeletons Are Out'.

65 Clendinnen, *Tiger's Eye*, p. 244.

66 Clendinnen, *Tiger's Eye*, p. 245.

67 Karskens, *The Colony*, pp. 13–14, 121–2.

68 Karskens, *The Colony*, pp. 461–2.

69 Karskens, *The Colony*, pp. 13–14.

70　Grace Karskens, 'Phillip and the Eora', presentation to *The First Governor: A Bicentenary Symposium on Arthur Phillip*, Museum of Sydney, 5 September 2014 (typescript kindly made available by the author).

71　Rhys Isaac, 'History Made from Stories Found: Seeking a Microhistory That Matters', *Common-place* 6:1 (October 2005), www.common-place.org (accessed 17 May 2014).

72　Gibson, *26 Views of the Starburst World*, Perth: UWA Publishing, 2012, p. viii.

73　Gibson, *26 Views of the Starburst World*, pp. 15–17.

74　See Tessa Morris-Suzuki, 'Unimaginable Pasts: The Horizons of Historical Fiction', chapter 2 of her *The Past Within Us: Media, Memory, History*, London and New York: Verso, 2005.

75　Barbara Kingsolver, *Small Wonder*, New York: HarperCollins, 2002, p. 203.

76　Eric Rolls, *A Million Wild Acres*, Melbourne: Nelson, 1981, p. vii.

77　Barry Lopez, 'Landscape and Narrative', *Crossing Open Ground*, New York: Vintage Books, 1989, pp. 61–71.

78　Alex Miller, 'Written In Our Hearts', *Weekend Australian*, 16–17 December 2006, pp. 8–9.

79　Bradley, 'Response to Clendinnen', pp. 75–6.

80　Pat Barker, interview with Phillip Adams, *Late Night Live*, ABC Radio National, 17 March 2005.

81　The quote is from the interview with Inga Clendinnen by Robin Hughes.

82　Tiffany Shellam, *Shaking Hands on the Fringe: Negotiating the Aboriginal World at King George's Sound*, Perth: UWA Press, 2009.

83　Kim Scott, 'A Noongar Voice, An Anomalous History', *Westerly*, 53, November 2008, p. 103. See also Tiffany Shellam, 'Tropes of Friendship, Undercurrents of Fear: Alternative Emotions on the "Friendly Frontier"', *Westerly*, 57, November 2012, pp. 16–31.

84　Mary Anne Jebb, 'Review of *That Deadman Dance* and *Shaking Hands on the Fringe*', *Aboriginal History*, 36, 2012, pp. 237–9.

85　Eleanor Dark, Untitled and undated typescript of a talk or essay about a novelist's 'autobiographical urge', Dark Papers, MLMSS 4545 Box 10.

THIRTEEN　The Feel of the Past: Grace Karskens

1　Grace Karskens, 'Public History – Academic History: The Common Ground', *Public History Review*, 1, 1992, pp. 14–25.

2　Karskens, 'Public History – Academic History', pp. 14–17.

3　Karskens, 'Public History – Academic History', p. 21.

4　Stuart Macintyre, 'The Writing of Australian History', in D H Borchardt and Victor Crittenden (eds.), *Australians: A Guide to Australian History Sources*, Sydney: Fairfax, Syme & Weldon Associates, 1987, p. 22.

5　John La Nauze, 'The Study of Australian History, 1929–1959', *Historical Studies*, 9 (33), November 1959, pp. 1–11, at p. 3. On the creativity of 'antiquarians', see Tom Griffiths, *Hunters and Collectors: The Antiquarian Imagination in Australia*, Cambridge: Cambridge University Press, 1996.

6　Stuart Macintyre, *History, the University and the Nation*, The Trevor Reese

Memorial Lecture 1992, London: Sir Robert Menzies Centre for Australian Studies, University of London, 1992, pp. 4–8.

7   Graeme Davison, 'Sense of Place', in Bain Attwood (ed.), *Boundaries of the Past*, Melbourne: The History Institute, Victoria, 1990, p. 31.

8   Karskens, 'Public History – Academic History', p. 21.

9   Karskens, 'Public History – Academic History', pp. 17–20.

10   Grace Karskens, *Holroyd: A Social History of Western Sydney*, Sydney: New South Wales University Press, 1991, p. 245.

11   Karskens, *Holroyd*, p. 3.

12   Grace Karskens, *The Colony: A History of Early Sydney*, Sydney: Allen & Unwin, 2009, p. 17.

13   Grace Karskens, 'Archaeological Sydney', Paper presented to *Whose Sydney? Reflections on the History and Memory of Sydney*, conference at Sydney Town Hall, 17 June 2003, and 'Nature City', unpublished paper.

14   Karskens, *Holroyd*, pp. 3, 245, 127, 246, 247.

15   Grace Karskens, 'Foreword' to *Four Essays about the Great North Road*, Sydney: Wirrimbirra Workshop, 1998, pp. 6–8.

16   Grace Karskens, 'The Construction of the Great North Road, NSW, 1826–1836', *Transactions of the Institution of Engineers – Multidisciplinary Engineering*, GE9, 2, October 1985, pp. 102–11.

17   Grace Karskens, 'Defiance, Deference and Diligence: Three Views of Convicts in New South Wales Road Gangs', *Australian Historical Archaeology*, 4, 1986, pp. 17–28; 'The Convict Road Station Site at Wisemans Ferry: An Historical and Archaeological Investigation', *Australian Historical Archaeology*, 2, 1984, pp. 17–26.

18   Grace Karskens, *Cox's Way: An Historical and Archaeological Study of Cox's Road and Early Crossings of the Blue Mountains, New South Wales*, Sydney: Crown Lands Office, Bicentennial Project Unit, 1988.

19   Grace Karskens, 'The Blue Mountains Crossings: New Stories from the Old Legends', *Journal of Australian Colonial History*, 16, 2014, pp. 197–225, at p. 201.

20   Siobhan Lavelle, *1813: A Tale That Grew in the Telling*, Blackheath: WriteLight, 2013; see also Richard Waterhouse, 'Commemoration, Celebration and "the Crossing"', *Journal of Australian Colonial History*, 16, 2014, pp. 186–96.

21   Eleanor Dark, *No Barrier*, Sydney: Collins, 1953; Karskens, 'The Blue Mountains Crossings', p. 199.

22   Karskens, 'The Blue Mountains Crossings', p. 211.

23   Karskens, 'The Blue Mountains Crossings', p. 218.

24   Karskens, 'The Blue Mountains Crossings', p. 203.

25   Grace Karskens, 'Engaging Artefacts: Urban Archaeology, Museums and the Origins of Sydney', *Tasmanian Historical Studies*, 7 (1), 2000, p. 39; Grace Karskens, *Inside the Rocks: The Archaeology of a Neighbourhood*, Sydney: Hale & Iremonger, 1999, pp. 69–70.

26   Grace Karskens, 'Revisiting the World View: The Archaeology of Convict Households in Sydney's Rocks Neighbourhood', *Historical Archaeology*, 37 (1), 2003, p. 34.

27   Grace Karskens, *The Rocks: A History of Early Sydney*, Melbourne: Melbourne University Press, 1997.

28 Grace Karskens, 'Seeking Sydney from the Ground Up: Foundations and Horizons in Sydney's Historiography', *Sydney Journal*, 4 (1), 2013, pp. 180–203.

29 Grace Karskens, 'Writing a History of Sydney', Seminar paper to the History Program, Research School of Social Sciences, ANU, 27 August 1998.

30 Karskens, *Inside the Rocks*, p. 17.

31 Henry Glassie, *Passing the Time in Ballymenone*, Bloomington and Indianapolis: Indiana University Press, 1995 (first published 1982), pp. 11, 603.

32 James Deetz, *In Small Things Forgotten: An Archaeology of Early American Life*, New York: Anchor Books, 1977.

33 Deetz, *In Small Things Forgotten*, p. 11.

34 Fernand Braudel, *Capitalism and Material Life*, New York: Harper and Row, 1967, p. 7.

35 Henry Glassie, *Folk Housing in Middle Virginia*, Knoxville: University of Tennessee Press, 1975.

36 Deetz, *In Small Things Forgotten*, pp. 259, 260.

37 Deetz, *In Small Things Forgotten*, p. 10.

38 Denis Byrne, 'Deep Nation: Australia's Acquisition of an Indigenous Past', *Aboriginal History*, 20, 1996, pp. 82–107.

39 Karskens, 'Engaging Artefacts', p. 51.

40 Graham Connah, 'Stamp Collecting or Increased Understanding? The Dilemma of Historical Archaeology', *Australian Historical Archaeology*, 1, 1983, pp. 15–21.

41 See Richard Flanagan's scarifying review of archaeology in museums in 'Crowbar History: Panel Games and Port Arthur', *Australian Society*, 9 (8), August 1990, pp. 35–7.

42 Susan Lawrence, 'The Role of Material Culture in Australasian Archaeology', *Australasian Historical Archaeology*, 16, 1998, pp. 8–15; Karskens, 'Engaging Artefacts'.

43 Karskens, 'Engaging Artefacts'.

44 Bernard Smith, 'History and the Collector', in his *The Death of the Artist as Hero: Essays in History and Culture*, Melbourne: Oxford University Press, 1988, pp. 95–100.

45 Karskens, *Holroyd*, p. 140, and 'Defiance, Deference and Diligence'.

46 Karskens, 'Revisiting the World View', p. 36.

47 Karskens, *Inside the Rocks*, p. 19.

48 Karskens, *Inside the Rocks*, p. 42.

49 Karskens, *Inside the Rocks*, pp. 36–9, 56.

50 Graham Connah, 'Pattern and Purpose in Historical Archaeology', *Australian Historical Archaeology*, 16, 1998, pp. 3–7.

51 Richard Mackay and Grace Karskens, 'Historical Archaeology in Australia: Historical or Hysterical? Crisis or Creative Awakening?' *Australian Historical Archaeology*, 17, 1999, pp. 10–15.

52 Connah, 'Pattern and Purpose', p. 5.

53 Jane Lydon, Review of *The Rocks, Australian Archaeology*, 46, 1998, pp. 54–6.

54 Mackay and Karskens, 'Historical or Hysterical?', p. 113.

55 Karskens, 'Engaging Artefacts', p. 60; Grace Karskens, 'Convicts and the Making of Australia', Allan Martin Lecture, ANU, 15 May 2012, www.youtube.com/watch?v=vP-Li2vvdkA (accessed September 2015).

56 Karskens, 'Engaging Artefacts', p. 42.

57   John Hirst, *Convict Society and its Enemies*, Sydney: Allen & Unwin, 1983, pp. 82–3.

58   Karskens, *Four Essays*, p. 80.

59   Grace Karskens and Susan Lawrence, 'The Archaeology of Cities: What Is It We Want to Know?', Paper presented at *Exploring the Modern City: Recent Approaches to Urban History and Archaeology*, conference at the Museum of Sydney, 2 May 2003; Karskens, Allan Martin Lecture, ANU.

60   Karskens, *The Rocks*, p. 17.

61   Alan Atkinson, 'Genesis: Recent Australian History Writing', *The Monthly*, August 2009.

62   Karskens, 'Seeking Sydney from the Ground Up'.

63   Paul Irish, 'Hidden in Plain View: Nineteenth-Century Aboriginal People and Places in Coastal Sydney', PhD thesis, University of NSW, 2014, p. 45.

64   Grace Karskens, 'Red Coat, Blue Jacket, Black Skin: Aboriginal Men and Clothing in Early NSW', *Aboriginal History*, 35, 2011, p. 20.

65   Grace Karskens, 'The Heritage of Aboriginal Sydney: Placing Lost Histories', Lecture presented on 24 September 2009 at the University of NSW, Sydney: www.youtube.com/watch?v=uNN5nlh3pvk (accessed September 2015).

66   Karskens, 'Red Coat, Blue Jacket, Black Skin', p. 20.

67   Heather Goodall and Alison Cadzow, *Rivers and Resilience: Aboriginal People on Sydney's Georges River*, Sydney: UNSW Press, 2009; Peter Read, *Belonging: Australians, Place and Aboriginal Ownership*, Cambridge: Cambridge University Press, 2000, chapter 1; Dennis Foley and Ricky Maynard, *Repossession of Our Spirit: Traditional Owners of Northern Sydney*, Canberra: Aboriginal History Inc., 2001; Maria Nugent, *Botany Bay: Where Histories Meet*, Sydney: Allen & Unwin, 2005; Irish, 'Hidden In Plain View'.

68   Grace Karskens, *The Colony*, p. 38.

69   Karskens, *The Colony*, pp. 38–42, 401–21.

70   Irish, 'Hidden in Plain View', p. 51.

71   Karskens, *The Colony*, pp. 401–21; Grace Karskens, 'Barangaroo: A Woman Worth Remembering', *Sydney Morning Herald*, 6 March 2010.

72   Karskens, *The Colony*, p. 378.

73   Rhys Isaac, *The Transformation of Virginia, 1740–1790*, Chapel Hill: UNCP, 1982.

74   Tim Bonyhady, *The Colonial Earth*, Melbourne: Miegunyah Press, 2000.

75   Inga Clendinnen, *Dancing with Strangers*, Melbourne: Text Publishing, 2003.

76   James Boyce, *Van Diemen's Land*, Melbourne: Black Inc., 2008.

77   Karskens, *The Colony*, p. xii.

78   Matthew C Strecher, 'Magical Realism and the Search for Identity in the Fiction of Murakami Haruki', *Journal of Japanese Studies*, 25 (2), summer 1999, pp. 267–8.

79   Greg Dening, 'A Poetic for Histories', in *Performances*, Melbourne: Melbourne University Press, 1996.

FOURTEEN   Dr Deep Time: Mike Smith

1   Billy Griffiths, 'The World in a Grain of Sand: The Malakanunja II Diaries', *Griffith Review*, 41, 2013, pp. 162–77.

2   Mike Smith, *Peopling the Cleland Hills: Aboriginal History in Western Central Australia 1850–1980*, Canberra: Aboriginal History Monograph 12, 2005, p. 85.

3   Mandy Martin, Libby Robin and Mike Smith, *Strata: Deserts Past, Present and Future. An Environmental Art Project about a Significant Cultural Place*, Canberra: Mandy Martin, 2005; R G Kimber, 'Tjungurrayi, Timothy Jugadai (1920–1988)', *Australian Dictionary of Biography*, National Centre of Biography, Australian National University, http://adb.anu.edu.au/biography/tjungurrayi-timothy-jugadai-15661/text26857, published first in hardcopy 2012 (accessed online 3 December 2015).

4   This and other unreferenced quotes are drawn from Mike Smith, interview by Tom Griffiths, 8 June 2012, National Library of Australia oral history recording and transcript available online at http://nla.gov.au/nla.oh-vn5981751.

5   R G Kimber, 'Journey to Alalya', 1989, unpublished manuscript in the Mike Smith Collection, National Museum of Australia Library.

6   Mike Smith, 'Reading Puritjarra', *Strata*, pp. 19, 22.

7   Mike Smith, *The Archaeology of Australia's Deserts*, Cambridge: Cambridge University Press, 2013, chapter 9: 'The Last Millennium: Archaeology and the Classic Ethnographies', p. 336. See also Peter Hiscock, 'Creators or Destroyers? The Burning Questions of Human Impact in Ancient Aboriginal Australia', *Humanities Australia*, 5, 2014, pp. 40–52.

8   Denis Byrne, 'Deep Nation: Australia's Acquisition of an Indigenous Past', *Aboriginal History*, 20, 1996, pp. 82–107.

9   Jeremy Long, 'Leaving the Desert: Actors and Sufferers in the Aboriginal Exodus from the Western Desert', *Aboriginal History*, 13, 1989, p. 11.

10   Smith, *Peopling the Cleland Hills*, footnote 173, p. 47.

11   Jeremy Long, 'Leaving the Desert', pp. 9–43.

12   M A Smith, 'The Pattern and Timing of Prehistoric Settlement in Central Australia', PhD thesis, University of New England, 1988, quoted in *Strata*, p. 6.

13   R G Kimber, '"Because it Is Our Country": The Pintupi and Their Return to Their Country', in Mike Smith and Paul Hesse (eds.), *23° S: Archaeology and Environmental History of the Southern Deserts*, Canberra: National Museum of Australia Press, 2005, pp. 345–56; Barry Hill, 'Where the Ice-Man Roamed', *Weekend Australian*, 23–24 July, 2005, p. R15.

14   Smith, *Peopling the Cleland Hills*, p. 82.

15   Deborah Rose, 'The Year Zero and the North Australian Frontier', in Deborah Rose and Anne Clark (eds.), *Tracking Knowledge in North Australian Landscapes*, Canberra and Darwin: North Australia Research Unit, ANU, 1997, pp. 19–36.

16   Mike Smith and Libby Robin, 'Archaeology, Ecology and Environmental History', in *Strata*, p. 31.

17   Smith, *Peopling the Cleland Hills*, p. 80.

18   Smith, *The Archaeology of Australia's Deserts*, p. 341.

19   Smith, *Peopling the Cleland Hills*, p. 83.

20   Daniel Lord Smail, *On Deep History and the Brain*, Berkeley: University of California Press, 2008, and Andrew Shryock and Daniel Lord Smail, *Deep History: The Architecture of Past and Present*, Berkeley: University of California Press, 2011.

Epilogue

1   Ian Coates et al., *Encounters: Revealing Stories of Aboriginal and Torres Strait
    Islander Objects from the British Museum*, Canberra: National Museum of Australia,
    2015, p. 49; Maria Nugent, *Captain Cook Was Here*, Melbourne: Cambridge
    University Press, 2009, p. 45.

2   Joseph Banks (arranged by B P Sandford), *The Endeavour Journal of Joseph Banks,
    25 Aug 1768–12 Jul 1771*, Volume 2, Sydney: State Library of New South Wales,
    1998, p. 243 (I am indebted to Billy Griffiths for this reference); Neil MacGregor,
    A History of the World in 100 Objects, London: The British Museum and Penguin,
    2010, pp. 490–4.

3   See June Oscar, 'Encountering Truth: The Real Life Stories of Objects from
    Empire's Frontier and Beyond', in Coates et al., *Encounters*, pp. 22–7.

4   Ernest Scott, *A Short History of Australia*, London: Oxford University Press, 1916.

5   Manning Clark, *The Quest for Grace*, Melbourne: Melbourne University Press,
    1990, p. 159; John La Nauze, 'The Study of Australian History, 1929–1959'.

6   For an eloquent and influential synthesis of this new biological story, see Tim
    Flannery, *The Future Eaters: An Ecological History of the Australasian Lands and
    People*, Sydney: Reed Books, 1994, where he also reflected on how quickly the
    factual world of his childhood had been overturned. See also George Seddon,
    Landprints: Reflections on Place and Landscape, Cambridge: Cambridge University
    Press, 1997; Libby Robin, *How a Continent Created a Nation*, Sydney: UNSW Press,
    2007; and Kirsty Douglas, *Pictures of Time Beneath: Science, Heritage and the Uses of
    the Deep Past*, Melbourne: CSIRO Publishing, 2010.

7   Darrell Lewis, *A Wild History: Life and Death on the Victoria River Frontier*,
    Melbourne: Monash University Publishing, 2012, p. xix, and Deborah Bird Rose
    and Darrell Lewis, 'A Bridge and a Pinch', *Public History Review*, 1, 1992,
    pp. 26–36.

8   Mark McKenna, 'The History Anxiety', in Alison Bashford and Stuart Macintyre
    (eds.), *The Cambridge History of Australia, Volume 2: The Commonwealth of
    Australia*, Cambridge: Cambridge University Press, 2013, p. 566.

9   Noel Pearson, 'Foreword' to John B Haviland with Roger Hart, *Old Man Fog
    and the Last Aborigines of Barrow Point*, Washington and London: Smithsonian
    Institution Press, 1998, pp. ix–xi.

10 Noel Pearson, 'Mabo and the Humanities: Shifting Frontiers', 1994 W K Hancock
    Memorial Lecture, in Derek Schreuder (ed.), *The Humanities and a Creative
    Nation: Jubilee Essays*, Papers from the Academy Symposium, November 1995,
    Australian Academy of the Humanities, Canberra, 1995, p. 52.

11 Marcia Langton, 'Prologue' to Rachel Perkins and Marcia Langton (eds.) *First
    Australians: An Illustrated History*, Melbourne: The Miegunyah Press, 2008,
    pp. xxiv–xxix, and Marcia Langton, 'A Fireside Chat', in Tim Bonyhady and
    Tom Griffiths (eds.), *Prehistory to Politics: John Mulvaney, the Humanities and the
    Public Intellectual*, Melbourne: Melbourne University Press, 1996, pp. 134–43.

Index

Lightning Source UK Ltd.
Milton Keynes UK
UKOW01f1059031216
288996UK00001B/161/P